THE
RED JOURNEY

AN ORAL HISTORY OF
LIVERPOOL FOOTBALL CLUB

To Richhie

Best wishes

THE
RED JOURNEY

AN ORAL HISTORY OF
LIVERPOOL FOOTBALL CLUB

Edited by
Mark Platt

deCoubertin
B O O K S

First published as a hardback by deCoubertin Books Ltd in 2017.

First Edition

deCoubertin Books, Studio I, Baltic Creative Campus, Liverpool, L1 OAH
www.decoubertin.co.uk

ISBN: 978-1-909245-63-1

A CIP catalogue record for this book is available from the British Library.

Cover design and typeset by Leslie Priestley.

Cover image by George Chilvers.

Printed and bound by Jellyfish.

Acknowledgements

As with the publication of any book, there have been so many people involved in the production process and I'm indebted to them all.

First and foremost, if it wasn't for the cooperation of the Liverpool players and managers over the years, this book would simply have not been possible. This is their story. Without them there would not be one to tell. So, to all those who, at some point over the years, have given up their time to be interviewed and shared their precious memories, I can't stress enough how much it is appreciated.

Then there are the good people from the publishers deCoubertin, notably James Corbett and Simon Hughes. It seems a long time ago now, but it was they who approached me with the initial idea for this book and who have offered encouragement throughout. Jack Gordon-Brown helped with a lot of the more recent interviews; Megan Pollard helped pull things together towards the end, while Leslie Priestley has done a great job on the design and credit to George Chilvers for the excellent colourisation of the iconic cover image.

To all the journalists, authors and producers who have previously documented parts of the club's history, among them some of my past and present work colleagues, you've made my job that bit easier and for this I'll always be grateful.

I must also acknowledge the fine work done by what is an ever-growing band of dedicated Liverpool FC historians. Through their diligent research, new light is now consistently being shed on the subject in terms of stories, quotes, photographs and facts. For that I salute the likes of Kjell Hanssen, Jonny Stokkeland, George Rowlands, Eric Doig, Arnie Baldursson, Gudmundur Magnusson and Adrian Killen, to name just a select few.

Honourable mentions too, for those who have experienced this 'Red Journey' with me. The mates I have known since the days when we swapped footy stickers in the school playground and dreamt of becoming the next Sammy Lee, and all the lads I know from the match – without whom football, for me, just wouldn't be as appealing as it once was. There are too many to name individually but you know who you are.

Last but not least, those closest to me who have had to live with my 'obsession' for the past 40 years. My dad for taking me to my first ever game and bringing me up as a Liverpudlian, my mum for putting up with us throughout and always being there; a baton that has since been passed onto my 'long-suffering' Evertonian wife Lynda who plays such a vital role in the background and, if she's been listening to me, would now know more about Albert Stubbins than Dixie Dean. And finally, my three kids – Jack, Ella and Tom – each of whom help me forget that it's been so long since Liverpool last won the league. They may know the words to 'Poor Scouser Tommy' but probably still wonder why I spend so much time sat in front of a computer.

Thank-you. This is for you all.

Contents

Introduction

Let's be honest. When it comes to the history of Liverpool Football Club, there is no shortage of suitable reading material already out there on the shelves.

For a club with such a proud and illustrious heritage, it's no surprise that so many words have been written about it.

As an author and historian, the challenge, therefore, is always to try and find a fresh way of approaching such a well-versed subject – one that I've long been fully immersed in.

Even before embarking on this project, I'd like to think that I already knew a fair bit about Liverpool's history and, with 'The Red Journey', I hope to have done it the justice it deserves, by curating a fascinatingly familiar story in a manner that is different to the traditional LFC history books that have previously been published.

Born in the shadow of the Kop, I've been a Red since as far back as I can remember; reared on tales of the legendary names and games that have long since passed into Anfield folklore. This club has played such a significant part in my life, in the process providing me with some of the happiest and most heart-breaking of memories.

I consider my upbringing as a Liverpudlian as similar to that of most fellow supporters I know. I didn't choose my footballing allegiance. That honour was bestowed on me by my dad. He'd supported them long before I arrived and had witnessed at first hand the club's meteoric rise from the Second Division under Bill Shankly. Liverpool was in his blood too. That I would follow in his footsteps was never up for debate. It was just an accepted rite of passage; one that I will be eternally grateful for.

In the year I was born, 1973, Liverpool won the League and UEFA Cup, a unique double that paved the way for a period of unprecedented domination, which I was lucky enough to experience. I grew up in an era when the words Liverpool and success went hand in hand.

Unfortunately, nothing lasts forever and I've since experienced the other side of the coin. When the Reds last won the league in 1990, I'd just turned 17. Little did I realise that for the remainder of my adult life to date, I'd still be waiting to see them reclaim their once proud mantle as the undisputed kings of English football.

My first game was a now famous First Division fixture at home to Tottenham Hotspur in September 1978. I was five years of age. I stood on a homemade wooden stool at the front of the 'Annie' Road.

Liverpool won seven-nil and Terry McDermott scored one of the greatest goals Anfield has ever seen. I may have been too young to appreciate the quality of football on show that day but I was transfixed by the spectacle; the vast crowd, the atmosphere and the vivid colours.

As we made the short journey back home along Oakfield Road that late summer afternoon, the only thing more certain than Liverpool winning the league against that season was that I'd soon be an Anfield regular.

It wasn't long before I found myself fully immersed in everything about the club. Back then it was to the pages of the 'footy' Echo and Shoot magazine that I'd turn to for my Red fix as I attempted to glean as much information as I could about this team that had begun to dominate my life.

One Christmas in the mid-to-late 1980s, I received a copy of Brian Pead's 'Liverpool: A Complete Record' book. The following year, BBC released the official club history video. I cite both as being hugely influential; for giving me an even greater appreciation of Liverpool's past and, in turn, helping to further stoke a passion that eventually developed into a career.

I've now been writing about Liverpool for the past quarter of a century, during which time I've delved deeper with my research and broadened my contacts; privileged to have met and, in most cases, interviewed almost every significant living person connected to the club.

It was in the autumn of 1992 that I set off on my first Liverpool-related journalistic assignment. I was a student at a local college and tasked with going out to find a story. Melwood was just up the road, so when placed in a group with four fellow Reds there was only one place we were heading.

Graeme Souness was Liverpool manager then. We knocked on the gate and asked if we could speak to him, were invited in and told to wait on the old pavilion, while training drew to a close. Ten minutes later Souness emerged and proceeded to give us half an hour of his time. I can't remember whether the subsequent interview that we typed up got us top marks off our tutor back at college, but it was good enough to be published in a popular national football magazine of the time.

The innocence of that breakthrough interview remains a cherished memory, of days when football was less complicated and the personalities associated with it were far more accessible. I've lost count of the number of interviews that I've conducted since but it's been great to draw on some of them in course of compiling this book.

For me, researching and writing about the history of Liverpool is a labour of love. My previous books have tended to focus on particular seasons [1946/47, 1965 and 1977], individuals [Joe Fagan and David Fairclough] or places [Anfield]. What sets 'The Red Journey' apart is the vastness of the topics covered and the in-depth conversational style in which the stories are delivered.

The concept of oral history is to record people's memories, experiences and opinions; then utilise them to form an informative and engaging narrative. Where books primarily relating to Liverpool are concerned, previous works that have fallen into the particular genre have generally focussed on supporter stories – Voice of Anfield [Eddie Cotton, 1996], Places I Remember [Dave Hewitson, 2104] and most recently Hillsborough Voices [Kevin Sampson, 2016].

In 'The Red Journey', the Liverpool story is recited, for the first time, solely by those who made it happen. From 1892 to the modern era, it is the complete history of club, told entirely in the collective voice of the men in the thick of the action at all the major moments, the pivotal people at the heart of the numerous triumphs and travails.

From John Houlding to Jurgen Klopp, it features the recollections of over 150 players, managers and other key figures associated with the club, past and present. Fresh interviews and archived quotes, painstakingly weaved together to form the definitive 'inside' story of a team that rose from humble beginnings to become one of the biggest and best in the game.

As 18-time champions of England and five time kings of Europe, unbridled highs, heroic deeds and unforgettable adventures are obviously plentiful. As with any compelling story though, it's one that is also tinged with its fair share of gut-wrenching lows, acts of villainy and times of trouble.

It's an emotional roller-coaster ride through 125 years of history, broken down into decade-by-decade chapters that allow the reader to casually dip in and out of with ease. Each individual chapter then follows a chronological trail through that particular period, focussing on the men, the moments and the matches that mattered.

Some chapters are obviously more populated than others. That's simply because there are either more key topics to discuss or more readily available voices to reflect. For this reason, the balance is obviously sways more towards the past half a century of Liverpool's history.

That's not to say the early years have been neglected. The heroes of the sepia-tinted bygone age may have long since passed, but as many first hand testimonies as possible have been sourced in an attempt to infuse the book with some rare insight from those who lit up Anfield in the days before Bill Shankly.

Events from the latter years will, of course, strike more of a chord but while that's a period that been largely littered with tales of triumph, I was conscious that this book shouldn't just be an endless list of title wins and trophies. There are more than enough to have done that but the importance of some history defining defeats should not be overlooked.

The Red Journey has been many years in the making and to condense everything into just 280 pages has been a massive task. I believe the end product though to be the first of its kind among the vast plethora of other books in the Liverpudlian library; one that will hopefully entertain as well educate, and act as a long lasting point of reference for future studies into the history of the world renowned institution that Liverpool Football club has become.

It's a story that is constantly evolving and one that will continue to fascinate. Enjoy the ride.

Up the Reds!

Mark Platt
Liverpool
October 2017

Early years

1892-1939

Beginnings

Between 1884 and 1892, Anfield was home to Everton Football Club. The land on which it was built had been acquired by Everton President John Houlding but when a row broke out over rent it led to the formation of Liverpool Football Club.

A bitter split

March 1892

John Houlding: You [Everton] must look for another site, here is the notice to quit my ground.

June 1892

W.E. Barclay: We [Liverpool] have joined the Lancashire League, and have thus provided a very interesting series of fixtures for our first team. We regret that we could not see our way to make application to enter the second division of the League, as we felt, after very careful deliberation, that the gates would be no better than the gates drawn with Lancashire clubs, whilst travelling expenses would have been very high. We hope to meet some of the league clubs during the season, and already engagements have been made with some of the leading Scottish clubs for odd dates. Cup ties – English, Lancashire and Liverpool – will fill vacant spots, and altogether I think the 'bill of fare' at Anfield will not disgrace the past. Our supporters may rely on it that we shall take to the field with men who can and will play football and good exhibitions of the dribbling code will be seen at Anfield.

The new club quickly prospered, joining the Football League in 1893 and gaining promotion to the First Division the following year. In 1896 the highly-rated Tom Watson was appointed secretary/manager and, as ambitions soared, he set about taking Liverpool to the next level.

The signing of Alex Raisbeck

May 1898

Alex Raisbeck: I remember when I first went to Liverpool I felt a bit shy and diffident. After all I was, after all, only a laddie, and a Scottish laddie at that. Although I had a guid Scottish tongue in my head, I did not let it wag too freely, the 'gift of the gab' not being mine. But when I got to Anfield I was received with open arms, and found myself in the centre of friends and brothers, maistly Scottish. I can tell you that I felt at home right away. Just let me mention one or two of the Scotsmen in the Liverpool team. There was Geordie Allan at centre and Barney Battles, two of the finest-built men who ever figured on the football field... Then there were the brothers Goldie, and Willie Dunlop, all Ayrshire callants; Hugh Morgan, Robertson, Cleghorn and 'Matt' McQueen.

Double disappointment

By 1898/99 Liverpool were well on their way to establishing themselves as one of the country's top teams and went close to landing both the First Division title and FA Cup. In the latter only Sheffield United stood between them and a place in the final...

Tom Watson: I never like to crow before the event, because football is a peculiar game, and the better team does not always win. But I have no doubts whatever that we are a better team than Sheffield United, and that we ought to win. Our halves will chop up any opposing combination, our defence is splendid, and our forwards are playing a deadly, determined game. You must not forget also that most of our players have youth on their side, and would naturally like to win distinction early in their career. But what encourages me most is the confidence of the men themselves. They know they have a heavy task before them, but they believe they are quite able to accomplish it. And I honestly believe they can and will win.

Despite Watson's confidence, Liverpool's cup dreams were shattered after four games of an epic semi-final tussle and more anguish was to follow in the race for the league title...

Alex Raisbeck: Although we failed to gain the League Championship in this ever-to-be-remembered year it was not until the last game with Aston Villa, who were neck-and-neck with Liverpool, that the decision was arrived at. The Villa had a better chance that day. They took the field comparatively fresh whereas we were exhausted by the strenuous tussles of the last few weeks. The consequence was that we were badly defeated and the honours went to the Villa.

Champions for a first time

West Bromwich Albion v Liverpool
The Hawthorns
Football League Division One
29 April 1901

Alex Raisbeck: It was a momentous match... we simply had to win. Time was wearing on and we still wanted that goal. At last! The ball was lying on the goal-line. Johnny Walker and the goalkeeper had got mixed up some way and were lying near the back of the net, and there was no friendly foot to put the ball through. I know I stopped dead. I was fascinated, I suppose, by the sight of both goalkeeper and Walker starting to wrestle towards the ball at the same instant. Which would reach it first? There was such a deathly stillness. I fancied I heard the tick of the referee's watch, although he was twenty yards from me, and it seemed as though half an hour had passed. But it must have lasted only a second or two. The goalie was on his hands and knees crawling towards the ball, when Walker, with a cat-like movement, wriggled his body along the ground and just tipped the ball over the line and the goal and championship were ours. What a night after the match! We got a great send-off at Snowhill Station by the Brummagen folks who were good enough sports to cheer us off as League champions, but we were unprepared for what was waiting us at Liverpool. I should imagine there was a crowd of between 50-60,000 packed in front of the Central Station, and right along nearly as far as Lime Street. The street was literally black with people, and in the time-honoured way the horses were dispensed with and our brake practically carried along by willing hands to our headquarters at the Sandon Hotel. As we went along the crowd yelled for me to make a speech from the brake. I was not to be found, however, as I found it convenient to lie low behind some of the others. Speechmaking was never in my line.

Relegation

1903/04

Alex Raisbeck: The match which sealed our fate was one in which we were not engaged. Stoke, who were running us neck-and-neck, as it were, for relegation had to play Everton at Goodison Park. It ought to have been a pinch for Everton as they were well up in the League and were very hard nuts to crack on their own ground. To the surprise of everybody, however, Stoke won the match and our fate was sealed. The result did not please everyone, as you will imagine, and I heard at the time that a great number of Everton's ticket-holders tore their tickets up after the game and swore they would never go to Goodison again.

Champions again, though cup disappointment

1905/06

Liverpool made an immediate return to the top-flight by winning the Second Division Championship in 1905 and were soon back challenging for the game's top honours.

Sam Hardy: It was on 16 June 1905, that I signed on for Liverpool, and even then, my prospects did not appear to be too bright, for Doig, the Scottish International, was first goalkeeper for my new club. However, I soon got a chance. To the best of my recollection my first match in the League team was in October, 1905, when we opposed Manchester City at Manchester. It was a very keen fight, the defence on both sides being exceedingly good, and I think we won by 1 to 0.

Alex Raisbeck: My best season with the Reds was undoubtedly 1905/06. We won the Liverpool Cup, League Championship and London Charity Shield, while we were only beaten by our near and dear neighbours, Everton, in the semi-final of the English Cup. The Cup tie took place on the Aston Lower Grounds, now the Villa Park. It was a very unfortunate day for Liverpool.

Sam Hardy: At the end of that season – 30 April 1906 – we were Champions of the First League, and it was at one time considered probable that we would have won double honours, viz., the League Championship and the Association Cup, but the latter was not destined to come to our side... and the game which put paid to our ambition was the semi-final, in which we had to meet our neighbours, Everton, who eventually won the Cup.

Arthur Goddard: Alex Raisbeck was the most outstanding player in the semi-final at Villa Park. He was magnificent, and so was Sam Hardy, the greatest goalkeeper I ever saw.

Sam Hardy: That was the greatest cup tie in which I have ever played... memories of every kick in the game will remain with me. It was at the same time, the greatest and the most disappointing. Yet, what a game! Think of it; Liverpool versus Everton, neighbouring clubs, and both eager to annex the trophy. Small wonder that 15,000 people travelled from Liverpool to Villa Park, Birmingham, to witness the fight, but, quite apart from local interest the ordinary football loving public were alive to the fact that the game would be worth seeing, and, altogether, there were 37,000 on the ground.

Alex Raisbeck: Prior to the match we were in special training at Southport and, along with the officials, made the journey direct to Birmingham on the day of the match. When we were in special training it was usual for the officials to pick the team prior to the kick-off. The officials had had little to worry about as we had been particularly lucky in the matter of injuries to players. It never rains but it pours. Cox and Raybould were both laid low on the eve of our Cup tie with Everton and although there was some hope of Sam being fit, there was absolutely no chance of Cox turning out.

Joe Hewitt: Just before the match, Secretary Mr Tom Watson asked me if I would play outside-left, as Raybould and Cox had cried off. 'You are my masters', I replied, so outside-left it was.

Arthur Goddard: If my memory serves me right, Robinson, our inside-right, should have scored in the first few minutes at Birmingham for he was right through with only Billy Scott to beat, only to shoot behind, much to our disappointment. They say fate does not look kindly upon you when you refuse her offerings. I know we never got another chance like that.

Joe Hewitt: I think I played the game of my life, Harry Makepeace could do nothing with me. I sent across a stream of centres which should have given us a three-goals lead, but in the end we were beaten 2-0 by Everton.

Sam Hardy: The battle ruled fast and furious for sixty-five minutes before a goal was scored. Then, Abbott, the Everton half, had a shot, which West, one of our backs, seeing that it was going behind, allowed to go. Dunlop, our other back, however, as if fascinated by the ball, had a kick, in the excitement of the moment, diverted it into the net before I had a chance to get anywhere near.

Joe Hewitt: I can well remember Everton's first goal. It was a long lob by Abbott, which Dunlop tried to hitch-kick and sliced the ball beyond Hardy, who was left helpless.

Sam Hardy: But for this the ball would have gone behind, and we were all left so astonished that before we quite realised it Everton swept down and scored again.

Joe Hewitt: The winner, I will never forget. Sharp had centred right across the goal face, and Hardman came dashing in to ram the ball home at great speed, and actually followed the ball into the net. It's a wonder the Everton amateur did not break his neck.

Alex Raisbeck: Everton beat Newcastle [in the final] so the League Championship and the Cup both came to Liverpool the same season. Our winning the Championship was greatly minimised by Everton's carrying off the Cup. As you know, a greater interest is taken in the Cup in England than in League doings. In fact, one would scarcely have known in Liverpool that we had won the League. Merseyside people went absolutely mad over the Cup coming to Liverpool for the first time.

Elisha Scott: the legend begins

Newcastle United v Liverpool
St James' Park
Football League Division One
1 January 1913

Elisha Scott: When I was seventeen I got my chance. I was with Broadway United and my brother Billy, who kept goal for Ireland, Everton and Linfield, was over in Ireland on a holiday. He came down and saw me playing against Queens Park, Lurgan, and he told me I was good and that he would recommend me to a first class English club. I thought it was too good to be true, but on his return to England he was as good as his word. Everton could have had me, for Billy recommended me to them first, but as I was only seventeen years of age they considered me too young and let the offer go past. Then my brother mentioned me to Mr McKenna, of Liverpool, who sent across to Belfast for me, gave me my chance in a practice game and I pleased him so well that I was played in the First League team against Newcastle United at Newcastle the following Saturday. I was not 18 years of age then, and I was quoted as having that day 'given the best display of goalkeeping ever seen at St James' Park'.

The road to a first FA Cup final

1914

Ephraim Longworth: In the first round we had to play Barnsley at home. When we failed to beat them at our own ground and had to travel to Barnsley for a replay, everybody was very dumpy about our prospects; but there was never a man dismayed, and we pulled through.

Kenneth Campbell: Everyone thought that was the finish of the Reds, as it was popularly imagined we would never survive at Barnsley. Barnsley was en fete for the replay. All the colliers and other industrial concerns closed down for the match, so the home team did not lack for support. Never have I seen a more excited crowd, and as the minutes flew without a score the excitement became intense. Just three minutes from the end Lacey, by an almost superhuman effort got through a goal, and we retired happy to be in the second round.

Ephraim Longworth: Our opponents in the second round were Gillingham, and this game we won, despite misgivings among various people. We had to go to West Ham in the third round, and that was a stiff fight if you like. The West Ham ground is on the small side – after Liverpool the spectators seem almost to be on the top of the players, and history had told us that such famous clubs as Manchester United, Middlesbrough, and one or two others had found the task at West Ham too great. But we managed to draw – very luckily, so it was said, though I do not agree.

Kenneth Campbell: I have reason to remember that day. It was my first introduction to Puddefoot, then making his name with the Hammers. What a duel between the pair of us. Syd peppered me with all manner of shots, and it took me all my time to keep my end up till the interval. A goal by Nicholl, the Middlesbrough man who played outside left for us, gave us some cheer just after half-time. It seemed a walk-over for us after this, but there's many a slip. And it was Puddefoot who eventually brought about my downfall. I had just saved a great swerving shot of his, when he was back again. He rounded Pursell and let fly with terrific force. My feet got stuck in the mud – it had been raining nearly all the time – and I was powerless to save.

Ephraim Longworth: In the replay we put up our very best game and beat them by a good margin. Against Queen's Park Rangers in round four we had a bit of luck – that I willingly grant, because our opponents missed a penalty late in the game, and lost by a goal. But, after all, we could hardly be responsible for their sins of omission, could we?

Kenneth Campbell: This brought us into the semi-final, in which we were drawn against Aston Villa, the Cup holders of the previous season. The match was to be played at Tottenham, and we went to Chingford, just outside London, for a three weeks' preparation.

Ephraim Longworth: It was against Aston Villa, however, that we recorded our greatest triumph – that we won against the greatest odds.

Kenneth Campbell: There could be no doubt who was the favourite for the final. Indeed, it was well known to us that hundreds of Birmingham people [Aston Villa supporters] had booked special trains for Crystal Palace, where the final was to be played. The London press was pretty severe on us. The odds were umpteen to nothing against us. However, this optimism helped us greatly. Few of us will forget the speech Old Tom Watson [as he was affectionately called amongst the boys] made at lunch before leaving for Tottenham. The continual slighting of his team by the press had got on his nerves. He got up after lunch to make a speech, and during all the years I had known him I do not remember ever having seen him so agitated. After calling the London press anything but sportsmen, he finished up by saying – 'Never mind, boys, I want you to turn out today and show them up. Show them there are more players than Aston Villa in the semi-final!' He was red in the face when he finished, and banged his fist on the table setting everything jumping. His speech did more than anything else to brace us up.

Ephraim Longworth: During the first twenty minutes or so at Tottenham against the Villa, we went through as hard a time of trial as I can remember in the course of my football career. The whole strength of the Villa side was put into their attacks. But, partly because such tactics were anticipated, we were enabled to withstand the attack.

Kenneth Campbell: It was a stirring encounter, I can tell you. What with Bache being in great shooting form and Harry Hampton ever ready to pounce on a chance, I had a hot time of it. For the first twenty minutes the Villa were [in football parlance] all over us, but, ably assisted by Longworth and Bob Pursell, I was able to keep our goal intact.

Ephraim Longworth: And, once the ferocity of it began to waver over so little, we bent to the attack in turn, and got that first goal which is so all-important in a Cup-tie.

Kenneth Campbell: Jimmy Nicholl surprised Hardy by heading a goal. Shortly after half-time the same player struck the bar, with Hardy beaten, and our boys claimed that the ball had rebounded over the goal-line. The referee decided against us, but afterwards Sam admitted that he thought he ball was over. However, Nicholl got another goal, and our chances looked extremely rosy for the Royal final.

Kenneth Campbell: We knew the King was going to witness the final and to present the medals. Excitement was intense right through, but our boys stuck it to the end... What a scene at the close. Old Tom was crying and laughing by turns. It was the first time he had piloted his favourite Reds into the final of 'ta coop'.

A trip to the Palace

Liverpool v Burnley
Crystal Palace
FA Cup final
25 April 1914

Kenneth Campbell: We went in taxis to the scene of the match. Four of our machines arrived at the Crystal Palace but one, with four players, was missing. What had happened to it we did not know. At first we were inclined to chaff. 'Somebody has kidnapped them,' said one of our boys and we all laughed. But as time wore on our banter ceased. Our officials were terribly anxious. What made the situation all the more serious was that we were to be already stripped to cheer the King at 3.20, ten minutes before the time for kicking off. I forget exactly who were in the missing taxi, but I do know that Tommy Fairfoul and Sheldon were two of them. At three o'clock Mr Watson got desperate and made another visit to the entrance gates. With a struggle he got outside and found his four missing players doing their best to get in. They had been trying to get past the commissionaire for quite a long time, but the official was adamant. He told them that all the players had gone in a long time ago, and he had heard the same tale before.

The winning goal

Kenneth Campbell: It was a really remarkable goal. The ball was almost breast high, and how Freeman got his foot on it and the force behind it I know not. It was one of these shots which might have gone anywhere. I certainly never saw it pass me. Anyhow, it was good enough to beat us, for no further scoring took place, and Burnley carried the cup home instead of us. In football I grudge no team their victory, but I have to confess I spent the rottenest time of my life during the subsequent proceedings.

Tom Watson

In May 1915, Liverpool Football Club was rocked to its core when highly popular secretary/manager Tom Watson suddenly passed away aged 56. During his tenure he had guided the Reds to two League titles and a first appearance in the FA Cup final. His 19 years at the helm remains a record and he's remembered as one of the greats.

Alex Raisbeck: [He] was more than a friend to me. From the day I became one of his players he took a particular interest in me; he fathered me, to tell the truth.

Kenneth Campbell: I remember Tom Watson, ever ready to further the interests of the club he had so much at heart, sent us to a firm of hatters in Liverpool to get rigged out in the club colours. We got straw hats, all the same style – different sizes, of course – embellished with ribbons of the club colours, and we had wide ties of the same colour.

Alex Raisbeck: Tom was as successful in bringing good players to Liverpool. It was Tom who came and saw me play when I was on loan from Hibs to Stoke. Jimmy Ross, Geordie Allan, Sam Raybould, the two Robertsons, 'Sailor' Hunter, Arthur Goddard and a host of others were discoveries of Tom Watson. He had a great influence over all players.

Back-to-back titles

The Liverpool team of the early 1920s is justifiably regarded as one of the finest in Anfield history. In 1921/22 they surprised everyone to win their first League title in 16 years and then completed a successful defence of that crown 12 months later, becoming the first Liverpool side to do so.

Donald Mackinlay: It was touch and go now and again, and one could see the boys felt the keenness of the position. We hope the public realised that we won again, in spite of being right on top early on... a big barrier to success in most cases, as teams came along with the avowed intention of making a league game a cup-tie business.

Elisha Scott: Liverpool was essentially a side that thrived on success. We could always play when we were winning. Not like others, who have to be down a goal, before they get really warmed up. A goal against in the good years was very unsettling to us, especially at home. Perhaps it was because it seldom happened.

Ephraim Longworth: I think we can claim to have performed a feat of rare strength. The man who makes the early running in a race has to suffer the knowledge that the man behind knows exactly how far he can come forward at a given moment, whereas the leader has no knowledge of what the people behind can do. We led the field for practically the whole of the time. We never had so many determined opponents to face. Everybody was lying awake and sitting up for us. However, we triumphed.

Elisha Scott: A good spirit always existed amongst us and the directors met us on every possible occasion with every fairness and consideration. We always went on the field, not as eleven players but as a team out to do our level best. We were all as one big happy family.

Donald Mackinlay: The only side that came near it was the one which won another championship in 1946/47. That was also a good side with some fine players, but I think we could have beaten it.

Anfield's star men of the 1920s

Elisha Scott: I was lucky in the fact that the club had such great players on their books when I joined them. I was singularly lucky that they had such great backs. Lucas, Longworth and Mackinlay are, in my opinion, three of the greatest backs I have ever had the pleasure of playing behind. They saved me a number of times, and it was seldom that the opposition were allowed to walk the ball in. Lucas had perhaps the best tackle of them all. He could leap several feet into the air. His heading away of dangerous centres was one of the main features of his play. Mackinlay playing right on top of his own half-back, seldom allowed situations to develop before he would nip things in the bud. His terrific drives were known not only to Anfield fans but habitues of all the leading football arenas. At forcing a game which was apparently lost and turning it in Liverpool's favour, no man succeeded more often than Donald Mackinlay. He was a good captain and under his leadership the club did exceptionally well. He rarely allowed the players to indulge in the slightest finesse.

Donald Mackinlay: In my day I had full control on the field and if there was any decision on changing of positions, I took it. I told my players, 'If I have to say anything to you, answer me back and don't start sulking.'

Elisha Scott: Longworth, 'Daddy' as he was known to the younger folk at the club at Anfield, may have been the greatest of the three. When I came to Liverpool, Longworth was established. The cry from behind the goal was 'Longworth again'. He had once more saved the Liverpool citadel. Longworth was the sheet anchor of the side. Anticipation and the power of his tackles were his best cards. By clever positional play, Longworth could bamboozle an opponent into giving him the ball without a tackle even being required.

Elisha Scott: In front of the backs we had men like Bamber, McNab, Wadsworth and Bromilow. No quarter was asked or given in this department. Dourness personified, with Bromilow adding the necessary daintiness and class. I have seen these half backs play some terrific games, especially away from home when they held up and thwarted some of the most brilliant forward lines in the land. As a sheer stopper, I have never seen anything approaching Walter Wadsworth. Too little of the credit for the Championships is laid at his door. He certainly was robust, I'll admit, but nothing more. I have seen him fling himself ten yards over the ground to stop forwards applying the crusher.

Donald Mackinlay: I remember one match in the early twenties when Wadsworth injured a leg and I saw blood coming out of his boot. I told him to get some attention to it and his reply was, 'Who's blood is it, yours or mine?' and went on playing. I think the game was tougher in my day.

Elisha Scott: Bromilow excelled, of course, in all parts of the game and was far from finished when he retired. In fact, I can recall but one occasion. His corner kicks were the acme of perfection and his cooperation with that famous left wing pair, Chambers and Hopkins, was a joy. Bromilow had a knack of going into the centre of the field and then swinging the ball out to the left again, having drawn the defence sadly out of position. This move worked time after time. Yes, he was a great half back.

George Patterson: His signature was obtained in the strangest manner. He came to the ground in uniform during the war and asked for a game. I asked George Fleming, who was in charge of the second team then, how he was fixed and he said he could do with another player. Bromilow played at outside right and was an instant success. When the war ended he signed as a professional. Eventually he took his place in the first team when Lacey was playing an international match for Ireland. I should think that it is one of the luckiest signings I have made.

Elisha Scott: Our best forward line was Lacey, Forshaw, Johnson, Chambers and Hopkin. The combination of Lacey centres and Chambers' heads resulted in dozens of goals. Lacey, to my mind, revolutionised wing play. He was so slow that to get down to the corner flag, he would have to beat the same man at least three times. To counteract this he introduced the idea of the forward centre. That is he would place the ball into the goal mouth from well down the wing there by cutting out all the wing play. Lacey rarely wasted a ball, and his corners invariably landed on the head of Chambers. They had a very business-like arrangement these two. Lacey would sweep the ball over from the corner flag with his left foot and Chambers, who had taken up a position on the edge of the penalty area, would rush in and crash it home with his head piece at an unstoppable speed. Yes, Chambers must go down to posterity as the greatest inside left Liverpool has produced. Many things about him were outstanding, his burly figure on the field – Liverpool were never the same team when he wasn't playing his bustling style, he simply glided the ball past the half back as if he didn't exist. He had a knack of getting his body in between his opponent and the ball, thereby, making it difficult to tackle him successfully. Finally he possessed a wonderful shot with either foot. The swerve he imparted leaving many a goalkeeper helpless.

Donald Mackinlay: We were playing at home and Harry Chambers, who lived in Hartnup Street, which is just behind Anfield, had not turned up when we were ready to go out. A deputy was getting stripped when Harry walked in. I asked him where he had been and without a smile, he answered 'Sorry, my taxi broke down.'

Elisha Scott: Hopkin, I am convinced, became a Liverpool player as a result of a brilliant display for Manchester United against us in a cup tie. Polly, as we called him, was a great character. One time he scored a goal and the stand went on fire. We advised him not to score any more. Dick Forshaw and Johnson completed a great side. By watching these players, I could tell after the first few minutes, what kind of an afternoon we were going to have. The first move of the individual was sufficient indication.

Elisha Scott: Gradually that wonderful eleven broke up. Lacey, Chambers, McNab, Wadsworth, were the first to leave. Forshaw went to Everton, and poor Dick Johnson, had in the meantime, passed on. At last only Lucas, Hopkin and I remained. Tommy was transferred to Clapton, leaving Polly and yours truly to keep the fort. Now we are all of the past, such is the way of things.

'Lisha' King of the Kop

Elisha Scott: My friends behind the goal were particularly generous to me. And to them, it may have appeared strange that I rarely recognised the crowd, or saluted them in the slightest manner, neither before nor during a game. Well, the explanation is simple. From the beginning of the game to the end of it, I was continuously in a state of nervous excitement. This tension lasted the whole of the 90 minutes and I could rarely get myself to relax to the slightest degree, whatever the state of the game: I was on tenterhooks. Hence it was that I never suffered the slightest distraction during the course of a match. My whole attention was concentrated on the play. The crowd was never part of my reckoning. I may have appeared to observers absolutely calm, cool and collected, but I can assure you that inwardly there burned always great anxiety to do the right thing at the right time. I dreaded making a mistake, and could rarely understand why others made them. For weeks on end, I prided myself on keeping my goal intact. I had a distinct disinclination to retrieving the ball from the back of the net.

Donald Mackinlay: A wonderful goalkeeper, the best I have seen. I put him above Sam Hardy. When Jimmy Jackson first played for us I told him Elisha would probably have a few words to say to him during games. "Don't take too much notice of him though, he doesn't mean it", I said. Jimmy replied, 'He won't say anything to me'. 'Won't he? He says them to me and I'm the captain.'

Elisha Scott: Any ball in the six yards area was my bird and it should be for every goalkeeper. If he thinks a full back or another defender is in the way, tell'em to get to blazes out of it. I did.

Donald Mackinlay: Elisha made his mistakes, like all of us. One I recollect was in a cup match at Newcastle when the only goal bounced in over his arm, but he was the man for me.

Elisha Scott: I remember it. It was a freak goal. Someone headed in from about 18 yards out and the ball bounced six yards from me, hit a hole in the ground and shot into the top corner. Funniest thing I have ever seen. It looked that simple that naturally I got the blame. The poor goalkeeper always gets blame, but the only simple thing about it that it made me look a bit simple.

Donald Mackinlay: Another great thing about Elisha was that if he thought he had made a mistake he admitted it. In one match against Tottenham, Arthur Grimsdell hit a free-kick which went into the net like a bullet. Elisha said, 'I should have stopped it'. All I could say was, 'It would have broken you into little bits if it had hit you'.

Upstaging Dixie

Everton v Liverpool
Goodison Park
FA Cup 3rd round
9 January 1932

Tom [Tiny] Bradshaw: It is usually difficult to remember individual matches, but one can't forget a Liverpool v Everton cup-tie. Everton were then doing very well and scoring a bundle of goals every week in the First Division. We expected to be flattened out and Everton started well when Dixie Dean, whom I had the responsibility of watching, put them in the lead.

Jimmy McDougall: At that time Everton were going great guns, scoring seven and eight goals a match, and our policy was to stop their gallop, but lo and behold Dixie Dean had the ball in our net in a matter of seconds. It certainly looked as though our policy was going to be torn to rags and tatters.

Tom [Tiny] Bradshaw: We eventually settled down and our outside-left, Gunson, made it 1-1 at the interval.

Jimmy McDougall: If I remember rightly, Gunson scored our first goal with his right foot, which was something of a feat because Gordon's right foot was alleged to be a 'swinger'. With his left he could hit a tremendous shot, but I don't recall him ever scoring another goal with his right.

Tom [Tiny] Bradshaw: There was naturally a very tense atmosphere as we struggled for the lead and there was tremendous enthusiasm among the Liverpool supporters when Gordon Hodgson headed the winner home from a cross from the left.

Jimmy McDougall: It was a hard game, not a great game, just a typical cup-tie – backwards and forwards. I cannot remember any highlights in connection with the game but I do remember that Jimmy Jackson was one of the outstanding players in our side.

Tom [Tiny] Bradshaw: After that both goals had narrow escapes, but we hung on to our lead to the end.

Jimmy McDougall: Dean was right at the peak of his form, but we managed to hold the scoring machine to that goal. In fact, Everton had a great side out so it was very pleasant to put a stop to their triumphal march.

Tom [Tiny] Bradshaw: There was talk at the time of Elisha Scott going to Everton but he was 100 per cent Liverpool. He was the most excited man in the dressing room at the end, and one of my memories is of Elisha throwing his boots up to the ceiling in sheer joy.

Nivvy makes his mark

Liverpool v Everton
Anfield
Football League Division One
30 September 1933

Berry Nieuwenhuys: Never before had I seen such a vast crowd, such brilliant football, or such clean football, and it was the thrill of my life when I managed to score the first goal. The point which struck me most was the cleanliness of the game. When we were leaving for England we were told that the game here was rough and dirty. Well, I can assure you that this match was 100 per cent cleaner that anything I have seen in Africa. I did not see one real foul in the entire ninety minutes. I confess I was rather staggered by the size of the crowd at the start but I did my best to forget they were there. That was hard in view of the continuous roar of voices. Still you could play in front of a crowd like that for years. They are such sportsmen. I thank them for the encouragement they gave me and also for the wonderful reception I was accorded when I left the field. I don't mind confessing it touched me.

Scott's fond farewell

2 May 1934

Elisha Scott: My final parting with Liverpool was one of the biggest breaks in my life, my broadcast to the spectators on that last fateful evening was a nightmare. While I was trying to say a few words into the microphone, the memories of the years crowded before me. My coming to Liverpool as a boy and all my varied experience covering those eventful twenty-two years, the famous players against whom I had striven so often, the glorious moments in cup and league, and the sorrow of leaving those faithful followers, who had stood by me through thick and thin. All these things swam before my eyes. I was tongue tied, and scarcely able to utter a syllable.

Pre-war Liverpool

March 1936

Matt Busby: Liverpool arrived with an offer which was accepted, and I was quite happy at the prospect of moving to Merseyside, even though Liverpool were having a bad time, being threatened with relegation to the Second Division. They signed me, in fact, to assist in the fight against relegation. The players were there, great players most of them, but many were obviously past their best. On the playing strength were such renowned names as Tommy Cooper and Ernie Blenkinsop, the finest pair of full-backs in England for a number of years, Tiny Bradshaw at centre-half, Jimmy McDougall [left-half], and a number of South Africans, including Berry Nieuwenhuys, Lance Carr, Arthur Riley and Dirk Kemp.

Ray Lambert: Part of my job on the groundstaff was to take the boots to the cobbler's. In those days, the football boots were heavy leather, with a very thick tongue, and we used to have to break them in. We sat with these boots in basins full of water to soften them and to get the shape of your foot. Now, Matt [Busby] didn't like this. He had this very old pair of boots. They were patched, they were stitched, they were in a right state. Just at the back of the Kop, just up the road, used to be the cobbler's where I took the boots, and this cobbler was a Scotsman. When I used to go in, he said, 'Ah noo whose boot you've got. It's Matt's. Will you tell the bugger to get a new pair. Tell the bugger to get a new pair'.

Matt Busby: Liverpool deserved success because they treated everyone on the staff as human beings should be treated, with kindness, consideration and understanding. Liverpool were always prepared to reward good service, even when they could so easily have evaded their obligations to players whose first XI days were ended. Jimmy [McDougall], a tremendous worker on the field, had completed a little less than the four years' qualification period for his second benefit when the club decided to replace him with Jimmy McInnes, bought from Third Lanark. McDougall was re-signed on top wages although he had lost his place, and the following year was again signed at the maximum when he was not playing at all. When he told the club he had decided to retire from football his second benefit was paid to him. I well remember Liverpool's handling of McDougall. It made a big impression on me, and indeed on all the players, because even though it was nothing more than just reward for a loyal servant there were few clubs who would have acted similarly in pre-war days. Before the war generosity was a rare occurrence.

Matt Busby: 'In addition... that Anfield Spion Kop is one of Liverpool Football Club's most precious possessions, I am certain matches have been won through the vocal efforts of its regular patrons. Only a man who has worn the red shirt of Liverpool, when the home team is attacking the Kop goal, knows and appreciates the value of the Kop supporter. The deafening roar that accompanies every attacking move carries sufficient volume to cause all but the most experienced of defences to panic and make mistakes. I know this is true because I have played at Anfield – for, and against Liverpool – and I know which side I would rather be on! It is to the credit of those wonderful supporters that, no matter how badly Liverpool are playing – and, frankly, the fans have been made to 'suffer' from time to time – in the eyes of the inhabitants of Spion Kop their team remains the finest in the world, and its players the greatest.

A new manager

6 August 1936

George Kay: I am proud to have been offered this post. I don't suggest I will win cups and everything else in my path, but I shall do my utmost, and I hope to find more players like Drake of the Arsenal, Light of West Brom and some others like Holt, who have been found for Southampton. I shall give every encouragement to the boys of the city and its surrounds. It is my plan to have matches three nights a week at Anfield to try and size up any boy who is worth nursing.

Matt Busby: George Kay's appointment was not made a day too soon, because the affairs of Liverpool Football Club were at a very low ebb, with a most obvious lack of discipline being responsible for many of Liverpool's problems at that time. The training routine was slipshod, players lacked the sort of supervision which I consider essential in every club, and the Anfield Road ship would most certainly have floundered on the relegation rocks without a strong man at the helm. George Kay was such a man, but he had to work very hard to pull the club out of trouble. No manager could have been presented with a more exacting assignment than the salvation of struggling Liverpool in the Spring of 1936, but George Kay was a real grafter throughout his managerial career. A man must be judged by results and it is a fact that from the day of his appointment until the outbreak of war, George Kay transformed Liverpool, and had it not been for the war, I feel sure this team would have been collecting the major honours in football in the early 1940s.

Other key signings of the mid to late-30s

Phil Taylor: I never knew Liverpool existed. I wasn't all that interested in League football. I was playing football myself. I was only interested in Bristol Rovers and what they were doing. Two Liverpool directors came down and I signed on and that was it. Mr Cartwright and Mr Richards came to my house. I remember old Richards. He came down in a bow-tie and a wing collar. My father did all the talking and the next minute I was on the train to Liverpool. All my family saw me off at Stapleton Road station.

When Ray Lambert joined Liverpool as an amateur, the same year, he was only 13 years and 189 days old, making him the youngest player ever to join a Football League club at that time.

Ray Lambert: I played for Flintshire Schoolboys. I was about thirteen and a half and I was playing in the fields down in the village. My sister came running after me and said, 'There's two gentlemen in the house, with a big car'. Well, you can imagine, in 1936, in a little village like Bagillt, some people coming in a big car. I thought to myself, 'What have I done now? I thought I'd been in some trouble or something like that. Anyway, I went home, and who was there but George Kay, manager of Liverpool, and George Patterson, the secretary. My father came to me first. He said, 'These gentlemen have come all the way from Liverpool'. Liverpool to me in those days was like going to Gibraltar or somewhere like that. It was that far away. 'Anyway, they've come to ask you if you'd like to sign on for Liverpool'. Well, I didn't know what to do. I was flabbergasted. My father said, 'Do you want to sign, son?' I said, 'Yes, I would love to sign'. So I signed on, there and then, thirteen and a half years of age. My photograph was in the *Liverpool Echo*, and I went to school the next morning, and we were lining up in school and the headmaster shouted, 'Lambert, I want you in my office after prayers'. I thought, 'Here goes again, what have I done?' Anyway, I go into the office. He said, 'What's all this I'm reading in the paper about signing on for Liverpool?' 'Oh', I said, 'Two gentlemen came last night and asked me to sign, and I just signed'. He played holy hell with me. 'You should never have done this', and all that sort of thing. You see, nobody was there to advise me in the beginning. Anyway, to cut a story short, I found out after a while that our headmaster was a big Evertonian. You see, I'd signed for Liverpool, and he wanted me to go to Everton.

27 July 1938

Matt Busby: One of the most important signings made by Liverpool during my playing days involved a boy from Lochgelly Violet, a Scottish Junior club; the name of the lad who left Lochgelly for Liverpool was Liddell.

Billy Liddell: The turning point of my young life came after I had been to a Youth Club dance one Saturday night. On returning home shortly before midnight I was surprised to see a light in the living-room. Normally my parents were in bed soon after ten o' clock. Both mother and father were still up and dressed, and were obviously not there to tick me off for being out so late. There was clearly something in the wind, though what it was I couldn't imagine. Certainly I was not prepared for the words which came immediately I had answered their questions about the dance. Mother could not keep silent longer. Neither could she prepare me gradually for the shock to come. Right out without any preliminaries, she asked: 'Willie, how would you like to live in Liverpool?' I could only stand and stare. I hadn't the slightest idea what the question conveyed. Football at that moment was far from my thoughts and Liverpool had never been in them at all. When I found words at last all I could say was: 'What on earth do you mean?' Then it came out bit by bit, and as it did I realized that, at the age of sixteen-and-a-half, I was at an important crossroads in my young life.

Matt Busby: I have always been happy to recall the part I played in that transfer. As a Liverpool player I still retained many connections with Manchester City and my playing colleagues at Maine Road. Alex Herd and I, as City players, used to play a lot of golf together in Scotland during the close season, and I saw no reason why my move to Merseyside should interfere with such enjoyable summertime activities. One day Alex Herd did not turn up for his round of the bunkers, and when I went in search of him, I was told that he had taken Willie McAndrew, the Hamilton Academicals manager, in his car to see a fifteen-year-old boy called Liddell playing football for Lochgelly Violet. No business was done with Hamilton because Billy Liddell's parents wanted some assurances about their son's future in the game, and Willie McAndrew's club were not really in a prosperous enough state to make lavish promises in that line. When Alex Herd told me the story, I immediately telephoned George Kay at Anfield and suggested he might succeed where Hamilton Academicals had failed. He did and Billy Liddell became a Liverpool player, a very fortunate day for Liverpool.

Billy Liddell: Let me add that it was also a very fortunate day for Billy Liddell. Whether or not I would have made a success in football had I remained in Scotland is pure conjecture. I might have been lucky, or I might not, but Matt did me a very good turn by putting Liverpool on my track. I well remember the day Mr Kay and Mr Billy McConnell, the chairman of the club, came to visit my parents at our home in Townhill near Dunfermline. They discussed my future and put at rest any fears that my mother and father had over the projected trip to Liverpool. Mr Kay said he would personally pick my lodgings and also keep a fatherly eye on me. That was my first meeting with the two men who were later to have much to do with my career. I liked them both from the start. Though widely different in temperament and outlook, Bill McConnell and George Kay had one thing in common – an intense love of the Liverpool Football Club and a burning desire to see it doing well.

Ten months after Liddell signed another youngster arrived on Merseyside and he too would have a big part to play in Liverpool's future.

8 May 1939

Bob Paisley: I was full of beans that day, but it was very quiet really. I was met at the station and after that long trek up Scotland Road in a tramcar, I found there were only one or two youngsters at the ground – Billy Liddell, Eddie Spicer and Ray Lambert. The rest had been recruited for the territorials.

Nice one Cyril

Liverpool v Chelsea
Anfield
Football League Division One
2 September 1939

As the threat of war intensified, a new local discovery made his mark in a game that was to be Liverpool's last competitive outing for six years.

Cyril Done: Well, you can imagine being chosen for Liverpool Football Club in 1939 – it was the greatest thrill of my life. I strived as hard as I could to score a goal and luck was with me, I headed the ball in and I can even remember the name of the centre-half – Salmond. The ball went into the net and I was the hero of the day. I got £8. I remember going down to a firm called Jackson's in London Road and buying myself a suit. They were about £3 in those days. And then war broke out...

War and Peace

1940-1949

Changing times

From the darkness of war to the light of a remarkable and unexpected League title triumph, this was a decade when new heroes emerged and Liverpool became established as a major force in the game once again.

Wartime Liverpool

As the Second World War raged across Europe and beyond, during the first half of the 1940s, football may have taken a back seat in terms of importance - but it continued nonetheless.

Phil Taylor: We were in the Infantry unit of the Ninth Kings, and at first we were deployed around Liverpool. I worked on a viaduct on the Liverpool-London railway line with a squad of the rest of our players. It was all the Liverpool players, and we were in bell-tents somewhere in Cheshire. We had to sort of guard this viaduct in case of sabotage. Tommy Cooper was our sergeant in charge. Good old Tom. There were two quick promotions made. Tom didn't know anything more about the army than the rest of us, but he was our senior so they gave Tom three stripes. The other sergeant was Arthur Riley, the goalkeeper, who had served in South Africa in the conscription days, so he knew a little about army procedure.

Matt Busby: It was a tragedy that, among all the Liverpool players who joined the Army as an entire club in 1939, Tommy Cooper became the only fatality... killed on a motor bicycle in this country.

Bob Paisley: My career as a professional with Liverpool had lasted just three months when I was called up. I had played in only two reserve games when the army beckoned. August Bank Holiday 1941 meant a departure for Egypt, and we arrived there after 10 weeks at sea. My first letter from home didn't arrive until it was nearly Christmas – and it was a note from Liverpool manager George Kay, telling me to report to the first game of the season against Preston! When I wrote back to Mr Kay, pointing out my whereabouts, he replied saying how lucky I was and how he wished he could change places with me. I felt the same way, wishing I could change places with him!

Billy Liddell: I wanted to qualify as a pilot but using my aptitude for maths I did so well in navigation that I was posted to the Air Navigation School at Bridgnorth in Shropshire. I was playing in a friendly scratch game with nothing at stake. We were winning with ease when, just before the end, I stumbled in a hole in the pitch and my ankle gave way. I was taken to hospital and learned I'd broken my leg just above the ankle. When I left hospital I went to the RAF Remedial Centre at Blackpool. After a month at Blackpool I returned to Bridgnorth and was posted to Heaton Park, near Manchester, where we were not allowed out of camp until 4.30pm on Saturdays. One week, when Liverpool were playing at Manchester City, I applied to get away at midday so I could turn out in the game. My application was refused but I still got to Maine Road. I just hopped over the camp wall when nobody was looking! I linked up with the Liverpool team at the station and went up to the ground in their coach. That was fortunate because there were scores of service police checking passes outside the ground. Luckily, they didn't check the passes of the servicemen on the coach and I got away with it.

Bob Paisley: My first derby game against Everton was early in the war, and at that time I was stationed in Tarporley in Cheshire, awaiting a posting abroad. It was a Liverpool Senior Cup final, and I was released to play in the game. But the army didn't provide the transport as well as a pass... so I cycled

30 miles to the ground. The crowd limit was supposed to be 15,000, but an estimated 30,000 saw the match – which Liverpool lost, 4-2.

Cyril Done: When we were in Leystone, some of us played for a works team on a Wednesday, to keep ourselves fit. And you can imagine a works team in Leystone, with players like Matt Busby, Phil Taylor and Jack Balmer. We quite enjoyed it.

Bob Paisley: The battery I was in went to the Far East. I should have gone with them but was transferred to another battery because I was the regimental soccer captain. That was a bit of luck because my unit was captured soon after it arrived and spent the rest of the war in a prisoner of war camp.

Billy Liddell: Wartime football did not mean long journeys for teams, but it did mean extra work for harassed managers. With players in the forces stationed all over the country, Mr Kay wrote thousands of letters and must have spent many hours on the phone to Commanding officers. Such was his personality that his own players and guest players would willingly make long journeys to play for the Reds. They helped to keep football going and the government said that in their view football was doing a service to the country in maintaining morale.

Cyril Done: We were in the entertainment business and obviously people in Britain wanted entertaining as much as possible. I think the powers-that-be thought it was good for the people of Merseyside that we should keep playing our game, the same as entertainers should carry on with their business.

Liddell's debut

Liverpool v Crewe Alexandra
Anfield
Western Division
1 January 1940

Billy Liddell: I was chosen at outside-left, we won 7-3, and I scored one of the goals after just two minutes... there was no happier youngster in Liverpool that day. My next senior game was against Manchester City at Maine Road, when I did even better by bagging a hat-trick in our 7-3 victory over a City side that included such starts as Frank Swift, Alex Herd, Bert Sproston, Les McDowall, Jackie Bray and others whose names were well known in the top sphere of football.

Shankly guests for Liverpool

Liverpool v Everton
Anfield
1942
Liverpool Senior Cup final

Bill Shankly: Before the game all the players, including Billy Liddell and myself, were in the passageway. But George Kay, the Liverpool manager, didn't speak. He just went round touching people on the shoulder. If he touched you, then you were playing.

Matt Busby's influence

Billy Liddell: Matt was a wonderful help on the field. You could hardly do anything other than play well with him behind you while off the field he was a constant source of good advice and valuable hints.

Phil Taylor: I must admit that I like to see a bit of style in a player – I tried to copy the likes of Matt Busby, who was an idol of mine for many years, and for a spell I played in the same side as Matt.

Billy Liddell: Matt Busby was never a robust player, although he had all the physical attributes. He never needed to use them because his ball control and distribution were second to none, while his positioning was such that he was always right in the game, without ever seeming to exert himself.

Phil Taylor: Matt was a player who played on the ground. He wasn't a big-boot player. He'd control the ball, bring it forward, bring it inside, more to the centre, and his left foot would go and the ball would go between the full-backs for Nieuwenhuys to run on to. You were looking for these things all the time and I tried to get myself doing the same thing later on.

Bob Paisley: I was deeply impressed by Matt Busby... a man you could look up to and respect. He'd played the game and people like him weren't solely tied down with tactics, which was a valuable lesson for me.

Laurie Hughes: Matt Busby was a nice fella, decent. We both loved the horses, so sometimes we'd go to the racing. Matt lived in Crosby, I was in Waterloo so we'd come home on the bus together.

But, as hostilities drew to a close Liverpool's revered pre-war captain contemplated his future in the game. The best years of his playing career behind him and, aged 36, he had a big decision to make.

Matt Busby: Liverpool were very keen to retain my services as a coach, and it seemed their offer of a five years' contract with the probability of promotion during that time, provided me with my main requirement... security. I agreed verbally to accept, but before signing a contract had a chat with the directors so as to leave no doubt in their minds that my hopes in soccer were centred on a managerial job, despite my keenness on coaching. The directors' plan was that, besides coaching, I could take some of the weight off George Kay. I was considering this offer, when quite unexpectedly I was informed that Mr JW Gibson, then chairman of Manchester United, would like to see me. The sequel was that his club offered me the manager's position at Old Trafford, this providing me with the opening I had been seeking. When I told the Liverpool directors of my decision they did not take it very well.

Post-war Liverpool

Laurie Hughes: The country yearned for top class football and nowhere was it more eagerly anticipated than in the city of Liverpool. For six long years Everton fans had all the bragging rights in the town. Merseyside was such an upbeat place back then, despite the horrors of war. Gradually things were turning back to normal, and that meant regular football. The game meant so much and to have it back brought a spring to the city's step. It got everyone going. After all, what else was there? As the season approached I remember just how excited the public were at the prospect of First Division action. There was a real buzz about the place. For our part, we were all just so glad to be back doing what we loved best; playing football and playing it competitively around the country. The city had been devastated by the sustained bombing of the Germans and it would take years to build it up again, but in the meantime, us footballers could hopefully put a smile back on the faces of our fellow Liverpudlians.

Eddie Spicer: In those days I never used to think about the money, and I don't think the other players did. They were just proud of playing for Liverpool. They were better off than if they had a job digging holes in the road or building houses. They were getting more money, and they were enjoying what they were doing.

Laurie Hughes: I don't think the players realised the amount of money they should have been getting. I never thought of it. I just wanted to enjoy my football which I did do, and get the rewards, which I thought at that particular time were good.

Cyril Done: If you went by bus or tram, you never paid. The conductor wouldn't take the money. It became embarrassing on certain occasions.

Stan Palk: Most of our training was done on the pitch at Anfield, that's why there was never any grass on it by Christmas. During the winter months when the pitch was covered in snow or the rain was falling heavily we used to run up and down the steps of the Kop. Albert Shelley and Jimmy Seddon were the trainers back then. We'd train every morning between 10 and 12 o'clock, unless you'd played on the Saturday. In that case you'd have the Monday off. And there was none of this warming up on the pitch before a match like they do nowadays. We'd just run out for the kick-off and get on with it. Anfield was mostly standing back then and held about 60,000-odd. The atmosphere was great and it was a privilege to play in front of such knowledgeable fans.

Laurie Hughes: We had a great spirit, a workaholic manager and, most importantly, some very good players. Liverpool had kept many of its key pre-war stars, but sadly lost the great Matt Busby. No matter, ours was a squad good enough, we hoped, to challenge the best of them.

George Kay: manager

Stan Palk: The manager, George Kay wasn't a bad fella either. You'd never hear him cursing and swearing. He was the type of manager you could talk to and I got along fine with him.

Matt Busby: A very fine man and manager whom I grew to admire, indeed I always regarded him as one of the best I have ever met in this great game... Often misunderstood because he could never control his feelings during a match, George was a familiar figure on the trainers' bench, shouting, beseeching, wringing his hands, holding his head in apparent anguish, and making an excellent attempt to kick and head every ball in the match. Perhaps George took his football too seriously, but a fanatical enthusiasm for his job – which should never be condemned – was entirely responsible for those odd manerisms.

Bob Paisley: He took Liverpool through the War to come out a bit like West Ham did after the First War. He was one of the people who laid the ground for the way Liverpool teams would play in the future... keeping the ball on the ground and passing it well, but being strong on the ball as well.

Laurie Hughes: To me, George was quite a dour man. I was one of the jokers in the team. I liked to play and train with a smile on my face, but George frowned upon too much fun so we didn't always see eye to eye. He was so desperate to achieve things that he often forgot to have fun and I found that side of his character hard to relate to. You had to respect him though. He knew what he wanted, he was football mad and that ultimately helped the team to succeed.

Albert Stubbins: George Kay was a lovely man, quiet and a deep thinker. He would read books about psychology and his first thought was always very much for his players. He would never criticise a Liverpool player in the press or tear a strip off us. He knew how to get the best out of his players. If we were trailing at half time he'd come into the dressing room and although he'd point out our errors he'd always say 'well played lads'. He knew and we knew that we weren't playing well but because he was so understanding we felt we had to play extra well to repay his faith in us.

Billy Liddell: He [Kay] had no other thought but for the good of Liverpool during his waking hours, and also during many of his nights. He told me often of the times he had lain in bed, unable to sleep, pondering over the manifold problems that beset every manager, but which can be a curse to the oversensitive or excessively conscientious ones... if any man gave his life for a club, George Kay did so for Liverpool.

Cyril Done: George Kay was the Shankly of his day. He ate, slept and lived for one thing only – football.

Breaking the bank for the 'Burning Stub'

Just weeks into the inaugural post-war Football League season of 1946/47 Liverpool caused a sensation in austerity-gripped Britain when they swooped to sign the prolific Geordie centre-forward Albert Stubbins for a club record £12,500.

Albert Stubbins: I was 27, Newcastle were in the Second Division, I wanted to play in the top-flight and, suddenly, I had a choice of two big First Division clubs [Liverpool and Everton]. It was a very difficult decision to make so I tossed a coin to decide which of the two teams I'd speak to first. It came down heads for Liverpool and I met George Kay and Bill McConnell. I was so impressed by their offer that I made my mind up without speaking to Theo Kelly. I explained to him that I'd decided to go to Anfield and I never regretted it.

Ray Lambert: I can remember playing for the reserves against Newcastle when I was 16. It was a Wednesday afternoon. We're all stripped and running on the field when I spotted this huge big fellow coming on with this huge red nose and a mop of red hair. I thought, 'Oh my God, what's this?' I thought it was a heavyweight boxer. It was Albert Stubbins.

Bob Paisley: Albert cost Liverpool a record fee at the time [and] he repaid it with many goals. He was a very good player and livened us up when he first came to Anfield from Newcastle.

Albert Stubbins: The fact that I'd scored goals for Newcastle gave me the confidence to think I could do it for Liverpool. In contrast to some players who later moved for bigger fees, I never felt any sense of strain over the price Liverpool had paid. It was never a worry to me. In fact, it was an incentive for me.

Laurie Hughes: We had signed a player who would complete a fantastic forward line and help us challenge for, and ultimately win, the title.

Albert Stubbins: The Liverpool team was such a good one, I never felt under any pressure. Maybe I should have done being the record signing but I never did. I remember on my debut at Bolton seeing how the Liverpool defence coped so well with their attack. This gave me so much confidence because I knew the players around me were all capable.

Bob Paisley: He changed his style to suit the First Division... and liked to wander out to the wing in a rather unconventional way for a forward of his day. He was a nippy little player in his younger days but was beginning to slow down when he joined us and redeveloped his all round game to compensate for that lack of searing pace.

Jimmy Payne: He didn't head many goals, but he was brilliant at bringing balls down. That was his greatest asset. He could get his foot up there and he could stop it and bring it straight down. With most people it would have bounced miles away.

Bob Paisley: He preferred the ball on the floor and wasn't the greatest header of a ball that I've seen – in fact, he would rather pull away from his defender as much as he could with the ball at his feet. He was very effective at that.

Albert Stubbins: The support of the fans also helped me settle when I first arrived. I always felt I had their support and I'll be eternally grateful to them for that. Even if I had a bad game the crowd would never crucify me like they would some players. As a player it is so important that the fans take to you. If they don't it can result in a very unhappy and unsettling time. Fortunately I had no such problems at Liverpool and everything went so well.

Balmer's hat-trick of hat-tricks

The sporting headlines in November 1946 belonged solely to one man; the often unpopular Liverpool inside-forward Jack Balmer, who created history with an unprecedented goalscoring feat.

Jack Balmer: Towards the end of a long career memories crowd thick and fast on one. That which remains most fresh in my mind was when I had the good fortune, thanks to the unselfishness of my team-mates, to score three successive hat-tricks in 1946-47.

Bob Paisley: I don't honestly think I've ever known a player so harshly treated by Liverpool supporters as he was – but he managed to smile his way through although it hurt him deeply.

Bill Jones: Jack was the experienced man in the team. He was a hell of a nice fella.

Bob Paisley: He was a local lad, born and bred in Liverpool, and he gave everything to his only professional club but there was a group of supporters who could never forgive him because he didn't get stuck into the tackle. He accepted the criticism but refused to change his style.

Jack Balmer: They were entitled to their opinion. Maybe I didn't go in for the crunch tackle but that kind of thing wasn't my idea of football. I was never a coward at the game but I got a shudder when I saw the boot going in.

Laurie Hughes: Jack wasn't the type of player who would battle alone up front and take the harsh treatment that could be dished out by the country's defenders. He didn't like the rough and tumble aspect of the game. Jack thrived on running onto balls and his speed often saw him race clear of those nasty centre-halves and that's how he got so many of his goals.

Bill Jones: I think that he had speed but his main sense was upstairs. He was a thinker.

Laurie Hughes: He was only a very slight chap really, nothing really strong about him, but he had a wonderful shot on him. Sometimes we'd think he'd shoot from ridiculous distances, but they still went in the net.

Albert Stubbins: He was very closely marked, but he still came through. He could turn very quickly, could Jack. Some players need a yard or two to manoeuvre, but Jack could turn in a very tight space and shoot very quickly. He was a quick thinker.

Bob Paisley: While a lot was made of his ten goals in three games – he scored a hat-trick at home to Portsmouth, four at Derby County and then another hat-trick at home to Arsenal – he should have been given far greater credit for his scoring run that season which saw him on target in seven successive matches between the beginning of November and the middle of December. In those games he scored 15 goals – a scoring rate that even Ian Rush, the greatest goal-scorer I've ever seen in the English game, would have been proud of. He was phenomenal for much of that season.

Laurie Hughes: At the time when Jackie Balmer scored these goals, you didn't realise what a big thing it was.

Charlie Ashcroft: I was playing for the reserves away at Derby the day he scored his third successive hat-trick. As we came off the pitch all we were interested in was events at Anfield and how many goals Jackie Balmer had scored. As we got to dressing room the director who had travelled with us came rushing in to tell us the news and the place erupted. Everyone was delighted for him and, coupled with our win that day, it was a very happy journey home.

Albert Stubbins: I think that was his greatest season. Certainly, he couldn't have performed any better, because he took the weight off me and in a way we took the weight off each other because the other team had to watch for two goalscorers - not just one.

The goal in the snow

Albert Stubbins registered 83 goals in 178 games during the course of his seven-year Liverpool career but there's one in particular that remains ingrained in Anfield folklore.

Liverpool v Birmingham City
Anfield
FA Cup quarter-final
1 March 1947

Albert Stubbins: The move that led to that goal actually came about because of something that had happened in the previous round against Derby County. During that particular match Billy Liddell made ground on the left wing and hit a terrific low ball across, which myself and Jack Balmer just failed to get to. I was annoyed because the ball needed just a touch and it would have been in the back of the net so I thought to myself that next time Bill put the ball over I would anticipate him hitting it low and hard. Anyway we won a free-kick on the left and he hit this low ball across the goalmouth. The Birmingham defence was certainly not expecting such a cross but, remembering what had happened against Derby, I threw myself full length at the ball and just managed to get my head to it.

Billy Liddell: When I put the ball over it was going a bit off course but Albert literally threw himself through the air to meet it with his head when parallel with the ground, about two feet above the pitch. It went in like a rocket, giving Gil Merrick absolutely no chance, and Albert slid on his stomach for several yards on the frozen surface before coming to a stop.

Albert Stubbins: With the pitch being so icy I skidded along on top of the ice and as I picked myself up my knees were all bloodied. Although at the time I didn't mind in the least.

Billy Liddell: It was an amazing goal by Albert. Nobody who saw it could ever forget it.

Albert Stubbins: I was still staying in a city centre hotel at the time and after the game I returned to collect my bags before travelling back up to the north east for the weekend. Some of the supporters must have seen me going into the hotel because I suddenly became aware of chanting outside. I looked out the window and there was a large crowd fans singing my name. It was one of the greatest moments in my life.

The original crazy gang

'Liverpool FC – styled the Crazy Gang – are not offended by such a title. The truth is everyone knows them to be an attractive and compelling side, with a strange mixture of the very good and the very bad when least expected. Hence the tag.' – The Sports Spectator, April 1947

Albert Stubbins: Wherever we played, George Kay wouldn't say to us, 'I want you back here at the hotel at such-and-such a time'. He'd say, 'You're Liverpool players, you're men and you're professionals, so go where you please but we expect you to have in mind that you have a game the following day'. That was the thing about Liverpool that I liked. They treated you as men. If there's one thing that stayed with me from my presence at Liverpool it is that.

Stan Palk: I was fortunate to play alongside some great players, the likes of Albert Stubbins and Billy Liddell. Billy was probably the star man at the time. He was a nice lad, strong and a good runner. Once he got the ball he was away. He could also play on the right or the left. Bob Paisley was another one. I used to be inside left and Paisley was behind me. Out of them all though I'd say the best player was Phil Taylor. He couldn't half pass a ball could Phil.

Albert Stubbins: That Liverpool team was a very good one. There was a tremendous feeling of togetherness. Cyril Sidlow was the goalkeeper; Ray Lambert and Jim Harvey were full-backs, Phil Taylor, Laurie Hughes, Bob Paisley. 'Nivvy' the South African, Jack Balmer, myself, Willie Fagan and a very unknown player... Billy Liddell! I'm joking, but at that time he was just a youngster coming up. He was a great player and a nice fella.

Laurie Hughes: We had a very good all-round side, solid and consistent. We were very good defensively and had a forward line with Billy Liddell and Albert Stubbins who took their opportunities quite well.

Albert Stubbins: When I first signed I expected to be playing my normal game but George [Kay] pointed out that as a high profile signing I would be well marked, with two or three players on me at times. His plan was for me to lie deep every now and again and let Jack Balmer come through the middle. We did this and it puzzled opposing defences. As a result myself and Jack scored a lot of goals between us. The manager, George Kay, used to look on Billy, Jack Balmer and myself as his heavy artillery.

Eddie Spicer: I always found it pleasant in Liverpool. I can't remember any ill-feelings in any dressing room. They were keyed up going out. They never used to talk a lot, never used to crack jokes. They were feeling serious. There was never a lot said before the game. There was plenty after the game... everybody was in the same frame of mind.

Albert Stubbins: We used to discuss the games, and how we played, light-heartedly in the bath afterwards. Any serious inquests were done later. After a match in the dressing room, amidst the piles of cotton wool, laces, boots and jerseys littering the floor, Phil Taylor's first move was for his cigarettes. He'd take two out of his case and flip one to Jack Balmer. Cyril Sidlow, from his long experience of catching trains after a game, was first in the bath, closely followed by his close friend and Wales compatriot Ray Lambert. Billy Liddell and I usually made straight for the vast tea urn to have a cuppa while our trainer Albert Shelley did about ten things at once!

Winning the title against all odds

Stan Palk: That was certainly a good team alright but it was only towards the end of the season that they made their charge for the title. I played a few times before getting injured, but they then went on this run that ended with us winning the league. It was a real achievement because it was a really strong division back then.

Bill Jones: We weren't favourites but Albert Stubbins came that season and Albert was really on song.

Bob Paisley: In the league we had moved from close to the foot of the table right up the ladder, after a run which took us unbeaten through a dozen matches.

Billy Liddell: Then we had a lean patch and lost ground. The championship hardly entered our heads because not only had we lost our place at the top of the table but seven of our remaining thirteen league games were away. We had to finish the season with four successive away matches, the last two being at Arsenal and Wolves. So it looked impossible.

Wolverhampton Wanderers v Liverpool
Molineux
Football League Division One
31 May 1947

Albert Stubbins: The season had been extended because of a very bad winter and icy grounds that couldn't be played upon and so it was May, going into June, before we finished the season. The last game of the season for us was at Wolverhampton and we had to win that game to win the title. Wolves were ahead in the table and they just had to get a draw. We were up against the finest centre-half that I ever played against, Stan Cullis, the Wolves and England captain. So it was a tough game for Liverpool.

Billy Liddell: But we were not a team to give up on anything and everybody was determined to have a go at it. Our team spirit during those last few weeks was as good as anything I'd experienced. There could have been no happier atmosphere anywhere.

Albert Stubbins: Everyone was very tense during the build up to the game at Molineux because so much rested on it. We had a couple of key players missing and Bob Priday a young South African winger was brought into the team at outside left.

Billy Liddell: The day was more suitable for cricket than football. It was extremely hot, with the thermometer somewhere in the eighties, and I remember remarking to Albert Stubbins about the vast number of spectators in short-sleeves or summer frocks. We were the first to score when Jackie Balmer steered one into the net and when Albert Stubbins got a second we thought the game was safely in the bag.

Albert Stubbins: I had a word with Bob before the game and I told him if he received the ball in a deep midfield position to knock it straight down the middle for me to chase. The first opportunity he got he did exactly that and it took the Wolves defence completely by surprise. Anticipating what he was going to do I had already set off and I left Stan Cullis and Billy Wright trailing in my wake. As I closed in on goal the keeper Bert Williams came rushing off his line but I just managed to get my toe to the ball and poke it past him into the corner of the net.

Billy Liddell: Wolves, however, were never a team to give up without a struggle. Cullis was a wonderful inspiration, urging his players on and making them fight as though their lives depended on it. Jimmy Dunn reduced the lead, but that was all Wolves could achieve, largely because our defence gave one of the finest exhibitions seen at Molineux for many a long day. It was ironic that the man who did most to keep Wolves from the draw, which would, as things turned out, have given them the championship, was their former goalkeeper Sidlow. Cyril made save after save when it seemed certain that he must be beaten.

Albert Stubbins: When the final whistle blew, Stan Cullis came up to me and shook hands. He was very, very sporting and the tears were streaming down his cheeks, he was so counting on winning a Championship medal. He'd won everything else and captained England, but that was his last big season and it ended in defeat for him.

Jack Balmer: It was a great day and a great feeling and I remember being carried off the Molineux pitch at the end shoulder-high.

Laurie Hughes: Although we were top of the league then, it wasn't certain that we'd won it though until somebody else played.

Billy Liddell: We were a happy party returning from Wolverhampton, but still had to wait a forthnight before knowing whether we were champions. Stoke had one game to play, against Sheffield United at Bramall Lane, which could not take place until June 14.

Liverpool v Everton
Anfield
Liverpool Senior Cup final
14 June 1947

Billy Liddell: Stoke had to beat Sheffield United to deny us the championship and, not surprisingly, our minds were more on what was happening there than in our game, although we managed to beat Everton 2-1. Loudspeaker announcements kept us informed about the score at Sheffield and the last ten minutes at Anfield were purely academic with the news that Stoke had lost 2-1. We were champions!

Albert Stubbins: We could hear some rustling among the crowd and all of a sudden a massive roar went up. Then it was confirmed over the tannoy and the fans swarmed onto the pitch. The game stopped and the Everton players went around shaking all our hands. They had won the last title before the war and it was great that it was staying on Merseyside.

Billy Liddell: 1946/47 was a great triumph because no-one expected us to win the league. It was a wonderful season right through.

Bob Paisley: I'd won a lot of cups and medals up in the north-east and then I found myself winning a championship in my first season of league football with Liverpool. I don't know about my ability but I must have been a lucky mascot!

Albert Stubbins: It was an amazing finish to the season. If you'd read it in one of the old comic books you wouldn't have believed it. So many players in that side reached their peak that season. We were the best team in the country and deserved to win the league.

Red neighbours

As Britain slowly readjusted to life after the war, an acute shortage of adequate housing posed major problems – even for footballers. So, in the belief that stability off the field breeds stability on it, Liverpool's board of directors boldly sanctioned the purchase of six newly-built semi-detached properties for their players.

Albert Stubbins: About eight of the players lived in one street. The club had bought these houses and they were newly constructed. Phil Taylor was in one. Phil was always a smooth, imperturbable man, the perfect Englishman. He lived on one side, Bob Paisley and Jessie, his wife, on the other. On my side there was Billy Liddell, Ted Spicer, Cyril Done and myself, so there were quite a crowd of us, and in the morning we would head for Anfield together.

Bob Paisley: We had a fine time then because most of the players lived near each other in Bowring Park. Willie Fagan, Ted Spicer, Albert, Cyril Done, Phil Taylor, Bill and I all lived in the Greystone Road-Westfield Avenue area and I think we paid 25 shillings a week in rent to the club.

Billy Liddell: Bob and I lived opposite each other and the day my wife and I moved in, Bob was the first person across our doorstep to welcome us.

Bob Paisley: Bill's wife Phyllis was the first one to get a washing machine, I think it was a Bendix, and we all went in to have a look at it because it was such a rarity in those days.

Albert Stubbins: Of course, petrol was short and none of us was running a car at the time. We travelled by bus. Phil Taylor was utterly unflappable. He was usually very prompt but one morning Phil had overslept. The rest of us got up to Anfield and, lo and behold, Phil came in about a quarter to ten, and we were supposed to be training at ten. Not only did he come in late but underneath his suit he had on his pyjamas and he was unshaven. But he'd brought a razor with him and was shaving in front of the mirror at five to ten, and Albert Shelley, our trainer, said, 'Here we are, supposed to be pushing for the Championship, and Phil Taylor's having a shave at five to ten', which we all took in good heart.

Bob Paisley: I can remember one incident when we all had to give Albert Stubbins a hand after he had bought a new bedroom suite which wouldn't go through the front door. We had to take out a window and hoist it up to get it into his bedroom!

Stubbins threatened

Liverpool v Huddersfield Town
Anfield
Football League Division One
6 March 1948

Albert Stubbins: On the morning of the match I received a telegram and although I can't remember the exact wording, the general consensus of it was that if I scored my legs would be broken. I did not want to unduly worry the rest of the team so I kept it to myself. It was obviously meant to frighten me but it didn't work. I went out and scored a hat-trick in a 4-0 win. I never did find out who sent it but maybe they should have sent me them more often! Perhaps it was George Kay's way of geeing me up.

Stubbins on strike

August-October 1948

Albert Stubbins: It had always been my intention to pursue a career in journalism once my playing days ended. When I signed for Liverpool the chairman Bill McConnell arranged for me to write a weekly column in the Football Echo. When Bill died the board felt they weren't responsible for his promise. There was some confusion and that is why I delayed signing on. It was all very amicable and at no time did the club and myself ever fall out. I always had a good relationship with the Liverpool board. It was a private matter and that is why so few people knew the real reasons behind the dispute, it was widely assumed that my family was unsettled on Merseyside.

Bust and Boom

1950-1959

The bad years

No-one could have foreseen the downward spiral that awaited Liverpool in the 1950s, certainly not at the very start of the decade when the Reds embarked on a run to their first-ever Wembley cup final. The woe experienced against Arsenal was a sign of what was to follow...

A grey day in the capital

Liverpool v Arsenal
Wembley
FA Cup final
29 April 1950

Albert Stubbins: To be a member of the first Liverpool team to play at Wembley was very special, even if the result did not go our way. I'd rather get there and lose than not get there at all because to play in the FA Cup final was a marvellous experience.

Phil Taylor: Even though we lost, in those days it was quite something for Liverpool to go to Wembley, and so far as I was concerned that final was the match to cap them all.

Billy Liddell: After the semi-final we had five weeks to wait for the final and they were the longest five weeks of my career. It got worse in the last fortnight, with the excitement mounting and it seemed that half the male population of Liverpool wanted to be at Wembley to cheer us on.

Albert Stubbins: Two weeks before the Cup final, we played Arsenal at Highbury and we beat them. And a few weeks previous to that we played them at Anfield and also beat them, without any bother, so we fancied our chances at Wembley. After winning the semi-final Phil Taylor would drum it into us that we were a better team than Arsenal and we all believed him.

Billy Liddell: A lot of people think we lost the match in the boardroom beforehand, because in those days the directors had the final word on team selection. They left Bob Paisley out, who had scored one of our goals in the semi-final.

Bob Paisley: I knew that George Kay didn't pick the team but I was so disappointed I could hardly look at him when he got on the team bus. I was with the lads at the time so I didn't say anything. I didn't want to upset them because I wanted them to win the cup. I had a good heart-to-heart chat with Albert Stubbins, who was a good friend, and I told him I was thinking of leaving Liverpool. I also had an offer from a Sunday paper offering quite a bit of money to have a go in print about being left out and saying publicly how I felt. I was tempted but I turned them down. I didn't want the big headlines.

Albert Stubbins: Bob was shattered to be left out and I don't think it was particularly wise for us to take to the field without him. Bob was one of our most consistent players and, of course, he'd scored a goal in the semi-final against Everton. He would have been a good man to stop Alex Forbes, who on the day was Arsenal's star player, because he was a great tackler.

Phil Taylor: Bob must have been the unluckiest player ever not to be in the team and if he had been I'm sure we'd have won. That's no reflection on any of those who did play, but Bob's qualities would have been invaluable at Wembley.

Jimmy Payne: We might have won the cup if Bob had played because he was such a hard worker. I played at inside-forward as well as on the wing and Bob played like two men. He was always feeding you the ball. Without that supply you can't play and Bob was a great supplier.

Laurie Hughes: Well I usually played centre-half and Bob played left half, but Bill Jones, who had played centre-half in the previous games went to left-half.

Bill Jones: I never heard the last of that. Whenever the 1950 final is mentioned so is the fact that I was chosen ahead of Bob. Bob and I were the best of pals. We more or less did everything together at the club. I felt sorry for Bob and it put me in a position. I know Bob felt it; he felt it very much.

Laurie Hughes: I don't know whether it was a good move or not, but I don't think the whole side performed as well as they could do on that day.

Bill Jones: I didn't have a good game but not many of us did. Stubbins and Payne each had chances and I hit the crossbar with a header which would have made it 1-1.

Jimmy Payne: Arsenal were one up after 15 minutes and got another after the interval. Even then we were not finished, and I think Arsenal owe more to goalkeeper George Swindin than they will ever realise. Liverpool flung everything into attack, determined to pull level, and Billy Liddell, breaking away, put across a peach of a centre. Swindin palmed the ball out and I flung myself forward to head. 'Goal! It's a goal'. The shout of triumph was in my throat – when the goalkeeper made an incredible save. How he got into position I will never know. I don't think he knew himself.

Billy Liddell: We had our chances but we didn't take them.

Bill Jones: The other side of it was that Billy Liddell took a bit of a hammering from Alex Forbes, which wasn't too good.

Ray Lambert: They had a lad there, Forbes, who did his job on Billy. He just hammered Billy everywhere he went, because he was that type of player, this Forbes.

Phil Taylor: I suppose they said, 'Billy Liddell's the danger man, so you get on to him and don't let him out of your sight'. Yes, they did have a go at Bill, although I don't suppose it made an awful lot of difference because Bill was that type of fellow who would get through anyway and would take some stopping once he got going.

Billy Liddell: Alec did come in a bit high, with his boot raised, and he caught me down the arm and side with his studs, but it was nothing serious. We lost because they were the better team on the day and we never played to our potential.

Albert Stubbins: Unfortunately Arsenal beat us 2-0. It was very frustrating to lose to them because I felt we were the best in the country at the time but Arsenal were on form that day and we weren't, it was as simple as that. They played very well. There was no luck about it, they scored two goals and that was it.

Liddell receives a lucrative offer

It was unheard of for British footballer's to try their luck abroad in the 1950s but in 1951 Liverpool star Billy Liddell was the subject of an audacious bid from a team in Colombia.

Billy Liddell: I was contacted by the English agent representing the Bogota clubs. The offer included a signing-on fee of £2,000 with top wages and hefty bonuses. It was enough to make anyone consider the matter seriously and I certainly gave it a lot of thought. Perhaps if my twin boys had been four or five years old instead of only a few months I would have had an even harder decision to make. The fact that the boys were so young finally decided me against accepting the offer. Later on, after hearing of the conditions in Colombia, I was jolly glad I'd decided to stay at home.

Don Welsh: manager

Just eight months after guiding Liverpool to a first Wembley appearance, ill-health forced George Kay to relinquish his managerial duties at Anfield. His successor was a former Charlton Athletic centre-forward who had guested for Liverpool during the war...

Don Welsh: Liverpool asked me to go for an interview. The next day I was told that they had agreed to appoint me. It was a wonderful opportunity to put my ideas into practice.

Phil Taylor: Don Welsh used to be very athletic, different to George Kay, who'd never worn a tracksuit. I think he'd got this through his army days, where he was a PT Corps instructor. We were given different exercises with the ball. We had the ball more often in those days than we did before the war. He tried to make training interesting, instead of the run-of-the-mill exercising.

Albert Stubbins: Don had this defensive theory. I remember a tactical talk he gave us. He said, 'Now, in football, if the others don't score, you can't lose'. He had us doing man-to-man marking. If their centre-half went up for a free-kick in our goalmouth, say, I had to go and mark him. In other words we had to play a negative game.

Ronnie Moran: In many ways he was ahead of his time. I was a part-time professional when he arrived and he had something in common with our later manager, Bill Shankly... he played in practice games and wouldn't allow the final whistle until his team were in front.

Cyril Done: When I was playing for Port Vale I was going to play against Liverpool on the Good Friday, so I rang Don Welsh on the Tuesday and said, 'Could you give me a lift down?' He said, 'Well, we're stopping at the Good Companion and I don't want you knowing any of our secrets'. Jokingly, I said,

'I know your secrets, Don, you've no need to worry'. Whether that upset him or not, I don't know, but he said, 'I'm sorry, I can't give you a lift down'. I thought, 'Good God,' because it was customary practise if somebody lived in their area. During the war I think most clubs helped out one another on travelling all over the place. Anyhow, that afternoon, I thought, 'I must get a goal by hook or by crook, because Don Welsh wouldn't give me a lift'. I got four, and even the Liverpool players came and congratulated me afterwards, but I don't think Don was very happy. When I was walking up the stairs after the game, he said, 'What the hell were you playing at?' I said, 'Serves you right, Don, for not giving me a lift'.

Alan A'Court: I'll always be grateful to Don Welsh because he introduced me to the game. He signed me by impersonating a police officer, coming down on to our local ground saying 'is Mr A'Court here because a bike has been stolen'. It was just for somebody to point me out and then of course he asked me if I would sign and that was it. He was quite a character, very likeable.

Ray Lambert: You never knew what Don was going to do. He was what I called a Peter Pan sort of character, he never grew up.

Laurie Hughes: He did some very wild things, like standing on his hands in public.

Jimmy Payne: He used to walk around the boardroom on his hands when we'd won a match.

Alan A'Court: He'd drive down Sheil Road banging his hands on the roof of his car! Mad things like that.

Ronnie Moran: I liked him. He's gone down in history as Liverpool's least successful manager due to the fact that he oversaw our relegation in 1954. He inherited a lot of players in their thirties when he arrived but gave me my chance and was always passionate about the game. I'll never forget him for that. He was a good bloke, someone I had a lot of time for.

A record Anfield attendance

Liverpool v Wolverhampton Wanderers
Anfield
FA Cup fourth round
2 February 1952

Billy Liddell: In the cup tie against Wolves, which drew Anfield's record attendance of 61,905, a tactical plan paid off handsomely. When our team was announced my name was, as usual, at outside left and Cyril Done's at centre forward. We knew that whatever schemes Wolves might contrive would be based on that formation. But Cyril and I received our instructions and when we lined up for the kick-off Cyril was on the left wing and I was in the middle.

Cyril Done: We walked on and I had number nine on and Billy had his number eleven on, and then as we walked on we just went into the various positions and just confused Billy Wright completely.

Billy Liddell: It didn't seem anything major but I think it temporarily upset Wolves' plans and made them reconsider what to do to clamp down on our attack. And it was during the crucial few minutes when they were readjusting that we did the damage. I don't know what Billy Wright's thoughts were when he saw me lining up at centre forward but people told me afterwards that he had a puzzled look! The surprise paid off, for Bob Paisley scored a goal within the first few minutes which was just the spur we wanted. When Cyril Done got a second soon after, I was doubly pleased because it was my idea he should be in the team. Our plan had been discussed in the week by our chairman, George Richards, Don Welsh and myself. Another player's name was mentioned as a subject for the switch but I suggested that Cyril was better suited for it. It was one of the very few times in my career that I was asked for my opinion on team selection.

Relegation

1953/54

Laurie Hughes: What happened was, the great players we had got old. And they were never replaced. Simple as that. We were in a poor way and had come close to it the previous season.

Billy Liddell: My memories of 1953/54 are all disappointing ones. For some time, in the words of the press, 'the writing had been on the wall' at Anfield. We had progressively declined from eighth place in 1950 to ninth, eleventh and then seventeenth.

Bob Paisley: Phil Taylor, Laurie Hughes and myself began the 1953/54 season as the first team half back line but, as a trio, we only ever played three games together that season. Phil dropped out after only five games and only ever made one further appearance.

Louis Bimpson: We got off to a bad start in 1953/54, later refound our confidence, and then a tragic incident hit us in a match against Manchester United. Full-back Eddie Spicer went into a tackle and didn't get up. He had broken a leg.

Bob Paisley: We could never decide on our best goalkeeper. Russell Crossley and Charlie Ashcroft had been in and out of the first team with neither of them able to claim the place for their own. We'd been shipping goals, had only won five matches, and were heading for the second division. At Portsmouth's Fratton Park, we were thrashed 5-1 by Pompey. Earlier in the season, we'd been done six at Charlton, five at Chelsea and also lost 5-1 at home to Preston North End. Manager Don Welsh decided it was time to do something about it. A few days before our trip to Old Trafford, Mr Welsh signed Geoff Twentyman for £10,000 from Carlisle United and Dave Underwood for £7,000 from Watford.

Eddie Spicer: We didn't know anything about him [Underwood] and after about 20 minutes I can remember Roger Byrne, who was outside left that day, going down the wing. I went with Tommy Taylor. Roger hit this ball, hard and low across the penalty box and I went for the ball expecting our goalkeeper to come out and drop on it. That's what our other goalkeepers would have done and that's what I thought Underwood would do. Instead he just took a woof at it with his boot, missed the ball and hit me. He was very upset about it afterwards and blamed himself for it.

Bob Paisley: That mighty blow shattered Ted's left leg. It disengrated just the way a piece of dead wood does if you tread on it. In all he had 19 fractures and he was in and out of hospital for the next 12 months having it set and reset and it took more than 12 months to get over it and to start to walk again. Ted never played another football match after that.

Louis Bimpson: He [Spicer] was a great clubman and the injury was felt by everyone in the team. I think we might have turned the corner but for that. Our position had reached a critical stage and we could not pull clear.

Geoff Twentyman: I made my debut at Old Trafford. It was 0-0 after about 20 minutes – then Eddie Spicer broke a leg, and our 10-man team ended by losing 5-1. At the Easter, we were on our way down... but we beat Middlesbrough twice, and took them down with us.

Roy Saunders: It was a sad blow for us all when we were relegated in 1954. Bad luck seemed to be against us all the time; we lost numerous matches by a single goal, and even the signing of a decent number of new players did not prevent the dreaded drop into Division Two.

Alan A'Court: The team was in slow decline and it was not a particularly nice feeling to be relegated, I can tell you that. But it was no use worrying about it. We just had to get on with it.

Bob Paisley: At the end of the season both Phil Taylor and myself were given free transfers but offered the chance to stay at the club on the training staff. I was asked to take charge of the reserves and Phil was appointed club coach.

Record defeat

Birmingham City v Liverpool
St Andrews
Football League Division Two
11 December 1954

Alan A'Court: I was barely 20 and had never known anything like it. It was a result that knocked me flat. When we got back to Merseyside I wouldn't even go home. I stayed sulking at my aunties. It was a game you had to see to believe. We went 3-0 down in the opening 15 minutes before Billy Liddell pulled one back for us. We conceded another goal before half-time and let in another five in the second half. The pitch at Birmingham was wet on top and rock hard underneath and we were slipping and sliding all over the place. We just weren't able to adapt to the conditions and it was an unbelievable result. Before we knew it the game had gone from us. It didn't help that the Birmingham players had trainers on and we didn't. But I don't want to make excuses. It was a day to forget all round, although I still say Billy's goal was the best of the ten goals scored that day! He kept his balance beautifully on that treacherous surface, turned like an ice-skater and hit a screamer past England goalkeeper Gil Merrick into the top corner of the net. The final score was Birmingham 9, Liverpool 1.

Restoring local pride

Everton v Liverpool
Goodison Park
FA Cup fourth round
29 January 1955

Roy Saunders: The best example of the use of tactical talks I have known, came in a cup-tie against Everton in 1955. We were not given a chance in this tussle which had set all Merseyside fans arguing. Everton were doing well in the First Division... we were not doing too brilliantly in Division Two.

Billy Liddell: We were very much the underdogs. We had failed to win an away game up to then that season while Everton were doing quite well in the First Division and were strong favourites. They'd just done a Christmas double over Wolves, winning 3-1 at Molineux and 3-2 at Goodison against the club who were the glamour side of the time after beating some of Europe's top clubs. So the tie looked a certainty for Everton. But certainties in football have a nasty habit of coming unstuck.

Roy Saunders: For some days beforehand our manager Mr Don Welsh had us practicing a special move.

Alan A'Court: A Liverpool supporter had actually written to Don Welsh explaining the tactics of the Everton defence. He wrote that when Everton defended a free-kick their defenders would all run out to catch the opposing forwards offside. For about three days prior to the match we worked on this at Melwood and on the day of the game it paid off, with me scoring the goal.

Roy Saunders: We arranged that wing half Geoff Twentyman would take the free-kicks on his side of the field and that inside forward Johnny Evans would lie back.

Alan A'Court: We were one up at the time when we got a free-kick. To the surprise of the Everton defence none of our forwards ran forward and as they charged out it left a hole for John Evans who found himself with the ball at his feet and clean through on goal with only the keeper to beat. He was eventually forced wide as the defenders chased back but he got the cross over.

Ronnie Moran: Eric Anderson ran through and managed to pass to Alan A'Court, who come in on the left and scored with an angled shot from about eight yards out. It was a crucial goal for us.

Alan A'Court: It came to me and I whacked it in. It was a practise move that paid off in front of 72,000 fans.

Billy Liddell: It was the only time I remember us practicing a set piece move [and] manager Don Welsh was so pleased he gave us 10 shillings each!

Roy Saunders: I'm certain that goal demoralised Everton and was the key in our surprise 4-0 win.

Laurie Hughes: I got a right clattering in that game but the best you could hope for was the magic sponge. There were no substitutes in those days so instead of being taken off I was switched to outside left with Alan A'Court moving inside, Evans operating at centre forward, Geoff Twentyman taking over at centre half and Bill Liddell dropping to left half. But we won – and, as captain, I was overjoyed!

Ronnie Moran: It was the best thing that had happened to Liverpool for years. But there were no prolonged celebrations in those days. After waving to the supporters at the end we got changed and made our way home.

Billy Liddell: It was a truly great day for us. We turned the form book upside down and ran Everton off their feet. In doing so we gave our delighted supporters ammunition for their arguments with Evertonians over the respective merits of the two teams.

Ronnie Moran: I think Billy and Laurie Hughes were the only two players in our squad who had cars and after that great win over Everton I walked down to Sleepers Hill to get the number eighteen tram to Seaforth, then caught the bus home to Crosby. The Liverpool fans I met on the way were delighted.

Alan A'Court: It was always nice to put one over on our near neighbours, especially with us being a division lower than them but sadly we lost in the next round at home to Huddersfield.

Young Melia's first team bow

Jimmy Melia: My debut was against Nottingham Forest in December 1955. In them days the directors still picked the team and we used to get the Liverpool Echo on a Wednesday lunchtime to find out who would be playing at the weekend. I was playing for the for the youth team against Bolton Wanderers this day and was on the bus to the ground when I saw the headline 'Young Melia Set To Make His Debut'. I couldn't believe it. That Forest game is one I'll remember for the rest of my life. The great Billy Liddell was playing. He scored a hat-trick that day and I was lucky enough to get one myself, from a cross by him. I hit it with my left foot and it finished up in the far corner, right in front of the Kop so it was a great start for me you know.

The goal that never was

Liverpool v Manchester City
Anfield
FA Cup fifth round replay
22 February 1956

Ronnie Moran: We drew at Maine Road on the Saturday and in them days you replayed on either the Tuesday or Wednesday afternoon because obviously there were no floodlights. It had been snowing and the pitch was frost bound.

Alan A'Court: It was played on a terrible pitch. In those days there was no messing about. If the pitch was bad they just brushed the snow off and you got on with it.

Ronnie Moran: We were doing well but they made it 2-1 late on. Then with the last kick of the game Billy, who was renowned for his long-range shooting, struck this ball from way out. As soon as it left his boot you could see that it was going in, I was right behind it.

Billy Liddell: With City leading and the last few seconds ticking away, Mr Griffiths [referee] was looking at his watch when I got the ball near the centre circle and made a bee-line for goal. The roar of the crowd was terrific. I knew this was our last chance and I just let fly with everything I had from just inside the penalty area, leaving Bert Trautmann helpless.

Ronnie Moran: But the referee, a Welshman called Griffiths, supposedly blew his whistle before the ball hit the net and so we lost 2-1. That was a big disappointment for us.

Billy Liddell: When I turned around I realised that the 'goal' had come just a few seconds too late. Though no attacking player had heard the whistle, and the City defence did all they could to stop me, apparently Mr Griffiths had blown for time while I was haring down for the visitors' goal.

Alan A'Court: There's still talk to this day that the ref only blew up then so he could get a lift home off the City skipper Roy Paul. He was standing by the tunnel when he blew. We all thought it was a legitimate goal but the ref was adamant that he'd blown and that was that, we were out.

Billy Liddell: When interviewed afterwards, he said he had whistled 15 seconds before I put the ball in the net, and pictures certainly showed him with his arms extended as I was about to shoot. How long he had stood like that I don't know, but I should have thought my goal was nearer five than 15 seconds too late.

Ronnie Moran: The crowd thought it was a goal and that we'd have to play extra time. They couldn't understand when all the players were walking off the pitch. There was nothing we could do.

Liddellpool

Such was Billy Liddell's influence at Anfield during the barren-years of the 1950s, the team was often renamed in honour of him.

Laurie Hughes: Billy Liddell was a giant of a man.

Bob Paisley: Billy Liddell would have been a star in any team, in any age. How I wish I could have had a Liddell in my successful teams. With him in the side I reckon we would have won the Grand National and the Boat Race! He was that good.

Jimmy Melia: One of the best players Liverpool have ever had. He was big and strong, and could hit the ball with both his left and right foot. He was everything to Liverpool at that time. He took all the corners, all the free-kicks and all the penalties. He had such power and was a great finisher.

Laurie Hughes: He could win a match on his own. Finney and Matthews were great footballers, but Billy was a match-winner. He had a great shot on him, he'd run down the wing like a rocket.

Bob Paisley: He was a naturally two-footed player. It didn't matter where he was playing, though I suppose his best position was outside-left. He could go round you, or past you, or even straight through you sometimes!

Matt Busby: Bill was aggressive. He took opponents on and had the shooting power to finish things off. There wasn't a weakness in Billy's game. He was as strong as a bull on the ball. Defenders found him a real handful, but always respected him.

Bob Paisley: Bill was so strong, even as a teenager, it was unbelievable. You couldn't shake him off the ball. In those days most wingers were fairly lightly-built players but Bill had absolutely no fear. I played behind him for most of my time but I never saw him use his strength for anything other than beating an opponent by fair means. He was never booked in a 15-year first team career.

Albert Stubbins: He made more than a few goals for me and was the most generous winger I ever played with. I can't think of a single weakness Billy had. He was a great player, fast and courageous. Strong as an ox and had the heart of a lion. He'd run through a brick wall but had abundant skill. Billy was a breed of player that later became virtually extinct – he moved head-on at defences.

Alan A'Court: Billy was a superb role model, a tremendous player and someone I looked up to immensly. It was a privilege to have played alongside him and great to follow in his footsteps. It was easy to see why people used to call the team 'Liddellpool'. He was one of the greats.

Albert Stubbins: Free-kicks were a tremendous part of Billy's armoury. In a game against Preston at Deepdale we got a free kick just outside the box, slightly towards the left flank. Billy came up to take it and was going to hit it with his right foot when the wind rolled the ball towards his left one. Most players would have stopped to replace the ball as Billy was entitled to do. But he just let it run, hit it with his left and it went in like a rocket. He was great with either foot. It didn't worry Billy at all.

Bill Shankly: Liddell was some player... He had everything. He was fast, powerful, shot with either foot and his headers were like blasts from a gun. On top of all that he was as hard as granite. What a player! He was so strong – and he took a nineteen-inch collar shirt!

Cyril Done: He was a thrilling player to watch. When Billy got the ball, the crowd hummed, and by the time he'd finished his run, they were cheering. When he collected the ball, the other team sat up and backed away and got worried because they knew Billy had something. He was not so much a dribbler. Billy was a speed merchant, and direct. He had the asset of being able to go both ways. He could go down the left and come in and use his right, or, as on many occasions for Liverpool, he's come in from the right on his left. He had the two-way system. A marvellous player and a marvellous man.

Ray Lambert: A credit to the game. He never drank, never smoked. Nothing like that. The man was a pleasure to know and to play with. He was so strong, like an ox. In five-a-side, sometimes you used to fool around. I'd go in goal, and Bill would let one go. Oh, let it go past. You wouldn't attempt to stop it. If anybody should have been decorated, there was a man. If he could help you, he would help you. He wouldn't see you down.

Bob Paisley: He was an exceptional person. He didn't smoke. He didn't drink. He didn't swear. And he wasn't even a full-time professional! Bill never trained with us.

Billy Liddell: I was one of the few professional footballers who had a job as well. I was an accountant and, all the time I played for Liverpool, I worked in an accountant's office. I trained with the other players at the start of the season, and then when the matches started I only trained twice a week, and I believe the others were training three or four times.

Bob Paisley: No-one would have known that Bill was, really, only a part-timer and I'm sure even if he had trained every day he wouldn't have been a better player than he was. He was certainly as good a player as we had in our time and was always immensely popular with the crowd.

Ian Callaghan: Billy Liddell was incredible. He was a god in Liverpool. When Billy got the ball the anticipation from the crowd was just huge. What is he going to do with it? Is he going to shoot from 30 yards or take it past people? He was wonderful. Billy played with a heavy ball on the heavy pitches. The way he used to kick the ball, wow! He was so strong.

Jimmy Melia: I remember a game against Bristol City at Anfield when we got a penalty. Billy had been our regular penalty taker for a number of years and had already scored two so was on a hat-trick. But on this day the boss had said I was on penalties. So I stepped forward to take it and the crowd start booing me. I could hear them, 'who does this cheeky little bugger think he is? Billy's out there and should be taking it'. Anyway, I put the ball in the back of the net and thought that would have won them over but no, they still booed me. It just showed how much they loved Billy.

Alan A'Court: If I put in a cross and he scored with a header, the papers would describe it as a great header from Liddell, then if he crossed it and I scored the goal, the papers would say what a great cross by Liddell. Haha! I couldn't win. But it didn't bother me. Billy deserved all the praise that came his way. There was no-one else like him.

Tommy Lawrence: He was such a gentleman, a wonderful, lovely, man. When I signed professional at 17 you got your photograph taken with a senior professional. Mine was with Billy. I've still got it in a frame.

Laurie Hughes: You had the Liddellpool thing, but we didn't mind. He earned that. If a Liverpool player got invited to a function, Billy always got offered the tickets first. We were getting a £2 win bonus though, so we'd a lot to thank him for.

Bob Paisley: He was often embarrassed when people referred to us as Liddellpool during the days of struggle but I think it was fair enough. He was a team rolled up into one.

Billy Liddell: I always went to the toilet before I went on the field, and I said a prayer before every match – to help me over the match – and I would do my best to live up to the reputation that I'd got.

Second Division doldrums

Billy Liddell: It goes without saying that the club's aim was to get out [of the Second Division] as quickly as possible. But as many others had previously discovered, it's far easier to drop down than get back to the first.

Phil Taylor: When I was promoted manager, we carried on in much the same way. I can't recall us ever having opponents watched before we played them. We concentrated on doing our own thing, and let them worry about us, with the emphasis very much on each individual playing his part.

Alan A'Court: We always had good gates – between 40 and 50 thousand but we [the players] used to wonder where all the money went because the directors were reluctant to spend it on transfers.

Phil Taylor: I can't remember that the board actually stopped me signing anybody I specially wanted, but they were not generally happy to pay out large sums of money.

Alan A'Court: People would say that Liverpool didn't want to win promotion because they would have to spend more if they went up but this certainly wasn't true in the case of the players.

Jimmy Melia: The majority of players that were brought in during this time were never quite good enough and it was a constant source of frustration to keep missing out on promotion.

Phil Taylor: At that time, teams at almost all clubs were picked by the board of directors, though they usually did ask the advice of the secretary or coach. I know both Don Welsh and myself had to present our teams to full board meetings, often involving eight or nine directors.

Alan A'Court: Always the bridesmaid, never the bride is what they used to say. We would always be in the running for promotion until Easter and I remember one season in particular, Doncaster scuppered our hopes by beating us home and away in the space of two days. That completely ruined our chances and we ended up finishing third.

Phil Taylor: I can remember times when the side that ran out was not really the one I had wanted to play. I was probably not a strong enough personality to be a good manager, because you really need to insist on being in charge if you are going to be successful.

Worcester humiliation

The name Worcester City will forever be associated with one of the most humiliating defeats in Liverpool history. On 15 January 1959 Second Division Liverpool - without talisman Billy Liddell who had been controversially omitted from the starting line-up - were infamously humbled out of the FA Cup by the non-league side.

Ronnie Moran: We went down on the Friday to play the following day and it was postponed so we had to go back on the Thursday and they beat us 2-1.

Laurie Hughes: Conditions weren't much better when it was eventually played. The ground was close to the river and it was waterlogged. But we didn't play well that day.

Jimmy Melia: The field was in such a mess that we could hardly stand up on it. Maybe it should have been postponed again. However, it went ahead and we ended up losing.

Alan A'Court: I suppose that was the beauty of the FA Cup, having to play at grounds like that. It was a horrible day and Worcester adapted to the conditions better than us. We just couldn't seem to raise our game. You don't like to make excuses but the pitch was sloping.

Ronnie Moran: A lot of people said that Billy not playing was the reason we lost, but over the years I've put it down to the fact that we had three or four players who weren't giving everything they had, especially when you went a goal behind. It wasn't a case of 'oh Billy isn't playing, we're going to get beat' because when you're picked you were thinking, 'I've just got to go out there and get on with my job'.

Phil Taylor: Worcester deserved to win. They outfought us on a pitch that may have reduced the odds against them, but… we lost because our forwards refused to fight.

Ronnie Moran: While I could say we were unlucky, at the end of the day, they scored two goals and we only scored one.

Hickson swaps blue for red

In the history of football on Merseyside there had never been a more controversial transfer than that of Dave Hickson's move from Everton to Liverpool in November 1959. Such was the furore, supporters on both sides of Stanley Park threatened to abandon their clubs if it went through.

Dave Hickson: Phil Taylor, the Liverpool manager, called me up and said, 'We'd like to sign you'. I was out of the side and just wanted to play. 'We'll play you every week', he promised, and he did. That's how the move to Liverpool materialised. As far as I was concerned it was quite straightforward.

Roger Hunt: Liverpool were in the Second Division and the players welcomed Dave because he was a noted goalscorer.

Dave Hickson: Despite the controversy there were huge queues waiting to get into Anfield for my debut against Aston Villa. With an attendance of nearly 50,000 Liverpool had 11,000 more fans than at any other league match so far that season. It was a strange feeling running on to the pitch wearing a red shirt and I was surprised at the welcome the Kop gave me. I remember on fan running onto the pitch and saying, 'You're one of ours now'.

Ronnie Moran: Everybody, players and supporters, were surprised at Dave's move across Stanley Park. But no matter where he's from, if the player gives his lot the crowd will always take to him. And Davie always did that. He was a great bloke.

Dave Hickson: Then to get the two goals [in a 2-1 Liverpool win] was a marvellous experience. I think that helped win a lot of Liverpool supporters over. It gave me a relationship with them that we maintained the whole time I was there.

Roger Hunt: I hadn't been in the team all that long and he was great, we played well together. He was very good in the air. I used to play alongside him, maybe just behind. He was tough, he was hard and always desperate to score goals. And if he didn't score a goal, even if the team won, he wasn't all that happy.

Dave Hickson: I could tell straight away that Liverpool had some really talented young players, like Ian Callaghan and Roger Hunt, and that they just needed time, but it wasn't always winning football.

Phil Taylor resigns

17 November 1959

Phil Taylor: It wasn't an easy job being manager. We had been demoted and we had to get back quickly. We had three seasons when we were fairly successful but we never quite made it back to the First Division.

Bob Paisley: You can look back now and see that Phil did a fair job during his three years in charge. In his first campaign we finished third, in his second we were fourth, and in his third we were fourth again. But that wasn't good enough for either the board or, in fairness, the fans and that time also included probably the most embarrassing result in the club's history when a team that included Scottish international goalkeeper Tommy Younger, veteran English international Johnny Wheeler and the newly capped Alan A'Court went down 2-1 at non-league Worcester City in the third round of the FA Cup.

Alan A'Court: Phil was a gentleman, a real nice guy. He'd been a Liverpool player himself, of course, not to mention a fine captain of this club, so he was a very understanding manager. He was never one to rant or rave, always quietly spoken, and he had the respect of all the players but unfortunately nice guys don't always get the success they deserve.

Jimmy Melia: Terrific man, totally dedicated to Liverpool. As manager he was unfortunate because he tried his best to change things and introduce new ideas but we had some bad results, not least at Worcester City in the FA Cup.

Bob Paisley: But at least he left behind a few gems as he had given a young striker called Roger Hunt his debut as a straight replacement for Billy Liddell and in the reserves he had two young men who were to play a major part in Liverpool's total revival under his successor – full-back Gerry Byrne and a young winger by the name of Ian Callaghan.

Roger Hunt: He was the boss who gave me my debut and I have very, very fond memories of him. I will always remember that when he gave me my debut, he rested Billy Liddell, who was the real hero. I'd always thought of myself as an inside forward but I came in more as a centre-forward. Jimmy Melia and Jimmy Harrower were the two inside forwards and I was the central striker. He called me to speak to me – and he was a real gentleman – and he said: 'We're very pleased with you and you're playing in the first team tomorrow'. I just thought 'Gosh, the Liverpool first team!' He was very, very nice to me after the game, too, which we won 2-0 and I scored the second goal.

Phil Taylor: I made promotion my goal. I set my heart on it and strove for it with all the energy I could muster. If the strain for the constant battle for promotion told a tale on the players, it also told on me. We had a long chat and it was made clear they had a new man, Bill Shankly, in mind, so I took the hint and agreed to call it a day. Resigning as Liverpool manager was a very moving experience. I had been at Liverpool since I was 17 and had so many good years at Anfield. But that's life, that's how things go and it was very pleasing to see my old club enjoy so much success later.

Bill Shankly arrives

1 December 1959

Ronnie Moran: No disrespect to the previous management but when Shanks came he was like a breath of fresh air. He completely changed the club around and took it to where it is today, renowned all over the world.

Bill Shankly: The potential was there when I arrived in 1959. I did what I could to make it flourish because Liverpool fans deserved only the best. I had watched the Liverpool supporters suffering in the shadows of Everton for years. I believed it was my destiny to get them out of those shadows. I knew Liverpool could be a great club with the greatest supporters in the game.

Billy Liddell: Bill brought with him to the manager's job the enthusiasm, drive, courage and energy he had shown on the field wearing a Scotland jersey. As well as being a great driver of men he was also a players' man. It didn't matter whether it was a cup-tie, a league game, a practice match or a kick-around. Bill Shankly lived for what he was doing.

Bill Shankly: Normally a new manager takes his own men with him to safeguard himself. I could have done that. But I didn't. I already knew Bob Paisley, Joe Fagan and Reuben Bennett. The first thing I did was to have a meeting with them. I told them that I'd lay down plans, then they'll have to pick them up and we'll all work in harmony. Then, one day, we might get the players we need and that will be it.

Joe Fagan: When I heard Bill was coming to Liverpool I was delighted. Not only would it be a pleasure to work with this man whose concept of the game I respected so much, I also knew that with his enthusiasm, Anfield would soon be buzzing.

Ronnie Moran: The very first thing Bill said to me and the players, in a team meeting on the Wednesday morning after joining, was that everyone had an equal chance and that he had no preconceived opinion about anyone at the club.

Jimmy Melia: His first game in charge was at home to Cardiff City and we got hammered 4-0. We didn't play well at all. I think we were all over anxious to impress him.

Ronnie Moran: How could I forget Bill's first game? It was Cardiff at home and we lost 4-0. Walking off at the end with Alan A'Court, I remember saying to him, 'I wonder what will happen now. I bet we get kiboshed!' But Bill wasn't like that. He wasn't one of those tea cups at the wall types.

Alan A'Court: We had a meeting on the following Monday or Tuesday and Bill said, 'Boys, I think there are some players who have been here too long', and I'm thinking to myself, 'Ooh, I've been here nine years, you know'.

Roger Hunt: When Bill Shankly came he made quite a few changes and more or less said if anyone didn't want to play for Liverpool they could leave anytime they wanted. He wanted everyone behind him.

Bill Shankly: We were overburdened with players. The maximum pay then was twenty pounds and the staff was too big. Within a month I had put down 24 names of players I thought should go and they went inside a year.

Ronnie Moran: He started getting rid of players and there was one player going out each week. We always used to be thinking 'I wonder when it's our turn'.

Bill Shankly: I made up my mind that we needed strengthening through the middle – a goalkeeper and a centre-half who between them could stop goals, and somebody up front to create goals and score them.

Alan A'Court: In no time at all, Anfield and Melwood were buzzing with an electric atmosphere. It was rather as if you were on board a powerful new racing car and he had just switched on the engine.

Chris Lawler: People forget what a good trainer he was. He introduced all new training methods. Like, summer training here was a joke. They used to run from Anfield down to Melwood. No ball work or nothing. So he stopped all that. He introduced training methods that went on for years.

Jimmy Melia: It needed someone special to turn things round. Reuben Bennett had us doing lots of running, but Bill immediately changed this. He installed the fundamentals of playing the ball and keeping it simple. It's something Liverpool have stuck to ever since.

Bill Shankly: What's the point of tearing players to pieces? We never bothered with sand dunes and hills and roads. We trained on grass where football is played. I brought out a bag of footballs. Jimmy Melia giggled with glee at the sight of them. The session was nothing but ball work, chipping, shooting, controlling, heading and movement... this was where a great team would be built.

Ronnie Moran: I learned more in the first season with Bill than I'd done in the seven years that I'd been a pro. I wish I'd been five years younger.

Roger Hunt: He also had this great enthusiasm for the game which he could transfer to the team. Also the crowd really took to him. He was one of them really. And he just changed the whole atmosphere around the club.

Ronnie Moran: Shanks always preached that we had eleven captains. He wanted to see players think things out and rectify things themselves if they were going wrong. You never got shouted at for trying to change something out on the pitch. You were always taught to work things out for yourself. Mind you, if you tried something stupid and it didn't come off, he had a saying that he would, 'hit you on the head with a big stick from the touchline.'

Bill Shankly: Knowing what needed to be done was one thing. Convincing the directors was another. It is difficult to believe how hard I had to fight to make certain people realise the potential of the club. It riled me and made me sick sometimes. They had been so unsuccessful that they were pessimistic, frightened to do anything... like gamblers on a losing streak who were afraid to bet anymore. I had to fight to make people realise that it was possible to be successful.

Red rising

1960-1969

New dawn

The 1960s is a decade that will forever be fondly remembered on Merseyside. Liverpudlian musicians took the pop charts by storm and an unprecedented era of success was about to be ushered in at Anfield. Liverpool would rise to the summit of the English game again, winning the FA Cup for the first time in the club's history.

Yeats & St John

Bill Shankly: Eric Sawyer [the director] was the beginning of Liverpool. He was willing to spend money. He said to me, 'If you can get the players, I'll get you the money'. One Sunday morning in 1961 the Sunday Post ran the headline 'St John wants to go'. I was on the phone straight away and we were in Motherwell on the Monday night. Charlie Mitten came on the scene from Newcastle and tried to sign him, but we arranged the fee of £37,500 on the Monday night and signed St John the next day. I said to Mr. Sawyer, 'He's not just a good centre forward, he's the only centre forward in the game'.

Ian St John: Newcastle were a First Division club and Liverpool were in the Second. They were also offering more money but when I met Shanks his personality, enthusiasm and manner just overwhelmed me. He was so charismatic, he just made you want to play for him. He talked non-stop on the drive down from Scotland to Liverpool, about his plans for the club and the team. How they were going to become the greatest and how I'd have such an important role to play. I felt as though I was going to a fantasy land.

Bill Shankly: My first great buy. Clever, canny, bags of skill, made things happen. Liked a scrap too. Jesus, did he like a scrap. I sometimes wanted to tie his fists behind his back. Great player though. Gave you everything on the pitch.

Ian St John: I had a quick temper which was a bad thing. The fact I wasn't frightened of anybody was a good thing. After just one training session the morning after I signed, I made my debut, away to Everton in the Liverpool Senior Cup. I scored three goals in front of a 70,000 crowd. He had hired me to be his hitman in the drive out of the Second Division and the supplanting of Everton as Merseyside's top club. We lost that first match against the big guns, 4-3, but everyone agreed that Shankly and his new man had issued a serious warning. We then went on tour to Czechoslovakia and when I returned a new but familiar face had arrived; Ron Yeats.

Bob Paisley: Everyone knows that The Saint was the first big signing of the Shankly regime but not too many people realised that we spotted Ron Yeats in the same game. We were more than impressed... his was a name which went into the book as a likely answer to our defensive problems.

Bill Shankly: Of all the hundreds of matches, both big and small, I watched in my career, this was undoubtedly the most historic. St John was playing for a Scotland team against the Scottish Second Division Select on the little Falkirk pitch. It wasn't much as far as games go. But there was a rare battle between two opposing players of great potential – Ian St John and Ron Yeats. Bouncy, dashing, full-of-courage St John had opposite him that night, raw-boned No.5, Ron Yeats. If I hadn't seen this match the history of Liverpool Football Club might have been written in a different way. Yeats and St John were the most vital signings for Liverpool. Just as Mr Sawyer laid the foundations in the boardroom, those two were the beginning of Liverpool on the pitch.

Bob Paisley: At the time he was playing for Dundee United in the Scottish First Division and was also doing his National Service with the Royal Artillery Service Corp, stationed in England at Aldershot Barracks. We made a few inquiries about the character of the man and all we got were glowing references.

Bill Shankly: Mr Sawyer and Sidney Reakes, another director, came with me to see about Yeats, and a Dundee director told me. 'No, we can't sell him'. But on the platform when we were returning to Liverpool another Dundee director whispered to me, 'I bet you could get him for £30,000'. I phoned Mr Sawyer and he said, 'Right, do a deal'.

Ron Yeats: I was happy at Dundee United. Although I was only young, I was club captain and I'd also skippered the British Army side, which had brought me a lot of recognition. I was aware that a few clubs were interested in me and I received a telegram telling me to report to a hotel in Edinburgh to discuss the possibility of a transfer but I was given no inclination about the identity of the club. It was there that I first met Shanks. He could have sold sand to the Arabs. He was unbelievable and after being in his company for a matter of minutes I knew he was the manager I wanted to play for. Liverpool was a sleeping giant he told me and his vision for the future excited me a great deal. I wanted to be part of it.

Bill Shankly: Big Ron was a fantastic looking man, with black hair. The first time I saw him he was wearing a light-grey suit and I said, 'It should be Hollywood you're going to'. He looked as if he could outclass all the film stars. When he came to Liverpool, I got all the press boys and said, 'Go on, walk around him, he's a colossus.'

Ron Yeats: I remember asking him, 'Whereabouts in England is Liverpool?' It was the worst thing I could have asked – it was like a red rag to a bull. Quick as a flash he replied, 'What do you mean, where's Liverpool? We're in the First Division in England, son'. I had meant whereabouts in the country but said back to him, 'Oh, I thought you were in the Second Division', to which he answered, 'We are at the moment but with you in the side we will soon be in the First Division'. How could I have refused to sign for someone like that, who had such faith in me?

Bill Shankly: He was a natural to be a captain; a big man who commanded respect and his position in the centre of defence meant that he could see everything going on in front of him. A captain should be like a puppeteer, with the other players on his strings all the time.

Ron Yeats: I got on very well with him. He was a lovely, lovely man. Even before I'd signed he told me that he wanted me to captain the side. 'You'll be my ears and my voice on the pitch', he said. I wasn't even 23 yet and I couldn't believe what I was hearing. It was a great honour.

Promotion

1961/62

Roger Hunt: We spent nearly £70,000 in the summer so suddenly it looked like we were a club hell-bent on promotion and that lifted everyone.

Kevin Lewis: The team that season played with no fear and the catalyst for that was the signings of Yeats and St John. They were great players and having them in the side helped everyone else play that bit better. There was suddenly a renewed enthusiasm about the place and it felt good, right from the first game. There was never any panic, not even when we lost the odd game or two. Shanks instilled a sense of calm and never tired of telling us how good we were. This created an air of confidence and, while never taking anything for granted, we sensed very early on that we were going up.

Ron Yeats: It was a great season for us. We fancied ourselves from the start. Shanks was slowly building the squad, buying better players all the time and I think we won it easy in the end.

Bill Shankly: We won the title in the first month of the season, when we were fitter than our rivals.

Ian St John: We won our first game against Bristol Rovers 2-0 and never looked back. We led from start to finish and had it wrapped up weeks before the end of the season.

Alan A'Court: We got off to a flyer. We went 10 games undefeated at the start of the season. We won nine and I think we drew at Brighton. We beat Newcastle home and away, and we beat Sunderland home and away. We got a little bit upset in the middle stages because Ron Yeats got injured and Ian St John, one or two key players like Jimmy Melia as well, but we came strong again after Christmas.

Roger Hunt: I was fortunate enough to score 41 goals. I was playing in a successful team and I was getting a lot of chances and it was a fantastic season for me. We were playing attacking football and weren't scared of anybody.

Jim Furnell: Shankly was just starting to get things going and although Liverpool were then in Division Two you just sensed it was waiting to take off. I went straight into the side, replacing Bert Slater, and made my debut at Walsall. I stayed in, too, and we clinched the championship. Playing for Liverpool, under probably the greatest club manager ever, was a fantastic experience. Being in goal in front of 15,000 on The Kop made you feel unbeatable.

Roger Hunt: Even though we had been well in front and always looking like we were going to get promotion it was great when it happened because that's where Liverpool belonged.

Liverpool v Southampton
Anfield
Football League Division Two
21 April 1962

Alan A'Court: It took eight years, 6 hours and 42 minutes I think it was! We beat Southampton in the mud and we were up!

Bill Shankly: Forty thousand supporters turned out to see this game on a really terrible day, but surely one of the most memorable in the history of the club.

Ronnie Moran: I was in the team then. We beat Southampton 2-0 and it took us up. It was pouring down that day and there was about six inches of mud.

Roger Hunt: It was raining and the pitch was heavy. There was also a lot of nervousness because Liverpool were so close to finally getting out of the Second Division.

Kevin Lewis: The desire among everyone to get back to Division One was so strong that it's hard for supporters nowadays to comprehend just what that day meant to the club. For me personally, it was great just to be part of such an important occasion and a hell of a feeling to score the goals that ended the long wait. My memory of them is a bit hazy now but one went in off the post and the other was a header. I remember the celebrations more, we had a great night.

Ronnie Moran: Kevin [Lewis] was only playing because Ian St John wasn't available but he scored the goals that took us up. I was particularly proud because I'd played a lot of games for the club in Division Two and we'd tried so hard for so long to get into the top league. Everybody was made up that we would finally be back in the big time.

Roger Hunt: I remember the scenes after the game more than the game itself. We went up to the directors' box and all of the crowd came on to the field.

Bill Shankly: The scenes which followed the game were quite unprecedented in my experience... the moment Ronnie Yeats showed himself, a tidal wave of humanity surged over the wall of the Kop, swept across the field and engulfed poor Yeats.

Ron Yeats: I can still remember the game against Southampton that clinched it for us. Just after the final whistle, everyone was going berserk and amid the celebrations I got thrown into the boys' pen! It took me about a quarter of an hour to get out and when I finally made my way back into the changing room I remember the boss saying to me, 'Jesus Christ son, I thought we'd lost you forever'.

Jim Furnell: Leyton Orient, who finished a place below us, went off for a long celebration break in Barbados. We were taken for a week in Dublin and it rained every day!

Ron Yeats: A lot of people ask me what was the highlight of my career. I won two league titles and was the first Liverpool captain to lift the FA Cup but the most important thing for me, in terms of the club's history, was winning promotion from the Second Division in 1961/62. Without winning that nothing else could have followed.

Thwarted by unbeatable Banks

Liverpool's ascent continued in 1962/63. They consolidated their top-flight status and embarked on an exciting FA Cup run that raised hopes of a first success in the competition. Unfortunately, in a tense semi-final at Hillsborough, the Reds suffered a heartbreaking 1-0 loss to Leicester.

Bill Shankly: A travesty of a result. It was the most one-sided game I have ever seen. Even the Leicester supporters were too stunned to cheer.

Ian Callaghan: That game proved to be one of the most agonizing I can remember. We swarmed around Leicester's goal for virtually the whole game, apart from one fateful moment after 18 minutes. Leicester won a free-kick and from it Mike Stringfellow put the ball past Tommy Lawrence.

Ian St John: Leicester had a good team, a terrific team, but we were unlucky. In Gordon Banks they had one of the best goalkeepers. We knew of his qualities but on this day he was unbeatable. He was like an octopus, tipping balls over the bar and around the post. He was everywhere. It was one of the games when we just couldn't get the ball past him. It was a bitter blow to lose that semi-final. I remember it as one of the biggest disappointments of my career.

Gordon Milne: That Leicester defeat hit us hard. We were the better team on the day but they had Gordon Banks in goal. The sixties team had never been to a semi-final before. The previous year we'd got to the quarter-final but lost to my old team Preston after a third game at Old Trafford. To then experience the crushing disappointment of losing in the semi-final just made our desire to win the cup even greater.

Chris Lawler: We were so close to getting to the final. It was a big day for us. I was only young, drafted in to play at the last minute because of an injury to Jimmy Melia, and not as nervous as I probably would have been in later years. It was a close game but Leicester were our bogey side at the time. Getting beat in the semi-final was worse than losing in the final itself. I always remember that famous photograph of Gordon Banks, looking as though he was laughing at us at the end of the game. The papers made out that he was but he wasn't like that. He was just made up that his team had won the game and was going to Wembley.

Champions Yeah! Yeah! Yeah!

1963/64

Roger Hunt: After getting promotion in 1961/62, then doing well in both the league and cup the following season, we were confident that we were good enough to win something this time around.

Tommy Lawrence: It was a great side. Very well-balanced. I think our strength was that all the lads got on so well with each other, on and off the pitch. We all played for each other and the team spirit was fantastic.

Ian St John: The nucleus of this title-winning team was already in place but on the eve of the season Shankly made one of his most important ever signings – Peter Thompson. Peter had been earning rave reviews with his performances for Preston and had been responsible for scoring the goal that knocked us out the FA Cup in a fifth round second replay at Old Trafford two years before so we certainly knew all about him. He was an old-fashioned style winger, in the Tom Finney or Stanley Matthews mould, so fast and skillful, a real entertainer. The crowd loved him and he was the missing link in our team.

Peter Thompson: The side had such a good mix. Cally and myself, for example, complemented each other perfectly. He was direct whereas I would tend to dwell on the ball a lot more and try to beat people. Some games, one of us would be struggling, the defender facing Cally may have been faster than him or the right-back could handle a dribbler like myself, so we'd simply swap flanks and it'd work.

Ian Callaghan: One of the essential things for any great team is that you all get on, on and off the field. And we did. We got on very well together. We also had a system of playing. We all understood what we had to do and knew what everybody else was supposed to do as well. It was these type of things that made it such a great side.

Ron Yeats: We were a very good team, and very confident in our own ability. In Shanks we had a manager who wouldn't comprehend the word defeat. It was a word that wasn't in his vocabulary. He'd only talk about winning.

Peter Thompson: Shankly must take a lot of the credit for bringing that team together and getting the best out of us. He'd build everyone up and we went onto the field genuinely believing that we were the greatest.

Willie Stevenson: There was a feeling among the squad that other teams underestimated us and even though we had a years' experience in the First Division, we still managed to catch a lot of teams cold.

Ron Yeats: We got off to a very indifferent start. I think that the first seven games produced only about seven points. It was pretty poor because I recollect the boss calling us together to discuss the situation, which turned out to be the turning point, because by mid-October we were joint fifth in the table. Points continued to come and in November we headed the list for a short spell.

Alf Arrowsmith: When I came into the first team Shanks said there wasn't enough firepower upfront. I'd scored 31 times in the Central League and when Jimmy Melia got injured Shanks changed things around. Saint dropped back into a deeper position so there was me, Roger Hunt and Peter Thompson upfront. We were going to take some stopping and to be honest with you; if I went past somebody they wouldn't catch me – simple as that.

Ian St John: Alfie's goals per game record was marvellous. He played in 20 matches that season and scored a remarkable 15 goals. That's how prolific he was. He was a Manc, mind, but the Scousers loved him all the same. He couldn't always play because of Roger and I, but Shanks occasionally played all three of us and that was hard for defenders.

Alf Arrowsmith: I remember we played Ipswich Town and we beat them 6-0. We were 1-0 up at half-time, Saint scored, but had missed about half-a-dozen. We went out in the second-half and got another five. I got two and I still missed a few more. In the dressing room afterwards Shanks said, 'Christ Alf, you should have broken Joe Payne's record today and scored about 13'. He was right in a way, but we won 6-0 and that was him. He knew that you'd do it for him, but he'd never praise you or anything, like my old chap didn't. He said, 'You've done alright', and that was it.

Tommy Lawrence: Alf was a great lad, all the players loved Alf. He'd been a prolific goalscorer in the reserves and certainly knew where the back of the net was. A bad injury later stalled his career but this was undoubtedly his best spell in the side and he scored some valuable goals for us during the run-in that season.

Alf Arrowsmith: At Easter you used to play on Friday, Saturday and Monday. On the Good Friday we had Tottenham away, Leicester away the following day and Tottenham at home two days later. Everton were top of the League at the time and, according to the papers, we were only going to pick two points up and Everton were going to get all six. Everton only picked two points up and we picked the six up.

Tommy Lawrence: We virtually won the league over Easter. We went to Tottenham and won 3-1, Roger getting all three. Then it was 2-0 at Leicester, our bogey team, Roger again and big Alf scoring the goals, before Tottenham came to Anfield and we completed the double over them with another 3-1 win. Alf scored in that one too, with the Saint also getting a couple. After winning those three games we were top and there was no stopping us. We were so confident then that we felt we could beat anyone.

Alf Arrowsmith: The key match though was the following one against Man United. We were top and they were second. Georgie Best had just got into their team, he'd have been about 19 and Harry Gregg, who was a good mate of mine, was in goal. United's team that day was Gregg, Brennan, Dunn, Crerand, Foulkes, Setters, Best, Stiles, Herd, Law and Charlton, and we beat them 3-0. Ian Callaghan got the first and I got the next two. It was 2-0 at half-time and I got the third at the Kop end.

Gordon Wallace: My best memory of playing in the Liverpool first team was the game against Burnley in that Championship winning season. Needing four points to win the league we went to Turf Moor on a Tuesday night. Roger Hunt was injured so I took his place. The atmosphere that night was incredible. There was massive crowds all the way from Liverpool and we won 3-0.

Liverpool v Arsenal
Anfield
Football League Division One
18 April 1964

Bill Shankly: We won seven games on the trot, running through teams and tearing them to pieces, and we rounded things off by drubbing Arsenal 5-0 at Anfield.

Ronnie Moran: We just went out there and had a go, like we did every game and I think we were three up by half-time. Then it was a good sing-song for the 'speccies' in the second-half and I think we even missed a penalty.

Alf Arrowsmith: We licked Arsenal 5-0. I got one, Peter [Thompson] got two and Roger [Hunt] and Saint got the others. Cally missed a penalty. We let him take it because he was the only forward that hadn't scored.

Roger Hunt: I remember that day well, it was a lovely sunny afternoon and we went around the pitch afterwards to celebrate with the crowd – fantastic. We were on top of the world as we did that lap of honour. I was so full of joy that I could have played another 90 minutes.

Alf Arrowsmith: There was a great atmosphere in the dressing room afterwards. Shanks then sent us out to run around the ground and the Kop was still packed out. We went up in the main stand and they gave Yeatsy this big cup. It was brilliant.

Ron Yeats: That we should clinch the championship on our own ground, before our own fans was perfect... when we ran the lap of honour round the ground, well that was like a fairy tale ending.

Roger Hunt: It was one of the most fantastic days of my life, the happiness on people's faces had to be seen to be believed. It was all part of a fantastic period in the city of Liverpool, what with the Beatles emerging at the same time. Whichever way you looked there was something happening.

Alf Arrowsmith: And we still had three games left. We had West Brom away, Birmingham City away and Stoke away and it's funny because we only took one more point. We'd won seven games in a row and won the Championship so after that we didn't bother that much.

Roger Hunt: We had won the league and we had won it well, playing attractive attacking football. Some of our critics, especially those down south, said we were too much like a machine, that our game was predictable and boring, but the players paid no attention to that – they knew it wasn't true.

Ron Yeats: Winning the league was a big thing. It was what Shanks had been building towards and it came as no big surprise to him; he forecast that we would win the league earlier in the season, when we were going through a bad spell.

Willie Stevenson: I don't think any of the players understood the magnitude of what we'd achieved. It was only when we finished seventh in 1964/65 that it made us realise just what an achievement winning the title actually was.

Into Europe

Winning the league meant Liverpool also secured qualification to European competition for the first time the following season, opening up an exciting new chapter for everyone at the club. And it all began with a trip to the capital of Iceland.

Ron Yeats: Most of us didn't even know where Reykjavik was. We flew from Manchester to London, then from London to Prestwick in Scotland and finally caught a flight from there to Iceland. When we got to Scotland, we had four or five hours to kill, so Bill Shankly decided to take us to the Butlins holiday camp in Ayr. When we got there Shanks said to the man on the gate, 'We are Liverpool Football Club, on our way to play a European tie in Iceland'. The fella just looked at him and replied, 'Oh aye, well you're on the wrong road here mate'.

Gordon Wallace: It was the club's first time in Europe and everything was new to us. On the trip over there I remember looking out of the plane at a volcano in the sea and the pilot telling us all about it.

Willie Stevenson: We were quite high up but close enough to see lava spilling everywhere. It's not every day you see an erupting volcano when you're on the way to a game.

Gordon Wallace: The Icelandic people were lovely people. It was, and still is, a beautiful country. I enjoyed the trip so much I went back there on holiday years later. In 1964 we were only there to play the match so we didn't get the chance to see it all so I made a promise to myself at the time that one day I would return and I did.

Willie Stevenson: The pitch was bobbly and the stands were really close to the pitch. There were more than 10,000 inside the stadium and they were making a right din.

Gordon Wallace: Obviously Reykjavik were only amateurs and we were expected to win. I remember Roger Hunt going to the by-line and squaring it back to me. I was only six-yards out and to be honest I miss-hit it. I shouldn't really say that but it's the truth. The ball went in between the goalkeeper and the near post. I don't have that many highlights from my career but that [scoring Liverpool's first ever goal in European competition] is something that can't be taken away from me.

Willie Stevenson: If you gave amateur sides like Reykjavik a bit of hope, they'd come on top and start kicking you. But as soon as we scored their confidence went and we ran out quite easy winners, 5-0.

Bobby Graham: I'd travelled with the squad to Reykjavik but did not play. Gordon Wallace was ruled out of the second leg with an injury and I was brought in to make my debut and scored two. It's a game I'll never forget.

Willie Stevenson: Their players were a really good bunch of lads. They brought all of their families over and treated it as a holiday. I think they had a few nights out in Liverpool after the game. The tie was won but we still managed to rattle six past them. The Kop took pity on Reykjavik and by the time we'd reached double figures on aggregate the fans started booing us whenever we attacked. It was typical Scouse humour.

Bobby Graham: We were winning easily, 6-0, and during the second half Shanks came out of the dugout and shouted to big Yeatsy, 'Let them score a goal'. We couldn't believe it but they were only amateurs and I think he felt sorry for them. Anyway, the next minute one of their players gets the ball on the halfway line and as he runs towards goal all our players are diving out of the way to let him through. He scores and all the crowd cheer.

Ron Yeats: We really enjoyed playing in Europe and so too did the Liverpool supporters. It was new and different. Everyone knew about the players in the First Division but they didn't know much about the foreign opposition. It was an exciting experience for us. I visited countries that I would never have visited had it not been for football. It was a learning experience for everyone at the club.

Bobby–dazzler

Liverpool v Aston Villa
Anfield
Football League Division One
26 September 1964

Bobby Graham: I scored a hat-trick on my league debut, the first Liverpool player to do so. I had a fair idea that I'd be playing against Villa. Ron Yeats hinted to me that I might be involved and I arranged for my parents to travel down from Scotland. I actually scored five that day but two of them were ruled out for offside. I remember the first one clearly. A long ball was played over the Villa defence and I ran through, beating the offside trap. As the ball bounced on the edge of the box the keeper came charging out and I just headed it over him and into the Kop net. I scored two more in the second half to complete my hat-trick and it was a marvellous feeling. My name may have been all over the papers but I couldn't celebrate too much because I had to be back in my digs before ten. If I was ever late home the landlady would be on the phone to the manager the next day. The house was just across the road from the Arkles pub and I never had my own key until I was 20! I remember just going over there with my mum and dad who were staying the night.

All red

November 1964

Ron Yeats: We'd just finished training one day and I was ready to go home when the boss called me into his office. At first I thought I was getting a wage rise but he wanted me to try on this all red strip, which he was contemplating using as our new first choice kit.

Bill Shankly: We used to play in white shorts with red stripes, white stockings with red tops and white piping on the jerseys. But we switched to all red and it was fantastic.

Ron Yeats: I got changed into this all red strip and came out of the dressing room. Bill and Bob were nowhere to be seen so I walked out of the players' tunnel to see if I could find them. They were both standing in the middle of the pitch and as I came out the boss shouted something like, 'That's it, that's our new kit – you look about seven-foot tall!'

Bill Shankly: It had a huge psychological effect. Our game against Anderlecht at Anfield was a night of milestones. We wore the all red strip for the first time. Christ, the players looked like giants. And we played like giants. I went home that night and I said to Ness, 'You know something... tonight I went out onto Anfield and for the first time there was a glow like a fire was burning'.

Ron Yeats: I think it was a big thing psychologically. It was amazing but it did make us look bigger. Personally, I loved playing in all red I must admit.

Flipping marvellous

Liverpool's European adventure continued against West German champions Cologne in a tense quarter-final. After two grueling stalemates the teams met for a third time in neutral Rotterdam. Still there was no separating them. Following a 2-2 draw Liverpool's European fate was decided on the flip of a disc.

Ron Yeats: I wasn't aware that we would have to toss a disc come the end of the match. No one had explained the situation to me. Knowing that our continuation in the competition rested on whether I chose right in a toss-up was a worrying situation. On my decision I could win or lose the club a fortune.

Ian St John: Anyway, up flew the disc to decide which of us would meet Inter Milan in the semi-final. I didn't go near the toss-up. I couldn't stand the tension. Instead, I stood with Peter Thompson some distance away. I saw the disc go up and come down, saw none of the red jerseys jumping in jubilation and said, 'we've lost.'

Ron Yeats: Amazingly the disc landed on its side in the mud when the referee tossed it first and I was frantically trying to blow it over in our favour.

Ian St John: Up went the disc again, down it came once more – and up into the air leaped Ron Yeats with his long arms outstretched with joy. I turned to Peter and said, 'We're through'.

Ron Yeats: Fortunately I chose right. When I was walking off the pitch Shanks asked me what I picked. I told him and was waiting for him to congratulate me but he just looked and replied, 'Aye, I'd have picked that myself'.

Ee-aye-addio we've finally won the Cup

Liverpool v Leeds United
Wembley
FA Cup final
1 May 1965

Ian Callaghan: I think the first time you do anything is always special because you don't know what to expect. When you do something again, although it is still a fantastic achievement, you know the procedure. In 1965 we hadn't won the cup before and it was without doubt one of the greatest occasions.

Ian St John: The one thing every player learned when they first came to Liverpool was that the club had never won the FA Cup. That was always our big target. The league was important but, at that time, the FA Cup was the big, big deal in English football, especially so at Anfield. You couldn't help but be swept away by the overwhelming desire to win this cup for the very first time. As we knew to our cost, the FA Cup was so difficult to win. We'd gone close, quarter-final twice and semi-final once, in the previous years so this time we were determined to bury the jinx.

Ron Yeats: I knew we were going to win the cup and the thought of getting beat didn't even enter my head. We were a better team than Leeds and were better organised. I actually spent more time worrying what I was going to say to the Queen than about the match itself. That may sound big headed but it is the truth. I didn't even suffer from pre-match nerves, I was looking forward to the game and couldn't wait to get started.

Tommy Smith: Liverpool and Leeds were two great sides who didn't mind kicking the living daylights out of each other, while at the same time playing a bit of football. We all enjoyed these type of games. Bobby Collins, Billy Bremner, Johnny Giles and Norman Hunter – they were all skilful players who also knew how to dish it out. Similarly, myself, big Yeatsy and Gerry Byrne were never slow to shirk out of a challenge and I suspected before the final that somebody might get sent off. I was just hoping that it wasn't going to be me. They had big Alan Peacock at centre forward and I knew that if need be, I would go straight through him.

Ron Yeats: Leeds had a hard reputation but we had done well against them in the league that season. The best team in the league we all felt was Chelsea and we had beaten them in the semi final. We had also beaten some very good European sides so facing Leeds held no fear for us.

Ian St John: On the coach driving up to Wembley we had a laugh listening to Shanks on Desert Island Discs. That helped take our minds off the game. We then got close to the ground and Shanks was waving to the fans and saying to us that we could not let them down. When we got to Wembley Jimmy Tarbuck and Frankie Vaughan came down to the dressing room and had a laugh and a joke with us. Our dressing room door was open and there was a really relaxed atmosphere. Leeds United on the other hand had their door locked and I remember Shanks laughing saying that they must be scared stiff.

Tommy Smith: There is no way anyone can prepare you for that moment when you first walk out in a cup final at Wembley. I had played at Wembley before, in an England youth international, but the ground wasn't even half full then. I walked out and everything just seemed to explode. It felt like my ears were going to burst and that the whole atmosphere was going to suck me in. For a minute I felt like I wanted to lie down and fall asleep, and I thought to myself 'I can't do this'.

Ian St John: There was no real banter between the two sets of players, even though the majority did know each other well. I don't think anyone knew what to say. Everyone was just keen to get out on the pitch and get the game underway. I also remember that we had these awful tracksuits. They were so uncomfortable, I think someone hand-knitted them.

Geoff Strong: None of the lads had played in an FA Cup final before and everyone was a bit overawed during the build-up. With Liverpool having never won the cup there was a lot of pressure on us but I was OK. I could always handle the big match situations, I used to enjoy them.

Tommy Lawrence: It was a hard game. There were some really hard tackles going in because Leeds could hand it out and we could hand it out.

Gerry Byrne: I went in for a tackle with Bobby Collins. He put his foot over the ball and turned his shoulder into me. I'd never broken a collarbone before so I wasn't aware of what damage had been done straight away, I just felt a sharp jagged bone moving about. It wasn't until Bob Paisley came on to treat my injury that I was aware of what I'd done.

Willie Stevenson: That wasn't a very good tackle on Gerry Byrne. But because Collins came in over the top we thought he'd done his leg, little did we know he'd done his collar-bone.

Bill Shankly: Gerry's collar bone was split and grinding together yet he played on in agony. It was a performance of raw courage from the boy.

Ian St John: If substitutes had been allowed then he'd have been subbed right away but of course they wasn't so he had to play on.

Gerry Byrne: It didn't cross my mind to leave the field and I played on with my arm dangling almost motionless by my side. I could move it slightly but the pain when I did was terrible. I remember accidentally taking a throw in, I could hardly lift my arm above my head and I never took another one during the match.

Ian Callaghan: For Gerry to go on and play the rest of the game, including extra-time, was just one of the most heroic things there's ever been on a football pitch.

Bill Shankly: He must be one of the toughest ever footballers... to have gone through such a painful injury ordeal with such dedication to the job in hand. I was proud of the way he kept his injury a secret from the Leeds team.

Gerry Byrne: I'm not sure whether the rest of the lads knew the extent of my injury until we got back into the changing room at half time. Whether any of the Leeds players knew, I don't know. Maybe they thought I played like that all the time!

Tommy Smith: A lot of people described the match as a chess game and I agree that it was tight with few chances. Both sides cancelled each other out.

Ian Callaghan: We pushed the ball around terrifically that day. I've heard people say it was a dull game but I didn't think so. I thought we played well, we really did.

Ron Yeats: When the game went into extra time I must admit I thought we might become leg weary because, after all, it had been a long hard season. But we showed no signs of tiredness.

Tommy Lawrence: Shanks' message to us was to just keep going. 'You'll get a goal boys', that's what he said. And he was right.

Roger Hunt: Willie Stevenson beat a couple of Leeds players, pushed it forward to where Gerry Byrne was out on the left. Gerry, who must have been in terrible pain, cut it back from the line and it came to me at about four feet high. I just stooped and headed it in. Maybe I've scored more spectacular goals in my career, but who cares? I felt ten feet tall. There were tears of joy.

Chris Lawler: There wasn't long left and I thought we'd hold out but when Bremner scored that goal I was thinking... well, it was the end of the earth then, wasn't it?

Willie Stevenson: Big Jack Charlton nodded it down and Billy Bremner blasted it first time into the back of the net. Tommy Lawrence had no chance. Oh our hearts sunk and you felt it right in the pit of your stomach.

Tommy Lawrence: It just flew past me into the top corner. I didn't see it. I still thought we could do it though. We'd had the better of the chances and just needed another one to come our way.

Willie Stevenson: We just re-doubled our efforts. Leeds hadn't had too much of the ball and I can't remember Tommy having many saves to make, so I was still confident. Then it came. A classic Cally cross and a classic St John header.

Ian St John: I could see the move developing. Stevo coming through the midfield and playing Cally down the right hand side. Cally did what he always did, you could bank on him. He beat the full-back and crossed the ball. The goal looked as big as the Mersey Tunnel when I headed it in. It was a momentous goal in the history of the club. The one that won the cup for Liverpool for the first time, so for the significance of it, it was the most important I ever scored. To tell you the truth, I couldn't have cared who scored it, so long as we won. But as kids all we ever wanted to do was score a winning goal in the FA Cup final... every kid who had ever kicked a ball anywhere; that was the ambition. And I'll be forever grateful that I was the guy on the end of the cross which enabled me to put the ball in the net that day.

Ron Yeats: When the final whistle sounded the whole emotion of the occasion began to take over. It was a great feeling when it began to sink in that we had finally won the cup for the first time in the club's history.

Gerry Byrne: The elation of winning the cup made me forget about the pain. But walking up the steps to collect the trophy was worse than actually playing in the match. People were slapping me on the back and every time the pain seemed to become more and more unbearable. I was trying to avoid them all in the end.

Tommy Lawrence: Not coming from Liverpool I didn't realise how much it meant for the fans to win the cup for the first time. My father was in the stands at Wembley, sat beside two Liverpudlians who had travelled over from Australia. They were in their seventies or eighties and at the end of the game they told him they could die happy now that they'd seen Liverpool win the cup.

Ron Yeats: Evertonians had always ribbed Liverpudlians about the fact that Liverpool had never won the FA Cup and I later received a tremendous amount of mail after the final congratulating me, as captain, on our victory. Some letters were from older supporters who actually wrote that they could now die in peace that Liverpool had won the FA Cup. It meant so much to everyone that success.

Tommy Lawrence: I actually lost the bottom of the cup. For some reason Shanks decided that I was in charge of it and I went and left it on the bus. We turned up at the after match banquet, there was the cup but with no base. The boss came marching up to me and said, 'What have you done with it son? You were in charge'. To him it was like the end of the world and I didn't know what to say. I had no idea where it was. The next moment he's on the phone to the coach company and thankfully it eventually turned up later that night.

Ron Yeats: We had a wonderful night in London and although I woke up with a hangover the next morning, I couldn't wait to get back to Liverpool and show off the cup. Everyone felt the same.

Tommy Lawrence: Coming home was fantastic. We were just outside Crewe when someone suddenly pointed out of the window and shouted, 'look at that'. There was a row of houses backing on to the railway track and every one had a red and white scarf hanging from the window. All the way from there until we reached Lime Street it was the same. Everywhere we looked it was red and white.

Ian St John: It was incredible. When we got to Lime Street we didn't know what to expect. We got off the train and onto a bus but we were still enclosed in the station. When we came out into the daylight we just couldn't believe the amount of people. There was thousands and thousands lining the streets. They were hanging out of windows and standing on the roofs of buildings. As we drove through them showing off the cup the cheering seemed as if it would go on forever. There's not another team in the country that would have got a reception like that. It was unique.

Bill Shankly: To think a club like Liverpool had never won the cup was unbelievable. So many had prayed for it to happen over all the years but it had never come to pass. So when we beat Leeds at Wembley in 1965 the emotion was unforgettable. Grown men were crying and it was the greatest feeling any human could have to see what we had done. There have been many proud moments. Wonderful, fantastic moments. But that was the greatest day.

Oh Inter 1, 2, 3...

Liverpool v Internazionale
Anfield
European Cup semi-final first leg
4 May 1965

Roger Hunt: The game against Inter Milan was just after we had won the cup and obviously we'd come back from Wembley and a quarter of a million people were there to welcome us back. Then two days later, we've got this game against Inter Milan so the atmosphere was electric. I've never known anything like it.

Ron Yeats: That was a superb game. Anfield was buzzing, absolutely buzzing. There was steam coming from the Kop. I never experienced anything like that, before or since. The hair still stands up on the back of my neck when I talk about the Milan game.

Willie Stevenson: We'd won the FA Cup for the first time a few days before and the crowd were right up for it. The atmosphere was unbelievable and the Italians froze.

Ron Yeats: When we arrived at the ground there was nobody outside. The police had actually requested that Liverpool open the turnstiles early to ease the congestion in the streets. The gates were closed by half past five and the noise was ear-splitting, especially when Gordon and Gerry paraded the FA Cup before the start.

Bill Shankly: I asked Milan to go out early, but they kept hanging about the dressing room. I said, 'It's time to go now', and eventually they made a move and went out onto the pitch. That's just what I wanted, psychologically, because I then sent out Gordon and Gerry with the FA Cup, followed by the team. Dear God, what an eruption there was when our supporters caught sight of that cup. The noise was unbelievable. The people were hysterical.

Gerry Byrne: I didn't know about Shanks' plan to have Gordon Milne and myself go round the pitch before the game to show all the fans the cup. Just before the lads were ready to come out and play he told us to go out there and walk round the pitch with the cup. So Gordon and I did exactly as we were told and while it didn't really make up for not playing it was an honour for the both of us. People say it was a masterstroke by Shanks because when the crowd saw us with the cup they went delirious. It set them off for the rest of the night.

Tommy Smith: Shanks never put any fear into us. He just said get out there and enjoy it. We'd won the FA Cup then went out and showed the Italians how to play.

Peter Thompson: We were lifted by a fabulous crowd and we forgot all about tiredness. We were inspired to raise our game. Inter hadn't conceded more than two goals in the European Cup – until we put three past them.

Roger Hunt: He [Shankly] told us the Italians would come strutting, full of self-belief, and he wanted us to go at them with a wave of early attacks. The crowd was alight and everything fell into place. Ian Callaghan put the ball over and it was about waist high. I hit it with my right foot on the volley and it flew into the top corner.

Ian Callaghan: Even when Mazzola equalized after ten minutes, I was still confident this was to be our night, and after 34 minutes I scored the most treasured goal of my career. What made it all the more rewarding was that it came from a free-kick plan we had been practicing for some time. It worked like a dream. Willie Stevenson and I lined up, then I dummied to shoot, ran over the ball and kept on running as Willie stroked it through to Roger Hunt, who side-footed it to me – and I hit it into the net.

Ian St John: With 15 minutes to go, I made my mark with the third goal when a hard shot from Hunt bounced off the Italian goalkeeper and allowed me to knock home the ball. There have been many great nights at Anfield, but I think when people look back, they will say that this was the night of nights. The night when Liverpool Football Club really came of age.

Bill Shankly: That's the greatest night that there had ever been. We met, technically, possibly the soundest team in the world and we beat them 3-1 and had a goal disallowed and it might have been 4-1. Herrera gave us credit for it afterwards. 'We have been beaten before', he said, 'but tonight we were defeated'.

Internazionale v Liverpool
San Siro, Milan
European Cup semi-final second leg
12 May 1965

Ron Yeats: After winning the first leg we were very optimistic going to Italy. Even though we'd beaten them at Anfield we knew they were a world-class side but not many sides had beaten us 3-0, which was the margin they had to win by. Half an hour before kick-off in Milan we went out onto the pitch and the atmosphere was electric. There were all sorts of fireworks flying down from the top of the stands, nearly hitting us and I think some of us capitulated.

Tommy Lawrence: When we came out of the tunnel they were throwing fireworks and spitting at us from the stands. We were used to deafening noise with the Kop of course but not this kind of animosity.

Bill Shankly: It was a war; I'd never seen such hostility.

Ron Yeats: The referee was atrocious too and I think it was proved in later years that he had actually taken a bribe and was given a villa in an Italian resort.

Tommy Smith: There was so much fiddling going on it was unbelievable. In Milan they scored from an indirect fee-kick and the ball was kicked out of Tommy Lawrence's hands for another. If pictures of the 1965 semi-final in Milan were analysed now, the ref then would be hung. He was so bent it was untrue.

Tommy Lawrence: I was at the centre of it all that night. For the first goal, the referee raised his arm to signal it was an indirect free-kick, then all of a sudden the ball was in the back of the net, and he allowed the goal to stand. Unbelievable. Then, as I was bouncing the ball in the area, I received a kick on the arm and the next thing I knew, their centre forward was putting the ball into the net to make it 2-0.

Bill Shankly: Of course, the decisions on the pitch were poor. Above all things in continental football, you expect to get protection for the goalkeeper. The referee never protected Lawrence in this case. Those goals were a disgrace.

Roger Hunt: We thought that if we could just hold them for half-an-hour we'd be ok but they were two up and level within nine minutes and both goals were disputed. It was a long time ago, but we were very upset. They were too good for us after that.

Ron Yeats: It was no consolation to us because the result can never be changed and on the day we didn't play as well as we should have but there's no doubt about it, we should have gone to the European Cup final that year. And had we done so I'm sure we'd have won it.

Willie Stevenson: It still hurts when I think about that game in Milan. I could tell in the first five minutes that the referee wasn't going to do us any favours. There were some very odd decisions. I'm sure if we'd beaten Inter Milan we'd have beaten Benfica in the final. We were terribly unlucky.

Tommy Smith: Everything was new to us back then and I honestly believe if we knew then what we know now Liverpool Football Club would have won the European Cup in 1965.

Ian St John: If there's one thing I could have changed it would have been that. We were the best team in Europe at the time and we all felt cheated by the hooky referee in Italy.

Ron Yeats: I had to go up to the referee at the end. When I saw him taking a bow, I just couldn't restrain myself.

Tommy Smith: Such was the set-up, if we had scored six, they would have scored ten. At the bottom of our hearts it was no use. I was so frustrated afterwards that I kicked the referee, but I got no reaction.

Bill Shankly: Of all the people that I've seen and I've met, he [referee, Ortiz de Mendibil] was the one person that haunts me, to this day.

Tommy Lawrence: At the end of the match Shanks just said, 'It was meant to be'. That wasn't like him but he knew that you just couldn't compete with cheats. We found out what playing in Europe was all about that night.

Bill Shankly: Afterwards, the people were sweeping the streets with enormous flags and I said to our players, 'All right, we've lost, but see what you have done. Inter Milan are the unofficial champions of the world and all these people are going mad because they are so pleased that they have beaten Liverpool. That's the standard you have raised yourselves up to'.

Triumph of the fittest

1965/66

Chris Lawler: Winning the league was always a great source of pride and satisfaction. The cup final is a one-off occasion where anything can happen, to win the league you have to perform consistently well over the course of the season. And that's what we did.

Roger Hunt: They always said the league is the hardest to win. It was played over 42 games then and Bill Shankly used to say it was our bread and butter.

Tommy Smith: Unthinkable as it would be today, Liverpool used only fourteen players throughout that entire season, with two of those – Bobby Graham and Alf Arrowsmith – making only four appearances between them. It was the team that ran off the tongue like a familiar nursery rhyme... Lawrence, Lawler, Byrne, Smith, Yeats, Stevenson, Milne, Callaghan, Thompson, Hunt and St John, plus Geoff Strong who would come in and plug any gaps if players were injured.

Chris Lawler: I think the use of substitutes had only just been introduced but there was no such thing as squad rotation then. It was virtually the same team every match. When asked for team news by reporters Shanks would say, 'Same as last season'. It became a running joke but such stability in the team was a big factor in us winning the league that season.

Ian St John: We had hard players, we had honest players. Players who played the game the right way and never tried to cheat people. We had players with pace, players with skill. And we were fit. The boss would forever preach the virtues of fitness. It's because of this that we used to score so many late goals.

Tommy Smith: Playing for Liverpool you had to be as fit as a fiddle.

Roger Hunt: We knew that all other things being equal, like skill, tactics and run of the ball, it was fitness that would count in the end. So we kept at 100% at all times, and it paid off for us. We found that there is more satisfaction in a good win than in a pint or a cigarette packet.

Ian St John: On one wing we had Peter Thompson with his marvelous dribbling. On the other, Ian Callaghan, who could run all day and was a terrific crosser of the ball. Up front, Roger Hunt's scoring record was phenomenal. Gerry Byrne and Chris Lawler were the full-backs. One was as hard as nails and the other scored over 60 goals, which, for a player in that position is amazing. We had good midfield players in Gordon Milne and Willie Stevenson. Ronnie Yeats was our captain, the colossus as Shanks called him. Alongside him was the Anfield Iron Tommy Smith. And, of course, the Flying Pig in goal.

Tommy Smith: The 1965/66 side was the best I ever played in, oozing with class. In those years, any one of probably a dozen teams might win the league.

Roger Hunt: We were a very good side by 1966. We had the benefits of experience, success and togetherness and were getting the rewards. Our game was more controlled, there was not so much charging into attack with gay abandon and the defence was much tighter than ever before.

Tommy Smith: We embarked on an unbeaten run of eighteen matches, from late October to late February. We then only lost one of our remaining ten. Such form allowed us to run away from our main rivals – who that season were Leeds, Burnley, Man United and Chelsea.

Ian St John: When we beat Everton 5-0, we played so well that it seemed we could do anything. We were not so much a football club as an empire. As well as slaughtering Everton, we put five past West Ham, Blackburn Rovers and Northampton Town. Our second title was virtually in our pockets by Christmas.

Tommy Smith: In the end we won it by six points, clinching it with a game to spare at home to Chelsea. On a personal level, I also broke into the England under-23 side that season but nothing could match that euphoria I felt at helping Liverpool win their second Championship in three seasons.

Battle of Britain

Liverpool v Celtic
Anfield
European Cup Winners Cup semi-final second leg
19 April 1966

Geoff Strong: Celtic's visit to Anfield was a truly magical night, which provided everyone who was there with a unique memory. The Kop was so tightly packed that it generated a steam, which meant that we couldn't see our own supporters. At first it looked as if there was smoke billowing around the ground. I have never seen that happen at any other ground, either as a player or a supporter.

Ian Callaghan: That was the Celtic side that went on to win the European Cup the next year, you remember names like Jimmy Johnston. They were a great team. I played against a guy called [Tommy] Gemmel who was a terrific player. So yeah, great memories.

Geoff Strong: It was a game I never expected to be playing in. I hadn't been in the side up at Parkhead for the first game when we lost 1-0 but then Roger Hunt was hurt and Mr Shankly told me I was to replace him. I was a bit nervous because it was such an important match.

Ron Yeats: Celtic were a bloody good side but Shanks had done his homework and in the first leg we sat back instead of adopting our usual cavalier approach.

Tommy Smith: We were satisfied to come away from Parkhead with a single goal defeat and I was confident we could take Celtic at Anfield but felt it would be far from an easy task.

Geoff Strong: The noise our supporters were making was deafening. You could hardly hear yourself think as the game got under way. It had hardly started before I thought it was all over for me. No-one was near me when I turned suddenly to watch the play and see if there was any space I should have been taking up. But as soon as I moved I felt my knee twist. This excruciating pain shot into the joint and I knew I'd hurt a cartilage. There was still no score but no substitutes were allowed. So I decided to try and play on. After that first flash of pain, it didn't hurt at all. The trouble was every time I put any weight onto the leg it just collapsed under me. But it didn't hurt.

Tommy Smith: The first half was evenly contested and tight; we knew we had to be patient. Not long after the break we were awarded a free-kick some twenty yards from goal. As the Celtic defence organized itself I noticed a gap and fancied my chances. Having picked my spot, to the delight of the majority in the crowd I had enough composure to drive the ball low and hard past Ronnie Simpson.

Geoff Strong: The boss and the trainers had given my knee a thorough examination at half-time and asked whether I wanted to go out for the second half. 'Try and stop me', was my answer. So they strapped it up and told me to stay upfield in case I could get a couple of headers in.

Ian Callaghan: The tie was very much in the balance and with Geoff Strong hobbling around we were virtually down to ten men and really up against it. But about 20 minutes into the second half I put a cross in and Geoff somehow jumped using his good knee and headed home.

Geoff Strong: Cally hit over a great cross. Two Celtic defenders went for it but it beat them. Anyway, the ball came over, I had a couple of yards of clear space to get my header in, and it flew into goal by the near post. My goal was to be the winner. The crowd went berserk – and who could blame them? I was as excited as they were.

Tommy Smith: Celtic, however, were far from done, Minutes from time Joe McBride had the ball in our net, only for both the referee and linesman to rule offside. It was then that it began to rain bottles. For a few minutes chaos ensued. There was no doubt in my mind that the goal was offside. The Celtic players' questioning of the decision was half-hearted, and the following days newspapers were in agreement, the referee had been right to disallow the goal. And we were through to our first European final.

Hampden heartache

Liverpool v Borussia Dortmund
Hampden Park, Glasgow
European Cup Winners' Cup final
4 May 1966

Ron Yeats: We didn't do ourselves justice and it was a very disappointing night. Not just for ourselves but for everyone at the club and the supporters who had made the trek up to Scotland.

Ian St John: It was hugely exciting for us all [to play in the club's first European final] and we thought it was great that the game was to be played up in Glasgow, on home soil, in a way. Everything was supposedly in our favour but that's also when you start to worry.

Ron Yeats: We all wanted to do especially well because it was in Britain, and we Scottish lads felt it a bit more keenly for being at Hampden. The unfortunate thing when we went up there was that the Celtic supporters, who we'd beaten in the semi-final, were all supporting Dortmund.

Tommy Smith: Rather than it being a balmy night as you sometimes get in early May, the weather in Glasgow was wet and windy. The famous 'Hampden Swirl' – the stadium's cavernous bowl causes the wind to circle the pitch in gusts – prevented either side from producing classic football.

Ron Yeats: It wasn't a great game. We pounded them at times, but they weren't a bad side and came back at us. We could have no complaints about the result.

Tommy Lawrence: It was a real shame, an anti-climax really, especially after beating that great Celtic side in the semi-final. We were favourites but Siggi Held put Dortmund ahead with a great goal, a volley from the edge of the box.

Ian Callaghan: It was so disappointing to find ourselves a goal down but we just had to roll our sleeves up and dig in. Luckily we managed to get back level quite quickly. Peter Thompson took on three players down the right and crossed it for Roger to score a terrific goal.

Tommy Smith: Although we had Dortmund on the rack for long periods we were not playing as well as we could. At times we lacked our usual edge and appeared disjointed. I still thought we'd do it though.

Roger Hunt: In the last few seconds of normal time the ball broke right for me to hit with my left foot, but I thought the centre half was coming to block it and I tried to take it a little further and overran it. Thinking back I think I should have hit it first time, but I did what I thought was the right thing at the time.

Ian St John: The goal that won it for them, how unlucky can you get on that one?

Ron Yeats: As everyone knows I scored the own goal that cost us the game. Tommy [Lawrence] had come rushing out to intercept a through ball and as the ball was hit back towards goal it came off the crossbar, hit me on the chest and went into the net. I'm very popular in Dortmund still.

Ian Callaghan: It was a great disappointment to get beaten by a goal like that and it took a while to get over it.

Willie Stevenson: I was so disappointed that in the shower room I picked up my medal and hurled it through the window. It must have fallen somewhere in the car park below.

Bill Shankly: We were beaten by a team of frightened men. It was obviously their plan from the start simply to keep us in subjection. They had no real attacking plan but they won. The two goals they scored were flukes. If Tommy Smith and Roger Hunt would have been fully fit we would have won easily.

Roger Hunt: It was one of our few poor displays that year. It was just an off night and to make it worse for me I was struggling with a bad ankle. It was probably the most disappointing defeat over the years because we just didn't play, though in fairness they were a very good team with some of the West German World Cup side.

Ian St John: I just wish we could have won it because our team deserved to be the first Liverpool team to win a European trophy. Unfortunately, we were destined not to and we've never forgotten it.

Lost in the fog

Ajax v Liverpool
Olympic Stadium, Amsterdam
European Cup 1st round first leg
7 December 1966

Roger Hunt: Little was known about Ajax in those days. When the draw was made they were thought of as one of the weaker teams in the competition so we were delighted to get them. We thought it would be easy.

Bill Shankly: Ajax had the makings of a team then, but they were not yet the great team that they later became. We played them first in Amsterdam, but the match should never have started. The fog was terrible. We were due to play Manchester United at Old Trafford the following Saturday, and that was a vital game for us. We didn't want to be delayed in Amsterdam, playing on Thursday and not returning home until the Friday. But it was not our decision to go ahead with the match. Leo Horne, the observer for UEFA, European football headquarters, was responsible for that. The referee, an Italian, said, 'If we can see from goal to goal, OK. If not, no game'. Leo Horne said, 'No. In Holland, if we can see from half-way line to goal, we play'.

Bobby Graham: That was a nightmare. The fog was so thick I only knew they had scored because I heard the roar of the crowd. I was playing left-back, so was close to the touchline and Shanks was on the pitch looking for the referee.

Bill Shankly: We couldn't see much of the game at all, sitting on the sidelines. We couldn't even see the ball. But the pressmen reported it in full. We were 2-0 down and Willie Stevenson and Geoff Strong started raiding. They were stung and went mad and tried to retrieve the game. So I went on to the pitch while the game was in progress and was walking about in the fog, and I said to Willie and Geoff, 'Christ, this is only the first game. There's another bloody game at Liverpool, so don't go and give away more goals. Let's get beat 2-0. We are not doing too bad. Take it easy'. I walked on to the pitch, talked to the players, and walked off again and the referee never saw me!

Roger Hunt: The poor conditions aside, we quickly discovered that they were a far better side than we imagined. Cruyff was only about 18 then but you could tell he had what it takes to become a superstar. He was unbelievable and it seemed like they were going to score every time they came forward. We didn't play well and ended up losing 5-1. It was a massive shock.

Ron Yeats: It was so bad we had to keep asking Tommy Lawrence the score! Seriously though, it would have been hard enough against such a fine team in any conditions, but not being able to see them made life impossible. It was possible, though, to see that Johan Cruyff was special. I just couldn't get near him. His first touch and running off the ball were magnificent, it was like chasing a shadow. He was a player who had everything.

Bobby Graham: Afterwards, Shanks was furious. He went around the entire team asking where we'd been hiding! When he eventually calmed down later he told us not to worry because we'd get the goals back in the second leg.

Bill Shankly: Aye, we lost 5-1 , but I still thought we could get through at Anfield. Candidly, I thought that at our best we might have beaten them 6-0 and I said so.

Bobby Graham: I was dropped for that game but I remember watching from the bench as Johan Cruyff took the mickey out of us. After that the boss had nothing but words of praise for Ajax, 'Some team them, they'll win the European Cup without a doubt', he said.

Roger Hunt: This was the start of a glorious era for Ajax and they went on to become one of the best teams in Europe.

Crazy Horse

In February 1967, Bill Shankly dipped into the transfer market and paid Blackpool £65,000 for a 19-year old who would go on to play a massive part in Liverpool's future success. His nickname was Crazy Horse. His real name was Emlyn Hughes.

Bill Shankly: I knew he was a winner. There are some players you go to watch and you really think they can play, but you're not too sure. I knew with Emlyn Hughes there was no risk.

Emlyn Hughes: We had to get to Lytham St Anne's to complete the signing so I could play straight away in Liverpool's next match and Shanks drove us both down there. It's only about 10 minutes from Bloomfield Road, but he was the worst driver in the world. He had this old brown Corsair and just as we left the ground he half went through a set of lights and a woman shunted into the back of us and smashed all the lights in. They got out of their cars and exchanged numbers and so on then we carried on. Next thing, a police car flags us down and the young officer comes up to the car and Shanks winds down the window, 'What is it officer?' he asked, 'I'm sorry sir you can't continue the journey in that car as you've got no lights' said the policeman. Shanks explained what had happened but the cop was having none of it. 'Do you know who's in this car?' said Shanks, and I thought he was doing the old do you know who I am routine. 'No', said the officer, 'I don't recognise you'. 'No, not me you fool', he said, 'I've got the future captain of England alongside me'.

The seven year itch

In comparison to the glory years of the mid-sixties, the latter part of the decade represented a barren spell for Liverpool as Bill Shankly set about rebuilding his team.

Bill Shankly: We had a mediocre time for a while in the late 1960s as we prepared for the 1970s. A lot of our players were about the same age and I had given them a set time as to how long I thought they would last. I thought some of them would maybe have gone on longer than they did, because of their experience. Maybe the success they had shortened their careers. They had won the League, the FA Cup and League again, and they had been in Europe so often. Perhaps they were no longer hungry enough.

Roger Hunt: Though we weren't an old side, perhaps a team only has a certain life span. Part of ours was spent trying to get promotion, and then adapting to the First Division the year after. Maybe you're not quite as hungry if you've won things. You still want to win, you hate to lose but it's not the first time any more and perhaps subconsciously you aren't so desperate for it.

Peter Thompson: In my fourth year at Anfield [1967] we finished third and Shankly called a crisis meeting. 'Christ, third is no good for me. Sell your big houses and your big cars because you're all no good to me', he told us. I went home panicking thinking I was about to be sold. Fortunately I wasn't but others were. That was the type of pressure we were under.

Tommy Smith: We just lacked that little extra something that we'd had earlier in the decade, up until about 1967. We were always there or thereabouts in the league – second, third or fourth – but were unable to replicate the success we'd had.

Ian St John: The break-up of the team was inevitable, but hard to take. Shanks actually said, 'The wind of change is coming boys'. When I was first left out, the team sheet was just left in the dressing room and the boss was nowhere to be seen. In fact, when it came to dropping players who had served him so well, Shanks found it difficult to tell them.

Roger Hunt: In some ways he was a bit soft underneath. He knew he had to break up the team which was going to hurt him a lot. He really didn't know how to handle it. The team he'd had for years, it was difficult for him to say, 'it's time you went,' and so it could take him a while to say he was leaving you out. He didn't like doing it because he was very loyal to the players. That was the spirit of the club. When you play for a club like Liverpool, you want it to go on forever. There's a lot of heartache involved at the end.

Bill Shankly: We had to say goodbye to players who had been great players. The changeover wasn't easy because it meant losing men who had been great servants, who had won the FA Cup for Liverpool for the first time and put them on the map.

Ian St John: Out of everything we did, the only thing we failed in was the European Cup. That was the one blemish on our part in Liverpool history. What we did do though was set the standards for the next lot who were coming through. They were always told, 'You have to be better than the sixties team'. Our team laid the foundations for the amazing success that followed.

European royalty

1970-1979

Seeds of change

The Seventies began with Liverpool still in the midst of transition but it would be a decade that saw the club rise to unprecedented heights at home and abroad.

Nadir

Watford v Liverpool
FA Cup quarter-final
Vicarage Road
21 February 1970

Bobby Graham: The pitch was very muddy that day. I went through, put the ball past their keeper but it stuck in the mud on the line. They had one breakaway and scored and we were out of the cup. Afterwards Sid Reakes, who I think was chairman at the time, came into the changing room and started slagging off all the players. Shanks went berserk and threw him out.

Bill Shankly: That defeat hastened the break-up of a once great team. After we lost I decided that was it. I realised I had to start again. It had to be done. If I didn't, I'd have been shirking my obligations.

Emlyn Hughes: After the Watford defeat he [Shankly] just came in and said, 'That's it, a lot of you have just played your last game for Liverpool'. It was sad to see the Sixties side go but it was inevitable. They couldn't physically compete with the kids any longer.

Bill Shankly: We had already dipped into the lower divisions to buy Larry Lloyd, Ray Clemence and Alec Lindsay. We couldn't buy £100,000 players and then put them in the reserves. We had to buy from the lower leagues to allow them time to play in the reserves. They were happy to come to Liverpool and learn their trade.

Tommy Lawrence: It was pretty obvious the boss had something in mind the Tuesday after the Watford game. When we reported to Melwood we were told that a friendly with Blackburn Rovers had been arranged behind closed doors, but when the squad was read out many of the names who had been regulars for years were not included. I was one of them. Ray Clemence was given my place and I knew then that my first team days were over.

Ray Clemence: I remember my first game as a regular. It was the week after the Watford game. Shankly went through the middle and took out Tommy Lawrence, Ronnie Yeats and Ian St John, and put myself, Larry Lloyd and Dougie Livermore into the side. It was against Derby at home, who were a good side then, and we lost 2-0. We were wondering what Shanks would do now but he continued to play the youngsters right through to the end of that season and in the last half dozen games we started to get things going.

Emlyn Hughes: I came to Liverpool in 1967 just when Mr Shankly was re-creating his team. I came in at the tail end of the great side of sixties, so I played throughout his team rebuilding. I could tell as early as 1969 that this team was going to be great. At that time, Ian Callaghan was the oldest player in the side and he was only 27 or 28. The average age of the rest of us would be around 21 or 22. We were developing together.

Gunned down

Liverpool v Arsenal
Wembley
FA Cup final
8 May 1971

Tommy Smith: We had one or two players left over from the old side. Cally was still there, as was Chris Lawler and I was now captain. Tosh [John Toshack] came and he gave the team something. Clemence in goal, Lindsay at left back, Larry Lloyd, Steve Heighway and Brian Hall. Things just started to happen and to captain Liverpool in an FA Cup final was another dream come true.

Brian Hall: We were still an in experienced side in 1971 and there was enormous tension on the coach from the Hendon Hall Hotel to Wembley. Shanks was building a new team and newcomers like myself were nervous. It was evident. We were looking forward to the occasion, of course, but found it almost impossible to relax.

Larry Lloyd: I remember walking out at Wembley and an unbelievable shiver went up my spine. There were 100,000 people at Wembley that day, my family were way up at the back of the stand but I somehow managed to spot them. The atmosphere was like nothing I had known before.

Ray Clemence: I froze on the day and so did a few of the other lads. I don't remember a thing about it. It was all a bit too much for me. Most big games, I remember certain aspects of them but that one, I only remember the goals.

Steve Heighway: There were no great expectations on us as we were such a young team and it was all a bit of a blur for me to be honest. I don't think it was a great game. I scored. It could have been the winner but unfortunately it wasn't.

Emlyn Hughes: It was a hot day. The sun was beating down. It drained all my energy. For some reason we were wearing heavy, thick, long-sleeved shirts. I may be accused of making excuses... but I'm convinced that our choice of shirts cost us the trophy – especially as we went into a gruelling extra-time.

Ray Clemence: To this day I still don't know what happened with their equalizer and the game just came and went. I remember sitting in the dressing room afterwards thinking, 'Christ, I've just played in a cup final, it might be the only one and I don't remember it'.

Tommy Smith: For many, the abiding image of that final was the reaction of Charlie George to what proved to be the winning goal, lying on the ground with that smug look on his face. I felt gutted.

Emlyn Hughes: For all that, I have to admit that Arsenal were the better side. We didn't deserve anything that day. The 1971 final goes down in history at Arsenal's victory. All I wanted to do was get off the pitch. I could not wait to get back to the hotel to hide and rest.

Larry Lloyd: You can imagine the crushing disappointment... we were all in tears and at a moment like that you feel as if you're never going to recover.

John Toshack: It was a disappointing end to the season, but looking back on it now, I don't think Shanks was too confident beforehand. We were still a very young side and we would get better. I don't think people could have realised how much better though.

Kevin Keegan: superstar

Kevin Keegan: I arrived at Liverpool from Scunthorpe with nobody having heard of me and nobody expecting anything from me either. From almost day one, my whole life just seemed to explode. One day I could walk down the street and no-one would recognise me, not even in Liverpool. The next day it was as if everybody knew me, whether it be in Liverpool, London, Manchester or Glasgow.

Bill Shankly: We bought Kevin for £35,000 – it ended up being robbery with violence. You could argue that Scunthorpe should have got another £100,000 the way this boy turned out. It's always difficult to go into the Third and Fourth Division and find players who can make it at the top. But in Kevin we found a man who had the one thing we wanted. Apart from his ability he had a natural enthusiasm – and that's what made him a special player.

Kevin Keegan: I didn't expect to get in Liverpool's first team so quickly. I came in at the end of the season [1970/71] and went on tour when a lot of the players were away with England. I got games, did well and forced myself into contention. It meant I never actually played a reserve team game for the club. That was the thing about Bill, he wasn't scared to put someone in. If he thought you were good enough that was it.

Bill Shankly: I said to him on Thursday did he want to play Saturday. 'Oh yes', he replied. It was just the answer I wanted to hear.

Ray Clemence: Kevin's sheer enthusiasm, bravery, fearless attitude and desire forced him into the team. First game of the season we beat Nottingham Forest 3-1 at home, and he was never out of the side after that.

Kevin Keegan: I will never forget my debut. There were 50,000 inside Anfield. Thirteen minutes in and I scored. In front of the Kop as well, it doesn't get any better than that. Peter Thompson crossed the ball and I went to smash it into the roof of the net but mis-hit it. Luckily it went in the bottom corner instead and that was me on my way. It was a great start. Everything happened so sudden. It wouldn't happen now. Unbelievable. Like a fairy-tale.

Ian Callaghan: Kevin Keegan was signed and made an unbelievable impact. He was the first superstar that Liverpool had. Kevin was a great player for Liverpool and I've nothing but admiration for him.

Title anguish

Arsenal v Liverpool
Highbury
Football League Division One
8 May 1972

Alec Lindsay: We went to Arsenal on the Monday night after they had lost the FA Cup final 1-0 to Leeds. We drew 0-0 but if we'd have won at Highbury we would have pipped Derby for the championship.

Brian Hall: Derby were in Majorca having a nice little break, they'd finished, they were top of the league. Leeds were favourites for the league really, they were going to Wolves and I think they only needed a draw in the two points for a win system as it was back then. By the time we're getting to the end of this game, word had come down from the terraces - because there were as many Liverpool fans inside Highbury as there was Arsenal fans - that Leeds were getting beat and I think that gave us that little extra push.

Bill Shankly: We were robbed of a goal. Kevin went through and gave a slanted pass to John Toshack who rammed the ball into the net. Everybody in the ground thought it was a goal, but it was disallowed for offside.

Brian Hall: Well when Toshy scored the roof came off the place; it was fantastic. And then... the referee Mr Fitzpatrick decided to disallow it.

John Toshack: I am still convinced it was a good goal. You see, when Kevin struck the ball I started to move in on goal from the far side. When the ball reached me, I looked offside for all the world to see, but I was there because I had reacted quicker than anybody else. When the ball was struck by Kevin, I was onside.

Brain Hall: Going from such heights of emotion to such depths of emotion in just seconds, it plays havoc with the nervous system and it was a very traumatic 20 seconds before I actually came to terms with it and thought, 'Wait a minute. What's going on here? We've scored a perfectly good goal and the referee has disallowed it'. Well to us it was a perfectly good goal. So at that particular moment, I have to say that Mr Fitzpatrick was not my favourite person.

John Toshack: I had been two seasons at Liverpool. We had been beaten in a Wembley cup final in extra time and now cheated out of a championship. That result was particularly hard to take.

Emlyn Hughes: I felt absolutely sick at the time. What sickened me in that game was that it ended a marvellous run we had made for the title – something like 24 points out of the last 28. I thought we had deserved to win the title. It was a much worse feeling than losing to Arsenal in the final.

Brian Hall: I was on the far side of the pitch from the dressing rooms at Highbury in the second half and it was the longest walk-off I've ever had. My legs were dead. I was physically tired, obviously, but it was that mental drain. I was absolutely shattered. Going into the dressing room, there was desperation and the desolation on everybody's face, dare I say a few tears, from senior professionals who had been around the game a while because we had been so close to winning the championship... so close.

Emlyn Hughes: I soon recovered because I knew that if the boys could be kept together we were going to be a great side, as good in my view as the team of the mid-sixties which won so much for Liverpool. We knew it was only a question of time before the team developed fully and we did something big. We knew we could only get better; we were not a team nearing the end of its great days, we were only approaching them. And we bounced back immediately.

Shankly's second great team

1972/73

Brian Hall: There was always great optimism in the camp and at the start of the 72/73 season it was no different. That was very much the nature of Bill Shankly. He inspired confidence in the lads. If he told us once, he told us a thousand times that we were the greatest. It gave us a tremendous self-belief, and I don't remember one time when we ran out with doubts that we wouldn't win.

Steve Heighway: Shanks was such a wonderful character, a manager who instilled in us the belief that we were the best; to believe in ourselves and never be frightened of anybody. He was totally supportive of us and would be dismissive of all our opponents. He'd do that to build up our confidence. And bit by bit, this group of players - supported by this incredible man and an incredible crowd, at a club with an incredible sense of history – began to believe that we were invincible. We were never arrogant about it but that's how it happened in the early seventies and results soon confirmed this.

Kevin Keegan: The closeness of the squad was amazing. Peter Cormack was the only new signing. He became my room-mate. Shanks called him the last piece of the jigsaw.

Peter Cormack: When I joined, I was just hoping that I would be picked for the team. The competition for places was intense, so to end up playing a prominent role was beyond my wildest dreams.

Brian Hall: With the exception of Keegan and Cormack, the majority of the side had been playing together since the 1970/71 season. Although we hadn't won anything, we'd come quite close and the 72/73 campaign was the continuation of this progression.

Larry Lloyd: I played the whole of that season, every minute of every game and we played 66 in total. Everything was going so well for us and at that point in my career it was the best season of my life. My head was in a good place, my body was in shape and I somehow managed to avoid any injuries and suspension.

Peter Cormack: It was a privilege to be at Liverpool during this time, with Shankly and also the many great players like Tommy Smith, Kevin Keegan and Cally. They played for the love of the club. It wasn't about money in those days. We'd have played for nothing. The club itself had won nothing for six years and there was a great desire to put that right.

Phil Thompson: There were some fantastic players in that side, for me household names; Tommy Smith, Chris Lawler and Larry Lloyd in defence, Keegan and Toshack up front, and the high energy of Ian Callaghan in midfield. For a young player like myself, trying to edge in alongside these guys was very special and you could sense there was something brewing with this team.

Steve Heighway: You never felt alone in that group. It had everything. It had talent, it had physical strength, it had so many unbelievably strong-willed people. The number of times I got pole-axed by an opposing defender only to get up and see the likes of Tommy Smith confronting the defender – and you have to remember that I played left wing and Tommy right back but he'd still sprint one hundred yards to get in his face. There was such an enormous strength of character in that side and that made room for my flamboyance. Without them I could never have done what I did. It all fitted together perfectly.

Kevin Keegan: The secret of Liverpool's success was teamwork. Individuals were ready to sacrifice a moment's glory that accompanies flash exhibitionism for the sake of making sure that movements flowed on a conveyor belt of passes that were stunningly accurate. The 1970s team were one of the greatest of all passing sides. The ball would be delivered – not clobbered – from the back. It would then become the property of accomplished midfield players... always ready to fetch and carry if required. The final point of delivery was usually either to me or to John Toshack. Tosh and I had an almost telepathic understanding and always knew where to be to get the best out of each other. During this championship season we scored 13 First Division goals each, and our little-and-large partnership proved too much of a handful for most defences. It was not always sweetness and light between the two of us, and there were times when we messed up moves and got annoyed with each other. But we were always lifted by the team spirit, and would forget our differences to produce the best efforts for the team.

Peter Cormack: Shankly would say before every season that whoever finished above Leeds would win the league and he was right. Along with Liverpool, Leeds were the dominant force and we were great rivals. We had some great battles. Amazingly, I don't think I ever finished on the losing side against them. It was the second to last game of the season and we knew that if we won, the title would virtually be ours. It was an unforgettable occasion and I scored the opening goal shortly after half-time in a 2-0 win. For us to be overtaken we had to lose our last game and our nearest challengers had to win by something like five or six goals, so it was never really going to happen.

Phil Thompson: I was only just beginning to get into the team that season. I'd played the previous two matches, and Shankly called me up to play. It was an incredible day, the passion everywhere was so intense. There were 55,000 inside Anfield. The noise was deafening. It was clear that we were the new champions. The game was then played out in a carnival atmosphere as the Kop celebrated. They knew we were safe. I remember the second half the Kop chanting my name. It was one of the first times they had ever done that. I felt like a million dollars. It was terrific.

Larry Lloyd: The point that won us the title came at home to Leicester. We were awful that day but thankfully held on for a goalless draw. Just a few years earlier, as a teenager, I'd been playing in the third tier of English football now I was playing an integral part in a championship winning team. It was boys own stuff. To be champions of England was an unbelievable feeling.

Bill Shankly: This title gave me greater pleasure than the previous two, simply because here we had a rebuilt side, some of them only two or three seasons in first team football and they stayed the course like veterans.

Phil Thompson: We had just won the title and were doing a lap of honour around Anfield. Shanks came out to accept all the plaudits, and the whole place went wild. There were scarves and hats and banners being thrown on to the field. Then a policeman down by the Kop end kicked a scarf out of the way and into the dirt. Shanks went mad. He shouted, 'Hey, someone's paid good money for that, don't be kicking it away'. He picked it up, wrapped it around his own neck and walked away. Suddenly he turned back towards the policeman. 'Don't you realise what you've just done?' he said. 'This scarf is someone's life'.

Kevin Keegan: Apart from a couple of medals I won playing for my school team I'd never won anything so this was unbelievable. The euphoria around the place was incredible. It was a great team and we all became big heroes, not just me. If you're successful and people see that you really want to win games then everyone's a hero.

Conquering Europe

Liverpool v Borussia Monchengladbach
Anfield
UEFA Cup final first leg
10 May 1973

Peter Robinson: I think Europe had become a challenge to Bill. He was obsessed with the Inter Milan game when I first came, and I know he was very hurt in '66 when we lost to Dortmund. Although he would never admit it – he used to say it was all about the domestic side and winning the Football League – deep down he really wanted to win a European trophy.

Steve Heighway: Shanks had gone on record as saying the league was his bread and butter but Europe was becoming more and more important to us. We always went abroad in pre-season and the more you travelled the more support you'd attract because it helped spread the club's name. By the early seventies, Liverpool, as a club, was accustomed to playing in Europe and it had become routine. We were used to it, lessons had been learnt from the past and nothing fazed us. We had a very mature outlook where playing in Europe was concerned.

Tommy Smith: The UEFA Cup was always regarded as the lesser of the three European competitions, but it was the hardest of them all to win. There was an extra round for starters, and the two-legged final didn't make it any easier. You'd also come up against emerging clubs who were on the verge of great things, like Monchengladbach for example.

Larry Lloyd: I hadn't realised that Liverpool had not won anything for seven years. Then, all of a sudden we'd won the league and we're going for the UEFA Cup. The first leg was abandoned due to a waterlogged pitch and it was difficult to know what to do because we were all geared up to play that night.

Bill Shankly: Brian Hall played, I didn't play big John [Toshack], I played the small men. There was terrible torrential rain and the ground was flooded. He [the referee] took the players off half an hour after the game had started and I said, 'Thank god for that'. So I said to John Toshack, 'You go home and get to bed and be ready for tomorrow night', because their defence wasn't very good in the air.

Tommy Smith: In the first leg at Anfield, the ground was so hard the water wouldn't drain away. It was like trying to play football in a pool. The ref called the game off, but Shanks had seen enough in that time to change his tactics for the following night. I think someone was looking down on us that night. We were struggling without the big man Toshack up front and the rain proved to be a blessing in disguise.

Bill Shankly: So, John came in the next night and we pumped the high balls into the box... he flicked them on and in no time at all it's three-nothing and the game is all over.

Larry Lloyd: I scored the third goal and it was to prove decisive in the tie. It was down at the Anfield Road end. Keegan, who'd scored the first two took a corner on the left, and I headed it home. Definitely the most important goal I ever scored.

Ray Clemence: We were 3-0 up and they got a penalty. Jupp Heynckes was a powerful striker of the ball but I'd watched him take a penalty a few weeks earlier when he put the ball to the keeper's right, and I made a mental note of that. As he kicked the ball, I was on my way and I managed to get a hand to the ball and push it around the post. At the time it didn't seem that important but in hindsight, given what was to happen in the second leg, it was probably the most important penalty save I ever made.

Peter Cormack: They were without doubt one of the best sides in Europe at the time and it was a great achievement to beat them. Without playing exceptionally well we pulled them apart in the first leg but we expected it to be much tougher away from home.

Borussia Monchenglabach v Liverpool
Bokelburg Stadium
UEFA Cup final second leg
23 May 1973

Alec Lindsay: As soon as the whistle went in the second leg we were on our heels. We didn't go there to play defensive, we were just pinned back and everyone had to defend, John Toshack, Keegan, Heighway, all of us.

Peter Cormack: I remember Tommy Smith, our captain, telling us to do whatever had to be done to stop their players getting past us. Well for the first twenty minutes we couldn't get anywhere near them, never mind stop them. I don't know what they were on that night but I had never played in game like that.

Tommy Smith: In the second leg the boss told us to contain them and hit them on the break. It was a real battle. We were 2-0 down after about twenty minutes. We hung in until half-time and got a real bollocking off Shanks.

Bill Shankly: The Germans oozed class in the first half and we couldn't keep up with them. I was worried – who wouldn't be – when our lead is suddenly only one. After they scored the second there was a thunderstorm, and I thought we were going to get beat by about 10-0.

Peter Cormack: They overran us and reduced the aggregate score to a single goal and we were thinking this can't be happening. If we'd have let slip a 3-0 first leg lead we would have been crucified, and rightly so.

Larry Lloyd: They murdered us to be quite honest, absolutely murdered us. Myself, Smithy and the rest of the defence had to work really hard that night, we really did.

Bill Shankly: But I knew they'd tire... just before half-time, I could see that the steam had gone out of them. And when we were in the dressing room, I said that we may even get a draw in this match.

Peter Cormack: By the time they come out for the second half it was like someone had pressed a button. They had nothing left in their tank. They were gone.

Bill Shankly: They blew up after ten minutes of the second half. They had no strength left after they put so much into the first half.

Tommy Smith: The second half started and I just started growling and snarling, getting stuck into a few tackles. I remember Joe Fagan came up to me afterwards and quietly said, 'Smithy, that was the best game you have had for a long time'. I thought, 'Fucking hell, Joe has never said anything like that to me before. That will do for me'.

Larry Lloyd: Towards the end of the game, as they frantically tried to get a third goal, we were just kicking the ball anywhere. Luckily, we just did enough. We kept them out and won the cup 3-2 on aggregate. Brilliant.

Peter Cormack: It was a tense finish but thankfully we held on. At the end of the game I just remember being totally drained and to be honest I don't recall too much of the celebrations. It's true what they say about occasions like that passing you by. We were just glad to have hung on and won our first European trophy. The rest is a blur.

Tommy Smith: I was so happy to be the first captain to lift a European trophy for Liverpool but I never realised how big the cup was. It had a big stone base and weighed a ton. I remember on the lap of honour some big fat guy jumped on my back and I nearly collapsed. After such a gruelling match I was absolutely knackered.

Bill Shankly: I would say that the UEFA Cup could be as difficult to win as the European Cup, because the teams that are in it are the teams that are promising to be great teams. It was great because we'd beaten a team that had five players in it that I thought were great players, very good players.

Tommy Smith: I eventually made it to the dressing room and I said to Shanks, 'Here you are boss, the cup's yours'. I handed it to him, but I don't think he realised how heavy it was either. He nearly dropped it!

Bill Shankly: When we came back on the plane, we arrived about one o'clock in the morning and the airport was full of people. That was the greatest thing of all. Now that was something really worthwhile and that was worth all the hard work and worry that I had been going through. To see these people at Speke Aerodrome at one or two o'clock in the morning, thousands of them. It was really brilliant.

Devouring Big Mac

Liverpool v Newcastle United
Wembley
FA Cup final
4 May 1974

Peter Cormack: It is everyone's dream to play in an FA Cup final and I was no different. It was everything I expected it to be and the entire build-up to it was something else. I was fortunate enough to play in many big games, for club and country, during my career but to play in the FA Cup final at Wembley was the biggest.

Steve Heighway: By now we were a very confident bunch of players. Most of us had been there in seventy-one so I think we took it all in our stride really. Malcolm Macdonald had told everyone what he was and what he wasn't going to do so all our players were well and truly wound up. There was no need for a team talk.

Kevin Keegan: Shanks just pinned up on the notice board at the team hotel the article Malcolm Macdonald had done. He said, 'There you are boys, that's what they're going to do to us'. We all felt like schoolkids going up to read it. Malcolm was saying things you shouldn't say before a match, that we had no pace and we were overrated, stuff like that. We were a club that didn't shout out about what we were going to do, we just did it, so it was going against everything we believed in. We were a very good side and it was a bit disrespectful to be honest. When we went out we just wanted to make him eat his words, and we did.

Emlyn Hughes: He was still shouting the odds when the boss Bill Shankly, myself and some of the other lads went on a pre-match TV interview with Newcastle manager Joe Harvey and his players. Their lads were immaculately dressed in their Wembley suits and ties. But it was boiling hot and you could see the sweat rolling off them. Just as the interview with Joe finished, Shanks turned to the camera and said, 'Boys... they're crapping themselves'. Newcastle heard it, as I'm sure Shanks meant them to, and it struck a psychological blow.

Tommy Smith: Supermac, as he was known, had also scored a hat-trick in a league game against us 18 months earlier when we'd lost up at Newcastle 3-2. The players in our team that day vowed he'd never score against us again. So we're lining up in the tunnel at Wembley and I growled at him, 'Don't come near me today son, I'm in a bad mood'. And you know what? He didn't come near me once.

Brian Hall: The 1974 cup final I think was a very defining moment, because on that day Liverpool played the way that Shanks and Bob, Joe and Ronnie had always wanted us to play.

Ian Callaghan: We'd learnt a lot from playing the top continental sides. They were more patient and we followed suit. We were the first English club to play possession football. Just pass to the nearest red shirt. It was really as simple as that.

Phil Thompson: The boss and his staff, they were ahead of the time. All of a sudden we were looking to play from the back. If it took fifty passes to score we didn't care. The coming together of Emlyn [Hughes] and myself in that partnership was the start of the Total Football that would be made famous by the Dutch that same year. I think the Dutch modelled it on what we were doing at Liverpool. We were Barcelona with attitude, keeping the ball for fun but progressing through the area. We'd play the ball sideways, backwards or forwards, whatever it took and we'd get through the lines very, very quickly by pulling people out of position, it was all about possession. It was the Liverpool way that we'd been taught. People thought it came from the 70s, but for me it had already been born out in the 60s by Shanks. Pass it to the nearest red shirt – that was his great motto. Pass it to the nearest red shirt. We took that on further in 1974 and literally nobody could get anywhere near us.

Bill Shankly: By the time we played Newcastle we were playing the Latin style, no big stopper centre-half. We had brought in young Phil Thompson to play alongside Emlyn Hughes. What Phil lacked in weight and heading power, he more than made up for in reading the ball and a magnificent positional sense. He, more than any other, set the style. We poked the ball about, used every inch of space, all teamwork and unselfish running, working for each other and the opposition didn't know what we were going to do next.

Phil Thompson: At Wembley, it was very even up to half-time and then just after half-time we took complete control. We played some great football. And at 0-0 there was the famous Alec Lindsay goal that was chalked off but which should have stood.

Alec Lindsay: It was quite funny because Keegan and me were celebrating on the greyhound track and we turned round to see the ref hadn't given it. He had called Kevin offside, Emlyn Hughes was rowing with him and we had to get back because the game had kicked off again.

Phil Thompson: But from that moment onwards we just got stronger and stronger. In the end it could have been five or six. It was a tremendous all-round team performance.

Steve Heighway: We were really on song that day. We were at the height of our powers as a team and we just blew them away really didn't we? You can run all day when you're in that kind of mood. The only thing that could possibly have stopped us was complacency but that was never allowed to set in with the likes of Shanks, Bob, Joe, Rueben and Ronnie about. The high standards, values and ethics that had been laid down were maintained at all times.

Peter Cormack: Newcastle never threatened to hurt us and once we scored our first goal the outcome was never in doubt. It ended up being the most one-sided cup final for years.

Phil Thompson: We were magnificent that day. We played marvellous football and won handsomely. I think everyone went home happy, even the Geordies. It wasn't like a scrappy 1-0 win that could have gone either way. They accepted defeat gracefully.

Kevin Keegan: It was so embarrassingly one-sided. The only amazing thing is that we didn't win by more. I don't even remember Newcastle having a shot, maybe Macdonald had one that went over the bar but that was it really.

Brian Hall: The last of the three goals, from Kevin, is the one I remember most because more than half our team was involved in the build-up. Shanks was a very proud man that day. I remember, because I wasn't too far away from him, that he was sat on the touchline, moving his hands backwards and forwards, backwards and forwards – like a conductor conducting his orchestra – in other words give-and-go, keep possession.

Bill Shankly: For me, that game was the culmination of things. The ground was suitable for play and we won 3-0. In one move we strung together twelve passes and on the thirteenth the ball was put into the net by Kevin Keegan.

Alec Lindsay: That has to be the outstanding memory of my time at the club because we won so easily. I know Liverpool have had some very good teams since then but that was a very good team too.

Brian Hall: We came out worthy winners but it was the manner in which we won the game. Everything we had talked about and worked on, throughout the sixties and seventies, came to fruition on that particular day. The model had been set and 1974 epitomised the way we would play in the future.

Shankly resigns!

12 July 1974

Bill Shankly: It was the most difficult thing in the world to make a decision like this and when I went to the Chairman to say I was retiring it was like walking to the electric chair.

Bob Paisley: Every year, virtually, he'd say he was going to pack in. You didn't take him seriously. When he finally did I was lost for words, shocked. It was the day I got back from holiday and it was like a bomb being dropped.

Peter Cormack: My wife and I were driving home from the Lakes when the news came on the radio and we just turned and looked at each other in amazement. I had no inkling of it whatsoever.

Ronnie Moran: I was with the wife shopping in Liverpool and posters were up saying he's finished. I saw it in the Echo and thought, 'No, this isn't right'. I was on the bench with Bill at the 1974 FA Cup final and didn't know he was going to quit. I knew nothing about it.

Steve Heighway: I don't remember where I actually was when hearing the news but I do remember being devastated by it. I had such enormous respect for Shanks and I always felt he had a soft spot for me, so on a personal level it came as a big disappointment because I just couldn't see the reasons for it. We'd won the league, we'd won the cup and I just thought we were then going to go on and win everything but all of a sudden our leader had announced his retirement.

Phil Thompson: It was devastating for me, because Shanks had been the godfather, the red father to everybody. We believed in him. He was at the hub of it all so it was like a bombshell. I couldn't believe it. Everyone's seen that television clip where the guy is interviewing people in the street and they're all saying, 'No you're kidding, you're joking', well, we all felt like that, even as players. It was hard to take in.

Peter Cormack: That was a big body blow and I think it was partly to blame for me leaving Liverpool, albeit two years later. If Shanks hadn't have resigned then I might have stayed on and fought for my place. No disrespect to Bob Paisley, because he went on to enjoy great success, but Shanks was a legend and one of the main reasons I joined Liverpool in the first place. My loyalties lay with Shanks and life at Liverpool was not the same after he left. I am sure some of the other older lads felt that way too.

Kevin Keegan: I just couldn't believe it and I remember just hoping it wasn't true. At the end of nearly every season he sat down with the board and threatened to resign over various issues. I learnt that off the older players. Normally it blew over and everything would be sorted out. The likes of Tommy and Emlyn thought this would be the case again. But it wasn't and he left. And, for me, when he left, half the club left and that's no disrespect to anybody else. It was such a shame and the beginning of the end for me at Liverpool.

Tommy Smith: I had spent a decade and a half in the Bill Shankly school of football. Now it was if a part of me had died. I took some consolation from the fact that Bill Shankly was getting out at the top, retiring as football's greatest winner. Chief executive Peter Robinson told us that Bill used to threaten to retire every year. They had always cajoled him out of it. This time there was no going back.

Bob Paisley: I tried to persuade him to stay, to have a break, go on a cruise and then come back. But he was adamant.

Bill Shankly: I think if you've got a pressurized job over a long period of time there comes a time when you are a little tired and fed up, if that's the word. You feel as if, goodness gracious, why should I carry on?

Steve Heighway: Once that initial shock subsides it was a case of sitting in the dressing room with the rest of the players and thinking about who's likely to replace him. 'Were they going to get Brian Clough or someone like him? What if he didn't fancy any of us and we had to find new clubs?' These were the thoughts going through our mind. I wasn't just a professional footballer, more importantly I was a Liverpool footballer. I'd never played anywhere else and had no inclination to. I don't know how I'd have handled that. So it was an unsettling time.

Bob Paisley: a reluctant successor

Peter Robinson: It was definitely a crisis time when Bill left. It was a bombshell and we had two options. One was to look outside the club, and Jack Charlton was one of the names Bill actually recommended to us. The other was to promote from within which, of course, was what we eventually opted for.

John Smith: When Bill resigned the only person we wanted to succeed him was Bob. We had no hesitation about that.

Peter Robinson: Bob was very reluctant to take the position as manager. When we approached him he said no. In the end the chairman, directors and I had to gang up on him.

Bob Paisley: I'd never even thought of being manager. I thought that if I accepted it would prevent the whole backroom set-up being disturbed. But I looked on myself as a buffer until they appointed a new manager and I told the players that.

Ray Clemence: I think when he first succeeded Shanks he was a bit overawed. I'll never forget him standing in the dressing-room in the summer of 1974 on the first day of pre-season training and telling us, 'Shanks has gone and they're giving me the job, even though I didn't really want it. But we must try to carry on what he's started'.

Bob Paisley: I knew, taking over from him, there would be difficulties to combat because of the type of extrovert personality Bill was and the fantastic record he had. I knew comparisons would be made.

Steve Heighway: Bill and Bob were totally different. Like night and day. When Shanks was in charge Bob was the one who fired the bullets so everyone was a bit frightened of him. We called him the Gunner. When he took over he was the complete opposite. He didn't want the job and told us so. At first he was shy and unconvincing. I have to say that the players were so mature that they got him through the early stages of his management career. I don't mean that in a disrespectful way but there's no question that we did. We sat together as a group at Melwood and said collectively that if we make life difficult for him there's no way he'll be able to handle it. Gradually he grew into the role.

Bob Paisley: I inherited a side of very good players and a successful pattern of training and playing which Bill and I had built up together during his years in charge. That aspect of my new position was fairly easy to maintain. The difficult part of the job was in handling the personal problems. I believe I had the respect of the players when I was in charge of the coaching but I had no experience of handling the players in other ways. Bill had always done that; that was the manager's job. Then, in 1974 I was the manager and I found that side of the job was no bed of roses. I found it tough.

Ray Clemence: For me, he was a better coach than motivator of men, but he could also pull a player apart. He was a decent man but he had a ruthless streak in him. He could assess all positions, even my speciality of goalkeeping. He knew a fair amount about that and he would play in goal in five-a-sides.

Kevin Keegan: We loved and respected Bob just as we had Shanks, but in a different way... Somebody else might have followed and wanted to make drastic changes, but Bob let the ship sail on, making adjustments as he went along.

Phil Thompson: It was same old, same old, nothing changed behind the scenes. The coaches, Joe Fagan and Ronnie Moran were still there, so it was exactly the same, it was just another voice. Bob knew the game inside out, probably more than Shanks, but couldn't convey that in team meetings and press conferences, and I think he felt a bit uncomfortable with that. Bob would always like to stay in the background.

Ian Callaghan: Shanks was the greatest motivator in the world, but Bob was the finest tactician. With his Durham accent he wasn't the easiest to understand. But he got his points across briefly and succinctly. He'd say things like, 'Their number four hits a good long one'. That meant you had to try to stop their right half getting the ball because his long passing was good.

Kevin Keegan: He wasn't as eloquent as others but he had his own terrific sense of humour and a million sayings. His use of the word 'doins' earned him the nickname Dougie Doins, also the Rat and the Gunner, because he'd fought in the war as a desert rat.

Joe Fagan: Whatever Bob said was always plain, straightforward stuff. He wasn't a flamboyant man. You didn't find Bob joking with the opposition as Bill did. The extraordinary thing about him was his ordinariness. There were no gimmicks with Bob.

Bob Paisley: I thought I'd failed in my first season as manager because we only finished runners-up. That's what it was like to follow the standards established by Bill Shankly.

Record win

Liverpool v Stromsgodset
Anfield
European Cup Winners' Cup first round first leg
17 September 1974

Brain Hall: There were only two players who didn't score in that game. Ray Clemence was one of them and the other one was me! Every other outfield player scored. Even Phil Thompson scored.

Phil Thompson: Phil Thompson actually scored two – the only time I ever did it – and they were two good goals. One was a simple header. For the other, I can remember Alec Lindsay chipping a ball through from the left back slot and I ran right through the middle of their defence, controlled it, the keeper came out and I slid it past him. I can still remember it to this day – one of the famous 13 I scored. But seriously, you always remember your goals and to beat any team 11-0, well... it doesn't happen too often so it was a fantastic achievement.

Brian Hall: When you play in a European tie and win 11-0 it's got to be a little bit special hasn't it? I've been ribbed about the game ever since quite frankly, particularly by my ex-team mates. It was just one of those nights when it wasn't going to happen for me. But I put it down to the fact that I had eleven assists. I'm not quite sure whether that's true or not but it's what I like to think.

Phil Thompson: We had a few other routs but that was probably the easiest one. We always gave teams respect and it was no different with Stromsgodset but on the night we tore them apart.

Brian Hall: We got on the roller coaster and just did not stop. We just kept going, going, going and completely buried this team. If we had played for another half hour we'd have probably got another five goals. It was one of those daft nights. And nobody gave in. Nobody kind of sat back on their laurels and thought 'well this game is won'. We just kept rolling.

Tommy Smith: What was it, 12-0 on aggregate? I don't think they got out their own half. I remember the second leg over there. The only reason we didn't score another eleven was because of the pitch, it was awful. It was like playing on Stanley Park.

Brian Hall: The second leg out in Norway, I can't even remember what the score was. I think it might have been 1-0. I know it was a formality. I think the Stromsgodset game proved to us how the first leg of a European tie here at Anfield should be played. You just keep going and going and you bury them. And if you can finish the tie off there and then, then do so. The second leg then becomes irrelevant because you know the likes of Stromsgodset are not going to beat you 12-0 in Norway.

First Division drama

Wolverhampton Wanderers v Liverpool
Molineux
Football League Division One
4 May 1976

Approaching the final league game of the season Liverpool needed a win to clinch the title, while opponents Wolves required maximum points to avoid relegation. The scene was set for a truly memorable night.

Phil Thompson: You can imagine, after not winning anything in Bob's first season, fingers were being pointed but Bob knew his players. He had a good nucleus. He'd also brought in Phil Neal and Terry McDermott, while youngsters like Jimmy Case and Davey Fairclough were breaking through. Things started to take shape and Keegan was to become one of the best players in Europe this season.

Kevin Keegan: QPR were our nearest challengers and they had finished the season. We needed a win to overtake them but Wolves, although they were struggling, was a tough place to go.

Phil Neal: I think the most enduring moment of my career was the night of our first championship under Paisley, my first medal. I remember that night at Wolves so vividly.

David Fairclough: When we got to the ground it was absolute chaos. There were huge crowds everywhere and just getting the coach to the players' entrance was a struggle. Fans were climbing up the floodlight pylons and everyone was desperate to get inside. Some were even allowed in through our dressing room, which was hilarious. Molineux was an old-fashioned stadium then and the big sash windows in the away dressing room opened out on to the street. We watched the scenes outside standing on the wooden benches and a number of us spotted lads we all knew. There were thousands out there but I managed to spot a couple of my mates, as did the likes of Thommo and a few of the others.

Phil Neal: It was hilarious because as we were getting changed, Phil Thompson asks the boss, 'Look, I've got four of my mates outside, can they come in?' They were on the other side of the massive door that led to the dressing room. Paisley has a think, and then he kindly says, 'Go on Thommo, let your mates in'.

So they open this door and 400 Liverpool fans must have paraded through the dressing room into the Paddock. They're walking through going, 'Good luck lads, you can do it'. Bob didn't close the door for a while. We just let them wander in. It was such a giggle, part of the perfect night.

Phil Thompson: It was a very, very tense night. Wolves also needed to win, and hope other results went their way, to stay up. But looking around the whole of the stadium, three sides were red and white, not the gold and black of Wolves. It was an incredible situation and you could feel it pounding.

David Fairclough: Liverpudlians always travelled in large numbers so we expected a more than decent following but this was just off the scale. The sheer size of our support really became apparent when we went out on to the pitch for our pre-match walkabout. Red and white filled all sides of the ground. The turnstiles had been locked hours before and we could have been forgiven for thinking we were back at Anfield.

Phil Neal: I didn't realise how tight the game would be and the level of tension we'd experience, but when we won it was just an incredible feeling.

Tommy Smith: They had big Steve Kindon up front. Steve would run through brick walls. He was whacking us, and they went one up. I wasn't particularly worried though, because we had plenty of time. We turned on the pressure in the second half and, really, it was just a matter of getting the first goal. Once we scored that, there was never going to be any doubt.

Phil Neal: A quarter-of-an-hour from the end however, it was still 1-0 so I was starting to feel a bit unsure. We'd hit the post, we'd done everything and it looked like being one of those nights when we were going to miss out.

David Fairclough: Lesser teams might have panicked but this Liverpool side was made of sterner stuff. Fittingly it was KK, the Footballer of the Year elect, who got the goal. Momentum had swung back in our favour and the travelling Kopites, who had backed us relentlessly throughout, spilled on the pitch in celebration. When Tosh and 'Razor' Ray Kennedy then put the outcome beyond any doubt with a goal apiece in the last five minutes the scenes were unbelievable.

Phil Thompson: I think everybody remembers the scenes, especially when the third one goes in. We were trying to get everyone off the pitch so that the game could restart. The supporters are then all lined up along the touchline and you were thinking, 'If they come on again we might not get this game finished'.

Ronnie Moran: The crowd had come onto the pitch for every goal but when the third one went in – with about a minute to go - they were jumping on the crossbar and the crossbar was starting to wobble. We were thinking, 'Oh my god, if they break the crossbar, the game will be finished and we might be forced to play it again'. I don't know who it was but one of ours went around to the back of the goal and warned them. Thankfully, we made it to the end of the game and then the celebrations could really begin. What a great night.

Kevin Keegan: I can remember it for the reason that we clinched the championship there and the jubilation that surrounded winning it. I can also remember my dad, who had cancer by that time, being in the dressing room with us afterwards. But I can't, for the life of me, remember the goal I scored that night. If I saw it on television the memories would no doubt come flooding back but off the top of my head I honestly can't recall it.

Phil Thompson: It was absolutely incredible. That was a fantastic achievement and we absolutely loved it. Coming home on the motorway, along the M6, it was just choc-a-bloc. I don't know how many times we had to stop because of the traffic.

David Fairclough: Going back on the coach took forever. Not that we minded. Everyone was in celebratory mood and the champagne continued to flow. For long stretches of the journey, traffic was at a complete standstill and supporters were partying on the hard shoulder of the motorway while we handed out bottles of bubbly. The scenes of jubilation were unprecedented. It was like Liverpool had never won the league before.

John Toshack: That is a night I will never forget. The fans must have thought the title was slipping away. It could not have been more dramatic if it had come out of a Boys Own annual. I felt very proud that night and it remains one of the greatest moments of my career.

A second UEFA Cup

Liverpool v FC Bruges
Anfield
UEFA Cup final first leg
28 April 1976

David Fairclough: European finals are often dull, cagey affairs. Not this one. For me, apart from a goal by myself, it had everything. And when I think back to it now I'm proud to say I was part of it. It was an amazing game.

Phil Thompson: Bruges were not one of the biggest names but they had some good players and we were caught out on the counter-attack a couple of times at the start. We found ourselves 2-0 down, which was an absolute massive shock.

David Fairclough: I was given the number eight shirt and asked to play out on the right side, with Tosh and Kevin as usual through the middle. This was the plan. But it was Bruges, attacking the Kop end, who were first into their stride with a stunning start that had them two goals up after just fifteen minutes. Anfield, normally such a cauldron of noise on nights like this, was temporarily silenced. Shocked into near submission.

Phil Thompson: But we still had this great belief and, knowing we had this knack of scoring so many late goals, we never gave up. It wasn't just down to luck. We would grind opponents down.

Jimmy Case: I started on the bench and, like everyone else, I couldn't quite believe it as Bruges went 2-0 up. I came on at half-time. John Toshack got taken off and it changed the game. During the break I thought I'm gonna get a big speech. But there was nothing tactical. They just said, 'Go on and cause fucking havoc'. These were the exact words from Joe Fagan and Ronnie Moran. So that's what I did.

Bob Paisley: We were like a gang of schoolboys in the first half. We committed hari-kari. We got off to a bad start and let our own mistakes upset us. I made the change to get more movement in our attack.

Jimmy Case: It wasn't that Tosh was playing badly, but manager Bob Paisley and the coaches felt something had to be changed, the pattern had to be altered. The Kop and the supporters were magnificent that night. Throats must have been red-raw with cheering. But you know what? I believe those fans liked to see us with our backs to the wall because they knew we could win.

John Toshack: I was bitterly disappointed at the substitution, but really Bob was to be applauded for what happened. The Belgians had not allowed us to get near their penalty area so any aerial advantage I possessed had been completely nullified. A change of approach was needed. The eventual scoreline was a tribute to the tactical knowledge of Bob Paisley as much as anything else.

Jimmy Case: It was a touch of genius... it allowed Ray Kennedy to move further forward and the Belgians couldn't handle Ray that night. He scored a blinder for the first, hit the post for me to bundle in the second and it was from his pass that Steve Heighway won the penalty which KK converted for a remarkable 3-2 win. I've never heard the Kop in better voice, they inspired that tremendous comeback.

Tommy Smith: It was the epitome of the old phrase a game of two halves. Having been shell-shocked by the Belgians in the first half we asserted ourselves in the second. We had a right rollicking from Bob Paisley, and it was a combination of that and the Kop that pulled us back.

Phil Thompson: To come back, as we did, was one of the great nights. Of course, there are so many other games in our illustrious history... but that deserves special mention. Because it was the Belgians of Bruges though, and not one of the great teams of Europe, it's not remembered as much.

David Fairclough: It's a pity it often gets forgotten about when people talk of Anfield's great European occasions. At most other clubs it would be hailed to high heaven and forever spoken about in revered terms. At Liverpool it's just recalled as another memorable match among a cast of thousands. For it not to be ranked that high just goes to show how great a continental pedigree this club has.

FC Bruges v Liverpool
Olympic Stadium
UEFA Cup final second leg
19 May 1976

Tommy Smith: We went away from home [for second leg] and I gave a penalty away - I still say it wasn't a penalty - and I then missed a good chance from a free-kick up in there half.

Jimmy Case: It was another nerve-tingling affair because Bruges scored first, and with their two goals at Anfield, they were ahead on away goals. But we soon got level on the night.

Phil Thompson: Even going 1-0 down away from home, we never ever were told to chase the game, we were more told to keep our shape, not to panic and that's what we did.

Jimmy Case: Kevin scored, and from that point on we went into professional mode, keeping the ball, squeezing the life out of Bruges to take the trophy, our second of the season, with a 4-3 win over the two legs.

Bob Paisley: When the chips were down we were able to edge back into the game. Bruges fought really hard but I thought, 20 minutes before half time, they were out of the game. The second half was another story. It was the longest 45 minutes of my life.

David Fairclough: We came under a lot of pressure in the second half and spent a lot of time with our backs against the wall. My instruction was to try and get Bruges running the other way and perhaps snatch a goal to put the outcome beyond reach of the hosts. That was easier said than done. Bruges knew just one goal would see them reclaim the advantage and they laid siege to Clem's goal. We found ourselves pinned back in our own half for long periods of the time that remained. Despite the best efforts of our travelling fans the atmosphere was so tense but thankfully we hung on. The feeling at the final whistle was sheer relief, quickly followed by a joyous burst of adrenalin as the scale of our achievement sank in.

Tommy Smith: Really and truly that was a long season and all I can remember for the last ten minutes was thinking, 'Jesus Christ I hope we can hang on, because my legs have gone'. Everybody was more or less the same but we managed it, which meant a second European medal so it was good.

David Fairclough: League champions, now UEFA Cup winners. Paisley had emulated the feat of Shanks three seasons before and issued an ominous warning to the rest of Europe that this Liverpool team was a force to be reckoned with. As the celebrations commenced we swapped shirts with our beaten opponents and Emlyn famously dropped the cup, leaving it without a base for our triumphant homecoming the following day.

Allez les rouges

Liverpool v St Etienne
Anfield
European Cup quarter-final second leg
16 March 1977

Joey Jones: For me it was the greatest atmosphere I ever played in. Older supporters will talk about the Inter Milan and Celtic games in the 60s, but there was no doubt in my mind that St Etienne was the best. There was a sense of anticipation about the game and it hit home when we heard that there were thousands of fans gathering around the ground early in the morning, never mind late afternoon.

David Fairclough: Pre-match tea and toast was served at around 4.30 and it came with the news that we'd be leaving for Anfield a bit earlier than normal due to unexpected numbers being up at the ground already. There were genuine concerns that it might take us some time getting there and they weren't wrong. The route from the Adelphi to Anfield took us along Great Homer Street, up Everton Valley and towards Anfield Road. As we edged up the hill it quickly became apparent that those early reports of crowd congestion were not exaggerated. The streets were absolutely rammed, similar to the scenes outside Molineux the season before. We later found that supporters had been queuing at the turnstiles since around midday. Many feigned illness to leave work early and I've since heard countless stories about how kids bunked off school to make sure they were there. It seems every supporter at Anfield that night has a story to tell, whether they were one of the lucky 55,000 in the ground or among the reported 10,000 locked out. It didn't take a genius to sense that this was no normal Anfield night. It had the feel of something very different.

Ray Clemence: The atmosphere that night was unbelievable. No one was sitting down. Everyone was stood on their seats. It was the most incredible atmosphere I ever experienced. There might have been only fifty-odd thousand in the ground but it felt like about 250,000.

Emlyn Hughes: I'd missed those European glory nights in the sixties that the other lads at the club were always talking about. I never really knew what they meant until the night we played St Etienne in the European Cup quarter final in 1977. There was steam coming off the Kop that night and the crowd were surging backwards and forwards.

David Fairclough: As Emlyn Hughes led us out, all those in a red kit reached up to give the 'This Is Anfield' sign another touch. Then came the first decibels of the Kop roar, three paces more and we were hit by a wall of sound that grew louder and louder as we climbed the final six steps towards the pitch. Once out into the open I was temporarily startled, the noise was deafening, and on a jam-packed Kop that was baying for victory there were more flags flying than I'd ever seen before. A red flare added to the sense of occasion, while clouds of smoke wafted their way across a goalmouth littered with masses of toilet roll. Whether as a supporter or player, I was no stranger to big occasions at Anfield but this all seemed new and so much more exciting. There was so much passion emanating from all four sides of the ground, it was almost frightening.

Phil Neal: I'd never known tension like it. You talk to anybody; it was the only European game where I was distracted by the crowd and the atmosphere got better and better as the game wore on. It was difficult to focus at times because when the ball was up the other end of the pitch I couldn't help but look up in amazement as the crowd. The whole stadium seemed to be moving, even the people in the stands. They were bobbing up and down, swaying and bouncing, You couldn't better that night.

Joey Jones: It was a real pressure game and the supporters played their part. I've watched the game on TV a number of times since and I'll admit that if the game was played today I'd have been sent off for some of the challenges I made that night. Of course, you got away with it back them.

Ian Callaghan: It was to go down as one of Anfield's greatest occasions – perhaps the most memorable of them all. When Kevin Keegan floated a cross-cum-shot over Curkovic and into the net with less than two minutes gone I thought that St Etienne might crumble.

Kevin Keegan: I just drove the ball across to the far post – and the wind did the rest.

Tommy Smith: Kevin's goal drew us level on aggregate and all appeared to be going well until Bathenay produced a piece of true class. In all the years I played football I was privileged to witness many fantastic goals but the one he scored for St Etienne that night is right up there with the best of them.

David Fairclough: Once Bathenay scored St Etienne's goal I, like many, thought that perhaps the French had a little bit too much for us, because they were a special side. Bathenay's goal was extraordinary, and when goals like that go in, you think to yourself that you're going to be up against it.

Ian Callaghan: We had it all to do again but in the 58th minute we made it 2-1 on the night when Tosh met my cross from the right and passed for Ray Kennedy to score.

Ray Kennedy: The ball came to me off Toshack's shin. I didn't hit it that hard, but I hit it true.

Ian Callaghan: Now it was a case of going all out for a winner, but at the same time watchful that Dominique Rocheteau, Larque, Bathenay and the rest did not snatch another goal for St Etienne.

David Fairclough: Fifteen more minutes passed without any further scoring and the time had come for a change. The call came for me to get ready. I was given no specific instructions. I took off the old training jumper and adjusted my shorts. As the Dutch linesman inspected my boots, Ronnie Moran patted me on the backside and told me, 'Just go and make a nuisance of yourself'. By now any nerves had disappeared. I was raring to go and, as always, the great welcome I received from the fans gave me a massive lift. We needed a goal and, so long as an opportunity came my way, I was always confident I could deliver.

Tommy Smith: With Bathenay's away goal. St Etienne were still in the driving seat but they found Davey's speed and direct running difficult to cope with.

Ian Callaghan: It was the introduction of David Fairclough as substitute for Tosh that was to prove the vital decision of the game and eleven minutes after coming on he was responsible for the most ecstatic moment I ever experienced at Anfield.

David Fairclough: Ray Kennedy put me through and I just chested it down. The ball seemed to hang a little and I remember shrugging off a heavy challenge from Lopez. I was thinking, once I'd got him on the wrong side, just to get the ball down and get it on target. I was quite aware that if I got the shot close to the keeper, he would have trouble getting down to save it. I put a spurt on, got clear of him and put it just where I wanted. I never had any doubt about it – I knew I would score. I had the whole goal to aim at and I made up my mind that it would go in. I let it tick over in my head and then put it in. It was a terrific feeling. The amazing thing is, it seemed so quiet as I homed in on the target but when the ball hit the back of the net the noise was just unbelievable. I remember Kevin Keegan leapt on me and I could hear him saying above the roar, 'Supersub you've done it again'.

Bob Paisley: I was banking on the fact that Liverpool never give in. I doubt if there was anyone better for that situation than Davie. It was a game in which you needed hearts, guts, stamina and determination. That's what won us the match.

David Fairclough: That word, St Etienne, it must be mentioned to me almost every day. It is incredible. At the time I never realised just what an effect it would have on people's memories and when I look back I feel lucky to have been given the opportunity to go on as substitute that night. It was a night I'll never forget.

Ian Callaghan: St Etienne was an unbelievable game, one of the best ever seen at Anfield. It was a fantastic night in every sense. There was an incredible atmosphere and, of course, we got the right result. St Etienne were a very good side. They had some great players and were without doubt one of the strongest in the competition. We were always confident that we were good enough to win the cup but beating a team of St Etienne's calibre was still great boost. That match was the highlight and even eclipsed the final.

Ray Clemence: St Etienne was probably the best team in Europe at that time and after beating them we all felt we could go on and win the European Cup.

The sacking of Rome [part I]

Liverpool v Borussia Monchengladbach
Stadio Olimpico, Rome
European Cup final
25 May 1977

Ray Clemence: Anyone associated with Liverpool Football Club, as a player or fan, will remember 1977 and the club's very first European Cup final. The first time always tends to be the best and this was no different. It came at the end of an incredible season. We'd won the league but unfortunately lost in the FA Cup final, so to go on to Rome and win the European Cup against Borussia Monchengladbach, in front of 26,000 Liverpool supporters was fantastic. It was a night I will remember for the rest of my life. That's an absolute certainty.

Ronnie Moran: We'd won the league but had lost in the FA Cup final to Manchester United the Saturday before. Everyone was disappointed about that, not just the players. We knew we had the big game in Rome on the Wednesday and had to lift ourselves for that. The lads were told to enjoy themselves on the Saturday night, we returned home from Wembley on Sunday and then began our preparations for Rome on the Monday. No-one needed a kick up the backside, everyone just rallied around. That's the type of lads they were and which is why we got the good result in Rome.

Emlyn Hughes: I remember walking out onto the pitch before the game and I thought to myself 'Jesus Christ we're back in Liverpool!' There was that many punters from Liverpool there, we were greeted by a sea of red and white. The support of the fans gave us all a terrific lift and all the lads were saying to each other how there was no way we could lose the match now. It was like playing at home. I can imagine what the Borussia players must have thought when they walked out. They must have looked around and thought they had no chance against such support. It must have seemed like they were playing at Anfield.

Terry McDermott: Rome will never fade from my memory. I'll always remember it until the day I die, walking out into the stadium and seeing the red and white chequered flags, I'd never seen anything like it, before or since. It was just an incredible feeling to see those fans. There must have been at least 30,000 Scousers there. It was just phenomenal. We walked on to the pitch about an hour before and thought 'Christ, how can we not win for these lot', and obviously we didn't.

Tommy Smith: The 1977 final was the one when I did notice the crowd. We went out to have a look at what was going on in the Rome stadium and three-quarters of it was red, I couldn't believe it and it hit you that we had more supporters than the Germans.

Joey Jones: There was one or two banners at Wembley the previous Saturday that had made me laugh, but when I walked out in Rome's Olympic Stadium and saw that banner [Joey Ate The Frogs Legs, Made The Swiss Role, Now He's Munching Gladbach] it made me feel about ten feet tall. I was given the banner when I left Liverpool and I think as much of that as I do the medal. It has been everywhere, so many people keep wanting to see it, it's probably more famous than me!

Phil Neal: Sitting in the dressing room before the biggest game of our lives Bob [Paisley] starts rattling on about how the last time he was in Rome it was in a tank during the war. I was thinking, 'shouldn't he be telling us a bit more about Monchengladbach'. Whether he did this consciously so not to worry us, I don't know, but he probably did, and it worked. We were all laughing and there is no doubt it helped us relax. Other managers preparing for their club's first ever European Cup final would have been so serious, but Bob was great. He was a one off.

Joey Jones: I'd get nervous before every game, but more so on this occasion because it was the biggest game of my career and the first time Liverpool had ever been in the final of the European Cup. People always remember the first time and that's what made this one so special. It meant so much to the fans and everyone within the club. On paper Borussia had a formidable side, packed with internationals. When you looked through the list of their players it was frightening. Vogts, Bonhof, Heynckes and Simonsen, they were world-class players. Liverpool though never worried about the opposition and we prepared for that game no differently to how we would have any other. Our attitude was always to let the opposition worry about us, although I don't think they'd have been quaking in their boots when they went through our team and saw Joey Jones at left back!

Tommy Smith: We got out there and it was untrue. I think on that night, we not so much became a European side, but we played like a European side. Terry McDermott's first goal was outstanding. The little one-two, bang, bang, and lifts it over the goalkeeper. Absolutely brilliant.

Terry McDermott: My goal I remember perfectly well. I've seen it that many times on television. It's just a great move. Cally passed the ball to Heighway and he's played a great through ball to pick out my run. I've got Wolfgang Kneib – he was about 9ft 2in – running out at me. I thought, 'Aye aye, hit it before he comes and clatters me'. It could have gone anywhere, but it went in the back of the net. It wasn't the best goal I ever scored but it was the most important.

Bob Paisley: Borussia were spread-eagled and it was a perfect example of Terry's awareness, anticipation and running. Kevin Keegan was giving that great professional Bertie Vogts a dog's life. He had the German selling programmes to the crowd – so far he had pulled him away from where the build up was taking place. Vogts was a key defender and he didn't realise what was happening until it was too late.

Kevin Keegan: I found myself, not unexpectedly, man-for-man-marked by Bertie Vogts. I loved that challenge, because I knew I would have to be at my very best to get the better of him. He gave me a lot of respect and followed me everywhere. In an odd way that built up my confidence. He stuck so close to me that after some pretty serious shirt pulling from him I told him I'd be happy to change shirts with him after the game but it wasn't usual to swap them during it!

Emlyn Hughes: Every team, no matter who you are playing, get at least a couple of chances in a match. Borussia were no different. They had a five-minute spell were they were on top and they took full advantage by grabbing an equaliser.

Tommy Smith: We'd battered them for the opening 40 minutes only to be pegged back shortly after half-time. It was a brilliantly taken goal. They then enjoyed a good spell and it crossed our minds that we could be in trouble. But we took the game to them. We were patient and didn't go gung-ho.

Ray Clemence: People often ask me, 'What was my greatest ever save?' I judge great saves not necessarily in terms of how spectacular they are, but how important they are in terms of having an influence on the game. That night in Rome, not long after they equalized, Stielike broke away and I found myself in a one-on-one situation with him. I just spread myself and luckily the ball hit me. If Stielike had of scored I'm not sure we'd have gone on to win the European Cup. A couple of minutes later Tommy Smith went up the other end and scored our second goal.

Tommy Smith: They failed to do their homework. We had arranged beforehand that I should go up for corners but they hadn't prepared for it and I was left unmarked. Stevie [Heighway] was expected to chip the corner in and the idea was for me to flick it on to Keegan and generally cause confusion in their penalty area. Instead he drove the ball into the centre, I ran to meet it and connected with a perfect header. The goalkeeper never moved. I'd compare it to serving an ace in tennis or hitting a hole in one in golf. Everything about it was perfect. My first thought was that I've got to get back before the ref disallows it for something. At two one up, I was more than confident that the cup was ours. The second goal took them by surprise and they lost a bit of heart after that. I was due to retire so this was supposedly my last game for the club and it seemed the perfect ending.

Kevin Keegan: I desperately wanted to go out on a winning note in Rome. I was enjoying myself very much against Bertie and when I got away from him on the halfway line, I simply set off for their goal. I made it all the way into the penalty area with Bertie chasing me, and then he brought me down.

Phil Neal: It was up to me to seal the victory and it was a long, agonising, walk up to that penalty spot. All the lads were saying, 'Come on Nealy, finish it off', while Cally, who had played a million games for this club, well, he's on the edge of the box saying a prayer. When I stepped up I wasn't nervous. I'd noticed that Wolfgang Kneib was about two or three inches taller than Clem so I had already decided that if I got a penalty I would keep it low because he would struggle to get down for it. This is what I done and it rolled in off the post.

Tommy Smith: I thought we won comfortably. We surprised Borussia by playing 'keep ball' while they opted to play more direct. It was by no means an open game but it wasn't as tight as previous European Cup finals. They tried their best but at the end of the day we were too good for them. It was a great performance by us. It was one of the finest games we ever played in Europe. There is no question about it. Everything we done that night in Rome fell perfectly into place.

Emlyn Hughes: I remember walking up those steps and I felt privileged to do so. I was captain of Liverpool because I was a mouthy shouter, not because I was the best player – I would moan at players incessantly to try and get that bit extra out of them. When I went up to lift the cup I was not thinking about myself, Kevin Keegan or the rest of the lads who'd just won the match. The names that were flashing through my mind were the likes of Roger Hunt, Ian St John and Ron Yeats, Shanks and Rueben Bennett. These were the men who had given us the chance to win the European Cup and who had put us in the position that we were in. This was the moment the club had been striving for since 1964 and we had learnt from them. As I reached out to collect the cup I knew that it was as much for them as for us.

Joey Jones: I remember watching the 1965 FA Cup final on telly as a kid and then going out to play afterwards, pretending I was St John scoring the winner. All of a sudden there I was playing in the first ever Liverpool side to win the European Cup. As a kid it was something I couldn't have imagined in my wildest dreams. It was unbelievable and I was so proud.

Bob Paisley: I've had some great moments in football, but nothing compares with this. Right from the start, we dominated the game – and turned in the best performance in the history of this club. I was the first English-born manager to win the European Cup and I couldn't have picked a better time or place to do it. Everything was perfect. Memories flooded back for me as the team bus left the stadium after the game and threaded its way through those ancient streets back to the hotel. I had driven into Rome on a tank in 1944. I was part of another conquering force then and came back as manager of another conquering force, thankfully in football not war.

Terry McDermott: I don't think there was many teams who would have played the way that we played against a top quality team like they were at the time, three days after getting beat in an FA Cup final, I thought that was just unbelievable.

Bob Paisley: To come away from Wembley and play like that was a feat in itself. Our win was a great team effort but Kevin stood out. He played his finest game for Liverpool in his last match for the club. I'm sure if Kevin had turned in a performance against Manchester United like the one he gave in Rome we'd have won the FA Cup, too. But the big question is, 'Could he have run like that twice in a few days?'

Joey Jones: I'd never seen the game in its entirety until a couple of years ago. I bought the video in Woolies and I couldn't remember much of it. For some reason there is only really one incident that sticks in my mind and that is the ball bouncing off my shin and going out of play as I tried to control it. I don't know why but, apart from the goals and the celebrations, that is my memory of actual game itself. Whatever people say though I firmly believe that the European Cup was harder to win back then than it is now.

Emlyn Hughes: We went back to the hotel afterwards and we were sitting around having a beer and a bite to eat. All the lads were there with their wives, having a laugh and a joke. The table of food was unbelievable. It was about 30 yards long by five foot wide and had everything on it. Ham, pork, lobster, prawns, all manner of foods. We were aware that there was fans outside and I said to our chairman John Smith that it might be a good idea to let them in because there was no way we were going to get through all that food. Half an hour later the doors are opened and the fans flooded in. These lads had travelled halfway across the world to support us and half of them looked like they hadn't eaten for a week. It was like a pack of locusts and within five minutes all the food had gone.

Phil Neal: The party in Rome was wonderful. The supporters found out where we were staying and at one stage it seemed as though the entire population of Liverpool was there. It got so busy that we ended up retiring to our rooms for a private party.

Bob Paisley: I like a drink and, in common with most people, enjoy celebrating a great victory. But this was different. It was no ordinary triumph. But I wanted to remain sober. I was drinking it all in – the atmosphere, the sense of pride, of achievement, of joy and reward for ten months hard labour. I wanted to savour every moment.

Tommy Smith: The major thing for me and Cally was that we had been in the team robbed by the referee in the 1965 European Cup semi-final against Inter Milan. It had been a long time but we had finally made up for that disappointment. True, we'd won the UEFA Cup in the meantime but this was the big one. That was my first thought when the final whistle went and I suppose it was fitting that it was back in Italy where we won it. I think that made it all the more sweeter.

Emlyn Hughes: The homecoming was absolutely brilliant but we always knew it would be. The Liverpool public had waited so long to see the club win the European Cup and they came out in their thousands. I remember coming along Queens Drive and you just couldn't move. There was that many people out on the streets to welcome us. It was fantastic.

Phil Neal: It was the best welcome home ever. I remember driving along Queens Drive and we had to knock on people's houses to use the toilet. We'd then get a lift back to the bus on the back of the police motor bikes that were escorting us. The scenes at the Picton library were unbelievable and the celebrations seemed to last for days.

Goodbye Kevin, hello Kenny

While Liverpool basked in the glow of being European Champions during the summer of 1977, Anfield found itself at the centre of two huge transfer stories – the departure of Kevin Keegan and arrival of Kenny Dalglish.

Terry McDermott: Kevin and Kenny were the two best players I ever played with.

Bob Paisley: I told Kenny when he arrived that I wished we still had Kevin too. Then it would simply have been a case of choosing the other nine players and a substitute and I'd expect to win the Grand National as well as cups and championships! There is no doubt in my mind that Kevin and Kenny together would have formed a lethal blend. Great players can always play together.

Bill Shankly: They would have to form a society for the prevention of cruelty to opponents if the two of them were in the same team.

Kevin Keegan: Six years is an awfully long time in football. It may only seem a short period of time to people outside the game but bearing in mind the average career only lasts between twelve and fifteen years, spending six of them at one club is a large percentage of a players' time in the game. The fact that I won so much during my time at Liverpool is something which will always give me a lot of pleasure but it wasn't that difficult a decision to leave in the end because I felt I was stagnating at Liverpool. Shankly had gone and I just felt that there was another mountain for me to climb somewhere.

Terry McDermott: We thought no-one could take the place of Kevin Keegan, he was the superstar of English football. Of course, he'd given the club a year's notice of his intention to leave but, still, when he left in the summer of 1977 we were all gutted because he was such a fantastic player and a terrific role model for us all.

Kevin Keegan: A deal had been done twelve months before. I'd signed on for one last year at Liverpool and a fee for me to leave was fixed at £500,000. It was a good deal for both of us and I think it would have been a mistake not to announce it. It was the right thing to do. I was just being honest with the punters and I think a lot of them accepted my reasons. It was out there and everyone knew what was happening. For Liverpool it gave them a year to find my replacement, to go out and head-hunt the right person. As it happens they didn't do too badly out of it because they went out and bought Kenny Dalglish. Having sold me for £500,000 and paying £440,000 for Kenny they banked £60,000, which, as it turned out, was a great piece of business.

Bob Paisley: I just hoped that after the trials and tribulations of my early years in management, someone up high would smile on me and guide my hand. My plea was answered when we got Kenny Dalglish. What a player, what a great professional. Just as Kevin had wanted a new challenge, so Kenny let it be known to Celtic that he was unsettled and wanted to embark on a new chapter of his career.

Kenny Dalglish: There was something very appealing about Liverpool. I was there briefly as a 15-year-old when Bill Shankly was manager, and I knew it was similar to Celtic. When the time came for me to leave Parkhead there was only one place I wanted to go and that was Liverpool. I also knew they'd give me the chance of success in Europe which I was yearning for.

Terry McDermott: We were all wondering who they'd bring in and there'd been rumours that it would be Kenny Dalglish. Obviously we knew about what he'd done up in Scotland. Everyone was aware of the goals he'd scored there but that was no guarantee that he'd fit in at Liverpool. It was only natural that we were a bit wary when he joined. Within half an hour of his first training session with us though we realised just what a talent he was. That's all it took. He was beyond belief really. What a replacement. Bob Paisley was a great spotter of talent but credit also to Geoff Twentyman who must have been to watch him.

Bob Paisley: It wasn't just Kevin's departure that made me go for Kenny. It was the fact that Kenny looked so much a Liverpool-type player because of his attitude to the game. He did the simple things and he was so consistent.

Phil Thompson: We'd always thought that Dalglish was a good player, we'd heard so much of him, but we didn't realise what a great player he was until he came to Liverpool. From the first games you knew of his ability, what he could do, not only for himself, he could create space, he could create goals, but what he could do for everybody else. He could hold the ball up, turn the ball into everybody and create things. He had assists galore and we knew that if we could get the ball into his feet, in and around the box, he'd cause havoc and he did that for the rest of his career at Liverpool.

Ronnie Moran: It was a lot of money to pay in those days and there was always a saying that players needed time to 'feel their way' when they came to a new club. Not Kenny. He went straight in. I think the Charity Shield was his first game, then we went to Middlesbrough on the opening day of the season and he scored. He was that good a player, he just muscled in to everything, you didn't have to ask him to work. He was a great player who worked all the time.

Tommy Smith: He came down and was as good as anybody I'd ever seen, one of the greatest players ever. There was no big fuss. He just got on with it and you could tell straight away that he was one of us.

Kenny Dalglish: I felt comfortable the very first time I walked into the place. That was the thing that struck me in training. They'd just come straight off two trophies the year before and they just said, 'You get nothing for last year'. The attitude was magnificent.

Phil Thompson: He settled very, very, quickly. He was quite shy, was Kenny, but I think Glaswegians and Scousers had always got along very well. They've got quite a similar mentality. He was a great laugh. He liked to laugh and joke. I couldn't understand him too much in those early days, but he went on to make himself a legend at the club.

Kenny Dalglish: The great thing about when I arrived is that there were a lot of people at Liverpool who were well set in their ways. When I got there it wasn't difficult to get into the Liverpool way of doing things because if I hadn't I would have been out of tune. Everything was set up for me to just slot in. But it wasn't like a machine because a machine doesn't have any feeling.

Phil Thompson: Because we were a good team with good players, we understood his ability and played to his strengths and he gave so much back, he was such a tremendous team player.

Ray Clemence: Kenny Dalglish was the best I ever played with. He could score, create, hold the ball up. I've played against Pele and Johan Cruyff, but Kenny was magical. He was a dream to have in your side, but a nightmare to face because you were always wondering what trick he'd come up with next.

David Johnson: What people don't realise is that he wasn't just a great player, he was also unselfish and his bravery, something no one ever mentions, was something else. In our playing days, players could tackle from behind and as Kenny's game was holding the ball up and linking the play, the amount of stick he used to get from defenders sliding in and tackling him from behind was unbelievable. I've seen him in the dressing room afterwards and his legs were cut to ribbons. It just shows you how tough he was because he hardly ever missed a game. So he was a great, great player, but brave as well.

Bob Paisley: The best buy we ever made.

Super Terry Mac

Liverpool v SV Hamburg
Anfield
European Super Cup final second leg
6 December 1977

David Fairclough: We'd drawn 1-1 in Hamburg and all the focus was on Keegan's first return to the club where he'd made his name and how he'd compare to new Kop favourite, Kenny. But on the night both were totally overshadowed by Terry Mac's treble in a stunning 6-0 win.

Terry McDermott: Someone was injured, I think it may have been Ian Callaghan. I was moved inside rather than be out wide on the right. Before the game I was urged by Bob Paisley to get forward more and link with Kenny Dalglish and on the night I scored one during the first half, then in the second half, kicking towards the Kop, I struck another two to complete my hat-trick, including one from 25-yards.

Phil Neal: Hamburg came to Anfield with Kevin Keegan as holders of the European Cup Winners' Cup. Liverpool were European Champions. Naturally we wanted to beat them, but on the night we overwhelmed the West Germans and fully justified our position as the best team in Europe.

David Fairclough: It might have lacked the electric atmosphere of St Etienne or the nail-biting drama of Bruges but it was as emphatic a performance against a top-ranked continental side that I was ever part of at Liverpool.

Retaining 'Ol' Big Ears'

Liverpool v FC Bruges
Wembley
European Cup final
10 May 1978

Emlyn Hughes: As holders, there was only one thing to do. We had to go out and win the European Cup for the second year in succession, which was something no other British team had achieved. People expected us to win the European Cup again and we expected to win it ourselves.

Bob Paisley: I told the players they had to forget about Rome and they responded magnificently.

Phil Thompson: Nothing will compare to 1977, beating Monchengladbach in Rome, that's very special in everybody's hearts and minds. But when you're a player and you missed out, as I had done through injury, it wasn't the same. I'd have given everything to have played in that game, so getting to the final again in 1978 was so important to me.

Graeme Souness: I joined Liverpool from Middlesbrough in early 1978 because they were the best club side in Europe and, I thought, they would give me my best chance of being successful not just as an individual but also as a member of a winning team. The nearest I had been to European competition before was watching the Eurovision Song Contest so it was a dream come true to win a European Champions' medal within four months. I arrived in the January, we got to the final against Bruges at Wembley and we won 1-0. Kenny got the goal.

Alan Hansen: It was a very special night. For five or six years beforehand I'd been watching the European Cup final and dreaming about playing in that match. The year before I was still at Partick and we watched Liverpool beat Monchengladbach with a six-pack, not thinking that the next year I'd be playing in the final myself. Running onto the pitch five minutes before kick-off at Wembley and I was thinking, 'This is what it's all about'.

David Fairclough: It was like a home game for us. The official attendance at Wembley that night was 92,000 and at least 80,000 of them must have been Liverpool fans. There were pockets of red everywhere and an unmistakable air of supreme confidence about the place. Liverpool Football Club ruled Europe and the pride that instilled in everyone, be it players or supporters, was huge. I was so desperate to play my part. Granted, it was no classic, but that wasn't down to us.

Graeme Souness: They [Bruges] never came to make it a game. We were a very good team then, and they were frightened of us, they didn't step out. We had most of the ball and I'm sure it was quite a dull game to watch for the neutral.

Emlyn Hughes: Bruges seemed beaten before they started. They were a disgrace. It seemed to me they were playing for a goalless draw, hoping in their wildest despair that the match might eventually be settled on penalties. What an attitude to take into a European Cup final. We were not at our best. I suppose we had the experience to do just what was needed.

Phil Neal: Football wise it was boring. The Bruges manager came to stifle us really and what a delicate touch it took from Kenny to earn the spoils.

Graeme Souness: I didn't have a bad game and the papers gave me a very good write-up, particularly over the ball which led to the goal. People said it was a wonderfully weighted pass but there was an element of luck about it. The reality was that I went to block the ball in a tackle. I thought I was going to get clattered. Fortunately the Bruges player pulled out and, without a great deal of finesse, I somehow managed to guide it to Kenny.

Bob Paisley: We needed a spark of individualism to give us victory and it was provided by Graeme and Kenny, two players comparatively new to our set-up. Graeme's sense of awareness allowed him to spot the opening and put Kenny in a one-on-one situation with the keeper that he thrives on. At the angle he was to goal, and the position in which he received the ball, many players would have snatched at the chance. But Kenny's ice-cool football brain delayed the shot until the Bruges keeper had committed himself – then Kenny tucked the ball away.

Kenny Dalglish: Seeing that goal go in was the greatest moment of my football life. Getting a European Cup winners' medal is every player's dream. I wanted to run to our fans and give them a salute. I don't remember jumping over the boards but I do know I couldn't leap over them on the way back because the emotion made my legs week.

Phil Thompson: People always remember Kenny Dalglish's dink over the goalkeeper but after that, although we'd dominated the game completely, I remember big Al trying a backpass that never reached Ray Clemence. The fella jinked around him and I just got back. My long skinny legs just happened to get there and I remember stretching my left leg out to just steer the ball away from goal.

Alan Hansen: It was a horrible moment. The ball bobbled as I was about to knock it back and when Thommo kicked it off the line, I was the most relieved man in the stadium.

Phil Thompson: That as much won us the game, because they didn't deserve anything out of it, we had dominated it completely, but it was a vital moment in the game. It didn't matter to me how we won. It was just about winning it. And winning it at Wembley in front of about 95,000 Liverpool fans, well, that was a very special moment for me.

David Fairclough: Nothing could have topped playing for Liverpool in a triumphant European Cup final. There are few higher accolades in football than a winners' medal in that competition.

Alan Hansen: It wasn't the best game in the world, but Kenny scored a great goal, we won 1-0 and I joined the ranks of the great players who had won the European Cup. I remember going through Wembley about half an hour after the match with Terry McDermott and just saying, 'This is the greatest feeling I've ever had'.

Seven up

Liverpool v Tottenham Hotspur
Anfield
Football League Division One
2 September 1978

Phil Neal: When we trained on the Friday you could sense there was a special buzz in the air. Maybe it was over who the opposition was and the players we were going to come up against, but we knew we were going to put up a performance, you could feel it. It's stuck in my mind that one because we thought we were going to take somebody for five or six.

Alan Kennedy: Entertainment wise, Spurs were the great pretenders and they had some great flair players in their midfield; two from Argentina in Ossie Ardiles and Ricardo Villa. They also had Glenn Hoddle in the team and it should have been a difficult game, but I think the way we played was just fantastic.

Phil Thompson: In Ardiles and Villa, we were playing against two players who had just won the World Cup and people were talking about Spurs challenging for the championship. When we had the bit between our teeth and people were saying things like that though we were really able to express ourselves. It was definitely one of the best team performances I can remember.

Phil Neal: Tottenham hadn't won at Anfield for donkey's years but there had been so much talk in the press about Tottenham and their new South American stars, we were like, 'We're going to show them what English football is all about'.

Steve Heighway: All of our players were absolutely right at the peak of their game that day. Tottenham had some good players in those days. I meet a lot of people who tell me that the last goal we scored, the one that travelled the length of the field in a matter of seconds, was the greatest goal they've ever seen.

Phil Neal: I scored a penalty to make it six-nil that afternoon, it had to be taken twice because the keeper moved the first time. But I just remember the Terry Mac goal really. One minute he's on the post defending a corner at the Kop end, the next minute he's ran the full length of the pitch to knock a header in at the Anfield Road end.

David Johnson: I will always remember this game. Not because I scored two goals, but because I played a part in what I think was the greatest ever goal to be scored at Anfield. Why Terry McDermott ran 80 yards to make it seven I will never know, but that really summed up Liverpool for me.

Terry McDermott: It started with a corner and I can't remember whether I headed it off the line or not, but the ball went to Kenny, Davey Johnson and then Steve Heighway. I'd run to the far post at their end. The Spurs players never touched the ball. It was three passes and the header at the end of it.

Phil Thompson: Everything seemed to go right that day and the goal from Terry was incredible. It was probably the greatest goal that has ever been scored at Anfield. All the more remarkable because he scored it with his head, that was very unusual.

Terry McDermott: Me scoring with my head... that never happened because I didn't like to ruffle my curls! Seriously though, it was the build-up to the goal that made it so special. From one end to the other, we broke so quick, about twelve to fifteen seconds or something like that, is all it took. The final ball from Steve Heighway was sensational and I just happened to be on the end of it. It could have been anyone. All I had to do was guide it in, just let it hit my head, which it did, and it flew into the top corner.

Alan Kennedy: I still remember Terry Mac turning to his right hand side, the Kemlyn Road stand were all up on their feet celebrating and I can just picture his permed hair. We all had permed hair in those days but his was perm was bouncing up and down as he ran back saying, 'I've made the run, I've done my little bit, now let's go for the eighth'.

Steve Heighway: I can remember thinking we could have achieved anything that day. It was the best team performance of my time at the club.

Terry McDermott: We really were outstanding that day. We ran them ragged, paralysed them really. But we were that good at that time. In that era, we were something special. The team was something special, the players were something special and the club was something special.

Champions again

1978/79

Phil Thompson: I know there have been some marvellous Liverpool teams but I would say the 78/79 side was the best. We beat teams with ease, up and down the country. I believe that was the best brand of football Liverpool supporters have ever witnessed throughout an entire campaign.

Ray Clemence: We conceded just sixteen goals all season, only four at Anfield and in those days there were 42 league games. We also scored 85 goals, so we weren't just a defensive side. We just played great football and it was a joy to be part of.

Steve Heighway: There wasn't any fancy dossiers on teams. Tom Saunders used to go and watch the opposition but that was it, we never spent much time listening to what he had to say about them. The style of play was simple and it was about everybody realizing that they were not indispensable. They were all just part of the collective so no-one ever got too big for their boots. That was important.

Jimmy Case: I remember one game against Bristol City, we were 2-0 up very early, we just kept the ball, passed it around. It wasn't that they were bad, but everything we did, every touch was there, so you don't end up getting a fifty-fifty ball. We did all that without doing the Leeds thing where they were flicking it up. Because that just entices somebody to kick you.

Graeme Souness: That 1978/79 season was sensational and I am tempted to say that team was the best I ever played in. It was not a case of winning games but a question of how many we were going to win by. We were knocking the ball about so well and enjoying so much possession that it was almost boring.

Ray Clemence: Concentration was a big part. I had very little to do, but I had to be alert to make the two or three saves I had to make.

Alan Hansen: Teams were coming here [to Anfield] and we were just pulverizing them. They weren't even getting a kick of the ball.

Alan Kennedy: The team never really changed much. Clemence in goal, a defence of Neal, Thompson, Hansen and myself, Kennedy, Case, McDermott and Souness in midfield, with Kenny and David Johnson in attack.

Jimmy Case: Some people might argue, but I don't think the midfield quartet Bob put together – Case, Souness, McDermott and Kennedy – could be bettered. It was the perfect combination of talents. We were there to win the battles first and then play football and we didn't lose many battles.

Phil Neal: It was the best side I played in. You couldn't beat that line-up. There was always someone to cover if you ventured forward. It was a wonderful machine, and the engine got better. He [Bob Paisley] had developed a team that, at one stage, I felt could possibly run itself. It had so many leaders.

Phil Thompson: Look at the age of the players in that team, that's why it was so special. It's said that players are at their peak between the age of 24 and 28, well... I was 24 in 1978, Alan Hansen was 23, Phil Neal was 26-27, Ray Clemence was the oldest – he was about 28, Alan Kennedy was same age as me, Jimmy Case was 23 or 24, Terry McDermott and Graeme Souness 26, Ray Kennedy 27, Kenny was 26 and David Johnson likewise. We were all the perfect age. That's what you call good planning.

Terry McDermott: We were frightening at times... I'm saying it was the best ever team.

David Johnson: We'd go away on international duty and the coaches would always be like, 'Come on, what's the secret? Something is going on there behind closed doors at Anfield and Melwood'. The Liverpool lads would just look at each other and say among ourselves, 'What are these guys on about?' All we used to do was the simple things. It was just common sense to us.

Ronnie Moran: We used to have a weekly joke. If we won we'd say, 'That's us OK for another week', but if we lost it was, 'Could be out of a job now!' There's no way you could afford to sit back.

Triumph and Tragedy

1980-1989

Highest highs and lowest lows

The 1980s was a decade that saw Liverpool Football Club dominate the domestic game, this was an era littered with unforgettable triumphs and countless memorable moments. Unfortunately, it's also remembered as being tinged with tragedies that would have a profound effect on everyone at the club.

Ending the 'Mickey Mouse' hoodoo

1981 League Cup final

Phil Thompson: We hadn't won the League Cup before. We'd found it difficult and thought, 'Is it ever going to happen?' We'd lost the final to Forest in 1978 and because we'd never won it we joked that it was the Mickey Mouse Cup. However, we were desperate to win it.

Sammy Lee: That was the first time I'd played at Wembley and it was an amazing game despite it only being 1-1. Not a lot of people remember that I actually scored a goal early in the first half which was unfortunately disallowed because Colin Irwin was standing in an offside position wide of the goal. However, they do remember how I was in an offside position much later in the game when Alan Kennedy scored the opening goal.

Alan Kennedy: We'd played 90 minutes and were deep into extra-time. I remember the clearance, I think by Billy Bonds, and it fell to me just nicely, it really did. I connected sweetly with the ball and I knew as soon as I hit it that if Sammy didn't get in the way it would find the back of the net. We thought, 'Yes, we've finally won it!' But they got a corner and from Alvin Martin's header Terry McDermott pushes the ball against the bar. It's a penalty and they score.

Ian Rush: I remember going down to watch the first game with all the reserves. We were winning one nil, and Ray Stewart scored a penalty right at the end. We were all absolutely gutted.

Phil Thompson: I didn't play in the first game at Wembley but I came back for the replay at Villa Park. I was fortunate enough to be captain and it was a sensational night.

Ian Rush: I travelled with the team for the replay. We trained on the morning, then had a meeting after lunch and Bob Paisley named the team. He said, 'Up front, Kenny Dalglish and Rush', and that was it. I was rooming with Kenny at the time, and so we got back to the room and I said, 'Is it right what he said then, am I playing?' And Kenny goes, 'Yeah, you're playing, and that was it'. I'm thinking, 'This is going to be only my second game, and I'm playing in a cup final.' It was unbelievable.

Phil Thompson: I was thrilled to be back and leading the side and we produced some top-class football. Even Hammers' manager John Lyall admitted that he had never seen a display like it for a long time.

Ian Rush: In contrast to the tight first meeting, the replay was full of open and entertaining football. Even when Paul Goddard gave West Ham an early lead, I was still confident we had enough to come back and overhaul them. Before the first half was out, goals from Dalglish and Hansen put us in the lead, a lead we were never to relinquish.

Phil Thompson: Suffice to say a good night was had by all. The next morning I received a call from Peter Robinson, our chief executive, who asked where the trophy was. I told him it was on the bus. 'Yes I know,' he replied. 'I've just had a call from the depot in St Helens – the driver found it on the back seat when he was cleaning up! Don't let the next one out of your sight!'

A magical night in Munich

Bayern Munich v Liverpool
Olympic Stadium, Munich
European Cup semi-final second leg
22 April 1981

Alan Hansen: That was a great night in Munich. We'd drawn 0-0 at Anfield in the first leg and Bayern had said some disparaging things about Liverpool on television, saying that we had no class, no touch and no technique.

Bob Paisley: I didn't have to motivate the lads – Bayern captain Paul Breitner did that for me when he was quoted after the first leg as saying that we didn't play intelligently. The players cut the article out of a newspaper and pinned it on the dressing room notice board at Anfield.

Howard Gayle: Breitner had slaughtered us after the first leg. He told the German media how poor we were, and what Bayern were and were not going to do to us in the return leg. We couldn't have afforded extra-time because we'd used our two substitutes.

Sammy Lee: We didn't do too well in the first leg, the home leg, and they rather conceitedly thought that they were through to the final.

Graeme Souness: When we arrived at the Olympic Stadium in Munich there were leaflets on all the seats explaining the quickest route from Munich to Paris, so they obviously thought they were going to be in the final. Bob Paisley stuck one of these leaflets on the wall in the changing room and said, 'Just have a look at that before you go out'.

Alan Hansen: It was typical German arrogance. They believed that they were through but because of that I've never seen a Liverpool dressing more fired up than it was on that night. It was incredible.

Graeme Souness: Then, as we were all lining up in the tunnel ready to go out, Bob goes, 'Oh I've forgotten something, Sammy tonight, you're going to mark Paul Breitner'. We all just looked around at each other in amazement. He'd never said anything like that before. Usually it was just, 'Go out there, you're better than everyone else and you'll win'.

Sammy Lee: They had a number of terrific players, one of them being Breitner. We knew what a good player he was. He was the focal point for all of their attacks, the playmaker. It's clichéd but I'd play anywhere for Liverpool and do whatever was asked of me, so it wasn't a problem.

Bob Paisley: We had so many injuries that it was almost our Central League side that toppled the West German champions.

Alan Hansen: I think the back four that night was, Phil Neal, myself, Colin Irwin and Richard Money we had so many injuries. To crown it all, Kenny went off injured after seven minutes and Howard Gayle came on and played magnificently.

Howard Gayle: I was made up just to be part of the travelling squad. I had no idea whatsoever that I'd play a part and to be named on the bench was a major milestone for me. Kenny was struggling with an Achilles injury and within ten minutes he took a knock on it so the gaffer said to me, 'Come on, son. You're going on'. I didn't have time to be nervous. It happened so quickly and with hindsight I think I benefited from it. If I'd have known the night before that I was playing in such a big game, I wouldn't have got any sleep and anybody who told you that they wouldn't be nervous in that situation would be telling you a lie.

Sammy Lee: As a midfield player he was ideal because he had such pace about him. You just had to look up and hit the ball into space knowing that Howard would run onto it. Not only did he have pace, but great ball skills and great vision and he was very aggressive in the tackle. He wasn't afraid of the challenge.

Howard Gayle: When Kenny went off everyone must have been writing off our chances. Ronnie Moran told me to stay wide and keep going at them and it worked. I remember ripping them to bits and we should have had a penalty in the first half when I was blatantly brought down. It was one of the great European performances by Liverpool.

Graeme Souness: Howie came on and ran the legs off the defender he was up against. They were all having a kick at him and, Howie being Howie, he wanted to have a go back. I'm not sure if he got booked, but he was in danger of getting sent off, so they took him off. The sub was subbed.

Howard Gayle: I'm the first substitute ever to be substituted and I'm in the Guinness book of records! I felt as the game went on that I had more to offer, but I got myself booked and I thought it was unfair. Basically I'd been kicked to death, but it was my first tackle in the game and the referee thought it was retaliation, but it wasn't. I think the most important thing though was that we got through.

Bob Paisley: We couldn't have afforded extra-time because we'd used our two substitutes and wouldn't have had anyone to send on.

Alan Hansen: David Johnson had a hamstring and was limping, Kenny had already gone off and we were virtually down to ten-men.

Graeme Souness: I remember we pushed Ray Kennedy upfront and he chested it down and volleyed it in to make it 1-0 and that was us going through.

Ray Kennedy: We had been doing well enough and we knew a goal would come if we just stayed patient. I'd been up front for only about five minutes when David Johnson played a great ball to me and the only difficult part was getting the bouncing ball under control.

Graeme Souness: There was only maybe 10 minutes to go and then in the 90th minute Rummenigge got a goal to make it 1-1. We'd done enough though. It was a really good night and because they had been so confident, I can remember a few of us ending up in their dressing room giving it a, 'See you in Paris, chaps!'

Alan Hansen: It was the best dressing room I'd been in. We were all battering down on the Bayern door. Everyone was going crazy. To be part of that was extra special. It was one of the greatest nights in Liverpool's history.

Scousers rule 'Gay Paree'

Liverpool v Real Madrid
Parc des Princes, Paris
European Cup final
27 May 1981

For this dream European Cup final, Scousers converged on the romantic French capital in their thousands and left declaring their love for a new Kop hero nicknamed Barney Rubble.

Alan Kennedy: I didn't even expect to be playing. I broke my wrist in the semi-final first leg against Bayern Munich and the club doctor said it was a ten-week job. I wanted to play but we couldn't find out what we should do - strap it up, plaster it or whatever. In the end I had a metal cast strapped to my wrist. It was a bit cumbersome and heavy and would undoubtedly be classed as dangerous in today's football world.

Kenny Dalglish: I hadn't played a competitive match for six weeks before the final but I was determined to play. I passed all the fitness tests and set out for Paris. I was never going to allow lack of match practice to prevent me from playing in a European Cup final.

Alan Kennedy: Bob told us the team when we got to the ground. It was a shock to be included and I probably wasn't fully prepared mentally. But once the manager gives you the go-ahead, you tune yourself in and get ready to go.

Phil Thompson: It was a wonderful occasion. The all-whites of Real Madrid – probably the biggest name in European football – against the all-reds of Liverpool. In a packed stadium, with me as captain. It was so special.

Alan Kennedy: I remember there being a dispute about shirt advertising that was only sorted out just before kick-off. A couple of hours before the game we were putting sticky tape on each other's shirts. I was doing Alan Hansen's, he was doing mine and Phil Thompson was doing Phil Neal's.

Phil Thompson: Allegedly, Umbro hadn't put any money into the UEFA sponsorship kitty and talks were taking place to resolve the issue almost right up until kick-off. We didn't have much say in it, even me as captain. Ronnie Moran was running around cutting these bits of tape up and telling us we've got to do it. But once the game started, out of loyalty to Umbro, some of the boys tore the strips of tape off.

Alan Kennedy: It was totally ridiculous and would never happen now, but Bob reacted in a good way. He said we should be even more determined to win the game. His attitude was always that if someone puts problems in our way, we'll get over them, and that's exactly what we did.

Phil Thompson: I'd seen Emlyn lift the European Cup twice and was so desperate to emulate him. I was trying hard to visualise me lifting it but in my dreams I just couldn't see it happening. I was having panic attacks over it.

Alan Hansen: I was even more nervous in Paris than I'd been in the 1978 final against Bruges at Wembley. Usually when I got out onto the pitch I felt better. But not that night.

Alan Kennedy: We respected Real but didn't fear them. We were always supremely confident. The thinking was if they play well then we had to be on our toes and play better. The most important thing was not to concede a goal and, obviously, not to get beat.

Phil Thompson: It was actually a bigger game for Real Madrid than it was for us because they were not the force they once were. We were the kings of European football then. Everybody wanted a piece of Liverpool Football Club.

Alan Kennedy: We were aware of Laurie [Cunningham] but Bob Paisley, the manager, never really bothered with that. He'd just say, 'Oh, he's fast, he's tricky', and that was it. Liverpool never worried about any players and rarely planned anything. We just played.

Phil Neal: I knew Laurie Cunningham from the England set-up and it was my job to make sure he had no impact on the game. Bob Paisley warned me beforehand that I would have a big defensive job on my hands in order to contain him. But looking back I'd say I put in as good a defensive job as I could that night and Laurie rarely troubled us.

Alan Kennedy: The pitch made it impossible to play good football, probably one of the worst-ever pitches I've played on. For a European Cup final it should have been a lot better, but it wasn't, and you've got to deal with it. So some of the football was probably poor, but we played what was called percentage football. We actually over-hit balls rather than give it away.

Bob Paisley: It was a very physical first half and some of the Real Madrid tackling was outrageous, to say the least. But at the same time they had players of real quality. We started quite well but we were upset, probably, by some of the tackles.

Graeme Souness: Some of their tackles were X-certificate and in the first few minutes we were knocked out of our stride by the violence of their challenges. I decided that they needed a little of their own medicine to slow them down and to show that we could not be intimidated. It was then that I picked out the nasty Camacho, but as I closed in to give him a little nip, the German Stielike came in on my blind side and left me a limping passenger for the remainder of the game.

Alan Kennedy: At half-time we've gone in the dressing room and it's 0-0 but Bob didn't want to change things, Bob was quite happy with 0-0, he knew Liverpool were capable of scoring away from home. But this was the final and I felt like we would never score.

David Johnson: It wasn't a great final but I remember it because there was this standing joke between me and Terry McDermott, whereby if anyone was going to be substituted it was usually one of us. We used to call it the pop-up toaster because they used to have the box with the numbers in and we reckoned that someone would kick the box and up would pop number nine or ten. Whenever we spotted the subs warming up we used to look at each other wondering who was going off. But, on this occasion, he took Kenny Dalglish off and left me on. So that was the highlight of my career, the night Kenny Dalglish was subbed and not me.

Phil Thompson: It wasn't the best final in the world but it's the winning that counts and Alan Kennedy sealed it to give me the most incredible footballing moment of my entire life.

Alan Kennedy: I wasn't trying to score. I was running to try to make space for others. Ray threw it to me. I ran into the area, García Cortés made a wild challenge on me and tried to take me and the ball out of the game.

Phil Thompson: What Al was doing up there I don't know. Saying that, I don't think he even knew himself. Davey Johnson said he should have pulled it back to him.

Alan Kennedy: Agustin [the Madrid goalkeeper] went to his left, thinking I would cross. I made my mind up probably in the last millisecond and I'm thinking, 'I can go for this'. David Johnson was making my decision for me. He's in open space, I could give the ball to him and he wouldn't miss from that distance. But I'm a bit of a powerhouse, if I see an opportunity I go for it. I saw the opportunity. 'Give it a strike and see what happens', I thought. 'I might get a rollicking from David Johnson saying I should have passed to him, but give it a go'. The ball went in the back of the net like a rocket and I was away, I was so fortunate on that particular occasion.

David Johnson: He was greedy wasn't he? We have a laugh about it now. I was the first player to reach him after he took off behind the goal in celebration. I picked him up. There was a moat between us and the supporters and jokingly I tried to push him in! I actually remember saying to him, 'Why didn't you pass to me?' and he said, 'If I'd have passed to you we'd have still been playing!' Meaning I'd have missed it. Seriously though, it was the most satisfying night of my European career. After being on the bench in '77 and on crutches in 1978, it meant so much to me.

Alan Kennedy: Honestly, I didn't know how to celebrate it. What are you doing?' I said to myself. Then I thought, 'Did the referee blow? Did they rule it out? Was it allowed? Who's running over? Did I really score?' I can picture the fans who were behind a big fence and had that not been there I would have been in with them, I'm sure of that.

Phil Thompson: I always remember as I walked up to collect the trophy that all the lights were reflecting off it and it was really gleaming. It looked superb. Then this old guy from UEFA, I don't remember his name, gets hold of the cup and I'm waiting for it. I couldn't wait to get my hands on it but he kept me waiting, and waiting. He even started to try lifting it himself! So I'm like, 'Just give me the cup, give me the bloody cup'.

Ray Clemence: I came into the dressing room afterwards and, as usual in these situations, it was mayhem, champagne everywhere and all the players bouncing around. It doesn't get much better than beating Real Madrid, 1-0, in Paris. But, as I sat in the corner with a paper cup full of champagne in hand and looked around, to me, it felt like just another game. Up until this moment I had never ever thought about leaving Liverpool but it was right there and then that I made the decision that I needed a new challenge elsewhere.

Phil Thompson: To have gone from watching my heroes from the Kop to captaining the team I loved and leading them to victory in the European Cup final was just unbelievable. There is no way I can express that feeling in words. Proud doesn't begin to describe how I felt. I remember lifting it towards my mates from my Sunday League team in Kirkby who were in the crowd that night – I could see them on the front row of the top balcony. It was for them, for me, for everyone in Liverpool.

Bob Paisley: It was a triumph for our character once again. We started with three players – Dalglish, Thompson and Alan Kennedy – short of match practice, and Souness was hurt shortly after the kick-off. I'm sure Real didn't begrudge us our victory. I was so proud to be the manager of the first British club to win the European Cup three times.

Graeme Souness: All the lads went out with the trophy after the game to celebrate. Hansen and I decided we'd stay in the hotel. So we went up to Bob's room. He's sitting there in a jersey with soup stains on it. He's got his slippers on because he always had problems with his ankles. And it's like a night in watching Coronation Street.

Alan Kennedy: I don't remember there being any major celebration. After the game, knowing Bob, he probably just said, 'Right, see you in July'.

Kenny Dalglish: I remember Alan Kennedy's goal but I don't remember too much about what happened afterwards. The good part about these nights was that we always had a good celebration, the sad part was you could never remember it.

Phil Thompson: For a Liverpool fan, to become the first Liverpool-born captain to win the European Cup, it was the most incredible night. Winning in Paris was something I'll always remember. It was the greatest personal moment of my career.

Alan Kennedy: You can't believe the feeling I had. Even when I woke up in Paris the next morning I thought it had all been a dream. It was quite a season for me to score a goal at Wembley [in the League Cup final] and then hit the one that won the European Cup.

Phil Thompson: So when we got home from Paris, Peter Robinson explained to me that as captain I was in charge of taking care of the trophy, even if it meant taking it home. Well I didn't need telling twice. It was in a big velvet bag so I put it in the back of my Capri and went straight to the Falcon in Kirkby. That was my local, and I ran the Sunday league team there. We moved all the trophies we'd won, and all the bottles of brown ale, and put the European Cup behind the bar. No one could believe it. There was a queue for the phone. Everybody was phoning their mates, telling them to come down and have a look.

Changing of the guard

1981/82

Phil Neal: One thing about Bob, he knew his players and was never afraid to break up a winning formula. You always knew there were two or three players waiting to come in every year.

Alan Kennedy: There was some big changes that season and a lot new younger players were brought in. Players like Ronnie Whelan, Ian Rush, Bruce Grobbelaar and Craig Johnston. It was a revolution.

Ronnie Whelan: It's very hard to pinpoint exactly when a player is in decline, and when a young player is ready to step up. I'd imagine at the start of 1981/82 Bob wasn't sure either. But he would have managed the process very carefully. He'd have been scrutinising the veterans for signs of age catching up on them, and he'd have been learning as much as possible about us reserves.

Mark Lawrenson: Let's be fair – Rushy, Ronnie Whelan, Craig [Johnston] to a certain degree, they were top, top players; they were as good as the players they replaced but a little bit quicker.

Alan Kennedy: The latter part of the 81/82 season was brilliant but the first half was horrendous, it was like, 'Fucking hell, what's going on here?' It was a weird time because it was unprecedented that we were so low in the league. We were as low as fourteenth or fifteenth.

Ian Rush: I think the main reason for Liverpool's stuttering form before Christmas 1981 was down to Bob rebuilding the team and the time it took for the newly-introduced players to bed in and make an impact, and I include myself in that.

Bruce Grobbelaar: I expected to start my Liverpool career in the reserves, I was startled when Ray Clemence left quickly and I was thrown in at the deep end. It took me time to get used to the defensive pattern and the lads playing in front of me.

Phil Thompson: Bruce had just arrived and no disrespect to him but I had been used to playing in front of Ray Clemence for so many years. Bruce would be coming for balls that I'd dealt with for years and this created all kinds of confusion.

Bruce Grobbelaar: What Bob Paisley did above all, particularly when the criticism was flying a round, was to encourage me to prove I had the ability to do the job. He gave me confidence that I could do it and I'll always be grateful to him for that.

Ian Rush: The way Bob Paisley went about it was tremendous. He just kept battling away and was saying it would come right. It gave us confidence even when results weren't going for us, as proved with what happened after Manchester City beat us at home on Boxing Day.

Bruce Grobbelaar: Phil Thompson skied a ball in the air and my powder-puff punch let in little Asa Hartford for one of his rare goals. Kevin Reeves then whipped in a cross-shot, which I pushed on to the post. With me flapping, the ball rebounded, hit me on the head and went in.

Alan Hansen: It was 3-1 and we were miles behind. People were writing us off. Some were saying it was the three points that had done us. It was the first season of three points for a win.

Ronnie Whelan: It was Liverpool's fifth home defeat of the calendar year, having been unbeaten at Anfield for the previous three years. I'd imagine Bob Paisley was a very worried man by Christmas 1981. There was a huge transition under way and it wasn't working for him. Those new players would remain part of the Liverpool set-up for practically the rest of the decade but he wasn't to know that at the time.

Mark Lawrenson: On the following Monday as we were getting ready for training Joe [Fagan] sat us all down at Anfield before we went on the bus to train at Melwood. Bob, Ronnie and Evo would all have been there in the dressing-room, but they all walked out after Joe spoke that day. He really went berserk. There was nothing they could have added, he said it all.

Phil Neal: He had a go at every single player. He said, 'We've had more meetings in the last month at this club then I've had in seventeen years. Hansen, start heading the ball; Souness, you haven't won a tackle; Dalglish, you should have twice as many goals by now...' We all got it.

Mark Lawrenson: It had an unbelievable effect. It had a far bigger effect than anyone else at the club doing it – even Bob Paisley or Kenny Dalglish afterwards.

Alan Kennedy: We got it back to playing the Liverpool way. The Liverpool way was pass and move, pass and move, pass and move all the time. Once we started that run, we just set our stall out. We said that's what we've got to do. Credit to Joe Fagan for realising we needed a good, stiff talking to, to get out there and do it.

New captain

Phil Thompson: I lost the captaincy on New Years' Day before we played Swansea in the FA Cup third round and it hurt immensely. But you have to grin and bare it. I was determined to show them, and probably that is how Bob Paisley wanted it to affect me. Although I was bitter to lose the captaincy I would have to say, team wise, the shrewdness of Paisley came right.

Graeme Souness: I can remember when we lost at home to Manchester City on Boxing Day we were twelfth in the league. I was made captain for the following game, which was away to Swansea in the FA Cup and, from there, we went on a fantastic run and won the Championship. When I was made captain it was just a title you had. The boss was the boss and you just wore an armband. I wasn't special because I was captain.

Milky Bar kid

Liverpool v Tottenham Hotspur
Wembley
League/Milk Cup final
13 March 1982

Phil Thompson: It was difficult coming up against Clem. We'd fought many battles together and I was shocked when he left in the summer of 1981. We were very close but I still wanted to beat him.

Ronnie Whelan: I couldn't sleep the night before but I remember saying afterwards that I had dreamt I would score the winner — there must have been some Irish logic in that! It was my first experience of walking out at Wembley, my big chance, so scoring two to win the game was schoolboy stuff and what dreams are made of.

Phil Neal: The Spurs fans were already toasting their victory when Ronnie Whelan popped up and whipped his goal in to equalize in the dying seconds. It took a good player to do that because Ray Clemence was still a great goalkeeper, he'd kept Spurs in the game.

Ronnie Whelan: It was a massive test. Tottenham had a great side with players like Glenn Hoddle, Micky Hazard and Ossie Ardiles. They looked like they had won the game until I squeezed a shot past Ray Clemence towards the end and we got stronger in extra-time.

Phil Neal: Paisley would not let us sit down before extra time started. He was bellowing, 'Get up off your feet, don't them let them see you are tired'. It stemmed from Shankly, who would never let an opponent see that you were weak. After that, we felt we had it in the bag.

Phil Thompson: It is part of Anfield folklore that Bob told all of our lads to stay on their feet in the moments before extra-time, with the Tottenham players all sitting or lying down. If you look at the video you will see that I started that logic. I thought, 'There is a huge psychological opportunity here', so I went round and said, 'Don't sit down, look at them, they are knackered, they are finished'.

Ronnie Whelan: We knew we were going to win then. They were looking very tired and I was so over the moon after getting my second that I ran over the running track to celebrate with our fans. Only when I got there did I realise it was such a long way back to the pitch and I was so tired that I barely made it.

Alan Kennedy: Spurs were beaten. Of course, they had to come at us a bit, but you can murder teams on that big pitch when they're stretched and in the last minute Rushie got our third. Our two new youngsters, playing their first games at Wembley for the club had got our goals and that again underlined that this was the new Liverpool up to its old tricks. That's why it was such a significant victory.

Sammy Lee: That Tottenham final was a terrifically open game and a great footballing spectacle. To come back the way we did was tremendous and people will remember Ronnie Whelan as the hero for the two goals he scored.

Ronnie Whelan: It was a magical day, and so special as it was my first major medal. I remember being called the 'Milky Bar kid' by Jimmy Greaves - which was a reference to the Milk Cup. It was a competition that really meant something special back then.

Sammy Lee: Winning the Milk Cup [in March] was the catalyst for us to go on and win that title. It qualified us for Europe, which was always what this club has been about and we then went on to bigger and better things, putting a very, very good run of form together to win the league.

Liverpool v Tottenham Hotspur
Anfield
Football League Division One
15 May 1982

Alan Hansen: We went on a phenomenal run [in the league] and, in the end, we won it at a canter. We beat Tottenham at home and there was a great atmosphere in the stadium. Hoddle scored first, but we just pulverised them in the second-half.

Ronnie Whelan: At half-time Bob told Mark Lawrenson that he was playing too close to Souey in centre midfield; he was getting in his way. He told Lawro to move further over to the left. Lawro did what he was told and it worked like a magic wand. He scored the equaliser six minutes into the second half and only four minutes later set up Kenny for our second.

Graeme Souness: In the second half Kenny was through one-one one and he stuck Clem on his arse and put it in the back of the net – which was not unusual for him. We won 3-1.

Ronnie Whelan: The fans were already celebrating another triumphant season when I finished off the scoring with three minutes to go. We wrapped up the title with a game to spare.

Sammy Lee: Having been so far behind at one stage, it was the manner in which we won it that made it all the more pleasing.

Alan Hansen: To win the championship at Anfield was always special. We did a lap of honour and it was just a great feeling again.

Bob Paisley: I said back in January that I hadn't seen a better team than us on our day, and that we could still do something if we put it together. A lot of people were shouting at us to bring in new players. Any idiot can do that. It's a matter of bringing them in at the right time and place so they fit in, and aren't murdered. I am proudest of this one because there was so much to do.

Ronnie Whelan: You look back on it now and it was the beginning of a new era for Liverpool. In hindsight we can see that the new generation was basically going through its growing pains in the first half of that season. In the second half, we clicked. Everything fell into place.

1-2, 1-2-3, 1-2-3-4, 5-0!

Everton v Liverpool
Goodison Park
Football League Division One
6 November 1982

Sammy Lee: I've got a lot of respect for Everton, some of my best friends are Evertonians. But, they're our local rivals and to beat them so convincingly... yeah it was wonderful.

Ian Rush: Merseyside derbies are always special but that was tremendous for me. I used to support Everton and my dream, growing up, had been to play for Everton at Goodison Park. But to actually go there with Liverpool and to score four goals against them was incredible. It's one of those things that, at the time, you don't realise how special it is but when you finish playing you realise how special it was for the supporters as well.

Graeme Souness: We absolutely mullered them that day and Jocky Hansen was outstanding. I can remember that, and Rush with the goals. It started off as a muck and boots type of game, but because we had better players who could mix it as well as play, we would win most of those games.

Ian Rush: It was one of those games in which everything we did turned to gold and I was just the lucky one to be on the end of them. There was some great passing to get me the goals. I remember Alan Hansen intercepting one, putting the ball into space for me and I managed to put it under Neville Southall.

Sammy Lee: Ian Rush with his pace and the acuteness of his runs, he'd make those angled runs in behind defences and the idea for me, as a midfielder, was to put the ball into the space, knowing full well that he'd run onto it and more than likely score, as he did four times that day.

Ian Rush: I think the last goal for me epitomises the way Liverpool played. If you look at it, I think Sammy Lee gets it, virtually from the goalkeeper and he runs with it. I made a diagonal run, Sammy puts the ball through to me and, this time, I just went around Southall. It went from box-to-box so quickly, which goes to show just how good we were at hitting teams on the break back then.

Bob bows out

Liverpool v Manchester United
Wembley
Milk Cup final
26 March 1983

The 1982/83 season was to be Bob Paisley's last as a manager. With Liverpool cantering to another championship, this was his last big occasion and goals from Alan Kennedy and Ronnie Whelan ensured there was a silver lining for English football's most successful boss.

Alan Kennedy: We were so used to Wembley by now, plus it was our third year running in the final of this competition and we wanted the run to continue. I remember a fantastic game between two closely matched sides.

Ronnie Whelan: It was the biggest game of the season. We were out of Europe and the FA Cup but here we were still playing at Wembley and against Manchester United.

Alan Kennedy: You can see all the Liverpool players laughing – almost in disbelief – that my shot was on target. They shouldn't have been; a couple of minutes earlier I'd had a crack from a similar spot that missed by inches, so I was just finding my range. It was only in extra time though that we got on top and Ronnie Whelan settled it with a fantastic goal.

Sammy Lee: It was always a difficult game against Manchester United and this was no exception. We always seemed to make things difficult for ourselves in these finals, but to fight our way back into the game again showed the terrific spirit that ran through the team at that time. When the chips looked to be down we would pull together and this obviously paid off in the end.

Bob Paisley: Once we scored the equaliser it was a question of taking the game to extra-time before we killed them off. I felt like a bullfighter going in for the last stab after the bull had 40 arrows in its back.

Ronnie Whelan: People still say I was crossing it for Rushie. Yes, he was in the box but I was going for goal, that's for sure. Everybody was tired and then Alan Kennedy made a run inside me. Frank Stapleton had gone to centre back so I tried to push the ball through his legs but it hit him and rolled back to me. I spotted Gary Bailey very far across over his goal and there was a big space to put it into. You don't even think about getting your technique right, it's instant. It's coming back at a nice pace and you hit it to that corner where you think he's not going to get it. Thankfully, it went in. To play against Manchester United and score the winner at Wembley... it was a huge day for me.

Alan Kennedy: As we had won it the previous two years, it had become a special competition and the gloss was applied when Graeme Souness insisted that Bob Paisley go up to collect the cup, as he was retiring at the end of the season.

Kenny Dalglish: Graeme said, 'Why don't we let Bob go up for the trophy?' It was unheard of then for a manager to receive the trophy. Everybody went, 'Yeah, that's brilliant'.

Mark Lawrenson: Bob at first said no. But Graeme insisted it was the players' wish that he did go up. I think that tells you something about what every player at Liverpool Football Club thought about Bob.

Kenny Dalglish: Bob went up the Wembley steps with one bit of a scarf over his front and the other over his back. It just summed him up. He was more interested in what he was going up to receive than how he looked going up there.

Ronnie Whelan: It was fitting for the greatest manager ever to go up those steps and lift the trophy. He'd won so much and it was great of Souey to let him do that.

Kenny Dalglish: It was a sad moment, Bob leaving, but he went out holding trophies.

Joe Fagan: manager

Peter Robinson: I had always thought of Joe as a potential manager, but there was a hierarchy in place at the club and the thinking was that everyone must wait their turn. That meant that the possibility of Joe taking the reins only really became an issue when Bob informed us he was stepping down. It was a case of natural progression.

Joe Fagan: When Bob decided to retire, it frightened me that they might ask me to take over. I said years ago that I'd never take on a manager's job, that coaching was my game. But things do change, don't they?

Graeme Souness: Bob had shown that promotion from within can work so I for one naturally assumed Joe would one day follow in his footsteps. I suppose it was just a question of whether the chance would ever come his way because Joe, obviously, wasn't getting any younger and no one knew when Bob was going to step down. When he did announce he'd be retiring then no other name came into the reckoning for me other than Joe.

Joe Fagan: I certainly had never given a thought to becoming manager of Liverpool FC. As a matter of fact, if the directors had appointed someone else it would not have made the slightest difference in my attitude towards this club.

Jan Molby: Joe was very, very quiet. And cleverly so. Joe just let things roll on from Paisley, with a lot of help from very experienced backroom staff like Ronnie Moran and Roy Evans, and other people who were still around the club like Tom Saunders and Bob himself. He trusted that what was already in place would be good enough, and that was very much the case.

Roy Evans: He basically did it to keep other people in a job.

Joe Fagan: My first reaction at the time was that I wouldn't take it. But I thought about it carefully and realised that someone else might come in and upset the whole rhythm. I finally decided to take it and keep the continuity going for a little longer.

Mark Lawrenson: Everybody loved Joe. Loved him. Everybody loved Paisley and respected him, but there was just something about Joe...

Alan Hansen: When Bob decided he was going, I think one hundred per cent of Liverpool players wanted Joe to be the manager. Sometimes it can be a bad thing if the board appoints the man the players want, but everybody knew that Joe was hugely respected. He knew all the ins and outs of the club, and what the players wanted was continuity.

Mark Lawrenson: As soon as we got back he asked for Graeme, as club captain, to go and see him in his office. Graeme came back out and closed the door of the home team dressing room, just the pros were in there, the young pros and kids were in the away dressing room because you all got changed at Anfield. He just said right, 'Joe's in charge, you all know what we think of him, let's just make sure that we give it a really, really good go'.

Graeme Souness: The transfer of power was as smooth as you'd expect.

Alan Hansen: We knew things wouldn't change much because he already ran the place, the training and the day-to-day workings of the club. Joe didn't change anything for the simple fact that he was part of the think-tank that had always regulated everything. He was a bigger part of that side of things than anybody was. So why would he change it?

Treble winners

1983/84

Ronnie Moran: It was a remarkable achievement. If you win one trophy you're delighted. If you win two trophies you are hailed as a team of magnificence. So to win three trophies in one season is an exceptional feat.

Ian Rush: It was definitely one of the greatest achievements I have been involved in. To go and win the treble in Joe Fagan's first season as manager was great. It was hard to believe at the time because no-one had done it. We were unlucky to go out of the FA Cup that season too so really we could have done a clean sweep.

Alan Hansen: It was great for the manager because if you look at the Liverpool managers throughout the years people will always remember Shankly, Paisley and Dalglish but they won't remember Joe Fagan too much. And this is a shame because Joe managed the side to an unprecedented treble. It took us 66 games and that was a lot of matches.

Sammy Lee: I know it's an old cliché but, basically, we took each game as it came and at the time it was just one big game after another.

Ian Rush: The treble winning side was a great one and the fact that I scored over 40 goals just goes to show how good it was. I had so many chances that season and I just managed to put a fair few of them away. Instead of one or two a game, I was regularly hitting three's and four's, both home and away. We were so quick, we were hitting teams on the break, and that's how I got most of my goals.

Alan Hansen: If you have a settled side and a settled defence then you are in front before you start. We had a lot of regulars in defence that season and that was obviously a big help to the side.

Sammy Lee: It is something that I can look back on with great pride. They were great times. Just being involved in that side was a special memory for me... playing alongside such great players as Dalglish, Hansen, Lawrenson and Souness.

Ronnie Whelan: Graeme [Souness] was brilliant that season. He didn't win player of the year or anything like that, mainly because other players didn't like the way he was out on the pitch. But he was the one who really led us as captain that year.

Sammy Lee: I was the only Scouser in the side but I never looked at it that way. We were all one, together as a team.

Ian Rush: Rather than eleven players, we were more of a squad and were successful because we all mucked in together.

Ronnie Whelan: It really was an exceptional team that year. To be part of it and win the treble was such a great experience because to win three major trophies in one season is so difficult.

Ronnie Moran: To a lot of people around the country the achievement went unnoticed, even at this club to a certain extent. If other managers would have won a treble in their first season they'd have been knighted.

Steve Nicol: We had a great side, there is no doubt about that. But I think at the time I was too young to realise just how good a team it was. It is easier to judge if you are standing back and watching. Being part of it, you are too busy doing your own job and your bit for the team.

Sammy Lee: Maybe it is for other people to say just how great an achievement it was and not ourselves who were involved. However, it was a very satisfying season for me personally. At the time it seemed to happen too fast and I really wish I'd have had an older head on my shoulders to appreciate it more.

Merseyside! Merseyside!

1984 Milk Cup final

Ian Rush: Our fans would have happily settled for us losing the League and the European Cup as long as we beat our old enemies. That's how important the rivalry is and in the weeks leading up to the game all we kept hearing was, 'You've just got to beat Everton'.

Graeme Souness: At about 4.30 on the morning of the match I was awoken by someone chanting, 'Everton, Everton'. Many of the other lads were woken up as well and Alan Kennedy chased the culprit as far as the lift. Needless to say my room-mate Kenny Dalglish was oblivious to it all, he just kept on snoring!

Sammy Lee: That was the showpiece of the four successive League Cup finals we played in. It was superb the way the fans mingled on the terraces and also how both sides lined up alongside each other at the end – it was a great occasion for Merseyside.

Ian Rush: Everyone went happy and came home happy but it would have been much more memorable for me if we'd won and I should have won it for us. I had a great chance to score but jabbed my foot at the ball too quickly, it hit my shin and looped over the bar. I should have done the simple thing and side-footed it home. I also remember having another great chance from which Neville Southall made an amazing save.

Bruce Grobbelaar: One save was really something special. It was a great volley from Ian and Southall could only have seen it at the last moment. He did really well to get to it, let alone save it.

Graeme Souness: We were lucky Everton didn't score in the opening 45 minutes and we got the slating we deserved at half-time. Joe told us that it looked as though only two or three of us wanted to play. He did not single out any one player, but used the Liverpool psychology of letting the players answer for themselves. So even the two or three who had acquitted themselves well would feel unsure and would try that much harder in the second period.

Joe Fagan: We could have been 3–0 down. It was basic stuff – not about tactics but getting a change in attitude. Of course, I'd have preferred it if we had won, but at the end when I looked around and listened to all the fans chanting 'Merseyside! Merseyside!' I thought, 'At least they are all going home happy'.

Graeme Souness: The replay was dour but memorable for me as I scored. I miscontrolled it and had my back to goal but flashed a leg at it and it just dipped in front of Everton keeper Southall before going in. It was a bit ad-hoc when we were presented with the trophy. A fan got in the way between me and Bruce Grobbelaar as I passed it down the line but it was all good fun.

Bruce Grobbelaar: That win really took the pressure off [Joe] and you could visibly see the change in him after that. It was as if a huge weight had been lifted from his shoulders. Any man would have been anxious following in the footsteps of Bob Paisley, and Joe, although he never showed it, was no different. Winning the Milk Cup also gave everyone the belief that more could follow.

League champions

Phil Neal: It was a difficult season. We won it by a mile the year before, and came through from twelfth in 1981–82, but this time we had to graft.

Joe Fagan: There were plenty of times, especially during April, when I wondered if we were going to make it. We lost at Southampton, and then later we were beaten at Stoke, and each time I wondered if we were going to let it slip. Fortunately, we got a very good result at Watford, in John Wark's first game for us, and then we managed to beat West Bromwich at Anfield after they had missed a couple of good chances. We never got really ahead. It may have looked as though we were quite relaxed, but I can tell you the tension was there. It finished up the right way in the end. I thought it would go to the final game. I was nearly right but thank God I was wrong.

Steve Nicol: We clinched the title in the penultimate league match of the season at Notts County. Normally, a goalless draw for Liverpool at Meadow Lane would be considered a poor result but this 0-0, coupled with Manchester United failing to beat Spurs at White Hart Lane, meant a third successive league championship for us with a game to spare.

Alan Hansen: The game that clinches the title is always special. We were always in control and near the top that season but it is like a sense of relief knowing that you have finally won the championship.

That is definitely the one trophy to win – the one you set your sights on at the start of the season. I remember sitting in the dressing room at Notts County and thinking, 'We've done it again'. It was a terrific feeling.

Graeme Souness: At other clubs it would have been deemed a great League season, but for us it was no better than a good one. Saying that, we were still better than anyone else. You don't win the title on luck and over nine months we deserved it.

Ian Rush: We were a better team that season than the previous two. I think some papers were just getting bored of us winning all the time.

The sacking of Rome [part II]

AS Roma v Liverpool
Stadio Olimpico, Rome
European Cup final
30 May 1984

Ian Rush: It was absolutely unbelievable to get Roma in the European Cup final and have to play them on their home ground. But we weren't worried about it because we were the best team and nothing bothered us. When you look back to it, you think, 'Oh my god, we shouldn't be playing this game here, Roma in Rome'. But, honestly, we were quite happy about it and confident that we were going to win.

Alan Hansen: Joe Fagan pulled off a masterstroke even before we flew out to Rome. While Roma were locked away in some Italian mountain training retreat we holidayed in Israel. Joe told us to just relax and let our hair down. We had a couple of Italian journalists with us and they couldn't believe what they were seeing. We were actually drinking beer two weeks before a European Cup final.

Ronnie Whelan: It was one hell of a bonding session and a great idea because it got us away from the pressure that was building back home. It was complete relaxation, a good laugh, a few drinks and some late nights.

Graeme Souness: It was a trip that summed up just how much he treated us like the adults we were. He imposed no curfews or restrictions on us out there. We were allowed to relax, enjoy the sun and have a few drinks.

Craig Johnston: I'd like to say we were the very essence of professionalism with our minds fixed firmly on the prize, but I'd be lying. We hit the booze from the outset in Tel Aviv. What the hell! It had been a tough season, we'd already won two trophies and nobody gave us a chance of winning the third with it being on Roma's own patch.

Graeme Souness: Our preparation couldn't have been any different to Roma's, but we were totally relaxed and that gave us a belief that we wouldn't be beaten. We may have been playing Roma in Rome but the general feeling among the lads as the game approached was that something unlucky would have to happen for us not to get something out of it. Four or five of us would have to have an off-day, and that didn't happen too often, or they would have to play exceptionally well to turn us over.

Mark Lawrenson: I remember being within earshot of a conversation between Joe and Ronnie Moran just a few days before we flew out to Rome and I overheard him saying that training would have to be toned down. Everybody was so up for the game that the coaches were ordered to hold us back in case we peaked too soon.

Graeme Souness: We knew the calibre of players they had in their team but that was about it. We were shown no video tapes of them, no one spoke to us about their set-piece routines and we were unaware of what formation Roma played. That's just the way it was at Liverpool back then, though, and it didn't do us any harm. Sometimes you can over-complicate matters and worry players. Joe Fagan was never big on pre-match speeches about the opposition. It was all about what we did on the pitch and his attitude was always, 'Let the opposition worry about us, rather than us worry about them'.

Mark Lawrenson: They took us to the training pitch on the day of the game, you wouldn't have let your dog piss on it. It was horrendous. Straight away Joe said, 'Ok, we'll just go for a walk, they obviously don't want to let us train because they're frightened to death of us'. He always spun it round. I also remember him having to inform us of a new directive from UEFA, instructing players not to run towards the crowd if a goal was scored. Joe amended that when he read it out to, 'When we score a goal', and not 'If'. 'When we score our goals do as UEFA say for the first two, but do what you like if we get any more'. It was a nice touch because apart from demonstrating his confidence it helped to ease the inevitable tension which was beginning to build up.

Graeme Souness: Just after we'd finished our pre-match meal Joe stood up in the dining room of the hotel and asked the waiters to leave the room because he wanted to speak with his players in private. We're all looking at each other thinking this is a first, but then he sort of started mumbling to himself about Roma and how they must be a good team because they'd reached the final of the European Cup. Everyone was glued to what he was saying and expecting this big impassioned speech, but then he just turns round and says, 'But they're not as good as us. Now the bus leaves at such a time so make sure you get plenty of rest before then and don't be late!' It was typical Joe and it put everyone at ease.

Sammy Lee: I always remember Graeme Souness taking us out onto the pitch in what was a fantastic atmosphere. As a team in unison we all just walked around in front of the Roma fans. This was the type of bonding and togetherness we had in the camp.

Alan Hansen: I've got to be honest with you, it was the most intimidating sight I've ever seen in my life. It was frightening how much those fans wanted Roma to win that match. It put fear into me.

Ian Rush: As regards the intimidating atmosphere, I remember Graeme Souness and Kenny Dalglish making sure it didn't affect any of the players. They were laughing and joking before the game and this increased our confidence.

Mark Lawrenson: When we walked out to sample the atmosphere there was a game on the pitch so we stood at the side watching for a few minutes, then Souey said, 'Come on, let's walk right around and wind them up by showing them we're not scared'.

Steve Nicol: We were all walking behind Souness and he walks toward the enemy, 30-40,000 Roma fans, with a big smile on his face. He actually wanted to climb the fence and stand even closer to them. When you're playing for a captain like that... your chest goes out and you just want to get in there with him.

Mark Lawrenson: As we made our way around, their fans were slaughtering us and the noise was unbelievable. We finally made our way back towards the dressing-room area, but once we got inside the tunnel Davey Hodgson starts singing this Chris Rea song that Craig Johnston had got us all into.

Craig Johnston: I had given Chris Rea's album a hiding to such an extent that all the players knew the songs off by heart, especially 'I Don't Know What It Is [But I Love It]'. When one of us would sing a verse, the rest would come in on the chorus, clapping and chanting, evoking those images of unity and victory. As we walked in silence down that dark corridor, the tension among the squad was palpable. Inexplicably, Davey Hodgson then broke into a solo rendition of the opening verse of that song. One or two joined in and by the time we drew abreast of the Roma dressing room the whole Liverpool squad had joined in. The Roma players just looked on bemused, thinking this must be the super relaxed Liverpool squad they'd heard about!

Mark Lawrenson: We get back in the dressing room and our lot [the coaching staff] are going, 'What are you doing?' 'Just singing boss, nothing else to do'. After the game, their manager, Swedish bloke, Nils Liedholm, apparently he came into the press conference and said, 'I knew we were beaten before we started'. All the journalists are going what's this all about? He said, 'I'm addressing my players, telling them the team and the opposition, and hear this singing, and it gets louder, and louder, and louder, I realise it's Liverpool players, I look at my players, and they all realise it's Liverpool players, and he said they all went white, oh my god'.

Graeme Souness: Alan Hansen was a great story-teller and after going out for the walk around the pitch we were back in the changing-room when he started telling this story. I can't for the life of me remember what it was about, but they were usually quite funny and when he started all the lads listened. I'm not exaggerating when I say this, but half an hour before kick-off we're all sitting there with our shirts and ties on still listening to him. Joe then had to interrupt and remind us that we had this big game to play and it was time to get changed. It was a sign of just how relaxed we were.

Craig Johnston: It was easily the biggest game of our lives for a few of us so, let's make no bones about it, yes, there were a lot of genuine nerves there. Here we were about to enter the lion's den, quite literally, and everyone outside the club was writing us off. If we'd let the tension get to us we'd have been a beaten team from the off. Singing Chris Rea and acting as though we didn't have a care in the world was our way of dealing with it.

Bruce Grobbelaar: From that moment we grew in stature and it just built from there. We were so pumped up it was untrue. Then we waited and waited and waited. The cheeky Italian so and sos. They were trying to pull another fast one by keeping us waiting, but it didn't work. All of a sudden Sammy Lee, Craig Johnston and Souey started singing the Chris Rea song again. One by one all the lads joined in and it wasn't long before the entire team were belting it out once more at the top of their voices. Every time we got to the chorus I would start banging on the door of the Roma dressing-room as if I was playing the drums! The next thing we know the door opens and a head peeps out, and mutters something in Italian to us that sounded like, 'You Scouse Bastardos!' When they eventually started to come out Souey looked each and every one of them in the eye and continued to sing in their faces. As they went past one-by-one the singing got higher and higher until it was so loud we couldn't even hear the noise of the crowd outside.

Alan Hansen: It was amazing. The Roma players just looked at us like we were off our heads, and we were!

Alan Kennedy: We're walking down, looking at them eye to eye, and I tell you what, they were the ones scared of us.

Ian Rush: I think the Roma players were more scared than us, because they also knew we were a good team.

Bruce Grobbelaar: These Roma guys were just looking around at each other and must have been thinking, 'Just what have we got here?' I don't know whether it was off-putting for them but it certainly put a feather in our cap and we felt invincible.

Mark Lawrenson: As for the game itself, I can just remember it being absolutely boring. It was awful, it really was. It was even awful to play in.

Phil Neal: Well that day, I joined the attack and I can hear Joe and Bob saying, if you're going to join the attack, stay with it until it breaks down, then get yourself back very quickly. Well I joined the attack and all of a sudden it continued, a ricochet falls in the six-yard box, and who's in there? Me! Unfortunately they scored to equalise, just before half-time, I think it was. Which was a bitter blow, and then it was down to penalites.

Ian Rush: We weren't the best at penalties and we struggled to get five to take them! We'd had a shoot-out in training before we went to Rome and I think only Phil Neal scored, so I think that's why everyone was reluctant to step up. I didn't volunteer. Only Graeme [Souness] and Phil [Neal] did. Souness then asked myself and Steve Nicol to take one but we were still one short so Alan Kennedy offered.

Alan Hansen: I was petrified about the prospect of having to take one. If there'd been two hundred players in the team I'd have still been the last one to offer my services.

Phil Neal: All of a sudden Stevie Nicol grabs the ball and starts marching towards the spot, and Souey says, 'Just let him, let him get on with it, he's a young lad and just wants to get it over with'.

Steve Nicol: It was an awful feeling seeing my shot go over and I just wanted the ground to open up and swallow me. That penalty miss was something I'll never forget.

Mark Lawrenson: Me and Hansen went, that's it, all over.

Ian Rush: So, Steve Nicol missed the first one but Joe Fagan did really well there because he said, 'Don't worry, you've done your best, you've taken the pressure off us'. I was still nervous though when it came to my penalty. That walk up to the spot, with 70,000 Italians whistling and booing, was very nerve-wracking, but as soon as the ball hit the back of the net I was engulfed by a great sense of relief.

Bruce Grobbelaar: Just before the shoot-out began I remember Smokin' Joe putting his arm around me. He gave this little speech, 'Now, son, myself and the coaches, the chairman and the directors, the captain and the players and even these fans are not going to blame you if you can't stop a ball from twelve yards. You've done your job, we can't blame you now'. I felt a massive weight lift from my shoulders. Then as I walked away he shouted, 'But try and put them off!' That was the last thing he said to me. The first penalty, of course, I did nothing. It was only when Conti stepped up that Joe Fagan's words came back to me. Conti was dancing around and I thought I'm not having this so started doing the old crossover legs routine. When he shot over I thought, 'Aye, aye, this might just work'.

Mark Lawrenson: Bruce was great with his antics on the line but we always take the mickey out him because he makes out he saved them penalties when, really, he never saved one, they missed them all.

Bruce Grobbelaar: When it came to Graziani I'll never forget him putting his arm around the referee before taking it. I was thinking, 'You can't do that, it's ungentlemanly conduct, so I went into the goal and started eating the net. It looked like spaghetti and so when I turned round I just started giving it all the spaghetti legs. I went to the right and my hand was actually touching the floor as I looked up and saw the ball hit the top of the crossbar. I knew what it meant and just started running around and jumping up and down like a lunatic. It was Joe who'd put it into my mind, though, so he must take some of the credit. When it comes to football he was a very intelligent man who knew which buttons to press and on which players.

Alan Kennedy: Bruce has done ever so well, he's kicked the post, he's bitten the net, he's done the spaghetti legs, and he's put Graziani off. Then he's clapped his hands when Graziani missed, give it what for, and then I'm walking forward and he's looking at me. He's looking a bit confused, he's like, 'Oh, it's you!'

Alan Hansen: Because I think I was the only one who could count to five, I said, 'If we score this we win', but then we all realised Alan Kennedy was taking it...

Alan Kennedy: I have thought about it on many occasions, I can still sort of see myself standing there thinking why did I do this? Why did I say anything to Joe Fagan about taking a penalty? If I'd missed that penalty I wouldn't have been able to live with myself so I'm in a situation where if I don't score I probably never play for the club again. If I do score, I'm a hero and I'm going to be carrying that cup around Liverpool. If I'm being honest I don't think he was confident in me taking it. He had seen me in the practice at Melwood and also when I took one in pre-season. I was shocking on both occasions, so I don't know why he picked me. What he must have seen was something that maybe the other players didn't have. It definitely wasn't ability, because I was limited in that. I suppose it must have been my bottle. Tom Saunders always said about me; if there was a cavalry charge I'd be at the front saying,

'Come on!' And then I would be the first to be shot! What he meant was you knew what you were getting with me, that I wouldn't let them down.

Phil Neal: I'd watched Rushie's and I'd watched Souey's but for some reason I just couldn't watch Alan Kennedy. For some reason my mind was just telling me, 'No'.

Mark Lawrenson: When it came to Al [Kennedy], me and Hansen just went, 'No chance now is there?' But, of course, he scored. It was just a mad night.

Alan Kennedy: Well, just as Grobbelaar had put Conti and Grazziani off, their goalkeeper tried to put me off and my legs were shaking. I didn't even look at him. I knew where I was going to put it and was confident. I chose the right way, the goalkeeper went the opposite way and I scored the goal. I peeled off to my right hand side and all the lads came over. I was the most relieved person – and I'm sure Joe Fagan was as well. The first thing he said to me was, 'Did you mean it?' And he followed that up with, 'Why did you change your mind? Because I remember last week when we played against the reserves, you went for the other corner'. I said, 'Boss, you wouldn't believe what I was thinking up there'. And then he just shook my hand and gave me his famous wink, as if to say, 'Well done', and that was it. That meant I must have done all right.

Graeme Souness: Joe knew what we were capable of. While a lot of fuss was made over the fact that we had to go and play Roma on their own ground I honestly don't think it worried him. Such was the character Joe had instilled into that team, he knew we had a fighting chance against anyone, anywhere in the world. I don't think he was the least bit surprised when we eventually won it.

The horror of Heysel

29 May 1985

Phil Neal: I couldn't wait to play my fifth European Cup final for Liverpool Football Club but it turned out to be such a tragedy. It's sickening really.

Peter Robinson: [the Heysel Stadium] wasn't right to stage a game of that size. We were shown the dressing-rooms and executive areas. I asked to go out on to the ground and we looked at the fan divisions – which were little more than a chicken-wire fence. It would not have got a ground license in England at that time.

Phil Neal: The club was in no way at fault and neither were Juventus. I want to know who was to blame for choosing that inept, dilapidated stadium for two massive clubs playing in a European Cup final. Surely, Barcelona was available and the Bernabeu, it could've been held anywhere really but not a rundown athletics stadium.

Peter Robinson: It worried me that the neutral area was in the middle of the Liverpool tickets and I expressed concern that if those tickets fell into the hands of Juventus supporters it was a recipe for problems. I asked why we couldn't have a complete end. But they were adamant the outlined system was the only way they could comply with UEFA regulations. They said they were well used to handling large crowds and said ticket sales had been totally controlled in Belgium. But I went back to Merseyside with great reservations.

Alan Hansen: My father had gone to the three previous European Cup finals. Wembley was fine. Paris, if you were a mile away from the ground and you didn't have a ticket they were hitting you on the head. Rome the same. Heysel, every man and his dog was getting in there. My dad said he went with his ticket, there was nobody at the turnstiles.

Bruce Grobbelaar: I remember remarking to Barney [Alan Kennedy] about the number of Italians in section Z. It was obvious to me that surely the authorities could see the same thing. Me and Steve Nicol went for a walk around the ground to pass time, and it was a mistake. Rather than the jeering we expected from Juventus supporters, they showered us with concrete blocks and flash bombs. I started to get concerned for my wife and family in the stands.

Kenny Dalglish: You go along to watch a game. You don't go along expecting that sort of ending, do you? Football's not that important. No game of football is worth that. Everything else pales into insignificance. Juventus fans should not have been throwing stones. Liverpool fans should not have reacted the way they did. Yet neither set of supporters could have anticipated the terrible outcome. If they had foreseen the dreadful consequences, or thought what terrible things might unfold, I'm sure the stones would never have been thrown by the Italians and that the English retaliation would never have occurred. Every single one of them, both Italian and English, must have regretted it. I'm sure they still do now.

Phil Neal: Joe Fagan had gone to address the fans and they suggested that I did as well, so about an hour later I made my way to the podium with a body guard at my side, being spat on. I had to walk up to the tannoy which was up the other end where the Italians were and it wasn't the best of passages to make your way through, particularly when you've got a Liverpool tracksuit on. I remember the UEFA official handing me a statement and telling me to read it. I looked at it and thought, 'Nah, I'm not having that, I'm going to say what I feel from the heart'. So I did do, I screwed it up and threw it on the floor and just appealed to our fans for calm.

Ronnie Whelan: Because of the delay we were at a loss as to what to do, and I just remember Joe constantly coming around trying to gee us up and keep us on our toes for when the call came to get out there. I must admit it was hard to keep focus, but he kept reminding us that all we could do in such a situation was 'be professional'.

Roy Evans: It was a very confusing situation and I don't think anybody can say they knew all the facts at that stage as we hadn't been told anything officially.

Alan Hansen: It sounds terrible to say it, but my overriding anxiety was that we had a European Cup final to play, and I had to get myself ready for it. I succeeded in getting myself so psyched up for the match that what was happening on the terraces was pushed into the background.

Joe Fagan: We knew that there was a lot of trouble out there, but none of the players knew about the deaths until after. I had heard something about it, but that was as far as it went and it was nothing official.

Mark Lawrenson: It was just a surreal scene and by now we were all beginning to realise something terrible must have happened. If anyone from UEFA had come in and said the game was off we'd all have been very relieved.

Peter Robinson: I wasn't happy about the match being played. But it was decided it was the only way of getting the security forces they needed.

Kenny Dalglish: Some people thought it would have been a mark of respect to those who died not to play the game. But UEFA decided it had to be played for fear of even greater trouble and at the time it was understandable.

Phil Neal: We were told we had to play but I think on reflection, it would have been better to call the game off. Even if you null and void the winners, I don't care, I think it would have been a better decision to have called that game completely off.

Jan Molby: In hindsight none of us should have taken part. The stadium should have been binned as a venue, and once the troubles started the game should have never kicked off, but that's in hindsight.

Ian Rush: After what had happened the match was always going to be a non-event. I think we should have had a definite penalty when Ronnie Whelan got brought down and they scored a penalty, which was outside the box. But that's all irrelevant really to what happened over there. Ask those who played in that game, even speak to the Juventus players who played in that game - it wasn't like a cup final. It was like, 'Let's get it over with and see that our families are okay and that everyone else is okay'.

Sammy Lee: I have no recollection of it whatsoever. All I remember is a feeling of numbness. I couldn't even tell you what our team was. It was all a complete blank.

Mark Lawrenson: I've not seen it [again]. The only thing I've seen of that game is the penalty and that came on somewhere where I wasn't expecting it. I've never watched a minute of it at all. I remember my stepfather and his mate going, and they saw all the body bags before they got to the VIP area. Mad.

Ian Rush: It was the only game, right from being a kid, when I wasn't bothered whether we won or lost. As a professional, I approached every game, even friendlies, with a fierce determination to win. That time, I honestly did not care. The game itself seemed almost unreal.

Joe Fagan: What is a game of football when so many are dead? The match itself just fades into insignificance.

Alan Hansen: He [Fagan] looked a broken man. Of all the men at Liverpool who went through the ordeal of Heysel, Joe was the one for whom I felt most sorry. It was his last game in charge and he deserved good memories, no matter what the result. Whenever I think of Heysel it's the expression on his face that first springs to mind. It was the night that the game which had been his whole life no longer meant anything.

Roy Evans: He was at a complete loss about the whole episode. He simply had no more words to say. He didn't understand and took it very badly. He carried it with him for the rest of his days.

Jim Beglin: The enormity of Heysel hit me like a train after the game. Dejection over losing the European Cup final to Juventus quickly gave way to disbelief when I learned that people had died. I walked with my Liverpool team-mates to where the wall had crumbled and the Italian fans were crushed. The remnants of people's lives, handbags and shoes, scarves and spectacles, were strewn among the rubble.

Phil Neal: I can talk freely about it now, but it was horrific. It was as if it was something that happens to other people, not in front of your own eyes.

Jim Beglin: Win, lose or draw, we usually had a party after a big game. But the atmosphere at our base in Brussels was very somber. We just swapped stories. Several of the wives and girlfriends were distressed by what they'd seen and the players all felt numb. We just wanted to get home.

Kenny Dalglish: We saw the Italian fans crying, and they were banging on the side of our bus when we left the hotel. When we left Brussels, the Italians were angry, understandably so – 39 of their friends had died. We needed a lot of police to protect the bus. I remember one Italian man, who had his face right up against the window where I was sitting. He was crying and screaming. You feel for anybody who loses someone in those circumstances.

Peter Robinson: It's a horror story that one has to live with.

Fagan steps down

On the morning of the 1985 European Cup final news broke that Joe Fagan would be stepping down as Liverpool manager immediately after the game. It was a decision that had been made months before but one that still took everyone by surprise.

Peter Robinson: We pleaded with him to stay on, but once his mind was made up there was no changing it. He felt it was right that he gave us enough to time to decide who would replace him. Again, this was typical of Joe – always putting the club first. We wanted him to do another year at least. We believed he was more than capable of steering the club to further glory, but he just felt he'd had enough and thought it was the best decision for everyone.

Jan Molby: I think he did start to feel the pressure during that season [1984/85]. Because of what they'd achieved the season before you could sense he was getting frustrated. It took a long time that season to get the team working at the maximum level it was capable of, and by that time it was too late. Everton had run away with the title and we lost crucial games in the cup competitions, notably the FA Cup semi-final replay against Man United.

Mark Lawrenson: Something happened to Joe, and it happened long before the Heysel disaster. I think he just got tired of the job and of the daily routine, and was happy to get out. This bubbly character had not looked his age in his first season, but looked considerably older in his second.

Ronnie Moran: I was sharing a room with Joe [in Brussels] and knew nothing about it, none of us did. I didn't find out until the morning of the game and it came as a massive shock. John Bennison [Liverpool youth coach] told me. He said it was all over the papers. But my initial reaction to him was, 'Don't believe everything you read in the papers'. I dismissed it as the press trying to cause mischief on the morning of an important game, which was nothing new. The night before, as we always used to do before big games, all the staff had been in our room talking about the game and having a little drink. I remember it would get to a certain time and Joe would say, 'Go on now bugger off, we've got a game tomorrow so let's get some sleep'. On this occasion he got the whisky back out and we had one more each, but still he didn't let on about him leaving. That was typical of Joe, though. He was so loyal and faithful to the club that if he'd been told to keep quiet he would.

Mark Lawrenson: We didn't know whether to believe the story or not. Nothing had been mentioned about him leaving, but we soon sensed something was going on and drew our own conclusions.

Peter Robinson: I did ask many years later about his reasons for this and, while there were no doubt other factors, what he said to me was that the one part of management he found very difficult was dealing with players who were not in the team. He wasn't comfortable with them knocking on his door, asking why they weren't playing. Having to tell players they were, for one reason or another, not good enough to play in his team was something he found extremely difficult. This maybe had something to do with the close relationship he once had with so many of the players when he was a coach.

The King inspires a double

The Heysel Stadium disaster cast a dark shadow over Liverpool Football Club and all eyes were always going to be focused on Anfield the following season, even more so due to the fact that in Kenny Dalglish the Reds had a new player/manager at the helm.

Jim Beglin: Kenny was hugely respected. There was a kind of aura about Kenny. Everybody looked up to Kenny. Not only was he a great footballer, he was also a very shrewd character as well. I think Peter Robinson and John Smith, at the time, knew exactly what they were doing.

Peter Robinson: When Joe told us he wanted to finish, the chairman [John Smith] appointed a sub-committee of four people - comprising himself, myself, Bob Paisley and Tom Saunders. Tom was little-known but had made a tremendous contribution over the years and was youth development officer. We had a situation with that little committee where we all knew Kenny Dalglish in different ways, we had all dealt with him in different ways. We did discuss it at length, it wasn't an immediate decision and at the end of the day we came down unanimously in favour of Kenny. In life you either get decisions right or wrong and that was one we got right .

Kenny Dalglish: Seeing as they were good enough to offer me the job, it was only right to say that I'd give it a go.

Craig Johnston: It was unheard of – a player-manager – back then. It was an abstract concept. All of a sudden, one of the players is a manager. That's kind of weird.

Alan Hansen: I think he thought long and hard about taking it. Going from a player into that job of player/manager was exceptionally difficult because it's always been like a, 'Them and us'. Now, he's 'them' and there's no halfway house.

Ronnie Whelan: Kenny had to step away from the players. When he walked into the dressing room it all went quiet, it was like, 'You can't let Kenny hear'.

Gary Gillespie: He was still one of the lads and you wondered how his mindset was going to change. And in fairness to him, it didn't change that much.

Bruce Grobbelaar: Kenny just took it in his stride and for the first time in a long while we actually heard Kenny Dalglish speak.

Kenny Dalglish: Things went really smoothly and that's a fantastic credit to the players, and everyone at the club. There was so much knowledge, help and support. Tom Saunders was there. Ronnie and Roy stayed, and old Bob came in to help me. If you're given a managerial job and you've got arguably the most successful manager in footballing history beside you, who's totally humble and supportive, appreciative and a fantastic help to myself then you're giving yourself a bit of a chance. But we never set any targets other than to do the best we possibly could.

Jan Molby: Training remained the same, he was, however, very, very interested in what was happening on the continent. He was a great watcher of great teams, so Denmark became a great source of inspiration for him and he came to watch many Denmark games. He liked the way we played, we played with a certain amount of freedom, reckless and naïve in attack maybe but we played some great football.

Kenny Dalglish: We never signed too many players but there were a lot of changes made and they appeared to be seamless. The new ones settled in, the existing ones accepted them and everyone was working for each other.

Alan Hansen: The team that year was not as good as previous teams I'd played in. We'd reached the European Cup final and FA Cup semi-final the season before but I always thought we were just a bit short. And with a new player/manager at the helm I maybe thought top four in the league.

Mark Lawrenson: We weren't sure. We really weren't sure what was going to happen. You looked around the dressing room and thought, 'We've been through Heysel and had a poor season', I'm not sure if we really fancied ourselves.

Kenny Dalglish: It was a trying time for everyone but a little bit of adversity doesn't half gel everyone together.

Mark Lawrenson: I remember the first game, we played Arsenal at home and the pressure before that game was just massive. The world's press was there. I think they were looking for us to slip up or for something to happen. I'd never known pressure like there was that day, bigger than the European Cup finals, FA Cup finals, having to win the league in your last game; far, far bigger. And yet, seemingly from the outset, Kenny just breezed through it. We beat Arsenal 2-0 and although it could never be business as usual because of Heysel we were back playing football.

Jim Beglin: Manchester United won their first ten games though and, in terms of the title race, that was it wasn't it? They were champions already according to the press. But there was no real concern. We kind of loved all that, if other teams were being talked up. It would get a little mention in our teamtalks, just to give us another little stir.

Steve Nicol: Come the new year, Everton had become our biggest rivals for the title but when they beat us 2-0 at Anfield at the end of February they went eight points clear of us with only 12 league games remaining. I struggled to see how we would make up the difference because they were playing so well and we weren't.

Jan Molby: I think that was what I always used to call 'the Liverpool moment', where all the players look at each other and go, 'Listen, there can be no more messing around, no more defeats, if we lose one more game, it's over'.

Alan Hansen: I just remember thinking that there was no way back for this side. I went out for dinner with Kenny Dalglish that night. And I said to him, 'Look, this is the worst Liverpool side I've ever played in, in my life. This team is going to win nothing'.

Jim Beglin: But that team had resilience. That team had resolve. And there was a determination that kicked in then.

Jan Molby: Call it a never-say-die attitude but there was a camaraderie between the players that season, the like of which I've never experienced anywhere else in my career.

Bruce Grobbelaar: Kenny came back into the side and that brought calmness, there was no panic anymore.

Alan Hansen: We went from being a side that never really knew where the next result was going to come from to thinking, 'We can't get beaten here'. It was absolutely amazing in the run-in. Every time we went on the pitch, I thought - we can't get beaten. And in football that's a wonderful feeling to have. There's no complacency there, but at the same time, we're going to beat everybody who is put in front of us - and we did.

Craig Johnston: Footballers, if they are up for it, they hunt in packs and they can smell blood. If you know the opposition is retreating, this animal instinct kicks in and it becomes like a tornado effect. It sweeps up stuff and doesn't stop.

Jan Molby: There's dressing rooms you could have walked into and said listen, to win the league title you need to win so many games, and the players in those dressing rooms would have gone but we've never done that before. A lot of those Liverpool players would know what it is like to be on one of those runs because they've done it before. So when you win four, you're not pressured, you say we'll win the next one.

Alan Hansen: In the end we came with this incredible run. We then won something like 12 out of the last thirteen, and drew the other one.

Jan Molby: It was almost as if we broke them [Everton]. If they drew, they'd go in the dressing room afterwards and find out we'd won. The pressure probably should have been on us because we were the ones having to chase but I think that pressure shifted to Goodison.

Mark Lawrenson: Everton slipped up. They were in control, going into the penultimate league game of the season, didn't they go to Oxford? We went to Leicester, and we beat them really comfortably. They lost and all of a sudden the pendulum swung going into the final league game of the season, if we beat Chelsea at Chelsea, regardless of Everton's result we'd win it.

Chelsea v Liverpool
Stamford Bridge
Football League Division One
3 May 1986

Alan Hansen: That was one of the great days. We had a horrific record at Chelsea and when the fixtures came out and you look and see Chelsea last game of the season, everyone was saying, 'Imagine having to go to Chelsea and win to win the Championship', but it happened.

Jim Beglin: The Kop basically turned up at Stamford Bridge. It was sensational to have that. The fervour and excitement was off the scale.

Gary Gillespie: It was just a sea of red and white and yellow behind one goal.

Jim Beglin: The pitch was poor, it wasn't easy to play football on it and Chelsea were a pretty good side with some good players.

Mark Lawrenson: Speedie and Dixon up front used to cause us lots of problems, especially Speedie because he was just a nark. But of course, you forget we had golden balls [Kenny Dalglish] in the team didn't we?

Jim Beglin: Because Chelsea had so many back I ventured further forward. From the corner, there was a partial clearance and I managed to smack one [which was cleared off the line]. Rather than back off I hung around because we managed to keep Chelsea pinned in. I always remember the ball arriving at Ronnie. He got a little header on it and I was aware of Kenny just to my right side, so rather than control it and try to turn, I just flicked it on first time.

Kenny Dalglish: I managed to score what people consider one of my greatest goals. Taking the ball on my chest, I let it drop and then caught it full on the volley. It could easily have gone in the enclosure but fortunately it flew past [Tony] Godden. 'How did you score that?' asked some TV reporter. 'I closed my eyes and I hit it'.

Alan Hansen: It was typical Dalglish. Flicked on, ball on the chest and then ball in the back of the net. In his first season as a player manager, to score the goal that wins the championship, especially after being so many points behind, was terrific.

Jim Beglin: After the goal I wouldn't say it was plain sailing. It was a tough game. Chelsea did have one or two moments when they troubled us but nothing major. We coped with the pressure really well.

Alan Hansen: I didn't think at any stage that we were in any sort of danger at all, but always in the back of your mind you knew that one mistake or one piece of whatever from them, and it goes to 1-1, then that's it – finished.

Ian Rush: Although we defended really well, I thought Chelsea gave us a few anxious moments and we had that little bit of luck.

Mark Lawrenson: Jimmy Hill on Match of the Day actually highlights a tackle where I got the ball but, you know, for a split second I was thinking, 'Oh my goodness', if the referee has only seen it from behind he might give a penalty, so it was a little bit, 'oops'.

Alan Hansen: The relief – you can see it on everyone's face when the final whistle goes. It was absolute euphoria. I went ballistic and the reason I went ballistic is because when we'd won every other title we'd always been in contention, always in front, always favourites. This time, we came from absolute nowhere and to go to Chelsea, last game of the season, and win was such a wonderful feeling.

Jan Molby: Personally, it was my first title in England, and there was great excitement, especially because of Kenny being player/manager. The unthinkable thing had happened really, he'd taken us back to the summit. Although I have to say that in the dressing room afterwards you could sense that the likes of Hansen and Kenny, Bruce and Rushie, had done all this before. They just kind of sat there and said, 'We're back, this is what we do'.

Kenny Dalglish: I think for everybody it was special because at the start of the season there was a real spotlight on the club, there was huge changes. I don't know if there was a great deal of optimism about ourselves. I don't know whether people were looking and hoping that this would be the demise of Liverpool Football Club. So for the boys to turn it around and win the title, was fantastic – especially knowing they had an FA Cup final to come the following the week. It really sent out a message that, 'No, we're not finished'.

Mark Lawrenson: No-one said we're in the cup final next week and we could win the double. It was like, 'Let's get on the bus and let's have a party'. The funny thing that happened then though was that our bus broke down just outside Birmingham. They had to send for a replacement and the bus that came to pick us up was another Ellisons bus that just so happened to be the Everton team coach. I mean, how ironic was that? The day we took the league from Everton, their bus actually took us the last 100 miles home to Melwood. It was all just a bit mad.

Liverpool v Everton
Wembley
FA Cup final
10 May 1986

Ian Rush: This was extra special, because the FA Cup was the one trophy that had eluded Liverpool for the past dozen years. The fact that we were facing our Mersey neighbours Everton in the final added extra spice. Ever since we'd both won our semi-finals Merseyside had been in a state of wild excitement at the prospect.

Ronnie Whelan: We'd had the all-Merseyside League Cup final in 1984 but this was the big one, this was the FA Cup, this was the one we all wanted to win. We're going there to win the double. Everton are going there to stop us doing the double.

Ian Rush: Of course, it was the first all-Merseyside FA Cup final and we were the top two teams, I'd say, in Europe at the time, not just England. But although we were chasing the elusive double, I felt that all the pre-match pressure was on Everton. We had a trophy to our name already. If we beat them at Wembley, they'd have nothing to show for their season.

Alan Hansen: Funnily enough, I'd gone out for dinner with Kevin Ratcliffe the week before we'd played Chelsea – it had been arranged by one of the newspapers – and we agreed that we'd be happy to settle for one [trophy] each. If they get the league we'll take the cup and vice-versa. But when we won the title we wanted the two of them.

Jan Molby: Although I had missed the last game at Chelsea in the league through illness I still felt Kenny would put me in, which he did. I felt nervous all week, not on the day, but leading up to it.

Ronnie Whelan: That was one of the most intense times I had going into a cup final. There was always a fear against Everton. I wouldn't fear playing against Manchester United or Tottenham in cup finals but playing against Everton... there was the fear that you were going to let so many people down within the city. You know, you're not going to get a load of Man United or Tottenham fans running around Liverpool shouting they've won but you would get a lot of Evertonians running around shouting if they win the game. That was the intensity of it.

Craig Johnston: The build-up to the cup final for me was not easy. It was like having butterflies in your stomach for a couple of weeks beforehand. The nerves of being in this goldfish bowl where you couldn't walk out the house without somebody making a comment either way – 'I love you' or 'I hate you' – I can still remember it now. I would physically feel a little bit sick and that's not ideal preparation for any game.

Alan Hansen: I was always nervous and the FA Cup final then was going to be probably the biggest game, at that time, that I'd played in my life. By the time the day came around I was drained.

Jan Molby: The reason I came to England was because of the cup final. I wanted to play at Wembley in a cup final. Not the League Cup, not an international match with Denmark – which I already had done

– I wanted to play in an FA Cup final. It's the one thing you remember from when you're a kid. Even in Denmark I used to watch them. And here it was. In those days, I believe, the FA Cup final was bigger than the European Cup final.

Alan Hansen: We get to Wembley and because it was Liverpool versus Everton I will never see a finer sight in my life than that of the Reds and Blues together on Wembley Way. It was magical. A great example to the world, I thought, about how a city could come together.

Jan Molby: So, we arrive at Wembley, 100,000 people. We go out to have a look at the pitch in our Wembley suits and, believe me, the Wembley suits were nothing special – off the peg, but it was a Wembley suit. We go back in the dressing room and I can't wait. Then, 15 minutes before kick-off you get the call to go and stand in the tunnel, the longest tunnel in football.

Alan Hansen: Of course, when you get in the tunnel the nerves disappear but they keep you in the tunnel for ten to 15 minutes. Then you come out the tunnel and there is just this crescendo of noise. By that stage of my career I'd played in four European Cup finals but I'd never experienced anything like that. This was like bedlam - the noise, and it was so hot. Everton got a corner after about seven minutes and I'm marking Graeme Sharp at the back post and he turned and said, 'It's hot isn't it?' And I just groaned.

Jan Molby: I think the occasion got to us a bit in the first half. None of us had played in the cup final before, whereas Everton had been there the previous two years and we didn't play well enough in the first half to give the impression that we were going to win the match. That wasn't necessarily down to us playing badly, that was just them being in control. They used their qualities. You see that with the goal, Lineker's pace.

Mark Lawrenson: He got in behind Al didn't he? I just remember Al chasing him. I couldn't have caught him.

Alan Hansen: Hansen the pundit would have slaughtered Hansen the player. It broke every rule in the book. When Reidy chipped the ball through, the golden rule was to push up and let him go offside or just turn and run. I just looked at it and he was away from me.

Bruce Grobbelaar: I went down to my left, got a hand to it and parried it. But he got there first and slid it in.

Mark Lawrenson: We forgot to play, we seriously forgot to play. Everton dominated the first half and I remember when we went in at half-time Ronnie Moran gave us a right talking to.

Kenny Dalglish: One of the most important parts of a manager's duty is to motivate the players at half-time. I told them, 'We've been magnificent all season, there's 45 minutes to go, let's go and give it our lot'. It was not quite Churchill but the players responded.

Mark Lawrenson: We had another fifteen minutes in the second half though when we were still crap. Brucie and Jim Beglin nearly came to blows over a defensive mix-up but in hindsight it was the wake-up call that we needed.

Jim Beglin: Bruce was telling me to let the ball run through but I put my foot on it. I was trying to shield it from Trevor Steven and ended up getting into a bit of a muddle. Bruce got excited and called me something, I called him something back and then he hit me. I was about to hit him back when it flashed through my mind that my friends and family were in the stand and there were millions on TV watching. I've heard people say that was the turning point so if it was the wake-up call we needed then great. We hadn't been in the game until that point.

Alan Hansen: Early in the second half I thought to myself, 'We could get stuffed here', but we all know what happened then…

Ian Rush: Jan Molby laid a ball just behind their defence and suddenly the chance was on. I reached it just before Bobby Mimms, took it round him and rolled it into an empty net. There was an explosion in my head like nothing I had experienced before.

Jan Molby: We were very tentative in the first half but after the equaliser everything clicked and we weren't going to lose then.

Craig Johnston: Everywhere I went, [Pat] Van Den Hauwe was with me. Box to box. Then one time, I remember going back to our box and he followed me. I saw a space down the wing and I started to sprint into it. The ball was on our left but Van Den Hauwe followed me all the way for 70 or so yards. By then Jan Molby had the ball. I knew he'd try to find Kenny first, but something prompted me to make that last ten-yard dash. Instinctively I went, and it was only because I had a bigger heart that I connected with the cross. Psycho Pat didn't have any legs left in him, and it was the easiest goal I've ever scored. It went through Kenny's legs and just sat up perfectly for me. I said to myself, 'This cannot be this easy'. It was like slow motion and everything seemed quiet. Then, all of a sudden, as I put the ball in the net, the whole place erupted.

Jan Molby: Of course, they [Everton] knew the history of Liverpool over the previous 20 years and somewhere inside their head they were probably thinking, 'I can't believe that's just happened, here they come again'.

Craig Johnston: I jumped up in the air shouting, 'I've done it, I've done it!' It was my dream to play in an FA Cup final and to score a decisive goal was unbelievable. If somebody would have shot me then, I'd have died a happy man.

Ian Rush: The last goal, our third, was a classic example of Liverpool at their best, with Jan Molby and then Ronnie Whelan carving out the chance for me. Jan had the ball and he passed to Ronnie Whelan, Kenny went to the left and I went to the right. So Ronnie had to decide whether to give it to Kenny or give it to me.

Ronnie Whelan: I knew Kenny had run across to my left because he was moaning at me as he went past. But I wasn't too sure about Kenny scoring with his left foot. I just felt if I could get it over Kevin Ratcliffe's head and right on to Rushie's foot he was going to score.

Ian Rush: Luckily from my point of view he gave it to me. I controlled it and smashed it past the keeper to make it 3-1. It's become famous for the way the ball hit the camera in the goal but it was special and once that went in I knew we had won.

Ronnie Whelan: I was so happy he scored because I would have got some stick off Kenny if he hadn't! Seriously though, we'd done it. We'd won the double. It was magnificent.

Kenny Dalglish: The Evertonians at the end of the game must have been absolutely gutted. They had lost the league and were 1-0 up at half-time in the FA Cup final only to be beaten 3-1. It must have seemed like a bad dream.

Ian Rush: When you're a kid, you don't dream about winning the league, you dream about scoring the winning goal in the FA Cup final. That was my first FA Cup final and I did it against the local rivals, Everton. It was just like everything rolled into one.

Jan Molby: Without wanting to sound big-headed the only thing missing from my performance was a goal, and I had a couple of chances to score. It would have been nice to have got a goal but football's a team game and it didn't matter who scored as long as we won. At the end of the day I had a hand in all three of our goals, which was great.

Kenny Dalglish: The lads put in a great effort and did everything that was asked of them. I was delighted for them as much as myself. All I did was pick the right team. It was such a proud moment. We did so well to win the league – the Wembley victory was just the icing on the cake for us.

Alan Hansen: It was hard to believe that for all the success achieved under Bob Paisley and Joe Fagan, the FA Cup was the one prize that had eluded the club since 1974. Somehow it had seemed as if there was a jinx on us. Then in Kenny's first year as boss, there it was. As a managerial debut for Kenny it could not have been bettered. It was an incredibly good season for us.

Ian Rush: His first season in management had been an incredible success; to achieve it while he was still playing as well made it all the more remarkable. Doing the double was next to impossible back then. No-one had done it since Arsenal in 1971. It was something very, very special and something I will never ever forget.

Jim Beglin: To go and do the double as we did was just incredible. I was in dreamland.

Jan Molby: I was absolutely delighted and I just thought, is there anything better than this? If the only thing I ever done in my career was win the double in 1985/86, then that would have done me.

Mark Lawrenson: If you'd have said to anybody involved in the football club, at the start of the season, that you'd win the double they'd have carted you off. It just doesn't sink in for ages and when I say ages, it's not months, it's years and years.

Bruce Grobbelaar: For us to produce a season like that showed the world that this football club was not going to go away.

John Houlding and Liverpool's 'Team of Macs' at the Sandon Hotel in 1892. Dressed in blue and white they went on to become Lancashire League champions and Liverpool Cup winners in 1892/93 before applying to join the Football League. [*Author's collection*]

Scotland international Alex Raisbeck was the driving force behind Liverpool's maiden League title triumph in 1901 and is regarded as the club's first iconic player. [*Adrian Killen*]

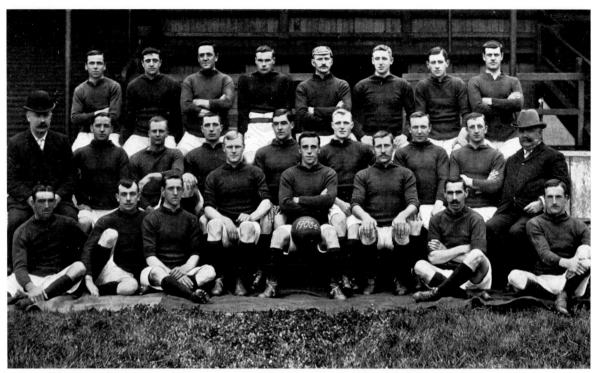

It was under the guidance of secretary/manager Tom Watson, pictured far right, that Liverpool first became an established force in the game. This is the team that went on to win the title in 1906. [*Getty*]

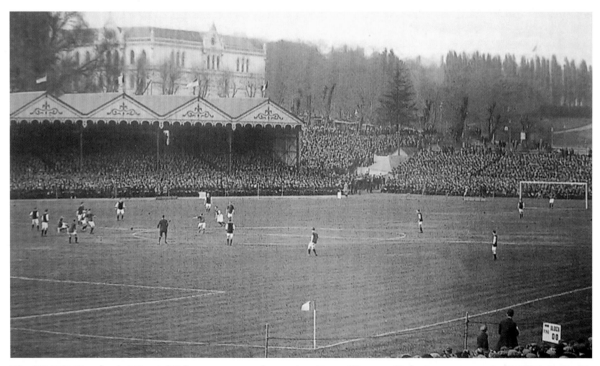

The 1914 FA Cup final at Crystal Palace was a grand occasion. It was Liverpool's first appearance in English football's showpiece and the King was on hand to present the cup. Unfortunately, Burnley won 1-0. [*George Chilvers*]

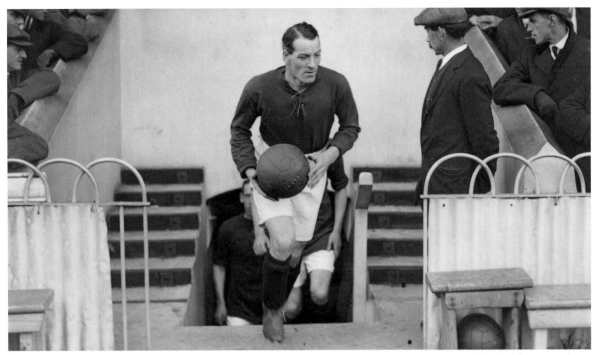

Donald Mackinlay served Liverpool for 18 years, during which time he captained the club with distinction and won two First Division Championship medals. [*Getty*]

The Liverpool team that won back-to-back First Division titles in the early 1920s is considered to be one of the finest in Anfield history. Back row [l-r] Chambers, McNab, Scott, Wadsworth, Bromilow, Forshaw. Front row [l-r] Lacey, Longworth, MacKinlay, Lucas, Hopkin, Patterson (Secretary). On ground, [l-r] Shone, Lewis. [*Getty*]

Legendary goalkeeper Elisha Scott saves a penalty in a 1923 FA Cup tie against Arsenal. Scott was a firm favourite among Kopites of the time and his pet hate was conceding goals. [*Getty*]

Liverpool's team of the late 1930s featured the likes of Matt Busby, Berry Nieuwenhuys, Phil Taylor, Jack Balmer and captain Tom Cooper [front row with the ball at his feet]. The latter was sadly killed in action during the Second World War. [*Getty*]

The Liverpool team were among the first footballers to sign up for action when war was declared in 1939. Here, Matt Busby and George Kay are among the onlookers as Arthur Riley gets to grips with a rifle. [*Getty*]

George Kay, pictured here with his players at Highbury, was Liverpool manager in the immediate pre and post war era. This team won the League in 1947 and reached the FA Cup final three years later. [*Getty*]

Albert Stubbins, a club record signing from Newcastle in September 1946 and a centre-forward whose goals helped fire the Reds to an unlikely title triumph in the first full season after the war. [*Getty*]

Manager George Kay, captain Phil Taylor, Albert Stubbins and Billy Liddell inspect the turf prior to the club's first ever appearance at Wembley in 1950. [*Getty*]

Flying Scot Billy Liddell was such an influential figure at Anfield during the 1950s that the club was often renamed 'Liddellpool' in honour of him. [*George Chilvers*]

The Liverpool squad of 1957 set off on a pre-season training run from the old Main Stand car park. Among the notable figures pictured here are Billy Liddell, Ronnie Moran, Tommy Younger and Geoff Twentyman, as manager Phil Taylor looks on from the left. [*Getty*]

After eight long years, Liverpool finally made their top-flight return in 1962/63 and in September that season Roger Hunt celebrated this last-gasp equaliser in a 2-2 draw with Everton at Goodison Park. [*Getty*]

The one and only Bill Shankly, Liverpool Football Club's modern day founding father, salutes the crowd at Wembley in 1965. [*Getty*]

A colossus and two-time League champion, Liverpool's inspirational captain of the sixties Ron Yeats with English football's most treasured piece of silverware. [*Getty*]

It's Wembley on the first of May and Liverpool's class of '65 have just won the FA Cup for a first time. The greatest day in the club's history it was said. [*Getty*]

'Sir' Roger Hunt helps send world club champions Internazionale packing with this goal on what was Anfield's first great European night. [*Getty*]

30 April 1966 and the kings of English football celebrate their second league championship in three seasons following a 2-1 victory over Chelsea. [*Getty*]

Bill Shankly built two great teams at Anfield. His second, featuring the likes of Ray Clemence, Kevin Keegan, Alec Lindsay and Emlyn Hughes began to take shape in the early seventies. [*Getty*]

Champions 1973! Shankly's second great team comes to fruition and it's two of the old guard, Ian Callaghan and Tommy Smith, who lead the celebrations in front of the Kop. [*Getty*]

Liverpool's breakthrough season in Europe came with the UEFA Cup success of 1972/73. Captain Tommy Smith believes it was the hardest of the three European competitions to win back then. [*Getty*]

Liverpool's very own 'JFK' moment, everyone remembers where they were on 12 July 1974 – the day Bill Shankly sensationally announced his resignation. [*Offside*]

Ecstatic scenes at Molineux on 4 May 1976 after a thrilling 3-1 victory clinched Liverpool's ninth League Championship, the first of Bob Paisley's managerial reign. [*Getty*]

Football's biggest superstar of the seventies was Liverpool number seven Kevin Keegan, seen here after scoring what proved to be the winning goal in the two-legged UEFA Cup final against FC Bruges in 1976. [*Getty*]

16 March 1977. This was the night Anfield was shaken to the core and the legend of Supersub was born as St Etienne were famously beaten in the European Cup quarter-final. [*Steve Hale*]

The sight that greeted the Liverpool team when they arrived in Rome for the club's historic first ever European Cup final against Borussia Monchengladbach. [*Offside*]

Bob Paisley was the first manager to lead Liverpool to European Cup glory and he went on to win it three times in total, the first man to do so. [*Getty*]

20 August 1977 and the soon-to-be new King of the Kop Kenny Dalglish trots out at Ayresome Park, Middlesbrough for his Liverpool league debut. He scored in a 1-1 draw. [*Offside*]

The decisive moment in the 1978 European Cup final against FC Bruges at Wembley as Kenny Dalglish latches onto a Graeme Souness through ball and prepares to break the deadlock with an exquisite chip over the 'keeper. [*Getty*]

The Anfield brains trust gather in the boot room to toast another title triumph. [l-r] Messrs Ronnie Moran, Roy Evans, Bob Paisley (Manager), Tom Saunders, John Bennison and Joe Fagan. [*Getty*]

Proud captain Phil Thompson celebrates after helping end Liverpool's League Cup hoodoo following a 2-1 victory over West Ham at Villa Park in a replay of the 1981 final. [*Getty*]

Reserve team rookie Howard Gayle, Liverpool's first ever black player, came off the bench to terrorise Bayern Munich's experienced defence in a memorable 1981 European Cup semi-final. [*Getty*]

As the final whistle goes at the Parc des Princes in Paris, Graeme Souness and Sammy Lee raise their arms aloft to acknowledge a famous 1-0 win over Real Madrid that secured Liverpool's third European Cup. [*Getty*]

'I don't know what it is but I love it' sang the defiant Liverpool team as they walked out into the lion's den to face AS Roma in the 1984 European Cup final. [*Getty*]

A stricken Joe Fagan appeals for calm after rioting on the terraces at the Heysel Stadium in Brussels overshadows his last game in charge of the club. [*Offside*]

Player/manager Kenny Dalglish shows off the spoils of his first season in the job – the 1986 League and FA Cup, the coveted double. [*Getty*]

Beardsley, Barnes and Aldridge: an exciting new era gets underway at Highbury on the opening day of the 1987/88 season, with all three involved in the opening goal. [*Offside*]

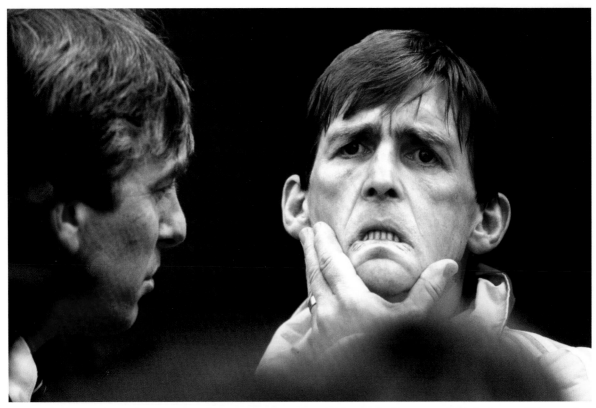

The look of anguish on the manager's face says it all as the Hillsborough disaster unfolds in front of him on that never-to-be-forgotten afternoon of 15 April 1989. [*Getty*]

Not even a 1-0 defeat to Norwich could ruin the atmosphere when supporters stood on the Spion Kop for a final time on 30 April 1994. [*Getty*]

Spice Boys: They were one of the most talented sides in Liverpool history but are unfortunately remembered more for the infamous cream suits that were worn at Wembley in 1996. [*Getty*]

Jamie Redknapp, Robbie Fowler and Sami Hyypia show off the three trophies Liverpool won during a remarkable 2000/01 season. [*Getty*]

Frenchman Gerard Houllier, the club's first-ever foreign manager, returns to the dugout after undergoing heart surgery. [*Getty*]

Ready, steady, go: Liverpool's players celebrate the miracle of Istanbul. [*Getty*]

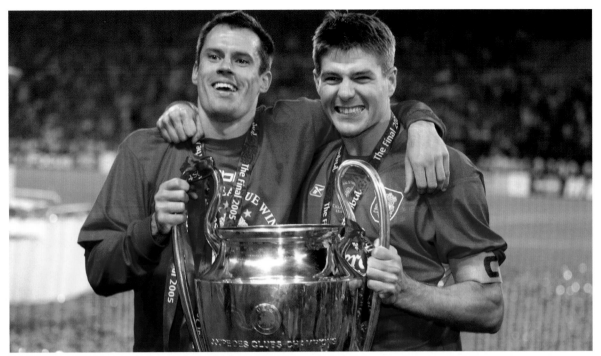

Local lads done good. Jamie Carragher and Steven Gerrard, the Scouse heartbeat of Liverpool's team throughout the noughties, proudly parade the Champions League trophy around the Ataturk Stadium in Istanbul. [*Offside*]

Time is almost up in the 2006 FA Cup final against West Ham in Cardiff and captain fantastic Steven Gerrard has just unleashed a trademark thunderbolt to rescue Liverpool once again. [*Getty*]

Liverpool's Spanish Armada: Fernando Torres and Xabi Alonso celebrate a goal in the 2008 Champions League quarter-final victory over Arsenal. [*Getty*]

Rafael Benitez: He came from Spain to make Liverpool great again and almost succeeded, leading them to Champions League and FA Cup glory but narrowly missing out on the Premier League title. [*Getty*]

In October 2010, a new regime was ushered in at Anfield after New England Sports Ventures [now known as FSG] assumed control of the club following the turbulent reign of Tom Hicks and George Gillett. Principal owner John W Henry and chairman Tom Werner are pictured here. [*Getty*]

Kenny Dalglish's return as manager in January 2011 was widely welcomed and just over a year later he guided the Reds to League Cup success against Cardiff City at Wembley. [*Getty*]

His four years at the club were controversial at times but there can be no denying that Luis Suarez was one of the most talented players to ever pull on a Liverpool shirt. [*Offside*]

Since Liverpool last won the League in 1990, no manager has gone closer to ending the club's long wait to be crowned champions again than Northern Irishman Brendan Rodgers in 2013/14. [*Getty*]

So near, yet so far. Devastation for Liverpool at Selhurst Park in May 2014 as the Premier League title slips agonisingly from their grasp. [*Offside*]

Jurgen Klopp has breathed new life into Liverpool Football Club following his appointment as manager in October 2015. [*Offside*]

Dejan Lovren rises highest at the far post to head home a dramatic late goal that completed an amazing comeback against Borussia Dortmund in April 2016. [*Getty*]

One of Liverpool's current stars is Senegal international Sadio Mane, signed from Southampton in the summer of 2016 and seen here celebrating a last-gasp winner at Goodson Park on his Merseyside derby debut. [*Getty*]

One for the future? At just 17 years and 45 days old, Ben Woodburn became Liverpool's youngest-ever goalscorer when he netted this goal in a 2-0 victory over Leeds United at Anfield in November 2016. [*Getty*]

Jan Molby: There are other teams in the history of Liverpool Football Club that would have been better, but we had a togetherness, we had a belief, we had a mentality – that just got the job done.

Ronnie Whelan: To put the scale of the achievement into perspective, you only have to think about all the other great Liverpool teams that never won the double, yet this set of lads came together and did it.

Alan Hansen: It was one of the biggest achievements of my time at Liverpool. We'd won the European Cup, we'd won the title but we'd never won the title and the FA Cup in the same season. To be lifting the trophy in May as a double-winning captain was probably better than anything I ever did at Liverpool. It was absolutely awesome.

Kenny Dalglish: It was a fairy-tale season for us. It's unbelievable to consider the amount of success that the football club had enjoyed but they had never won the double. It was a fantastic achievement. If you don't enjoy winning the league, then going to Wembley and win the cup, to complete a double; then you've got a problem. It doesn't get any better.

Better than Brazil

1987/88

Having endured a season without silverware and with Ian Rush leaving for Juventus the future wasn't looking good for Liverpool – until Kenny Dalglish responded by assembling one of the most exciting teams in Anfield history.

John Aldridge: I was the first part of the jigsaw, then came John Barnes and Peter Beardsley, and Ray Houghton shortly after. It just all gelled. It was a fantastic team to play in and be part of.

Steve McMahon: What a team. Magnificent. Aldo was born to score goals, that's all he did. We used to have some great fun in training and off the pitch, but he could score goals.

Mark Lawrenson: You can't replace Rushie but Aldo came damn well near to replacing him.

John Aldridge: Once Kenny had made the changes, to suit my way of scoring, getting chances from wide positions, with Barnesy and Craig Johnston, and later Ray Houghton, with Peter Beardsley in behind, we were just scoring for fun. It was good management.

Steve McMahon: He was wonderful to play with; you knew that anything in that six yard box he'd be there. He used to know exactly when the ball would go near post or far post, because Barnesy would put things on a plate for him.

Jan Molby: I had seen Barnes play for Watford and England, and thought he was okay. But then he came to Liverpool and I realised he was magnificent. There was nothing he couldn't do. Playing out on the left, helping the left back and defend, getting forward, scoring goals, creating goals. As much as he was left footed he had a great right foot as well. He saw things but also had the ability to execute things.

Mark Lawrenson: Barnesy was just sensational, he had a spell for two or three years where he was as good as Kenny.

Steve McMahon: When we bought Barnesy he was a revelation. He was a great player at Watford but at Liverpool, he must have had his three best years in football, in my opinion he was the best in Europe at the time.

Alan Hansen: I think Barnesy, in all my years at Liverpool, would be in the top three or four players ever. I don't say that lightly. He had everything. He had pace and he had strength. It used to be that when I picked the ball up at centre-half, the first person I looked for would be Dalglish, then when he retired and Barnesy came, the first person I looked for would be Barnesy.

John Barnes: If you're a good player you are accepted at Liverpool. But I wasn't the only one coming in at that time so it wasn't that hard for me. Any dressing room is going to be happy if things are going well, and from day one things went well. We, the new players, all felt at home immediately. From the first week of training it was like we had been playing together forever.

Steve McMahon: Peter Beardsley came in as well, he was a wonderful player for Liverpool.

Jan Molby: I was excited about Beardsley: I really rated him as a footballer.

Mark Lawrenson: Peter could win a game on his own for you.

Jan Molby: Peter took that to a different level, he had ability and a sharp mind, he saw things and he tried things, and when they came off he was from a different planet.

John Barnes: As the club's record signing, there was probably more pressure on Peter to perform than me but, you know, Peter did perform and exceptionally so.

Steve McMahon: We had quality all round and throughout the team, which is why I say that when one of the players had a bad day, there was always three or four others that would come into the equation. Teams couldn't mark one or two players out of the game for Liverpool, because everyone could play.

Jan Molby: I broke a bone in my foot pre-season. The boys went off to Scandinavia and I was put in plaster. Kenny rings me and said come out, don't sit at home, because in those days you did no rehab, you just sat in plaster for six weeks. As soon as I went out to Scandinavia and watched them play, I thought how good does this look? It was amazing, the way they were playing.

Kenny Dalglish: That team was fantastic. Peter Beardsley, John Aldridge, John Barnes, Ray Houghton, Steve McMahon, Ronnie Whelan – top quality in every position. Alan Hansen, Gary Gillespie, Steve Nicol, Barry Venison... it was just fantastic to watch them play and see their movement.

John Barnes: I didn't play as an orthodox left-winger for Liverpool. I used to come in off the line, I used to play in the way that I always wanted to play, the position I thought was mine since I was eight, nine, ten years old. When I came in Peter would go wide so we had a good movement and understanding. We just had intelligent players who could play that way. So that is why I think Liverpool were very fortunate because I don't think we envisaged that happening – me not playing as a left-winger, Peter Beardsley not staying in that position, just to play with John Aldridge, us moving around – and one of the biggest factors to that working was Ray Houghton because he came to play on the right as a typical Liverpool right-sided midfield player.

Mark Lawrenson: Little razor was an absolute bonus, he was the archetypal Liverpool midfielder playing on the right, he was just a bundle of an energy, never gave the ball away, lots of vision. Those signings were all top drawer.

John Aldridge: He [Kenny] must have had the easiest job in the world with that team. He put it all in place, so he'd already done the hard job. There was no team talks as such, he'd make you aware of one or two of the opposition beforehand, but as a manager you don't have to say much when your team is winning every game.

Kenny Dalglish: It was about individual ability within a team framework and the training we did, not least the five-a-sides.

John Barnes: We didn't play at home for the first three games. We had to play away at Arsenal which we won, I can't remember where else, but we played really, really well. By the time we got to Anfield to play the first game the crowd had taken to me, so it was just fantastic.

John Aldridge: It just clicked from that first game at Highbury. I think we quickly realised it was going to be good, the pattern of play was very fluent, very attractive and we all had an extra expectancy that season.

Peter Beardsley: It was the beginning of an incredible run which saw us equal the First Division's best-ever start, the 29-match unbeaten record which Leeds had set up fourteen years earlier.

John Barnes: We played QPR in October. They were top of the table and that was a fantastic day. We took them to pieces and I managed to score two cracking goals. More importantly, the result put us top of the table for the first time that season, even though we still had games in hand over the other sides. By Christmas, the pundits had already crowned us champions but we never got carried away, it was always just a case of taking one game at a time. The unbeaten run was great but we knew it would come to an end at some point. Unfortunately, it came against Everton, but it's how you react and, fortunately, we'd react the same whether we won or lost.

Steve McMahon: We knew nine times out of ten that we'd win the game. And the best thing about that team as well was that we could mix it up. If people wanted to say before the game do you want a scrap, do you want a fight or do you want to play football? We'd say it's up to you, we can do both, and we had the players to do that, and that made us a great team. It was wonderful knowing that we all had confidence in each other to play. We were a proper team.

Ray Houghton: It was simple. At most clubs when you get the ball you only have one or two options, but all of a sudden I had eight or nine. The staff instilled in us the importance of workrate and earning the right to play, but when you look at that team everyone was quality.

Peter Beardsley: I scored the goal against Spurs that actually clinched the championship when the season still had a fortnight and four more games to go. Ray Houghton played the ball across to me on the corner of the 18-yard box. I cut inside Gary Mabbutt and bent the ball inside the far post past Bobby Mimms. Anfield erupted in a mass of red and white. The fact that the supporters were used to success did not make it any less sweet.

Gary Gillespie: The 1988 side was even better than the double team. There was talent all over the pitch. Barnes, Beardsley, Aldridge, teams just couldn't cope. We knew we were going to win, it was a case of how many goals today.

John Barnes: The unfortunate thing is that we were obviously not in Europe. That is one challenge I would have really looked forward to with that Liverpool team. I know AC Milan had a very good side around this time – with Gullit, Van Basten and Riijkaard – but I'd like to think we'd have been good enough to win one, maybe two, of those European Cups. Who knows?

John Aldridge: AC Milan were the dominant team in Europe then but I'd have fancied us against anyone. Gullit, Van Basten and co... no problem, they would certainly have known they'd been in a game against that Liverpool team, take it from me. I think Van Basten even said that they knew they only won it so many times because we weren't in it.

Liverpool v Nottingham Forest
Anfield
Football League Division One
13 April 1988

Steve McMahon: People who watched that game have often said it was the best game they'd ever seen, footballing wise, and I can't disagree. We'd played Nottingham Forest on the Saturday in the semi-final at Hillsborough, and we'd beaten them. They were no mean outfit as well; they were a decent team. They had a lot to prove at Anfield on that Wednesday night, after getting knocked out of the FA Cup. We thought it was going to be a lot harder than it was, but the way we played was incredible. It really was football at its best, and that summed up the team at that moment in time. We were just on fire.

John Aldridge: For the first fifteen minutes we never really got going but once in our stride we were unstoppable.

John Barnes: Sometimes you win 6-0, sometimes you win 8-0. Sometimes you only win 1-0. But you don't have a 90-minute performance like that one, especially against a side as good as Nottingham Forest were at that time.

Alan Hansen: We were going for the Championship and it was just one of these nights where everything came off.

Ray Houghton: You look back on that night as a game when everything clicked. Sometimes things click for 60 or 70 minutes of a game, but that night for 90 minutes we were relentless.

John Barnes: When you play some of the lesser teams, that's when you can score goals and really dominate them. But Nottingham Forest, they were a good hardworking side, probably one of the top sides in the country at the time. So to totally dominate them in that way, and to score five goals was very pleasing.

Alan Hansen: We passed and we moved, we had Barnes and Beardsley playing right at their peak. There were a couple of times when Beardsley shimmied and about 10,000 people at the Anfield Road end were sold the dummy as well.

John Barnes: We didn't have to defend because every time we got the ball, we didn't give it away. It was the best all-round performance I've been involved with for 90 minutes. I think I have played in teams where Liverpool have played better for 20 minutes, but in terms of a sustained, 90 minute, quality performance, that was it.

Alan Hansen: It was an incredible night and it could have ended up at anything. It could have been nine, could have been eleven. We had so much possession, so many chances and quite rightly people say it's one of the greatest performances of all time.

John Barnes: Every time we got the ball we looked like we were going to create something and every time we attacked I felt we were going to score.

John Aldridge: The 5-0 against Forest, I never tire of watching that. It was one of the ultimate performances, as the great Tom Finney said. It was just a joy to play in that side, in any game, not just that one.

Gary Gillespie: That was virtually the perfect game. Everything clicked and each player performed to their maximum. I even got a goal, a rasping left footer in front of the Kop! But we never got carried away with the way we were playing, the backroom staff would knock you down a peg if we began to. You'd win 5-0 and Ronnie Moran would say, 'Don't think you've done it all now, big-heads'.

Liverpool v Wimbledon
Wembley
FA Cup final
14 May 1988

Ray Houghton: There was a lot riding on it. There was a chance to do the double. And I remember being really nervous before the game. I could hardly sleep and I don't know why. Maybe because most of the pundits were saying this was a mismatch and we were hot favourites to win. We never thought that though. Not for one moment did we think that. We knew what to expect from Wimbledon. We knew it would be competitive. We never thought it was going to be easy and we gave them the respect they deserved.

John Barnes: Liverpool didn't play particularly well and so we lost the game, it was a bad performance, but it wasn't as big an upset as people make out. Wimbledon finished seventh that season and subsequently concluded a campaign in the top ten for another decade. Ok, some of the skill levels have not been so high, but they were a very good, effective side who knew each other's function and contribution as well as any other team in the country.

Ray Houghton: People say we were too casual and they psyched us out of the game. That all makes a good story, but the truth is we didn't produce enough individual performances on the day. Player for player we were better than them but on the day they took their once chance and we couldn't break down their defence.

Steve McMahon: Wimbledon stuck to their task and you've got to give them credit. Not many people do, they think good old fashioned Wimbledon getting stuck in. Yes they did, but they played to their strengths and they won it from a set piece which is what they worked on.

Jan Molby: Sometimes when you come up against that type of football, and you're not on your game, they can hurt you. What annoys me about that Wimbledon game is that I believe if we played that game 100 times we would have won 95 of them. I would rather replay that game than the Arsenal game in 89, because Arsenal won the title over 42 games, fair dues they get enough points in that time to win it. Wimbledon was a one-off, and there's a lot of unnecessary rubbish attached to what happened in that game.

Steve McMahon: They say they psyched us in the tunnel – no chance. As I said before, we could mix it; the Ronnie Whelan's of this world, he was the assassin. He could put himself about when he wanted to, and we had lots of strong players. Not just physically, but mentally they were very, very strong. So no, we wouldn't allow Wimbledon to put us off mentally or physically.

John Barnes: That didn't happen. Liverpool were the top team in the country because we had one or two players in the team that could mix it if necessary.

Steve McMahon: People talk about the tackle, it was pre-meditated by Vinny but it didn't affect me. They say he won the game for Wimbledon because of that. Rubbish! We had a goal disallowed, I think that's what cost us in the end, it shouldn't have been disallowed.

Peter Beardsley: There was a long ball played forward and although Andy Thorn had fouled me, I managed to get away from him and was in on goal and just lifted the ball over Dave Beasant as he dived. He made out later that he knew the whistle had done but I wasn't sure whether I believed him. I certainly didn't hear the referee Brian Hill blow for a foul. I was celebrating the goal but turned around to see Mr Hill pointing to the place where he wanted the free-kick taken from.

Kenny Dalglish: Just before the Beardsley incident the referee had let another one go and he did play advantage. Then Wimbledon breakaway and score, and the Cup is won and lost within a minute.

Ray Houghton: If you're being analytical, they got a goal out of nothing. They had one or two chances in 90 minutes, scored one goal and then hung on. Peter's goal should never have been disallowed. The ref should have played the advantage and if we'd have got that first goal then I think we'd have gone on to win the game comfortably.

Steve McMahon: Tasting defeat at Wembley was obviously very disappointing but it was just one of those games. We had chances galore and, of course, Aldo missed a penalty.

John Aldridge: First and foremost, it was never a penalty. [Clive] Goodyear was the defender and he got a toe to the ball. It was a great tackle, well timed. I was surprised the referee gave a pen to be honest but I suppose he was only making up for wrongly disallowing Peter Beardsley's goal in the first half. He knew he'd slipped up there so probably gave us this to make up for it. But I fancied it. I'd scored ten out of ten penalties for Liverpool that season and I knew where I was going to put it. Unfortunately, Dave Beasant had done his homework. He took a gamble and it paid off for him so he deserves credit for that. Although have you seen how far out of his goal he was? When I kicked the ball he was only two yards from my feet!

Ray Houghton: There are certain things you try to erase from your memory and for me that day is one of them.

John Aldridge: It still hurts. I don't have nightmares about it but I do have regrets.

Hillsborough

15 April 1989

John Aldridge: If I hadn't become a footballer it is almost certain I would have been in the middle of the Leppings Lane terrace at Hillsborough on Saturday, 15 April, 1989. In the days when I was a fan I would never have considered missing an FA Cup semi-final involving Liverpool so I have to assume I would have travelled with everyone else to Sheffield for the game against Nottingham Forest. But fate decreed that John Aldridge be elsewhere that day. I was not on the Leppings Lane terrace, I was on the Hillsborough playing field, oblivious to what was going on among the Liverpool contingent.

John Barnes: Saturday, 15 April, 1989 should have been a day of excitement when a compelling FA Cup semi-final between Liverpool and Nottingham Forest was played at the home of Sheffield Wednesday. I try not think about the day itself, but I will never forget it. The events were like a nightmare unfolding.

Kenny Dalglish: I will never, never forget 15 April, 1989. I cannot even think of the name Hillsborough, cannot even say the word, without so many distressing memories flooding back. I find it very difficult to write about Hillsborough. The memory will remain with me for the rest of my life.

Alan Hansen: In the opening few minutes I felt happier than I could have anticipated. Two months short of my 34th birthday, I had been out of Liverpool's first team for nine months - the result of a dislocated left knee sustained in a pre-season friendly against Atletico Madrid in Spain - and had only started playing again, for the reserves, four days before the semi-final. The Liverpool fans gave me a tremendous reception as I came on to the pitch, and I made a great start to the game. In those opening minutes, I hit three good passes - two long balls over the top of the Forest defence to Steve McMahon and the other to Peter Beardsley, who hit a shot against the Forest bar. All my fears about my fitness evaporated. I felt as if I had never been away. Then, suddenly, I started to fall into the blackest period of my life.

John Barnes: I didn't realise anything was amiss on the Leppings Lane terrace until a couple of fans ran on to the pitch shouting, 'There are people being killed in there'. I thought they were exaggerating, like when players say, 'That tackle nearly killed me'. I just thought the fans were getting a bit squashed. But Bruce Grobbelaar, who was closest to the Leppings Lane terrace, quickly realised there was something terribly wrong when he went to retrieve a ball and heard fans screaming. Bruce shouted at the stewards to do something.

Bruce Grobbelaar: I knew exactly what was happening from the pitch, so why couldn't the people who had the power to make the right decisions change things? I told a policewoman to open the gates, but it seemed to take a long time to register with her the desperation of the situation.

Alan Hansen: The first inclination I got was when two guys come on the pitch, and I go to them right away and said, 'You'll get us in trouble here'. The guy looked at me, and you could tell from the sadness in his eyes that he wasn't making it up, and he says, "Al, there's people dying in there'.

John Aldridge: I was the Liverpool player furthest away from the Leppings Lane terrace when a fan decked out in Liverpool red approached Ray Houghton and shouted something at him. I assumed it was some kind of pitch invasion. The last action I could remember was Peter Beardsley hitting the crossbar with a fierce shot. But soon a policeman with a look of concern approached referee Ray Lewis and began talking to him. The game was brought to a halt. I remember Steve Nicol saying something to the referee, though I was too far away to hear anything. I didn't have a clue what was going on.

John Barnes: Six minutes into the match, a policeman ran on to tell Ray Lewis, the referee, to halt the game. Lewis immediately led the players back to the dressing-rooms. The scale of the tragedy was still unimaginable. We thought a few fans had been squashed but that we would be playing again soon, once the stewards had sorted out the problem. Lewis kept coming in and saying, 'Another five minutes'. Each time, we all got up and started jogging again until he finally came in and said, 'That's it, lads, match off'.

Kenny Dalglish: Nobody knew the scale of the disaster. I ordered the players to stay inside and went out into the corridor. A few fans had gathered there. They called out to me, 'Kenny, Kenny, there are people dying out there'. News of the horror filtered through. People who had been outside began to give a hint of the unfolding disaster. Like any man, my first reaction was to check my family was all right.

John Aldridge: The confirmation that Liverpool fans had died reached us while we were getting changed. Some of us were showering, though some had already put their clothes back on. Again, I don't remember exactly what I did. I cast my eyes over to John Barnes and could see tears in his eyes. He was sitting there quietly, not wanting to be disturbed. A few of the other players looked stunned. I couldn't talk. Nobody could, there was a strange sort of silence. Usually there is much conversation and banter when the lads are all together in the dressing-room. Not now. Too many thoughts were flashing through our minds. The sense of logic was disappearing.

Alan Hansen: Somebody comes in and says, 'There's 18 dead'. Then there was like 32, and then the numbers went up. It's a sense of shock. Then you go upstairs and you see the girls, and they're like crying their eyes out. They're watching coverage of the events unfolding. But you still never really knew the enormity of what had happened.

John Barnes: All the rumours of crushing and deaths became desperate reality when I heard Des Lynam say, 'There's been a tragedy at Hillsborough. There are many dead'. I went numb. I couldn't believe it. Complete silence seized the room. Every face turned towards the television screen. No one sat down. No one spoke. Forest's players were also in the lounge. What could they say? 'We're sorry your fans have been killed?' The fact that they played for Forest and we played for Liverpool was irrelevant. These were human beings who died. We watched the television for an hour in silence. Many in the lounge were crying. Each of the players wondered whether he knew anyone who could have been in that terrible cage. I had only been at Liverpool for two years and knew hardly any of the fans. It was far worse for the local players like John Aldridge and Steve McMahon. Aldo was very agitated. He was desperately trying to make phone-calls. Eventually, we got on the coach, each player sitting next to his wife, holding hands, still numb and speechless. Everyone drank heavily all the way back to Liverpool. I got completely smashed on brandy. People wept all the way home. All the wives were crying. I was crying. Kenny was crying. Bruce said he was considering quitting.

Kenny Dalglish: The next day people began coming up to Anfield. They just wanted to leave tributes and flowers at the Shankly Gates. Peter Robinson got in touch with the groundsman and told him to open the ground. Liverpool Football Club didn't want supporters standing around on the street. That was a magnificent thing to do. At 6pm we all went to the cathedral. Bruce Grobbelaar read from the scriptures. There was an awful sense of loss, confusion, frustration. So many emotions were felt. The players and their wives were determined to do something. We all went into Anfield the next day. The wives were brilliant. Everything just stopped, and rightly so. It comforted people coming into Anfield, talking to the players, the wives, and having a cup of tea. Liverpool Football Club was the focus of so many people's lives that it was natural they should head for Anfield. It gave them somewhere to go, something to talk about.

John Aldridge: When the full extent of the disaster that eventually claimed the lives of 96 people unfolded, my emotions were of great sadness for the victims whose only mistake was choosing the wrong day to watch a football match; a football match in which I was playing. I remember giving an interview to the Liverpool Echo in which I said I didn't care if I never played again. I meant every word. For the two weeks following the disaster I was in a state of shock, helpless to do anything, I feel no shame in admitting Hillsborough affected me mentally for a time, a long time. I couldn't cope. It weakened me physically, emotionally and mentally. The thought of training never entered my head. I remember trying to go jogging but I couldn't run. There was a time when I wondered if I would ever muster the strength to play. I seriously considered retirement. I was learning about what was relevant in life. I didn't really see the point in football.

John Barnes: Hillsborough made me realise what is really important in life. Before Hillsborough, I had always tried to keep things in perspective but what happened on the Leppings Lane terraces made me question so much in my life. Football lost its obsessive significance; it was not the be all and end all. How could it be when 96 people died, when parents lost children and children lost parents? Bill Shankly's comment that 'football is not a matter of life and death, it is far more important than that' sounded even falser after Hillsborough. Football is a game, a glorious pursuit; but how can it be more important than life itself?

Steve McMahon: Difficult, difficult times. It's hard to describe, especially being from Liverpool and knowing lots of the families, knowing lots of the people that went to the games. We were all doing our bit, rallying round each other and the families; going to funerals and going to houses, trying to console people and be there for them. Do the best we could basically.

Jan Molby: It was a very testing time. A lot of us were relatively young men in our mid-twenties. We were good footballers; some were great footballers. But we were badly equipped to deal with a disaster and the aftermath of it – meeting families and going to funerals – but I do believe everyone wanted to be part of it and everybody did their best.

Alan Hansen: I went to about twelve and I remember saying to Janet [his wife] after the first one, 'This will get better'. It never. It got worse.

Ray Houghton: I went to a lot of funerals with John Aldridge. It was so upsetting seeing the families, but I think John felt it more than anyone. Being a local lad it really hit him hard. Liverpool as a club and a city is a family. The way things transpired, with flowers on the Kop, really underlined the closeness of the place. As players, we didn't want to play football for a while. The game had to take a backseat. It was the families that were all-important.

John Aldridge: Hillsborough was a real tragedy on a real day involving real people. We often talk of nightmares in our lives, of disaster, of tragedies, but most of us don't really know what we're talking about. I was injured playing for Liverpool the season before Hillsborough and I called it a personal disaster. Disaster? When you know people have died in your vicinity you realise missing a football match or two through injury is irrelevant.

Kenny Dalglish: I was offered the manager's job at Sheffield Wednesday after I left Liverpool but I couldn't take it because of what had happened at Hillsborough. The person who offered me the job said, 'I never thought of that'. But I can never be in the stadium without thinking of all those people who died on the Leppings Lane terraces.

Liverpool v Everton
Wembley
FA Cup final
20 May 1989

Kenny Dalglish: Fate decreed it would be Liverpool and Everton, helping the healing process, and fate also knew Liverpool must win. A final weighted with such emotional significance proved a classic.

Ronnie Whelan: We had to win it, we knew we had to win it, and we knew Everton weren't just going to give it to us, that's for sure. So there was a lot of pressure on us that day.

John Barnes: I must admit, I felt slightly sorry for Everton. In different circumstances everybody would maybe have wanted Everton to win because they were underdogs and in this country everyone loves an underdog. But because of Hillsborough everybody, apart from the Everton fans, wanted Liverpool to win. It was just good that it was an all-Merseyside final because Everton fans would have lost loved ones at Hillsborough too so it was only right that they were there with us at Wembley.

Steve McMahon: Only one team was ever going to win that cup final that year and I'm glad we played it because there was talk of cancelling it. But that wouldn't have been right, there would have been a big hole. And it was fitting that Everton got to the final too. The city of Liverpool was the winner that day.

Steve Nicol: No way were we losing that. Not for one minute. It just meant too much to too many people. And the game couldn't have started better.

John Aldridge: It was actually my first touch of the game, so I was a bit wet behind the ears when it came to me. It was a great move. Steve Nicol put a great ball in behind and Steve McMahon made one of his fantastic runs from midfield. He squared the ball to me and I put it exactly where I meant to put the penalty the year before. It was a nice way to start the game. Especially after all that went on, it meant an awful lot to me.

Ray Houghton: Everybody felt for John the year before when he missed the penalty against Wimbledon so I was absolutely delighted that, so early on in the game, he got that opportunity to make amends. Once John was through you just knew he was going to score. It was a clinical piece of finishing.

Ian Rush: In the last 20 minutes I came on for Aldo and Everton scored a lucky goal in the last minute. You're thinking, 'What's going on?'

Ray Houghton: Bruce didn't have much to do during the 90 minutes but we took our eye off it for one moment and paid the price.

Ian Rush: Fortunately, I then scored to put us 2-1 up. It was the one that broke Dixie Dean's Merseyside derby goalscoring record, although I didn't realise until afterwards when somebody told me. That was great for me but they went back down and scored again.

Ray Houghton: Give Everton credit, they got themselves back in it with another Stuart McCall goal to make it 2-2 but our third goal, the winning goal, was a fabulous header from Rushie and the ball in from John Barnes was as good a cross as you will see.

Ian Rush: Only John Barnes could have put the ball in there. He's looked up and actually bent the ball around the defenders. It came at me medium height and my first reaction was to control it then shoot. I was never the most powerful header of the ball so I just got direction on it. To score another two against Everton in the FA Cup final was a brilliant feeling but, at the time, it was just about giving something back to the supporters.

Ray Houghton: Everton must have been sick of the sight of Rushie, given all the goals he scored against them. That one just knocked the stuffing out of their players. They'd come back twice but you just thought they are not going to do it for a third time.

Steve McMahon: I'm glad we won it. But having said that, if Everton had won the FA Cup, I think we'd have just been happy for the cup to be brought back to Merseyside. I think that was important, it was Merseyside united and in the face of adversity came a wonderful, wonderful cup final. That was for all those families that suffered.

Ronnie Whelan: When you're a kid growing up I watched the FA Cup final every year, up early and watched it all through the day until the captain went up to collect the cup. All of a sudden there I was, leading all those great players up the steps. It was a huge moment for me. One I'll never forget.

Steve Nicol: The triumph was made so much more special because of the Hillsborough tragedy. If somebody said to me that I was only able to win one trophy during my time at Liverpool – and I would have to give the rest of my medals back – then the FA Cup final in 1989 would be that trophy. It's the one I cherish the most.

Kenny Dalglish: It was the best. Even now, the Hillsborough Cup final was the trophy that meant most in my career, above even the European Cup. This trophy was for the 95 [later to become 96] who had died and for their families, who bore the tragedy with such dignity. It cannot have been easy for the relatives who travelled to Wembley, feeling the sadness amid the celebrations, knowing their loved one would have been there to see Ronnie lift the cup.

Ray Houghton: We wanted to share it with the Liverpool fans and the Liverpool public, including the Everton fans because they had also made it such a special day. They wanted to be there and pay their respects to the people who died and I think they done that extremely well. It was such a special occasion.

It's up for grabs now...

Liverpool v Arsenal
Anfield
Football League Division One
26 May 1989

Kenny Dalglish: Privately, I was deeply unhappy about Liverpool being ordered to play on that Friday. The fixture had been scheduled for several weeks earlier, but the fixtures had been rescheduled and re-ordered after Hillsborough. I understood Liverpool-Arsenal offered the perfect showdown, a dream for ITV, but it was unfair on us. The League and ITV contributed to Liverpool losing the double because they made our run-in too difficult. The lads were magnificent but there's only so much the human body can take. We were shattered by Hillsborough and by the intense demands of an unforgiving final week.

John Aldridge: It was a strange affair. We could actually afford to lose 1-0 to Arsenal and still win the league. After what we'd gone through as a team after Hillsborough... we'd fought our corner and got our season back on track, won the FA Cup and now had a chance of doing the double. I don't want to make excuses but I think if perhaps we needed to get a result, a draw or a win, we'd have probably won it. We didn't know whether to go and attack or to defend and in the end we did neither.

Ronnie Whelan: We were never sent out to play cautiously and we weren't that night against Arsenal either. But maybe it was the unspoken thought in the back of our minds; we don't need to win here, a draw will do. Maybe that thought infected our minds in some way, without us even knowing.

Kenny Dalglish: Sensing their exhaustion, I urged the players to take the game to Arsenal, knowing a goal would kill them off. The heart was willing but I feared the legs might be weak. The game unfolded in a blur and, looking back, it's still like peering into the mist.

Steve McMahon: It would have been better if we'd have needed to win the game, 1-0 or 2-0, because we'd have done that. The problem was we could afford to get beat and subconsciously you tend to take your foot off the gas. We didn't play our natural game that night. I know that and we weren't told to play that way. But where I would normally go for a forward run I found myself holding back, thinking there was no need to. And it was the same with the other lads. We just froze a bit on the night, if you like. We didn't do ourselves justice at all.

John Barnes: We just didn't play our normal game and the fact that we could afford to lose meant that even after they scored the first goal, we thought, 'Oh well'.

John Aldridge: Rushie went off in the first half, which was unfortunate because we'd been enjoying a good run of form together. I believe if he'd have stayed on then one of us would have scored but as it was we ran out of steam.

Ronnie Whelan: There was nothing left in the tank. I know I was running on empty. I was plodding along, trying and trying to get into the game, but nothing was getting me there. And once they scored after half-time they had all the momentum and we couldn't raise a gallop. Just contain them and maybe catch them on the counter. And we nearly, nearly, nearly made it. We were seconds away.

Steve McMahon: I was trying to rally the troops by saying, 'Look we've only got one minute to go in the season'. We stood on the brink of another famous double and just one last effort was needed.

Kenny Dalglish: What I recall most about Arsenal's decisive second goal was the criticism of John Barnes for trying to take the ball past Kevin Richardson and losing it. I resented this condemnation of Digger. Why shouldn't John attempt to go past Richardson, who was hobbling? John had been racing past people for fun at Liverpool, and I'd never slam anybody for expressing themselves – that's what I bought Digger for in the first place.

Steve McMahon: Nine times out of ten Barnesy keeps that ball by the corner flag. We'd normally give him the ball and he'd keep hold of it for a couple of minutes, he was that strong and that good. On this one occasion he tries to cross it when he should have kept it, or got a free-kick or thrown-in out of it. He never, we lost the ball and they went down the other end to score.

John Barnes: Ninety-two minutes on the clock and we thought that that was it. I don't think we would have been particularly happy winning [the league] having lost 1-0, but nevertheless it was better than losing 2-0 and losing the league. But the game was winding down to nothing. I think Arsenal had even thought that we had won it, and they were going to take some credit from the fact that they had beaten us 1-0 and that they'd only lost by winning 1-0 at Anfield. So I don't even think that they could believe it.

Ronnie Whelan: And then Mickey T goes and makes a name for himself! I could see it happening as it unfolded, almost in slow-motion. The ball going through the middle, Michael Thomas running on to it, Bruce coming out, Ray sprinting to get back.

Steve Nicol: [Alan] Smith plays the ball over to Michael Thomas. He miscontrols it. It hits me. Then it hits him again and falls right into his path. By this stage none of us can get to him in time. He shoots, He scores. Game over. Title lost on goals scored.

Ronnie Whelan: It was a difficult chance to take and I was thinking Bruce would get a block on it or Ray would get the tackle in or Thomas would take a bad touch. So much could have gone wrong with that chance. I couldn't believe it when the ball hit the net. Could not believe it. You're seeing something right in front of your eyes but you're not taking it in.

Ray Houghton: I can still see it now, Mickey Thomas charging through. And I always think to myself, why didn't I just bring him down? I should have done. There was a split second when I could have brought him down. I'd have given away a penalty but what's to say they'd have scored it? I've got a picture at home that shows how close I was to him and to this day I wish I'd have brought him down, and I said that to him when he later joined the club. It was so disappointing. And still is.

John Barnes: By playing the way we did, we left ourselves open to the sucker-punch and when that happens in the 92nd minute there's no chance of coming back from it. I happen to believe that had they scored their second with half an hour to go then we would have come back, but there was no chance of us coming back after that.

Steve Nicol: Sometimes in life you just don't have any say over what happens. Only someone above decides that. The ricochet off him could have gone anywhere. I was where I should have been. Big Al was where he should have been. Gary [Ablett] was where he should have been. The football gods decided that was the way it was going to end.

Steve McMahon: It was just unreal. It just flashed before you, the goal. It was like, 'Nah, is this really happening?'

Kenny Dalglish: I once watched a clip of that Michael Thomas goal and heard that great commentator Brian Moore say, 'Dalglish just stands there'. I did. The shock froze me to the spot. I was numb, the fuel gauge showing empty as dejection set in.

Steve Nicol: When referee David Hutchinson blew his whistle 38 seconds after the restart to signal the end of the game we were numb. Totally numb. I can't remember what I did in the immediate aftermath but I do remember the Liverpool fans staying behind and, after showing their appreciation for us, applauding Arsenal when they were presented with the championship trophy. Of course, they were hurting too, really hurting, but I don't think another set of supporters in the world would have shown the class that the Kop and the rest of Anfield showed that night.

John Aldridge: The way we lost it was heart-rending. It was just one game too much I think. Everything took its toll. We looked shattered on the night. We were so tired.

Steve McMahon: The season dragged on for obvious reasons and I think it was one step too far if truth be known, what with all the emotion of what had gone on in the weeks before. It was very sad. It hurts me. It hurts me so much.

Ronnie Whelan: For me, the hurt really started to seep in over the next few weeks. To have it taken away from you like that, in the last seconds of the season. The Arsenal lads deserve every credit in the world for going to Anfield and taking the title from under our noses. It took serious bottle to do that. It's a legendary game now, but it still hurts and always will.

Kenny Dalglish: When people talk about that remarkable match at Anfield as an epic moment in the history of football, I struggle to feel any pride or pleasure. I just feel pain. Doing the double would have been a fairy-tale, an unbelievable achievement after what Liverpool had endured.

Paradise lost

1990-1999

The big change

Following a long period of success, the harrowing events of the late 1980s were to take a toll during what was to be a turbulent last decade of the twentieth century. Cracks would soon appear in the once impregnable Anfield empire. But first, there was one last title.

Happy eighteenth

1989/90

Ray Houghton: I think the lads were still hurting after what happened with Hillsborough the season before, and I'm not so sure that everyone had recovered. Typical of the players though, they responded to adversity. We'd lost out on the league the previous season and that wasn't good enough. We had to rectify things and that's what we done. Once again, we came out on top, there was a demand for it at Liverpool. First is everything and anything else didn't matter.

Gary Gillespie: That's what it was all about at Liverpool at the time. You have a setback, you get knocked down a little bit, and it is how you bounce back. Liverpool always tended to have that ability to do that. That was kind of ingrained in you. In the eight years that I was there, I can't recall finishing lower than second, we either won the league or were runners-up. In its own right that's quite a good record to have. But I think it gives you impetus and ambition to do better than what you did the last season.

Jan Molby: It was kind of a strange season in the fact that previously we always had very settled teams – you could name the one to eleven – but in 89/90 a lot of different players played, so you wouldn't be able to say bang, that was the team. There seemed to be a lot of changes. There were a lot of injuries and a lot of people came in. Beardsley played some games but not others. Kenny had this thing about Ray Houghton and Peter Beardsley not playing in some of the away games. In the end we had enough quality, really good players who were maybe not at the top of their game like they used to be, but who still had the knowledge.

Ronnie Whelan: In 1989/90 we went back one more time for the league title. But I don't think we ever quite touched the heights of 1987/88. We won it with nine points to spare over Aston Villa and we still played some devastating football along the way. But we weren't as consistent. There was a lot of chopping and changing at the back and we didn't find our groove until December. We went on a long unbeaten run then and just when we needed an extra push in the final furlong, up stepped the bold Ronnie Rosenthal. Ronnie appeared out of the blue and smashed a hat-trick against Charlton.

Ronny Rosenthal: Kenny was disappointed with Peter Beardsley and told me an hour before the game I'd be playing. After 10 minutes, I scored with my right foot, then again immediately after half-time with my left and finally with my head after combining with John Barnes. The perfect hat-trick, I believe they call it. Yes, an incredible feeling. And I've still got the ball upstairs.

Kenny Dalglish: When we began slowing up a bit, with injuries, I brought in Ronny Rosenthal. Ronny gave us momentum. He had five starts, three appearances as sub and seven goals. That was a very good return which helped to win us the championship.

Ronnie Whelan: Talk about a hot streak! Ronny scored seven in the last seven games and the man became a cult hero at Anfield forever.

Ronny Rosenthal: I was one of the most expensive foreign players to join an English club from abroad at the time. The fee did not bring unreasonable pressure. I think I gave back to Liverpool what they paid. When I analyse my career, I would admit that I was not a prolific goalscorer. But I was someone who could change the game at any time.

Steve McMahon: Again it just showed the character of the players and the squad we had to bounce back after such a horrendous season. But it showed what we were all about. Winning the league is magnificent, there's no better feeling.

Steve Staunton: I don't remember any special celebrations. It was typical Liverpool. Ronnie Moran came in with a box of medals and said, 'If you've played more than 12 games, take a medal. Make sure you're ready for next season because it's going to be a lot fucking harder'.

Ronny Rosenthal: We had some champagne and there was a bit of singing. But there was not a night of massive celebration. We had a meal with our families. Hey, we were expected to win. Had I known then that it was going to be Liverpool's last title, I would have made more of it.

Kenny quits

22 February 1991

Kenny Dalglish: Against Everton in that famous 4-4 fifth round replay, I was the only person at Goodison that night who knew it was my last match. Before the game, I lay on my hotel bed and decided that I had to get out. The alternative was going mad. I promised myself that I would inform Noel White and Peter Robinson of my decision at our usual meeting the following morning. Irrespective of the outcome against Liverpool's oldest rivals, I was going to tell them that I was resigning the next day. I could either keep my job or my sanity. I had to go.

Ronnie Moran: We were due to play Luton away on the Saturday and I'm sat at home on the Thursday night when the phone goes. It was Kenny and he was upset. He said, 'I've packed in'. I didn't believe him. I knew he could be a practical joker so I replied, 'Come on, what do you really want?' 'No', he said. 'I've packed up, I've really packed up. I've finished. I've resigned'. I still couldn't believe what he was telling me but then he started getting a bit overcome with emotion and put the phone down. The wife asked what the matter was so I told her, fully believing that he was still taking the mickey. A couple of minutes later, the phone goes again. It was Mr White, the chairman then. He said, 'Kenny has packed in, we can't get him to stay on, he wants to finish and he's had enough'. And that was when I realised the seriousness of it.

Phil Thompson: It was a major shock, absolute major shock. I can remember coming in – this was when we used to get changed up at Anfield – and going into the bootroom and Ronnie and Roy were sitting there. I came in, put my keys down and was about to go out when Roy said, 'Ronnie you best tell Phil'. And I said, 'Tell me what? And he said, 'It's the boss, Kenny. He's packing in'. And I thought, 'Oh yeah', I thought it was another joke, a normal thing of a morning and he said, 'No, Phil, he's packing in'. It was a massive shock. I was very close to him because we'd been playing colleagues and got on ever so well. You could only see the club going from strength to strength with him in charge so it was very sad to see him go.

Ray Houghton: Kenny was never down. He was always lively and until the end he just wanted the club to succeed. When he resigned it was like a bolt out of the blue. He called a meeting and just said, 'I'm off'. We couldn't believe it.

Ian Rush: He kept his emotions to himself. We'd had that 4-4 draw against Everton and then before leaving for Luton we had a meeting. Kenny just came in and said he was leaving and that was it really. I think he did have a tear in his eye so he just left the dressing room and we just couldn't believe it.

John Barnes: It was very shocking, but for me particularly because the players heard about it before I actually did it. They were told at Anfield on the Friday before travelling to Luton but I'd gone straight down to Watford after the Everton game and was due to meet them. The first thing I heard about it was when I got to Luton. I was there ahead of the team and was met by all these reporters asking me questions about Kenny resigning. At first I didn't know what they were talking about. It was a big shock to me. I couldn't believe it and initially thought it was a bit of a wind-up. Only when the players arrived and they told me did it start to sink in.

Jamie Redknapp: I'll never forget it, because when he resigned, I was in tears, I was gutted. I'd come up here as a 17- year-old kid. I was back at my digs in Anfield Road when the landlady picked up the phone and said, 'There's a phone call for you.' This was the afternoon he was resigning, he had a-million-and-one things on his plate, but he found time to ring me and say, 'I'm sorry, but it was something I felt I had to do. But don't worry, you're going to be in safe hands here and I'm sure you'll be here for a long time to come'. I'll never forget that because he didn't need to ring me at all and it really meant an awful lot to me.

Gary Gillespie: We used to still go out with Kenny; myself, Alan Hansen, Steve McMahon and Ronnie Whelan, and he never really, at any stage, gave us the impression that he was ready to pack it in, which made it all the more surprising. It was a massive shock, a really big shock.

Steve McMahon: I was actually in hospital, I got injured in a game against Everton. I was having an operation. I couldn't get my breath when I heard that he had resigned. It was a devastating blow, because he had done a magnificent job. But, he did it for the right reasons. Everyone thought he had an ulterior motive, but he did it because he wasn't well. Everyone says it's the best job in the world and yes, it probably is, but your health is more important, and he felt at that moment in time, that was the right decision for him and his family so you've got to respect that.

David Speedie: I was so upset, nearly in tears to be quite honest. I got a phone call from the club, because they were picking me up on the way to Luton. I got a phone call from Kenny's secretary and she said, 'Have you heard the news?' I thought somebody had died or something, or been killed in a car crash. She goes, 'Kenny's resigned'. I was gobsmacked, I was stuck for words. It was like a death, for me, personally, because he'd bought me. He'd brought me to the club. But I could understand the reasons why Kenny did what he did.

Steve Nicol: It came out of the blue, yeah, but thinking back it shouldn't have come as that much of a surprise. Everyone was sort of a little off kilter at that time and not really where they should have been mentally. Kenny obviously wasn't. he needed a break and that's why he decided to quit. But yeah, when it happened, it was a shock, a real surprise.

Kenny Dalglish: In truth, I had wanted to leave Anfield in 1990, a year before I eventually resigned. In the 22 months between Hillsborough and my resignation, the strain kept growing until I finally snapped.

Steve McMahon: It's a build-up of pressure and that's why when these managers get paid big money, they deserve it, because you live and breathe it. It's 24/7. You take it home with you. Your family life suffers as well. It's very, very difficult.

Gary Gillespie: We obviously didn't understand the pressure and stress he was under, and maybe the players themselves should have taken a little bit of responsibility. He maybe thought we weren't doing what we should be doing and giving him what he expected. He was a perfectionist and was under pressure to maintain Liverpool's status as England's top club. Maybe our levels of professionalism were a little bit less than what he was expecting at the time.

Ian Rush: Knowing Kenny, he probably took the pressures too much. Instead of laying them off on other people, and asking other people to do it, he took them all on himself. He was good at looking after the players and if the players had any problems, Kenny Dalglish would look after them and help sort them out. Looking back now, he probably took too much on and he maybe should have helped himself a bit more, but he just wanted the club to be successful and by doing that, he put more pressure on himself.

Steve McMahon: I think over time... he maybe regretted that decision. Maybe he could have taken time out, which he was offered, take a few months break and see how he felt about it'. But he didn't do that, because he expected if he did it, then players would expect the same thing, so he decided that was the right thing to do for him and his family.

Gary Gillespie: He later told me what finally broke the camel's back for him; he was finding it difficult to make key and decisive decisions that he could previously make with ease. This inability to make these decisions in the way he wanted was probably the trigger for Kenny to step down. Knowing Kenny, he would have thought this wasn't the way forward, neither for himself nor, more importantly, for Liverpool Football Club.

Kenny Dalglish: Resigning was a decision made primarily in my best interests, but I was also thinking of Liverpool, a manager who cannot make decisions has to go. Some people could hide or con people or get others to make decisions but I couldn't do that. Not to Liverpool. I would have been glad if it had never happened, but it was inevitable, given the strains and stresses of the previous few years.

I left the club I loved out of necessity, not choice. Events and emotions had overtaken me. I was no longer in control. I said I felt my head was going to explode. That's what it really felt like. There was a feeling of intense relief throughout the afternoon before the Everton game, because I knew respite was hours away. It was like emerging from a darkened room.

Jan Molby: It's very difficult to derail a team. So when Kenny resigns it's like, 'What a shock that is and we're going to miss him, but we'll be okay, we'll rally around'. But we obviously never did – we never rallied – you kind of think something is happening that isn't happening, so the rallying that we thought was happening wasn't happening. It was almost like it was falling apart. The first league game after Kenny resigned I think we were three or four nil down at Luton, and the writing was on the wall.

Souness returns

John Barnes: Liverpool wanted someone steeped in the club's tradition so Graeme Souness returned in April 1991.

Ronnie Whelan: I thought he was exactly the manager Liverpool needed. I was thrilled he was coming back. There was no one better to take over from Kenny. We all thought the same, especially the old pros who'd soldiered with him during his playing days. He was steeped in Liverpool. He knew how the club worked. He knew how we played the game. He had five years of high-level management under his belt. He was the ideal man. This was a new era and we were going to win things. I had no doubt about it.

Graeme Souness: My spell at Anfield as a player had left me with nothing but happy memories. It was a job that I felt I had to do. Though I took it at completely the wrong time. I was blinded by my feelings for Liverpool. Since leaving Spurs as a teenager, everywhere I'd gone it was success, success, success; medal, medal, medal; trophy, trophy, trophy. I thought the pattern would continue at Liverpool. I didn't stop for a minute to think about what I was doing, to analyse the situation.

Ian Rush: I was delighted to see Graeme return, as I believed if anyone had the qualities to keep Liverpool at the top it was him. It had been seven years since Graeme had last set foot in Anfield and many of the players didn't know him. 'Don't worry, he'll be perfect', I told them.

Graeme Souness: I drove into the car park on that April day at Anfield to see many familiar faces waiting for me. That felt good – a sign of the stability which has been one of the great strengths of Liverpool over the years. I could not wait to get started. I was so excited at the prospect.

Gary Gillespie: When Graeme was appointed manager he came in and gave us a big speech. Everyone at the time thought, 'Woah, I've never heard that before and here we go, this could work'.

Peter Beardsley: Nobody would argue that he was the right choice, with his previous record as a player at Liverpool; his experience in Italian football and his achievements as manager at Glasgow Rangers. At our first team meeting after his appointment he talked about his ambitions for Liverpool. He told us he had been a success wherever he had been, and he wanted more than anything to continue that at Anfield.

Nick Tanner: I was delighted because it was a fresh start. It gave people a big kick up the arse. I used to watch him play as a kid and think, 'Fucking hell – he's a real man'. I wanted to be him. In the first few weeks, he told everyone in a meeting that he would reward effort. It was a fair day's pay for a fair day's work. It's the way it should be. You couldn't afford to be in cruise control.

Steve Nicol: In all honesty though, our former captain was returning to a club that had lost its way. I don't think he quite understood the situation we were in when he first arrived back at Anfield. What he actually inherited was a team on the decline. So it was his job to resurrect some life back into the place.

Graeme Souness: Peter Robinson spelled out the size of the task facing me once I had agreed to take over from Kenny Dalglish. He said to me, 'You do know what you're taking on don't you? We are not a good team and we don't have many great players'. Peter warned me, "This is a big, big job", and that opinion was echoed by another director, Tom Saunders. He knew his football and so when he said, 'Do you like a challenge? Because you have certainly got one here', it was a gentle reminder that he did not expect it to be all plain sailing.

Ian Rush: Knowing Graeme, I felt he was going to stamp his own impression upon the club, but I never appreciated how different this would be. Graeme shook the club up from top to bottom. Players adapted to the new regime but results did not go particularly well.

Graeme Souness: Over the next two and a half years there were many occasions when Tom would sidle up to me and whisper, 'I told you it would be a challenge and now you know'.

A classic comeback

Liverpool v Auxerre
Anfield
UEFA Cup second round second leg
6 November 1991

Nick Tanner: We lost 2-0 over in France and everyone expected us to go out. We were terrible. Alan Hansen slated us in the press. But at Anfield, we won 3-0 and went through.

Mark Walters: That was a great night. We were 2-0 down from the first leg. It was live on TV and because of that the crowd wasn't as big as it should have been given the magnitude of the game but the atmosphere was electric.

Ian Rush: It sounded like there was a full-house; it sounded like the European ties of old.

Mike Marsh: It was fantastic, I would have loved to have played at Anfield on those great European nights of the past, when there was a full-house and singing from start to finish, but even though there was only 23,000 there on this night they could see something was happening and produced a special atmosphere.

Graeme Souness: The players felt hard done by, having lost 2-0 in the first leg, so they had the bit between their teeth.

Mike Marsh: I didn't start the first game, I was on the bench over in France. We come back with a two goal deficit but if I remember rightly we got away with murder, it could have been four or five. They played really well and we were expecting the worst when we got them back to Anfield.

Mark Walters: Not many teams had overturned a two-goal deficit in Europe and I don't think there were many people who fancied our chances so the task we faced was a very difficult one.

Mike Marsh: Ahead of the game the manager pulled me and told me that I'd be playing right-back, which was a new experience for me; I'd never played there in my life. But it all turned out well in the end, I played really well that night.

Graeme Souness: Jan Molby got an early penalty down at the Anfield Road to put us 1-0 up and that was just the start we needed. It gave everyone a lift.

Mike Marsh: Once we were awarded the penalty no-one expected Jan to miss and within five minutes of kick-off the deficit had been cut. The players played their part as well as the crowd. We played at a very good tempo, got the fans behind us right from the start and carried it through.

Mark Walters: We had a dream start with a goal after four minutes and didn't panic when it would have been easy to start pumping the ball upfield. We showed patience and got our reward.

Mike Marsh: I don't know whether it was a cross or a shot from Ray Houghton on the left-hand side. We were attacking the Anfield Road end and for some reason, maybe because I wasn't a natural defender, I found myself in an advanced position running towards the far post. As the ball came across I headed it back towards the direction it came from. I was so happy to see it go in and just remember running away waving my arms.

Ian Rush: When we got to 2-0 it was incredible. We thought, 'Come on we can do it'. You could see then that the opposition was crumbling and that was because of the supporters. They could sense that we could win the game and really it was their support that won us that game.

Mark Walters: The fans were the vital factor. The noise they created put fear on the faces of the French players. You could see it. It was nice for us to give them something to shout about.

Mike Marsh: Jan slid Mark Walters in at the Kop end, Mark's managed to get to the ball before the keeper and slotted it in. And that was us through to the next round.

Mark Walters: Luckily that chance came my way. I broke through from the middle, ran towards goal and just managed to slip the ball past the keeper. It was a great moment for myself and the team. We silenced a few of our critics that night.

Mike Marsh: It was a fantastic experience to turn it around and win 3-0. It had never happened before at Liverpool so that shows how big an achievement it was.

Graeme Souness: Considering our injuries and the four foreigners regulation the performance was immense. In terms of the silky football this club is famous for, there wasn't much of that. But in terms of grit, determination and will to win I could not have asked for more.

Nick Tanner: It was a defiant performance, really emotional. It felt like an achievement because we'd come through a fair bit of adversity. Unfortunately, Anfield was only half full that night in a period when Graeme was getting lots of abuse. So the game isn't remembered.

Graeme Souness: I remember in my office after the game, Terry Littlewood, who used to look after my office when I was there, said, 'There's someone outside to see you', so I said to him, 'Who is it?' And he said, 'It's a Frenchman and he wants to recommend a player to you'. It was Michel Platini and he said, 'Can I have a word? I've got a player for you, he's had a few problems back in France, but he'd love to come and play for Liverpool'. It turned out to be Eric Cantona, and I said, 'Well at this time, we don't exactly need any more problems'. That was one that got away most definitely.

Souness and '*that*' newspaper

The problems continued to mount for Souness and in April 1992, as he recovered from an emergency heart operation, he became embroiled in a scandal for which many Liverpool supporters have never forgiven him.... as the third anniversary of the Hillsborough disaster approached, he gave an interview to a newspaper that spread lies about the actions of Liverpool supporters on that dreadful day.

Graeme Souness: There were a series of circumstances. I agreed to have a picture taken after the FA Cup replay against Portsmouth. The game went to extra-time. I said you can only have a picture if we get through. I was in hospital with my girlfriend, who is now my wife. We had our picture taken but that was after extra-time and penalties. That picture was meant to go in [the paper] on the Tuesday but because it had gone to extra-time and penalties, it missed the deadline. So it went in on the Wednesday. The Wednesday was the anniversary of Hillsborough. The local journalist for the newspaper at the time was Mike Ellis, who was away on holiday and he was the one person who could have said to the newspaper's office, you just can't do that. So I hold my hands up. I accept I made one almighty rick. At the time I didn't realise the strength of feeling against it. When I was manager of Liverpool, there were players in my team dealing with that newspaper. There were ex-players dealing with that newspaper. My problem was that I agreed to do an exclusive with them. The thing that really killed me, and makes me sad today is that the last thing I want to do is upset any Liverpool supporter – especially the people damaged by Hillsborough – in whatever shape of form. So I hold my hands up. I'm still a Liverpool supporter. They are still my team. I can only apologise and it's something I have to live with.

A silver lining?

Liverpool v Sunderland
Wembley
FA Cup final
9 May 1992

Graeme Souness: It was just after open-heart surgery and all that went on around that. I was apprehensive I'd be badly received. We won but it's not a day I look back on and think, 'Oh, I really enjoyed that'.

Ray Houghton: That was a poor season, other than the fact that we won the FA Cup.

Ian Rush: In Graeme's first season in charge results were not too bad but, by Liverpool's previously high standards, not particularly good either, which resulted in Graeme coming in for a lot of criticism.

Dean Saunders: The injury situation was unbelievable. Nine key players had Achilles operations that years and I had nine different strike partners. But considering the turmoil it wasn't a bad season. We won the FA Cup, returned to Europe and I scored 23 goals, which I'd have taken if you'd offered me that at the start of the year.

Mark Wright: We lacked consistency in the league that year. On our day, though, we could beat anyone and that's what the cup is all about, even though it only papered over the cracks.

Jan Molby: It was very much, 'Ah here we go again, we've won a trophy'. It might not be the league, but the second biggest trophy in those days was the FA Cup, it was a big thing, we'll win the league next year. But it was great to win the FA Cup. It doesn't matter how you win in it, does it? We played only one top flight club in Aston Villa, all the other teams we drew were from the lower leagues.

Mark Wright: We were losing to Ipswich and I said to Souness, 'Get Steve McManaman on the right and get him running at them'. He tore them apart, of course, and scored the winner. The major game though was Portsmouth. At 1-0 down and not long to go we looked out of it. But all of a sudden we took our chance and we were back.

Dean Saunders: The Portsmouth semi-finals were two very close games. The replay at Villa Park was exhausting. Rob Jones had terrible cramp so I finished off covering at right-back! It went to penalties, which are bad enough, but for a place in the cup final... so tense. It should be impossible to miss shouldn't it? But try with 40,000 lunatics screaming at you. You can go to pieces and Pompey did. Liverpool's class and experience showed. I took my kick at 2-0 up. Their keeper went the wrong way and we were off to Wembley.

Steve McManaman: I'd got injured in the first semi against Portsmouth at Highbury. I watched the Villa Park replay in a pub in Liverpool, we won on penalties. I didn't think I'd be fit enough to make the final, I played a reserve game but was still wondering about Wembley.

Jan Molby: The final was against another team from Division Two but we won it. It wasn't memorable, but it was an FA Cup, and it was fantastic.

Rob Jones: Sunderland were obviously the underdogs as they were struggling in the old Second Division, but we weren't going to take anything for granted. We had an extremely tough semi-final against Portsmouth and we were expecting them to follow Pompey's example.

Ian Rush: Before the final we stayed at Sopwell House near St Albans. Graeme joined us on the Friday afternoon and we were all delighted to see him, but more delighted that he appeared to be looking well.

Graeme Souness: In a perfect world the doctor said he would rather I stay at home, but he understood how much I wanted to be at Wembley. It was the first time I had been to an FA Cup final. I never made it as a player and I wasn't going to miss it as a manager.

Mark Wright: The mere fact he turned up lifted me and I'm sure it did the rest of the team. Most of the Liverpool players in that side had won things before. There was only the likes of Rob Jones, Deano and myself who hadn't won anything, so for us it was fantastic. Everything about it was so special, as it would be for anyone doing it for the first time.

Dean Saunders: If you asked me what my most memorable moment was, it would have to be that day. Watching it still makes the hairs stand up on the back of my neck.

Steve McManaman: As a kid you dream about playing in FA Cup finals. I remember Ronnie Moran led us out because it was just after Greame Souness' heart operation.

Ronnie Moran: I knew the day before that I'd be walking them out. I'd rather it have been Graeme because he was the manager but the doctors wouldn't let him because of his recent heart operation. I walked out in my club suit but quickly got changed into a tracksuit because I couldn't jump up and down in a suit.

Michael Thomas: I always remember the nerves kicking in as we come out the dressing room then as we got to the end of the tunnel the noise and colour just hit me, as did the realisation that this is the day, the day everyone all around the world is watching. That this is massive.

Rob Jones: Surprisingly I wasn't nervous at all; just excited about representing Liverpool in a cup final like my grandad did 42 years earlier. He was in the stands that day and later told me he was an extremely proud man.

Dean Saunders: The final was the most nervous I've ever been in my life. You really don't want to mess up your part of the day with so many eyes on you. It's the only chance you're going to get. Luckily we played very well on a lovely sunny day. I think the last Sunderland player to touch the ball was in the first half!

Steve McManaman: The first half was quite evenly matched but at half-time Graeme switched me to the right wing and it was a comfortable 2-0 win in the end.

Ronnie Moran: Our passing wasn't sharp enough in the first half and give credit to Sunderland, they had a couple of chances to score. I even thought they might have had a penalty but then right on half-time we could have had one too so it evens itself out.

Rob Jones: Sunderland had the better of the first half and we wouldn't have complained if we went in at the interval behind. However, in the second half we stepped it up a gear and Michael Thomas brilliantly put us 1-0 up with a fantastically taken half volley. From my point of view his goal goes down as one of the greatest FA Cup final goals of all time.

Michael Thomas: You can't really explain that moment. That is the moment you play football for. What else can I say about it, other than it was all down to McManaman really, he did fantastic work to set me up, but to score in the final was my greatest moment, the best ever.

Steve McManaman: I never saw much of Michael's goal. There were two players on me and I knew I just had to flick the ball through before they could get in a tackle. I just aimed for the space and Michael did the rest.

Ronnie Moran: It was Steve's switch in the second half that changed the game for us. Once we got the breaks we were on our game and we never eased up because more goals are always needed before the cigars come out.

Rob Jones: Rushie then made it 2-0 and we knew the cup was ours.

Ian Rush: As the ball came to me I had my eye on the bottom corner of the net and I decided to place the ball rather than blasting it. It was a nice side-footed finish and what a feeling that was, not only did it put us firmly in the driving season but it also meant that I had scored more FA Cup final goals than anyone else.

Dean Saunders: I hit the bar with a header. It was a shame not to score but the result is the main thing. You see the other team walking off having lost and I'd have hated to have experienced that feeling after all the hard work it took getting there.

Ian Rush: When the final whistle sounded we all headed for Graeme. I was delighted he had a trophy in his first full season as manager. It had been an arduous season, particularly for him, and though winning the FA Cup was a crowning moment, the fact he was returning to health pleased me more than anything.

Graeme Souness: What I should have done is resigned after the FA Cup final both because of the mistake I'd made and because of my health. Looking at pictures of myself, I shouldn't have been there, because I was still fragile.

Rob Jones: It was a good game and the main thing was we won. To get an FA Cup winners' medal was a really proud moment, although we were actually given runners-up medals at first because there was a mistake during the presentation and the boxes had been laid out wrong!

Mark Wright: It was a boyhood dream to win the FA Cup and, to realise that dream as the captain who walks up to collect the trophy, was a real honour for me. I couldn't get up those stairs quick enough and as I did I actually tripped. It could have been embarrassing but I didn't care because I was going up to lift the FA Cup for Liverpool. As the Duchess of Kent went to hand me the cup I said to her, 'I apologise for what I'm about to say', then I turned, held the cup aloft and I think everyone knows what I shouted… let's just say it wasn't, 'Jolly good show!'

Dean Saunders: I remember Michael Thomas buying a bottle of brandy on the way home. We just stopped the coach in the middle of a street outside Wembley and he got out, went in an off license and came back with it. I didn't drink any of it.

Mark Wright: All I know is that we celebrated by drinking far too much alcohol.

Dean Saunders: I'll always be grateful for winning the FA Cup with Liverpool, but their expectations were so high you always had the sense that nothing short of winning the title was really good enough… as if everyone knew they weren't quite matching up.

A famous fightback

Liverpool v Manchester United
Anfield
Premier League
4 January 1994

Graeme Souness: It was a wonderful game. Man United were just emerging as the team who would go on to dominate for the next 10 years and they found themselves 3-0 up before we had even got started. Not that we played particularly badly, it was just that United were so hot at that time.

Neil Ruddock: United were flying at the time. They had three shots and scored with each of them. We were three down after 24 minutes and thinking, 'We can't let them score again or this could end up 8-0 or something'. It could have been so humiliating. But Cloughie scored two to pull it back to 3-2 just before half-time and that changed everything.

Nigel Clough: The game against United was special because the team came back from 3-0 down and the atmosphere at Anfield that night was so inspiring.

Graeme Souness: Once Nigel scored the first goal, I felt there was something in it for us because the history of this club shows that we are capable of coming back from anything.

Neil Ruddock: The atmosphere in that game was unbelievable. Something I'd never experienced before. And the pace of the game, that was relentless. It was end-to-end stuff.

Robbie Fowler: That was some night, an incredible game to play in when you're an 18-year old kid. The fans were baying for blood because it was United, and as each goal went in it got louder and louder, until the hairs were standing up on the back of my neck, never mind theirs.

Graeme Souness: I can remember Razor Ruddock getting a smack on the head when he equalised. It was such a brave header.

Neil Ruddock: I was only doing my job, that's what I got paid to do. I banged heads with Pallister and if I could relive that moment I'd bang my head again. Scoring that equaliser against Manchester United was one of the highlights of my time at Liverpool. It was a great comeback.

Robbie Fowler: When Razor scored at the end the roof came off. Seagulls died. It was incredible.

Ian Rush: Having been taken apart by United in the early stages, we galvanised ourselves to turn the tables and, but for the width of a post, could have achieved a remarkable victory.

Neil Ruddock: Just to get back to 3-3 after what happened at the start was great though and at the end it felt like we'd won.

Ian Rush: The press saw our performance against United as proof that Liverpool were at last starting to turn the corner under Graeme. But this was not the case.

The end for Souness

That heroic comeback against United was to offer just a brief respite for beleaguered boss Graeme Souness and, just a few weeks later, a humiliating FA Cup exit at home to Bristol City brought one of Anfield's most turbulent managerial reigns to an end.

Neil Ruddock: Brian Tinnion scored a worldie and that was the end of Souey. I was gutted for him. He brought me in and you partly feel that it was your fault.

Ian Rush: I sensed that not too many Liverpool supporters were sad to see him go. They loved Graeme as a player, but the general feeling was he hadn't cut the mustard as manager.

Ronnie Whelan: I think Souey went into the job the way he used to go into tackles, full steam ahead, not caring whether he hurt himself or anyone else. Everybody was sorry to see him go when he left as a player; I'm not so sure it was the same when he left as manager.

Graeme Souness: I lost the dressing room and that hurt me, because it started with some of the players I'd worked with and looked after as young boys. I was disappointed in a lot of people but I was far from blameless.

Bruce Grobbelaar: Souness was the best player I've ever played with – the best in the world for a time. For that, I admired him. But his skills as a manager and his judgement were questionable. For a long time, we didn't see eye to eye because of it. Maybe if he managed today, he'd be the best manager in the world as well, because now I can see that a lot of his ideas were visionary. He could see what way football was going, but the problem was he tried to change too much too soon. He always demanded instant success as a player and was intolerant of people who didn't feel the same. As a manager, when you come in, it takes patience and time to change things, but Souness was impatient.

Jamie Redknapp: The problem was, the older pros still at Liverpool from Graeme's time as a player remembered him and what he was like – someone who loved socializing, someone who was a bit of a glamour-puss. His nickname was Champagne Charlie, wasn't it? Graeme used to be one of the lads and got away with a lot – being the captain, supremely confident and strong-willed. Suddenly, he was laying down the law to people like Bruce Grobbelaar and Ronnie Whelan, who thought it was hypocritical.

Neil Ruddock: He was managing his friends. He's come back and telling his mates not to do what he used to do with them. He wanted really to do the right thing. He wanted it right now. He couldn't wait. He couldn't see the full picture. The players were talking behind his back. That's what I'd seen.

Robbie Fowler: I heard plenty of talk in the dressing room about him from some of the players – mostly the ones who had fallen out with him – but how can I say a bad word against him? He gave me my chance in football for a start, and for all this hard man approach – and he was hard, believe me – he cared about Liverpool, and he cared about those players who put it in for him.

Nick Tanner: It can be the players on the sidelines that ruin the morale of the squad. Big characters not in the team would get together over a few beers and slag everyone off. Maybe they were a little bit worried about getting back in because we trained harder and took Graeme's fitness programmes more seriously than they did. They'd argue that league titles had been won eating pie and chips. But in those times, everyone else was eating pie and chips.

John Barnes: Life was difficult for Souness. The English scene was not as simple as in Scotland. A mass turnover of players was not considered healthy practice in England. Souness got rid of too many Liverpool players too soon. All these drastic changes ran counter to Anfield's tradition of continuity, of bringing players in and phasing others out. Souness obviously felt radical steps were required and wanted his own men in.

Graeme Souness: When I arrived the team wasn't good enough and neither was the squad. There was a need for urgent reconstruction. The ability wasn't there and the attitude was bad. I oversaw three or four testimonial matches in my first two years and that shows you how old the players were and where their priorities lay.

Jan Molby: There was absolutely nothing wrong with the knowledge that Graeme had gained in Italy and in Scotland, absolutely nothing wrong with that. It was the way he approached it. Nothing wrong with having opinions about players, but you can only make changes when you're ready to make changes; he inherited a team where you still had Grobbelaar, Nicol, Hansen, Rush, Barnes, Whelan, McMahon, Beardsley, myself. I don't think those players – even at that age – would have been capable of finishing outside the top two, we might not have been good enough to win it but we weren't capable of finishing outside of the top two.

Steve Nicol: Whether it was Graeme or anybody else that took over at that particular time, we'd have found it tough. Most managers pick up a team that needs a little bit of sorting out, but Graeme walked into a club where the focus, from top to bottom, had been centred on Hillsborough and not on the football team. That would have been a tough task for anybody. And when you take over a job like that, you're expected to win the title, so it's not easy.

Mark Wright: It was a transitional period with a lot of the old guard leaving and the club adjusting to rule changes. The team that had won everything in the past were all experienced internationals and they ran Liverpool. But when we had to start from scratch it was always going to take time. I think what Souness did all those years ago was the start of the rebuilding process.

Ray Houghton: Liverpool's training, I used to call it groundhog day. Every day you could say right we're going to do this, we're going to do that. It never really changed, whereas I think when Graeme came in, Graeme wanted to do try and change it around. So there was a lot more fitness work. In pre-season we were doing a lot more longer runs, players weren't used to it. It was quite strange to go from where we were and go from what really was very, very, very successful.

Tom Saunders: People resent change, they do not take to it easily. They have to see that that change is going to benefit them and it's not easy to convince people when the change is a drastic one. It has its teething problems. Sadly in the football game you do not have a lot of time.

Graeme Souness: You are asking supporters to be patient, and this is at a time when the expectation levels are still enormous. It has to be managed. You've got a club with twenty-five years of success. The first manager in is a bringer of bad news, where he's telling players – in some cases legends – that their time is up. Nobody goes quietly.

Roy Evans: No one ever tried harder at Liverpool than Graeme. I've never seen anyone so distraught when we lost games than he was. Sometimes you would fear for him getting into his car after a game, he looked so bad.

Tom Saunders: He was an outstanding competitor as a player and couldn't possibly understand why it was that when a player put a red shirt on he did not have the same commitment as Graeme Souness had when he played. That to him was a hell of a problem.

Graeme Souness: In management, I expected my players to feel the same as me. But the world was changing. Players were expecting a shoulder to cry on. The players were holding more power than the manager. I wasn't cute enough sometimes, or political enough.

Roy Evans: What Graeme wanted was for the more senior players to behave towards the younger more inexperienced players the same way he and Kenny had done a decade or so earlier. We had this system of the older pros policing and looking after the younger ones, guiding them along and putting them straight when they needed it. That started to go a little bit and Graeme got frustrated by that.

John Barnes: I never got on with Souness. Some people thought I tried to undermine him but that was not the case. He and I didn't agree on many issues, particularly in terms of the way Liverpool played, but I never questioned him. I had to respect him as a manager. He never saw the best of me. Because of the Achilles injury I was never able to give him what he wanted. That frustrated him. I felt he didn't rate me. But everything Souness did was for the good of Liverpool.

Neil Ruddock: People can blame the manager for this and that, but at the end of the day it's down to the players to go out there and perform, and we weren't performing as well as we could of, that's for sure.

Dean Saunders: It was upsetting because Graeme loved the club and he risked everything returning to Anfield. He could have stayed at Rangers as a legend for the rest of his career.

Graeme Souness: It was the most difficult period for the club in its recent history. We managed to win the cup in my two and a half years, but my timing was all wrong. Players like Redknapp, McManaman and Fowler were waiting to flourish, but were still too young.

Mark Wright: I've got a lot of time for what Graeme did at the club. He took the bull by the horns. He knew a lot of the older players were coming to an end and he had to change it and he did. Maybe he did it too quickly, but he brought players in and he had the bottle to put the likes of Robbie Fowler and McManaman in. I think it would have been a matter of time before it clicked for him.

Mark Walters: At the end of the day you are judged on what you win so I can understand why people think differently but I thought Souness did well. He brought through a lot of great young players like Robbie Fowler and Steve McManaman, but one thing he was maybe guilty of was splitting the team up too quickly and making too many changes too soon.

Jamie Redknapp: I love Graeme, but when he came into Liverpool, he was a different Graeme to the one I now know. He was very aggressive. He was having wars with everybody when he didn't need to, really. If he had his time again, I'm sure he'd have been different with the players. He would have been a bit more relaxed. He's a legend, Graeme, and he knows it. He has an aura. He's intense. If he'd gone in there with a feather rather than a sledgehammer, he might have been more successful. He tried to take on too much too soon.

Graeme Souness: I went into Liverpool probably believing I knew everything there was to know about management because I'd been successful elsewhere. As a manager it felt like I could win everything in a rush and I'm not blaming anybody but myself, because if I did it again now, I'd do it a lot differently.

Back to the Boot Room

The departure of Souness brought about a return to the tried and trusted methods that had served the club so well in the past, with Roy Evans completing his ascent through the ranks 20 years after curtailing his playing career to join the backroom staff.

Roy Evans: I'd spoke to Graeme at the end, we played a cup tie and got beat. Graeme was obviously really upset and said he was going to leave. The day after I got a phone call off the chairman, who invited me around to his house. I had a chat with him and a couple of the directors. They offered me the job and I took it straight away.

Mark Wright: He was the only man for the job. The figurehead at Anfield.

John Barnes: The board's decision to name Roy Evans as Souness's successor did not surprise me one bit. I thought Roy could possibly have been appointed before, perhaps even as far back as 1985. When Souness went, Roy finally got it. Roy never really struck me as an obvious manager but Liverpool's board sought sanctuary in the Boot Room, hoping that a return to the principle of succession from within would restore former glories.

Ian Rush: I was delighted to see Roy take over as manager. He's been at the club since the sixties. He was very knowledgeable about the game, rational, fair-minded and had the respect of all the players. I felt the team was in good hands.

Roy Evans: On the way home in the car I thought to myself, 'What have I got myself into'. To be honest I had never really thought about being the manager before, because I would never be looking for someone else's job. It was now my time to implement everything I had learnt from Joe, Bill and Bob.

Jan Molby: I remember on the first day of training after he took over, the old coaching manuals from Shankly's time were out. And over the summer, Roy and Ronnie went through all the training sessions that had been practised and we followed the same process. Maybe I was naive but I figured that the results would get better. Most of the boys [Rush, Nicol and Whelan] were still there. Then the younger ones like McManaman, Fowler and Redknapp were making their mark. It did not feel like a terminal illness.

Roy Evans: The club was in a reasonable state. On the pitch we weren't great; we hadn't had the greatest of seasons. We weren't challenging for anything. There had been so many changes under Graeme, I wanted things to settle down and give everyone a chance to prove themselves. Maybe that was the wrong thing to do. In my mind, I knew what needed to happen. Like when every manager takes over, you always need an extra two or three players. But if I had any regrets about that time, it would be that I was probably a little bit pedestrian – I got into the job and thought well let's get it through till the end of the season in a safe way. I should have been more proactive in that first season really from day one and if I had my time again, I probably would have got rid of people sooner, bringing others in; enabling us to hit the ground running the next season.

The Kop's last stand

30 April 1994 marked the end of an era at Anfield as Liverpool entertained Norwich City in the last ever game to be played in front of the standing Kop. For once the game was of secondary importance.

Robbie Fowler: Everyone in football knows what the Kop's all about. We all knew it had to come down and what that meant for everyone, Liverpool as a club and certainly the fans who stood on it.

Ian Rush: There was an incredible atmosphere and that's probably why we lost, because we were concentrating more on the Kop than we were on the actual game! Norwich were up for it. They probably felt that this was the best time to beat Liverpool and they did beat us.

Robbie Fowler: We weren't focused on the football and as a result we lost to Norwich 1-0. I know it sounds like I'm looking for excuses as to why we didn't win but on that day the occasion – saying farewell to the Kop – took over. It was bigger and more important than the match itself.

John Barnes: I can't remember the game, no. I remember we lost 1-0 and it was disappointing because it was a big occasion, but I can't remember anything about what happened on the pitch apart from the fact that we weren't very good.

Julian Dicks: We were all disappointed in the performance against Norwich. It would have been nice to have finished off with a good performance in front of the Kop for a final time. Everyone was so buoyant on the Kop that day and we should have added to that party atmosphere by winning the game but unfortunately it just wasn't to be.

Roy Evans: It was a great goal that beat us from Norwich, but it was such a shame because it would have been nice to go out with a win, obviously for the fans and the players. To be fair to our fans, though, they turned it into a great occasion.

Ian Rush: It was incredible, flags and everything. It just goes to show how much the Kop meant to the supporters because I think they would have given anything to be in there for the last game ever in front of the standing Kop.

Robbie Fowler: All I can recall is the Kop singing throughout it and the noise that was generated. It was just a sea of people, flags, scarves and banners. It was all about people celebrating a terrace that had been such a big part of Anfield.

Roy Evans: Over the years it had been a fantastic thing. No other club had had anything like it and it was so sad to see it go.

Kenny Dalglish: Everything has to come to an end sometime and if that was the price we had to pay [to ensure safety] then so be it. The Kop will always be there and the passion generated by those on the Kop will always be the same. Sometimes in life you just have to move on and I think it moved on for the better.

Fowler: record breaker

On 28 August 1994, 19 year-old Liverpool striker Robbie Fowler set a goalscoring record that stood for over two decades when he fired three goals past Arsenal in the space of just 273 seconds.

Robbie Fowler: Arsenal at the time probably had one of the best defences in England, probably even Europe. I was a young lad playing against them and obviously I did quite well. I scored a goal and then the other two followed really, really quickly.

Jan Molby: Arsenal of that time was a very difficult team to play against. Defensively they were very strong so you tended to get very few clear cut chances against them.

Jamie Redknapp: I remember it was one of the first games of the season. Robbie was so sharp at the time but Arsenal had their famous back five; Seaman, Adams, Dixon, Keown, Bould and Winterburn. At the time they were impregnable, nobody could get past them, but Robbie just tore them to shreds, he only looked about nine at the time as well! He was so good.

Robbie Fowler: They came to Anfield on the second Sunday of the season, in front of the Sky cameras. It was a tense, tight game against one of the title favourites, then on 26 minutes Jamie Redknapp floated one into the box. Tosh [Ian Rush] got above Martin Keown and when it fell I lashed it into the corner of the net.

Steve McManaman: He found himself in the right place at the right time. Whenever anything fell in the box, whether it was a ricochet or whatever, nine times out ten Robbie would be there. And if that happens to be in the six-yard box then there's only place the ball is going to end up and that's in the back of the net.

Robbie Fowler: Three minutes later Macca rolled one across to me, I beat Keown and put it right into the far corner through Lee Dixon's legs. Even I was impressed with that one. The whole place was in uproar.

Steve McManaman: Number two was a different type of goal. There wasn't a lot of power but there didn't need to be. It was accurate, as most of Robbie's shots generally were. His first two goals suddenly opened the game up for us because until then it had been a very close.

Robbie Fowler: For the hat-trick, Barnesy sent me through. The shot was saved by David Seaman, but I was the only one left standing and I put it into the empty net from a tight angle.

Steve McManaman: His hat-trick goal was a strange one to some extent. He needed a huge amount of composure, a huge amount of patience and some class. I think it took a ricochet or two, then he had the ball on the by-line and there wasn't much space to squeeze it in. Even though it was for his hat-trick, he didn't slash his boot at the ball. In a high-pressure situation he remained ice-cool. He knew what he needed to do and where it had to go.

Robbie Fowler: A hat-trick in four minutes and 33 seconds, the fastest in Liverpool history, in Premiership history and the quickest since the war. All that against the legendary Arsenal back four. That was a great achievement, one that will live with me forever. I guess that hat-trick cemented me in the public eye and it was around then that the *God* nickname began to stick.

The McManaman final

Liverpool v Bolton Wanderers
Wembley
Coca-Cola Cup final
2 April 1995

David James: The Coca-Cola Cup final in 1995 represented a great day for everyone at the club as we won our first trophy under the management of Roy Evans.

Roy Evans: We had a really good bunch of lads, including a lot of young players. They were obviously really excited going into the game and they fulfilled that on the pitch. Happy memories.

John Scales: I was determined to enjoy that moment at Wembley. It's always important to win silverware, especially with the heritage and tradition Liverpool has.

Rob Jones: The League Cup is seen as a trophy that isn't as important as others but it was important for us at that time. We were a young squad and we were in our first full season under Roy. It had been three years since the FA Cup triumph against Sunderland and that was regarded as a real drought for Liverpool Football Club.

David James: Bolton provided tough opposition on the day and it certainly wasn't an easy game for us. We were obviously, and rightly, the favourites going into the match but we knew anything could happen in a one-off encounter and we had to be professional. Our preparation was good and thankfully our performance on the day was enough to earn us victory.

Steve McManaman: We went into the game under a little bit of pressure because Bolton were from a lower division. We'd had a tough run to the final, beating some good teams along the way; the likes of Arsenal, Blackburn and Crystal Palace. Bolton was supposed to be the easiest game and we were expected to win.

Phil Babb: I just remember Steve McManaman on that day was unplayable. He was phenomenal.

Steve McManaman: I felt good throughout that game. It was a good game to play in and certainly in the position I played because there was a lot of space. We were two attacking teams who were having a real go at each other.

Roy Evans: He was always a danger Steve, because he had great energy and, for a player of his physique, he also had great strength.

John Scales: Steve is up there with the best I played with. He was a tremendous dribbler of the ball. There was a directness about him and he had unlimited levels of fitness, he'd just go and go and go.

Steve McManaman: It was a sigh of relief really when we scored the first goal. I picked up the ball fairly central. I ran towards goal and had shot. In hindsight I think the goalkeeper should maybe have stopped it but that wasn't our concern and we felt elated to go in at half-time 1-0 ahead.

Rob Jones: It was an occasion that proved Macca had arrived as a world class performer. We all knew how good he was but on that day at Wembley he was at his best and ran the show.

Roy Evans: Down at our end they had half a chance but the ball goes to Jamo who throws it out to Macca. He lays it off, runs forward and gets it back, wide left, cuts inside to go past about three or four players on his way into the box and then just side-foots it in. That's the type of goal Macca was always capable of scoring. It put us 2-0 up and in control of the game.

Steve McManaman: It was a nice goal the second one. It was about the 67th minute but it felt as though it was the last minute because the game was so stretched and it looked like everyone was out on their feet. There were only a couple of players I had to beat. When that went in we could relax a bit. I was confident the cup was ours then.

David James: At that stage we were coasting and should have killed the game off there and then, but instead Bolton attacked right away and scored with a terrific shot from Thompson. I didn't have a chance of saving it as it flew into the top corner of the net. From then on it was game on again and we expected to be put under pressure as Bolton were obviously going to throw men forward to get an equaliser.

Neil Ruddock: I then gave a free-kick away in the last minute right on the edge of the box. I was thinking, 'Oh no, please don't score'. Thompson had a great left foot. He stepped up to take it and, thankfully, put it over the bar. I just remember the whistle going soon after and I was in tears.

Roy Evans: It was a bit nervous towards the end and when the final whistle went the feeling was one of relief at first then excitement. It was a pleasure to win that day, not just for myself but for the players, staff and the supporters.

David James: In the end we deserved to climb the Wembley steps to collect the trophy. It was a good team performance overall, but naturally Steve McManaman earned the man-of-the-match award as a result of his two goals.

Steve McManaman: Obviously it was great to score two goals and get the man-of-the-match award off someone like Stanley Matthews. He said a lot of nice things about my performance and that was very special. I think I played better games for Liverpool really, but a lot of people say that was one of my best.

Phil Babb: For me, to play my first cup final at the old Wembley and win some silverware was magnificent. I mean, that's what you want to go to a big club for and it happened in such a short space of time.

Robbie Fowler: I remember getting my medal then seeing my dad in the crowd so I made a beeline for him. I've showed him the medal and he's gone, 'I'll keep hold of that'. So he's put it in his pocket. I thought okay, fair enough. It wasn't until a few days later that my dad told me he nearly lost it. Because when he was going out of the stadium, people had seen me give him the medal and people wanted to see it. So my dad's opened the box and tried to show them, but as he's opened the box, the medal's fell out, and honest to god it's gone an inch away from the grid. So my first medal nearly went into the sewers!

Steve McManaman: Everything about Wembley was special so to get there and lift a trophy was the pinnacle, without a shadow of a doubt. Playing for Liverpool is based on success so when you win something, regardless of what it is it's the greatest feeling in the world.

John Scales: You win a final and you feel proud. But it was our ambition to win leagues and FA Cups. No way did we feel it was an achievement that put us back to where we wanted to be at. It was satisfying but it wasn't enough.

Roy Evans: People may look on it as only being the Coca-Cola Cup but, at the end of the day, it's still a nice trophy to win. The first one you win is always important and to win it for the club I'd supported all my life made it extra special. It was also a great way to celebrate my first full year in management. We had high hopes of going on to better things and it's just a pity we didn't go on to win the next one really.

The Premier League's greatest game

Liverpool v Newcastle United
Anfield
Premier League
3 April 1996

Roy Evans: It was a great game. Nobody knew which way that was going to go, it was backwards and forwards, great goals and great football. Obviously the crowd were right on the edge of their seats. Everybody on our bench and the Newcastle bench were the same. It was a great advert for football, the way it was played. End-to-end stuff, with some magic moments.

Jamie Redknapp: We played 3-5-2 and that system really suited us. You could tell it was going to be organised chaos from the first whistle. We made the perfect start and if you look back at that goal, you will see it was total football. David James played it out to John Scales, we kept moving it forward and I switched it wide to Rob Jones, who cushioned it to Stan Collymore. His cross to Robbie Fowler was just sensational and the finish was what you would expect of Robbie. There wasn't a better striker around at that time. Honestly, that goal was as good as you could wish to see.

Robbie Fowler: That game was typical of the rivalry we had with Newcastle. We'd played them twice that season and lost both times, once in the league and the other in the League Cup. We were both committed to playing proper football and there was never a chance it was going to finish 1-0.

Stan Collymore: It was a fantastic game and I just remember everybody, all 22 players on that pitch, having a really good game that night. I think that's what made it so special.

Roy Evans: To be fair, it was kamikaze defending. Managers would be dead within six months if every game was like that.

Stan Collymore: I've never been allowed to forget the winning goal; that made it 4-3. It was at the very end. I've seen the footage with Martin Tyler's commentary about a million times now. The ball got passed around in midfield. I was actually out of camera shot. Way out on the left hand side of the 18-yard box and it was like, 'Barnes to Rush, Rush to Barnes', and it came to Digger and he saw me coming in on the left hand side and played the ball across.

John Barnes: I had changed position at that point in my career and was playing central midfield, while Jamie, Stan, Robbie and Stevie Mac did all the attacking. At the end of that game, though, I'd got a bit fed up of how it had turned into a basketball game. I told that to Rob Lee and he said the same. We'd been running our balls off just to get the ball forward so I decided to join the party. I played a one-two with Ian Rush and wasn't expecting him to give it back to me. I thought he was going to pass to Stan. I knew he was free, so when Rushie gave me the ball I was ready to give it to Stan as I could see him steaming forward. That's the only reason it looked like I had eyes in the side of my head! Still, it was some finish.

Stan Collymore: I remember I just had one touch to steady myself and then just hit it. As a striker, really, you're taught to shoot across the goal, but I hit it that hard, it went past the keeper as soon as I hit it.

Roy Evans: It was a good goal from Stan. He came in from the left hand side and smashed it in. One of the great moments.

Stan Collymore: I just ran off, I remember running off and pulling some strange faces just past the Kop. Then I remember the whistle going, the flags in the Kop and the relief, because we needed to win if we had any chance of staying in the title race.

Robbie Fowler: There was an old man in the Newcastle end who looked close to tears at the final whistle. I couldn't help but feel so sorry for him. It genuinely could have gone either way. It was unforgettable. But, sadly, it didn't take us to the title.

Roy Evans: Elation, disbelief, so much had gone on in that game it was mind-boggling. To win it, you go away feeling fantastic, obviously. I did feel a little bit sorry for Kevin though because that result was a big blow to their own title aspirations.

Stan Collymore: I think everybody watching remembers Kevin Keegan draped over the advertising board. He got another couple of grey hairs that night.

White suits

The 1996 FA Cup final was one to forget. As a spectacle, it was one of the worst in living memory. Liverpool lost 1-0 to Manchester United in a game no-one deserved to win and the main talking point to this day remains the player's pre-match attire.

John Barnes: They had nothing to do with me. At the age I was then I wanted nothing other than a nice sensible grey or blue suit but I was out voted. People who say it was my decision are trying to pass the buck. I can tell you now I would not have voted for cream suits or those ray band sunglasses. There were some other people involved in that.

Ian Rush: Jamie Redknapp, David James and Neil Ruddock were all involved in choosing those suits. They were only young at the time and in hindsight I think the older players in the squad like myself should have perhaps had a word. They were excited at going to an FA Cup final for the first time but we did stand out a mile in those suits. I don't think any of us have got them now.

Jamie Redknapp: I don't laugh about it to be honest. I don't find it that funny, it's a bit embarrassing really but that's life isn't it? People have tried to blame certain players for it but we done things as a team. I don't think we realised just how bad the suits were until the day.

David James: Let me put the record straight, the suits were not my idea. We were having the discussion and someone said, 'Jamo, you know Giorgio Armani', so I got them a phone number and that was as far as my involvement went. Armani brought in the colour swatches and the club captain was in charge of FA Cup attire. Personally, I was so excited about going to the cup final I would have gone in a plastic bag. Saying that, I did think the white suits looked good and I maintain to this day that had we won we would have been known as the best-dressed FA Cup winners ever.

Robbie Fowler: A lot has been made about the cream suits but if we had won the game then they'd have been the best suits in the world. It was not one specific player who wanted the cream suits. It was a collective thing. Obviously, it was a mistake. We should have just wore a black suit but that's easy to say in hindsight.

Steve McManaman: Oh yeah, the cream suits. Admittedly you look back and realise perhaps it was wrong, gave off the wrong message, but it was immaterial. It doesn't matter what suit you wear, it's what you do when you pull on the shirt that matters. We didn't play well enough on the day and that's why we lost. Simple as that.

Jamie Redknapp: If knew then what we know now then I'm sure we would have just worn our normal club suits or something similar. If we'd have won that game no one would have cared about the white suits. They'd still be in fashion today. I'd have probably have worn mine out! The fact is we didn't and we ended up with egg on our face. We looked like ice-cream men.

David James: On the day of the final everything is different to a normal match, your usual rhythm is all messed up. You get there early to walk around on the pitch and wave to friends and family. With the history between the Liverpool and Man United boys I remember there being a stand-off and none of the players spoke to each other. Then we lost - a late Eric Cantona goal from a corner we shouldn't have conceded.

John Barnes: The biggest disappointment for me was the performance because it was a bad performance. It was a bad cup final. Manchester United didn't outplay us, in fact I don't think they played particularly well. It was a game between two good sides, both of whom didn't play well. Unfortunately for us Manchester United won. If we had won playing badly then, of course, it would have been fine. We'd have won the cup and people would then have only remembered the poor performance of Manchester United.

Rob Jones: United had just clinched the title so all the spotlight was upon us to deliver. The game itself turned out to be awful and we failed to recreate the type of performance that had seen us outplay United home and away earlier in the season. One goal was always going to win it and unfortunately for us they got it through Cantona's volley.

Steve McManaman: Some people forget we'd played a lot of good football that season as well. Losing to them was a massive personal disappointment. Eric Cantona's goal has been shown so many times, a very scrappy goal that we should have defended far better.

Rob Jones: I was actually on the goal line and didn't react in time. When I watch the slow motion replay back now, I always expect myself to chest the ball to safety or to get my leg to it. The only real option I had to keep the ball from hitting the back of the net was to handle it, which would have resulted in them being awarded a penalty, myself an early shower and left us relying on David James to save the spot kick. It's easy to analyse it now. It all happened in a split second and sadly I was unable to prevent them from scoring and ultimately from winning the cup.

David James: Losing that FA Cup final, against Manchester United in 1996, was the most profoundly depressing experience I have ever had. When I came off the field I remember being in shock. We had been expected to win. A whole summer stretched before us with nothing to look forward to. At least when you lose a game in the league there's another one along in a week - you can refocus. I spent that summer with my head up my arse. I couldn't accept it was only a game. All I could think was, 'Why didn't I?', 'Why didn't we?'

Jamie Redknapp: It was a shit final. United were shit. But we were shit too. It was a terrible game. The football was poor. Maybe the pressure got to everyone. Gary Neville. said years later that Alex Ferguson didn't need to do a team talk after he saw our suits. He claimed that Fergie told them to target crosses into the box because Jamo would be too busy focusing on waving to the Armani people in the stands. Fuck off. That's rubbish. You were shit, we were shit, you nicked it. If Jamo catches that corner, Cantona doesn't volley it in. It wasn't as if we were diabolical. It should have gone to a replay.

David James: You get your runners-up medal and then you're supposed to do a lap of honour for the fans. Well I got to the halfway line and went in. I was fuming. That evening a few of the lads went out on the town, but I couldn't. I just sat in my hotel room. I couldn't understand how anybody could go out after something like that. The next day we had to do this open-top bus tour of Liverpool and it was awful - everyone on the bus was miserable.

Spice Boys

John Barnes: Robbie and Macca, Jamie and David, Stan and Jason McAteer all had the Spice Boy label loaded onto them. The Spice Boys criticism was purely down to the players not being successful. The press thought the reason Liverpool were not winning trophies was because the players were going out modelling all the time. It made good headlines but it was unfair. Accusations of not caring about Liverpool, of being obsessed only with money, women and modelling, were far from the truth.

Jason McAteer: Well football at the time... It had gone through this lull, hadn't it? And then all the money had been ploughed in. Sky came along and the Premier League kicked off. The next thing, footballers were like film stars, and everyone wanted to be a footballer, and we become very, very accessible to the media.

Robbie Fowler: I just think it's a stupid tag, and we as players would never ever call ourselves it. I knew a few players went into London and socialised, but we done everything properly. We trained right, we went out and played games properly.

Jason McAteer: Magazines wanted to fill pages so they'd want to do interviews. Years before, apart from George Best, no one was really bothered about footballers, especially what they did outside of football. But all of a sudden, we became personalities, and people wanted to know what we were doing. We were young, and we weren't doing anything we shouldn't have been doing, People just wanted to know what our lives were about.

Phil Babb: It was a name made up by tabloid hacks just to get sensationalism. If you think about what they were trying to attach it to: yes, we were young. Yes, we had good lifestyles. Some lads were doing modelling; some lads were going out with glamorous girlfriends. But it was nothing that lads weren't doing at Liverpool in the 1980s and even 70s; Keegan with his Brut advert, and stuff like that. It's nothing new but because Sky had just come on the scene and the exposure surrounding footballer's was getting bigger, it was an easy tag to label with us.

Mark Wright: Firstly, every player takes football seriously, but I must admit I couldn't agree with the modelling contracts and players flying off to Rome to do Armani shoots. Players should have fun, of course they should, but there should only be one focus and that should be football. They represented a new generation of young players though.

Roy Evans: Listen. You can call them Spice Boys or whatever you want, but when they played football matches, they wanted to win. Yes, some of them started doing bits and pieces, adverts, modelling and so on, but it wasn't a problem. The attitude was always good when it came to the game. We had a great set of lads here and, if anything, the social life they had helped keep the togetherness of the team. It didn't affect the performance on the pitch. We had a no drink rule after Wednesday when the team was announced and they respected that.

Neil Ruddock: We did sometimes party too much but we'd never drink two days before a game before a game.

Phil Babb: We worked hard and we played hard. We had a very, very tight group. We went out together socially and there were no bad eggs in the group. I don't think that tag hindered us

Jason McAteer: When you're winning trophies you can justify going for a night out. When you're winning trophies and you're winning leagues, you can justify maybe going out with somebody who's in the public eye or being caught out on the town.

Robbie Fowler: It was a tag that the media come up with and it just stuck, rightly or wrongly. You're always going to get that. If a team that is not as successful as it should be, I think you're always leaving yourself open to that little bit of criticism.

Phil Babb: We were close, but Man U were winning trophies, winning European Cups, etc. Those boys had just as fruitful a lifestyle as we did, but we just got tagged.

Steve McManaman: It was a media invention, a load of garbage in reality. It was very insulting to the players and most of all Roy Evans, who I always respected. Obviously you had some lads modelling and things like that, but football always came first. To suggest otherwise is a terrible slur.

Evo's entertainers: the nearly men

Under Roy Evans, Liverpool played a brand of football that won them many admirers. Frustratingly though, it brought little silverware.

Roy Evans: They had great ability. But did we fulfil our promise? Probably not. On our day we were as good as anybody but our day didn't come quite often enough. We got caught out too many times believing we could attack any team and outscore them. It was my choice to go that way. Attacking was our strength. Just look at the players we had.

Robbie Fowler: I love Roy Evans. I've played under some unbelievable managers, and although Roy maybe didn't have the tactical nous of some, to me he was better because he gave us freedom to go out there and play the way we wanted to play. His ethos was more on what we could do as opposed to what the opposition could do. We went out there and played the best we could, and, at times, no team could stop us. I loved the fact that he trusted us and it made me want to go out there and perform that little bit better. His man-management skills for me were superior to the other managers.

Jason McAteer: We were a very, very attacking team, especially with Macca, because the system that Roy wanted to play gave Macca this free role, and he was the best dribbler of his generation, Steve McManaman. If we could get the ball to him we would always have a chance. Robbie Fowler was the most gifted striker of his generation. You've got experience with John Barnes, you've got me down one flank, you've got Rob Jones down the other. It was just a matter of when we were going to gel and we did, we gelled very, very quickly attacking wise. Maybe defensively we were caught.

John Scales: Roy chopped and changed it a lot. I played in a back three alongside Neil Ruddock, Phil Babb, Mark Wright, Dominic Matteo and Steve Harkness. Then on the flanks there was Stig Bjørnebye, Jason McAteer and Rob Jones. Every week, it was a different combination. I felt that we were never allowed to settle. It's no wonder there was an inconsistency, especially at set pieces, when your responsibilities change depending on who you are playing with. You look at the stats and it worked pretty well, but not well enough.

Phil Babb: But back then we had Rob Jones, arguably one of the best full-backs in England at the time, Stig was a flying left-back or left wing-back, so we had the tools to play that system, with me and Scalesy marking as central defenders, and then Neil Ruddock sort of sweeping behind. With Razor's range of passing, it worked. It certainly let the boys in front of us express themselves.

Jason McAteer: This is not detrimental to the lads who played in them positons because everyone's a defender when you haven't got the ball, and maybe at times we could have done better. Maybe concentration lapsed in certain players and as a team, as a unit, concentration maybe wasn't what it should have been and we lost games that we should have easily won. We lost titles and cups because of it.

John Scales: It is sad because Roy is the nicest fella you'll ever meet. But unfortunately, in my opinion, he didn't have the respect or gravitas that he needed to meet the expectations of the club just when football was changing. I think it frustrated Ronnie Moran, who was the opposite of Roy in terms of temperament. It must have frustrated Sammy Lee and it probably frustrated Roy inwardly too. I regret it. We missed a great opportunity to be something special. I honestly feel that group of players could have defined the era and reclaimed the glory of the eighties.

Jason McAteer: This is the Liverpool team that should have won the league. It was there for us and we blew it, all on our own.

Roy Evans: The only regret I have as manager of Liverpool Football Club was not winning the Premier League. We came close in 1997, but in the end it wasn't meant to be. We suffered a couple of home defeats towards the end of the season, most notably to Coventry City, which sent us off track.

Mark Wright: We were the best side that season and we really should have won the league, a couple of things went against us and we made a couple of mistakes, but even Alex Ferguson said we were the best team that year.

Jason McAteer: Europe was no better, all promise and no delivery. We get all the way to the semi-final of the Cup Winners' Cup but when we play Paris St Germain in April, our confidence is low. We've all but conceded the title to United and Roy's plan going to France is to play our own game and try to win it. We could have gone for the draw but didn't, and we ended up losing 3-0.

Robbie Fowler: We were woeful…and there were no excuses, because we were a much better side than they were and we should have stuffed them. Of all the games under Roy Evans, that was the one we should have been ashamed of, because no one played that night and we came away embarrassed by our performance. In the second leg we battered them, and could have scored five or six, but only managed two and were out.

Jason McAteer: Maybe the game was evolving too quickly, not just for Roy but for Liverpool. Football changed so quickly. The money, the media, the TV, fitness, diet – everything. Whether Roy was up to speed with all that, I'm not sure. But he had a young team who never questioned him on anything. In the dressing room, the voices were John Barnes, Mark Wright and Rushie. Never ever did one of the young lads pipe up. Otherwise Ronnie Moran would be in your face. Roy built some team. When he left, it was reaching its peak.

Boy Wonder

As the 1996/97 season petered out, Liverpool blooded a 17-year-old striking sensation by the name of Michael Owen. The previous season he'd fired the Reds to glory in the FA Youth Cup and he didn't disappoint on his senior debut away to Wimbledon, coming off the bench to become the club's then youngest-ever goalscorer.

Michael Owen: It was a big deal making my debut. I couldn't wait. I was nervous, I was excited, I was everything you'd expect. As I ran onto the pitch a surge of self-belief ran through my veins. I believed I was better than any other player on the pitch.

Steve Heighway: He was tactically aware and technically ready. I'd worked with Michael since he was a young boy and nothing was ever going to faze him.

Jamie Carragher: He was a star-in-waiting. But to score on your debut and put your name up in lights is what top players do. And Michael didn't disappoint.

Roy Evans: As the saying goes, if you are good enough you're old enough. Michael had the right temperament to handle that step-up to the first team. He deserved his chance and I had no reservations about putting him in.

Michael Owen: Ninety per cent of football is between your ears. It's how you view it. How confident you feel and how fearless you are. I had all these things as a kid.

Jamie Carragher: As soon as he went into the team he got goals. His pace was blistering. Physically he wasn't as powerful as some of the defenders he was up against be he was so quick they couldn't get near him.

Jason McAteer: The emergence of Michael was a real bonus for Liverpool fans at that time. He played in the last two games of the season and immediately had the look of a player who was going to be around the first team for a long time.

Karl Heinz Riedle: I signed in the summer of 1997 and Roy Evans said to me, 'Karl, I have a new young talent that I want you to see'. And then, of course, I saw Michael playing in training, and I said to myself, 'This boy is not just a young talent, he is going to be a bloody great player!'

Paul Ince: Normally a young kid playing for Liverpool would get nervous but it seemed like he'd been playing for years. The quality of his finishing was unbelievable.

Michael Owen: It was just so exciting to be playing real football for a great team with great history and great fans. And to have my name sung on the Kop was just everything you dream about really.

The odd couple

Following two near title misses and an FA Cup final defeat, Roy Evans's reign in sole charge of Liverpool was over. The club's solution was to appoint Frenchman Gerard Houllier in a joint tenure. It was an ill-fated decision and the relationship would be over quickly.

Roy Evans: Back in them days only the top two clubs used to qualify for the European Cup from the English League. Therefore, the club was finding ways to get back into Europe's elite competition. Principally, the role they were looking for was a director of football. They approached John Toshack at first, as not only did he understand Liverpool Football Club but also, he had experience in Europe, where he won La Liga with Real Madrid and the Spanish Cup with Real Sociedad. John, therefore, was considered the best man for the role; however he declined, as he was only really interested in being number one. Anyway, I went away on holiday and the club met Gerard on their own without me.

Gerard Houllier: David [Moores] came to see me in Paris, along with Rick Parry and Peter Robinson. They wanted me to join Liverpool for one particular reason. They told me that the club needed to change but it also needed to rediscover the culture of winning trophies – silverware. Rick, particularly, was very clear about that.

Roy Evans: Arsène Wenger had revolutionized Arsenal, and France had just won the World Cup. It seemed like a sensible idea to get Houllier in. As the discussions went on, somebody mentioned the title of joint-manager. It was sold to me that it would be in the best interests of the club. It hadn't worked before but, the way football management was going, there were so many obstacles so maybe it would ease the pressure. I let my heart rule my head. Deep down, I knew it wasn't right.

Rick Parry: It was a genuine attempt at the time, I think, to match the old and the new. Liverpool have never been a club that believes in revolution it's always been evolution and always has a loyalty to its people. But I think being a joint leader of anything is very difficult.

Paul Ince: I loved Roy Evans. I thought he was great for the lads. When Houllier came in I didn't understand the reason behind that. I think it affected myself and the other players. Having joint managers didn't really work. You know, who do you go to? Who's making decisions? That affected us big time.

Patrik Berger: My impression was that the club accepted Roy's time was over but did not really know how to deal with it. The solution was to recruit Gerard as a joint manager. He had time to evaluate the strength of the squad and plan for the future before Roy's inevitable departure.

Roy Evans: For the first three to four months it worked well and we were top of the league. The one thing I will say about me and Gerard is that we both had the same ideas about playing football. We both wanted to play the type of football where we kept the ball on the ground and passed it. Gradually though, other things started to get in the middle and the players could probably sense that. It became difficult because we had exactly the same job. There weren't certain things that I did or certain things that Gerard did, we both did the same and I felt it became difficult. At the end of the day there can only be one boss who carries the can.

Jason McAteer: It was a very confusing period. The players did not know who to go to. I'd been dropped from the team along with Robbie [Fowler]. The usual procedure would be to go to the manager's office and speak to him. But whose office did we go to now? Roy told me that he and Houllier had agreed to speak together whenever they dropped a player. But when it came to that time, Houllier always seemed to go missing.

David Thompson: Naturally, I'd go to Roy but I feared that might piss the other fella off. The players could see it was a marriage of convenience rather than something both Roy and Houllier really wanted. It wasn't a healthy environment.

Robbie Fowler: We went every year to Norway. We'd played this Norwegian team [in a friendly]. After the game we go upstairs, get changed and all come down the lift in our jeans, shirts and jackets. Gerard Houllier is by the front door and he says, 'Where are you all going?' 'We always go out for a drink'. 'Not tonight', he said. Next minute there was a 'Bing!' The lift opened and it was Roy Evans in his suit. 'We're with him', and we go out.

Roy Evans: People would start looking at you and the players were thinking, 'Who's in charge?' We were getting mixed messages from people. I felt it was starting to get to the players. While I was still there, all of them still called me, 'Boss'. I picked the team – the final decision always fell to me. Most of the players were on my side when it got into a bit of a war towards the end. The lads who weren't in the team were always going to go with Gerard. It was messy.

Gerard Houllier: Picking the team was not the main problem. It did not work because we had different opinions on how the team should prepare and maybe how players conducted themselves. I was the hard one and Roy was the easier one. We'd put a session on and some players would say, 'Roy, I'm staying in the gym'. It didn't work. It worked at the beginning. But soon it did not.

Danny Murphy: Even if you appoint two people who are great friends and have similar views on football, to be in charge of a team, a decision still needs to be made and there will be disagreements. Everyone has different opinions on one player, never mind eleven players or sixteen players. So I can't imagine the amount of time Roy and Gerard must have spent picking a team or a squad. It must have been a nightmare. I could imagine Gérard saying, 'Let's go defensive, we'll hit them on the break'. Then Roy chipping in, 'No, let's have a go here'. It was an impossible working situation.

Roy Evans: In the end it came down to roles, responsibilities and titles. At the outset, I'd said something about not having an ego and that I'd do whatever was better for the club. It was a massive mistake. I should have been sharper or brighter than that. I wasn't strong enough to insist that he would only be a director of football. I should have said that under no circumstances can two men do the same job. The board should have known that too. It had been tried at other clubs and it hadn't worked. At the end of the day, you can sit down with your best mate and talk about football and you don't have the same opinions. There's always going to be a clash. And that's what happened.

Gerard Houllier: I went to speak to the people [directors]. I said, 'It's Roy's team'. If Liverpool still wanted me in the summer, I would come back. But Rick Parry stepped forward and made a point about how the players would feel like they were the rulers if that happened.

Rick Parry: It wasn't working as we'd hoped and we needed to move on, but it happened in a relatively dignified way and again it was a difficult time for the club and a difficult period for Gerard. He was concerned about taking sole charge partway through the season. I think he recognised that there was a major rebuilding exercise as far as the team were concerned, if we were to challenge for the honours. I wouldn't describe it as a low point as such, because that wasn't how it felt, but it was certainly a very, very challenging time.

Robbie Fowler: Rightly or wrongly, from Roy's point of view, I think he would be the first to say we did need a sole manager, because it was just never ever going to work.

Roy Evans: Because I was a supporter of the club, I realized somebody had to go. It was never going to be Gerard. It was going to be me. Yeah it was a very difficult decision. I loved the job that I had; it was fantastic. I obviously loved the club because I had been here 35 years in total and to make that decision it was very, very difficult. Regrets? Of course. Should I have stayed and fought it out? At the time I thought it was the right decision and I still have no doubts about that to this day.

Rick Parry: Ultimately one person has to be held accountable, one person has to set the style, but perhaps it was a useful experience in initiating Gerard in the first place. It would have been a lot more difficult if he would have come in on day one in sole charge. Maybe it was something the club had to go through just to convince itself that change was necessary.

Jason McAteer: I respect Roy a lot for taking himself out of the situation. He only did it because of his love for Liverpool. He could see the team, the players and the results were suffering because the joint managerial role wasn't suiting anyone. It was clear Houllier was going to stay, because he'd just been brought in by the board. So there was only one option. There was no other solution. Roy could have carried on and taken another job at the club probably, but he did the big thing with a clean break.

Phil Babb: He'd been a fantastic servant to the club and I just felt it was harsh on him. He hadn't done badly. But sometimes things just need freshening up, and that seemed to be the club's philosophy. They wanted to give him maybe a little bit of help, and ultimately bypass him and make Gerard the single manager.

Rick Parry: In fairness it was Roy's decision to go. I've always had a lot of respect for Roy and I think every Liverpool supporter has. It was typical of Roy that he came to us and said, 'Look this isn't going to work, and this isn't the right structure. Gerard is the future so it's right and proper that I should go'. That's pretty commendable because that's not an easy thing to do.

The French revolution

Suddenly, Gerard Houllier was in charge all by himself. He would be the first foreign manager in Liverpool's history. Sweeping changes were afoot.

Gerard Houllier: We changed the habits in terms of the way the team prepared and practised. We brought a different attitude to training, demanding that the players looked after themselves in terms of diet. I personally think we also signed a group of players that went on to play together for a long time: players from different countries, different leagues and different attitudes – probably more in tune with what was happening elsewhere in football. This is not a criticism of what happened previously. But sometimes you need to change to evolve.

Jason McAteer: The way Houllier was speaking, it was as if we were on the verge of relegation. It was as if we were a gang of lads on the Club 18–30 circuit. But the season before, we'd gone as close to the title as any Liverpool team had since 1990. He had an exciting group of young players at his disposal, with talent that just needed harnessing a little. But Houllier came out with loads of comments about us being technically inferior. He made out we were crap. Then he spoke of a five-year rebuilding job to make us 'contenders' again. We were 'contenders' five months earlier. He was getting his excuses in, buying himself time.

Phil Thompson: I knew the people above at the football club needed somebody to wrestle control back from the players, and it is very difficult for a manager to do that and still retain the trust of the players, so it needed to somebody else. I'd gone in there as a whirlwind, I'd gone in there to make enemies and whether that's right or not... I'd gone in there and I was playing the part of a villain, of the bad cop. I sit here and know now that I'd played the role that I'd gone to do, and I did for 12, maybe 18 months, and we succeeded in exactly that... we brought discipline back to the football club, everybody knew where they all stood. Gerard was the boss; he was the good cop, I was the bad cop.

Danny Murphy: Senior players, recognized internationals, boys like Razor Ruddock or Robbie [Fowler], were wandering out two minutes before training was due to start with a bacon sandwich in their hand. I'm sure that happened at many other training grounds. But the clubs like Arsenal and Man United – where they'd clamped down on player freedoms – were the clubs winning the trophies.

Gerard Houllier: It is a very difficult decision to get rid of the captain. In the long term, it proved to be an important call. Why? When I got rid of Paul Ince, then Steven Gerrard, Michael Owen, Jamie Carragher, Danny Murphy and David Thompson, they all blossomed. Paul was a huge player and a fantastic player. I liked him a lot. He was captain of the national team and captain of Liverpool. Why did I get rid of him? Because I felt the other younger players needed to be able to breathe. Paul was the organizer of the social occasions. There were parties, not just ones arranged by him. I wanted this to stop and for the players to focus.

Paul Ince: I loved it at Liverpool. We had a great team spirit and camaraderie. We knew we were getting close and just felt we needed three or four new players in to make it happen. I thought I was pivotal to that so to find out I was leaving after just two years was a huge wrench for me.

David James: It was such a turbulent time and a lot of players suffered. I don't know how Ince's relationship was with Houllier but I knew mine was not the best. He had very different plans for Liverpool to what Roy Evans did.

David Thompson: I'd been brought up by managers that had preached the 'Liverpool way'. Houllier was different. Steve Heighway had always taught us to prepare properly and drill our own game plan: let the opposition worry about us. Suddenly, this manager comes in and he's worried about the opposition. I was thinking, 'We've got fantastic players here, I'm not used to not going forward'. Instead, we were camping out and parking the bus.

Erik Meijer: Gerard was very demanding. He was very French, very difficult to figure out. I never knew what he was really thinking. Yet he had strict rules. Hard. Tactically, he was very clever, always looking for the right mixture in the team.

Phil Babb: Gerard soon brought in his own players and ultimately got rid of some of the stronger characters in the dressing room; the likes of Ince, McManaman, myself and eventually Fowler. He wanted to impart his own influence on it, which he did.

Phil Thompson: I remember Gerard said to me, 'Phil we need a new, big, tall, commanding centre back'. And I said, 'No Gerard, you're wrong – we need two'. He agreed and we got Stephen Henchoz and Sami Hyypia who, for a couple of years, were one of the best defensive pairings in the Premier League. They were good signings. We made other good signings. And some bad ones too, which people will always level at us.

Gerard Houllier: We signed players for the long term: Hyypia, Henchoz, Hamann. We used young British players. I think the best way is to leave behind a way of thinking and put the club one step forward, where everybody contributes. Because of your style, your management and your personality, you can leave an imprint on the club. We improved Anfield, we built a different Melwood and, as David Moores said, we took Liverpool into the twenty-first century. The players we had were not all old at the same time.

Jason McAteer: A huge rebuilding job wasn't necessary. There was no need to go and spend nearly £100 million on foreign players and get rid of the young internationals Liverpool had on their books. Under Houllier, the promotion from within all but stopped. He tried to solve all problems with a chequebook.

Danny Murphy: Because Houllier signed a lot of foreign players at the beginning, there was a perception on the outside that Liverpool's soul was being stripped away. There's no doubt the setting of standards was helped by the signing of foreign players like Sami Hyypia, Markus Babbel, and Didi Hamann to a degree. But the heartbeat of the team was English: Stevie, Carra, Michael, myself, Robbie, Jamie Redknapp and Emile Heskey.

Jamie Carragher: I think I was always going to work well with Houllier because, although I liked a night out with my mates, he didn't have to make me train better. I'd always trained well and he loved me from day one because of that. Maybe it wasn't the case with other players. There's no doubt, though, that Houllier came at the right time. He was all over me. I was a bit-part player under Roy Evans but as soon as Houllier arrived I was in. He was talking to me all of the time and one of the first things he did was sort out a new contract for me with Rick Parry. He'd only been there a month. I think he loved my aggression and intensity compared to the others. He probably thought, 'He's someone I can work with and improve'.

Gerard Houllier: I would say Carragher progressed. I would say Murphy became a better player. I had to put him on loan at Crewe to learn a different way and come back with different values. Michael [Owen] became Ballon d'Or. Hyypia – nobody knew him before. And Heskey, nobody believed in him but I did. If he had had more belief in himself, he could have achieved more. Sometimes you do not succeed absolutely with everybody. Robbie [Fowler] had some good times and bad times.

Danny Murphy: Houllier gave a couple of lads a lot of opportunities to change, possibly more than other managers would have. Now they might say, 'Danny Murphy – well, he's agreeing with Houllier because he played him'. But there has to be some framework of discipline at a club. If a manager keeps allowing someone to step outside it – even if it's for daft things like turning up late – the indiscipline spreads quickly. Houllier was a fair man. There comes a tipping point. I disagree with some people who might claim they were pushed out of the door unfairly. They were pushed out of the door for a reason.

Jamie Carragher: Houllier was massive on the team. Nobody would stop him creating a spirit. He used to do this thing with pencils to emphasize his point. He'd get one pencil and snap it. Then he'd get eleven pencils and say, 'Try to snap that'. You couldn't. The strength of eleven pencils was greater than one.

Phil Thompson: He was incredible, because he was so knowledgeable. He may not have had a proper footballing background in terms of playing at a high level but, watching and listening to him, you'd never have known. Initially, the players were probably looking at him and thinking, 'Does he really know the game'. But his coaching drills were absolutely fantastic, he tried to make them entertaining and different. I thought that was quite fascinating how somebody could be so be worldly wise in the game of football having not actually played at a high level.

Jamie Carragher: His team meetings were unbelievable. I'd never seen anything like it before. I was in awe of him. Even someone like Gary McAllister, who was thirty-six, said he'd never seen a manager speak with so much passion. Before every season he'd do a big presentation, mapping out what he wanted to happen, explaining his values. It wasn't done by PowerPoint. It was a really aggressive, rousing speech. Jamie Redknapp didn't get on great with Houllier. But I always remember him saying that if Liverpool had had Houllier in the mid-nineties, they'd probably have won the league and wrestled back the initiative from United.

Stevie G

November 1998

Just weeks into the sole managerial reign of Gerard Houllier, a new hero emerged from Liverpool's academy. Steven Gerrard was his name. He was only 18 but destined for stardom.

Gerard Houllier: Steve Heighway asked me to watch a game at the academy. I wanted a right winger and he thought he may have had the answer. However, in the middle of the park there was a player who was very lean but who was very aggressive, running from box to box, shouting at players. He was playing like a natural leader. He was also quick, good on the ball and his touch was brilliant. I said to Steve Heighway, 'I don't know who he is but if he belongs to Liverpool Football Club then he needs to start training with us at Melwood tomorrow'.

Jamie Redknapp: I can remember we were having a full 11-aside practise match one day but were a couple of players short so these two young lads from the academy came over, one of being Steven Gerrard. The match got underway and I passed this ball to him. Normally a youngster would just give it straight back so you can play the next pass. But he received the ball and just hit this 40-yard diagonal pass straight to someone's feet. There was a different noise to it. It was like a ping. And I just thought, 'Who is this kid? Who is he?' Then, about two minutes later, he's gone in for a 50-50 with Paul Ince and cleaned him out. I just thought, 'This guy's got it all'.

Steven Gerrard: It all happened so quick. I moved from the academy to Melwood along with Stephen Wright and began training full-time with the first team. It was all just unreal. Eventually we started travelling with the squad. There were a few injuries and then suspensions after Paul Ince and Steve McManaman had been sent off in a European game. That gave me my break.

Gerard Houllier: He needed to strengthen and fill his body out but he was ready. Even at a young age he was a true competitor. To succeed at the top level you need to work hard, have great desire, obvious talent and great game intelligence. He had all that.

Steven Gerrard: Within a couple of weeks of training at Melwood, I was named as a sub for the home game with Blackburn and the feeling that ran through my body when I was told I was going on for the last couple of minutes is something I've only experienced two or three times in my career. The first time is always so special, even if I wasn't on for that long. I came on late in the second half and I remember being anxious to impress in those first few minutes so I tried to just kept things simple. I made a few passes that were short and safe, but also over-hit a couple of crosses. I was running on adrenaline and trying too hard to make an impact.

Jamie Carragher: When he first came into the squad a lot of the first team players wouldn't have known much about him. Like with all top players who come through the ranks they'd have heard his name mentioned but that's all really. So when he first came up to Melwood he was a little bit shy but in no way was he inhibited. He was very driven and focussed on the pitch. He knew what he wanted to do and always stood out.

Steven Gerrard: When I first broke into the side I was sitting next to the likes of Stephen Wright, Davey Thompson and Danny Murphy who, like me, were squad players trying to break into the starting eleven. I remember being very nervous, but excited at the same time. I was also very respectful of the big names and personalities in that dressing room. It could be an intimidating place so I used to keep myself to myself, just watch, learn and take everything in. I only spoke when I was spoken to really and just hoped that my performances on the pitch would be good enough to ensure that I was invited back into the dressing room again and again.

Jamie Carragher: Although I was a bit older than him, I'd known for years that he was a special talent but it was not until he broke into the first team that it became apparent to everyone that he was going to be a really special player.

Steven Gerrard: It was just a great feeling to know that I'd played for Liverpool's first team and achieved the first part of my dream. I thought about all the hard work that had gone before, all the sacrifices I had to make; the times on the street when your mates are up to no good and trying to get you to stay out. Just to get to this stage had been one hell of a journey. The pressure had been intense. Everyone had been talking. 'Would I make it, would I not?' so in that respect, it was almost a relief to have got my debut out of the way. The ball was rolling, I was a professional footballer, playing for Liverpool. I had a future and if I did things right I knew it could have been a big one.

Back among the elite

2000-2009

Restoring past glories

The new millennium brought fresh hope for Liverpool Football Club and its supporters. After a turbulent decade the Reds were playing catch-up but a brighter future beckoned.

Cup treble

2000/01

Gerard Houllier: I knew one day we would win some trophies but I didn't think we would win three in the same season. You need to have a vision. That vision was not a dream. Just a target. I would say aim for the moon and land among the stars.

Gary McAllister: Within the dressing room we all felt that we could win a cup. We sensed that we were good enough players to go on and win something. There were other teams ahead of us in terms of winning the championship, but Liverpool must always be capable of competing for honours. The fans demand that.

Jamie Carragher: At the start of the season, you've got 38 Premier League games, your two domestic cup competitions and we were in the UEFA Cup as well. You never imagine that you'll play every game, somewhere along the line you think you're going to lose at least one cup tie. But that season, when we won the trophies, we played every game we possibly could. 63 games in total and I played 58 of them.

Steven Gerrard: I didn't realise we would do quite as well as we did in 2000/01, a season that became defined by, 'The Treble', but I had an inkling that we would compete at the top. It was easy to see the quality we had in every position, but Gerard Houllier underpinned that by the mentality he was creating.

Jamie Carragher: It wasn't the easiest side on the eye. I know Houllier used to get upset with that, pointing out that we'd scored 127 goals in the 2001/01 season. He should have embraced it and celebrated the fact we were resolute. We loved going to places in Europe, playing shite football, drawing 0-0 or winning 1-0. When we were at our best, we could go anywhere and do a job. It didn't matter who the opposition was.

Gary McAllister: The set-up meant that we were made for cup competitions. Liverpool were criticised under Gerard for the counter-attacking style of play, but it could win us matches. He was very precise, very measured. You did your job, in your part of the pitch. Be careful; don't get caught in case they break. I was used as a more defensive midfield player whilst my mind-set was to get forward and support the attack. In our team the two wide men were the most offensive of the midfielders. The two central guys were asked to sit back. It worked though.

Jamie Carragher: If you looked at that Liverpool team without knowing who was in charge, you'd probably think it was a British manager. The size and power; we had four centre-backs in defence. Babbel played right-back and had been a centre-half at Bayern Munich and I was at left-back and I later developed into an established centre-back at Liverpool. Babbel got forward more than me but I certainly wasn't a flying full-back. Then you had Hamman in the centre of the park along with Stevie. Heskey was a big lad too and up front he helped it tick. Deep down, Houllier must have known he'd created a bit of a monster.

Dietmar Hamann: It put Liverpool back on the map. Gerard Houllier did a great job bringing a lot of foreign players in, we also had a lot of homegrown talent and we gelled very quickly.

Michael Owen: I had my best season that year when we won all those trophies – five in the calendar year – it was a time when trophies were scarce around Merseyside so yes it was a fabulous year.

Steven Gerrard: It was a dream season for myself personally and also the club. I think you realise when you're older how difficult it is to win just one trophy, so to do three in one year is some achievement.

Jamie Carragher: I rank it higher, in terms of achievement, than maybe winning the Champions League. The Champions League will always be the greatest moment but every year someone wins the Champions League. How often do you see one team win three cup competitions in the same season? It's unique really and certainly a fantastic memory.

Liverpool v Birmingham City
Millennium Stadium, Cardiff
Worthington Cup final
25 February 2001

Dietmar Hamann: Unlike some managers Houllier, this particular year anyway, took the League Cup seriously. I think he thought he had to get the monkey off his own back and off the back of the club by winning something and this was a real chance to do that.

Robbie Fowler: It all started so well for us. Some days you know it is going to be your day. I went onto that pitch feeling ten feet tall, leading out my hometown club into a major final, with 75,000 fans there cheering me. I knew I was going to score... I could see the keeper had strayed off his line a little and the ball bounced up at the perfect height for me to get a proper contact to smash it over his head. It was one of those that if you connect with it properly, it goes in. I knew it was in, the moment I hit it. I was turning even before it had gone in, and I was off down the touchline. I ran towards our bench and charged into the group of them standing there, all going mad.

Phil Thompson: We were cruising in the 90 minutes and should have won 3-0, but they got a last-gasp penalty that Darren Purse converted. It was incredible and we knew they would be up for it in extra time. When you listen to people from Birmingham recalling that day, it's as if they murdered us from start to finish. That is ridiculous. The result should have been put out of sight. As it was, the result was settled by penalties.

Dietmar Hamann: I was down to take the fourth penalty. By the time it came round to me we were 3-2 up. If I scored Birmingham would be up against it. Usually I will try to place a penalty. On this occasion I think I got a bit too excited and I decided to hit it as hard as I possibly could. I smashed it against the keeper. I was in danger of looking like an idiot as Birmingham pulled level with their next kick.

Jamie Carragher: People remind me about my run-up for the penalty I took in the shootout and how it must go down as the longest in history. It was sudden death but I didn't have any nerves. I knew where I wanted to put it and thankfully it went in. My Dad missed the moment, though. He left his seat because he couldn't watch. It had been a difficult game but we battled through and deserved it.

Phil Thompson: When Andrew Johnson's penalty was saved by Sander Westerveld the red army erupted and the scenes in the stadium were amazing. We were so proud to have our first trophy in the bag.

Robbie Fowler: We danced around the stadium that afternoon, relieved really that we had brought some silverware back to Anfield after a six-year gap.

Jamie Carragher: It was my first trophy with the senior Liverpool team and it was the catalyst for us to go on and win the cup treble. Gerard Houllier told us to remember how winning felt and urged us to use it as an inspiration. It was and we did.

Dietmar Hamann: It was the start of something.

Liverpool v Arsenal
Millennium Stadium, Cardiff
FA Cup final
12 May 2001

Michael Owen: I think it was one of the finest days of my footballing career. The drama of winning the FA Cup is enough, but how it was won and scoring twice in the last 10 minutes or so is what the FA Cup is all about.

Phil Thompson: You know sometimes you win games that you shouldn't do and this was one of them, it didn't matter whether it was cup final or not. I wouldn't say we played particularly well but we showed tremendous character, commitment and passion, and we never knew when we were beaten.

Jamie Carragher: It was a game we went into as slight underdogs and, to be fair, we should have lost. We got battered really. Arsenal were a level above us at that stage, as proved in the league. They were a great side then so for us to win it was incredible. It turned out to be the Michael Owen final. He got us out of jail.

Michael Owen: How we hung on to only being one down was amazing. You almost look back now and think it was fate. The thing is, at the time I was in a real good goalscoring run. Funnily enough, my boot manufacturers Umbro, just before the game gave me these special boots that I was supposed to wear in the final. I put them on two or three days before and Gerard Houllier looked at me as if to say, 'What are you doing?' He was adamant that because of the goals I'd been scoring in the weeks leading up the final I mustn't change from my old tatty boots. So, anyway, I bowed to the manager's judgement and they stayed hot for that last game.

Gerard Houllier: As soon as Michael scored the first goal I knew we would win it.

Jamie Carragher: The second goal that Michael Owen scored, I think it's something that everyone will forever remember, it's part of Liverpool's history. I'll never forget the scenes in the crowd when that winner went in. My dad was in the stands and he said people were crying and everything, so I can imagine what it would have been like. I wouldn't have minded being in that crowd, just to go a bit mad with them.

Phil Thompson: I remember one of the pundits saying it was a long hopeful ball from Patrik Berger. It was a fantastic ball! And Michael took it. His two strikes were fantastic.

Michael Owen: I'd say it was right up there, for excitement. To score a goal in an FA Cup final was a dream right from when I was a kid, so it was extra special.

Phil Thompson: It was a great day, the weather was wonderful, it was our second time down there in Cardiff and it was a fantastic occasion, it really, really was and I'll never forget the scenes at the end of the game because the goals came so late. It was wonderful.

Jamie Carragher: Before Istanbul this was the game that everyone talked to me about. It was such a great feeling for us and, of course, it was my first FA Cup winners medal – something I'd always wanted.

Michael Owen: If you went to the four corners of the world and asked what my career is best remembered for, the answer would most probably be the goal for England against Argentina in the 1998 World Cup. Not for me. It would have to be this FA Cup final. If I could relive one day again it would be that. It was just the most amazing, magical day. The heat, the stadium, the build-up – it was all brilliant, even, in a perverse kind of way, the way we got battered, was brilliant. Then, to score two in the last few minutes... it was even better than I envisaged when playing in the garden as a kid, re-enacting great moments. The feeling afterwards, lifting the trophy and the party that night, it was just amazing.

Liverpool v Alaves
Westfalenstadion, Dortmund
UEFA Cup final
16 May 2001

Gerard Houllier: The players played for history, played for immortality really because I don't think any club anywhere, not only in England, had managed to win three cups in one year.

Phil Thompson: The pundits were labelling us as boring and that it was going to be a 0-0 game with it going to penalties or whatever. As it happens we gave one of the best European finals since a certain 7-3 game in a European final [Real Madrid v Eintracht Frankfurt in 1960].

Gary McAllister: It was a game in which we started off very comfortably and it was a case of how many were we going to score in those early stages. We came out at a frightening pace and began to open them up. I thought, 'This is going to be five or six-nil', I really did because they didn't know what had hit them.

Steven Gerrard: We set off like a steam train and after Markus [Babbel] had given us an early lead, I crashed home a second goal. I played on the right in Dortmund, but with a fair amount of freedom to go where I wanted because we had Didi and Gary McAllister holding in midfield.

Phil Thompson: It was unbelievable because we started so well and everyone thought that it was going to be great and then they made a change within their team, which meant they had to come out after us and they showed what great qualities they have in their team.

Gary McAllister: All credit to Alaves, they came storming back. Tactically it was a strange game. We'd scored twice, but then they pulled one back and throughout it all, the Alaves coach was changing formations, changing tactics and that was very brave. It caught out our guys at the back.

Danny Murphy: Carra was left-back and I was left-midfield. Houllier wanted to stop Cosmin Contra, the Alaves right-back. from raiding forward. Neither me nor Carra were left-footed and neither of us really wanted to play there but Houllier knew that both of us would die trying to stop him.

Gary McAllister: It was just one of those games where I didn't want it to end because it was so enjoyable to play in. It was attack versus attack. Big flowing attacks from both sides. With half-time approaching we managed to gather our senses and we picked them off again. Michael was brought down in the box by their keeper and I scored from the penalty spot. On my run up I slipped a wee bit but, whilst the keeper got a hand to it, the power I generated saw it home.

Steven Gerrard: However, there was a pattern emerging to our appearances in finals that still holds true today. At Liverpool we seem to enjoy making life difficult for ourselves. The scoring was crazy that night. Twice we threw away two-goal leads.

Phil Thompson: Having been in control it was now 3-3. Thankfully for us the dangerous Moreno was subbed after 64 minutes while Robbie came on for Emile. These were both significant changes. Within nine minutes Robbie had put us back in front.

Robbie Fowler: To get on in a UEFA Cup final and score a goal like that, for me, it was unbelievable and I think everyone, including me, thought it was going to be the winner. My heart sank when Cruyff's header hit the back of the net. I think it was about 5 seconds before the final whistle.

Gerard Houllier: If you look at what happened after the equaliser, which came about 2 minutes before the end of the game, you could have thought we would have collapsed. We could have, but we didn't. We stood up and as soon as the extra-time started we got back into the job and tried to score a goal.

Gary McAllister: When they went down to ten men you could see that they were flagging a little bit and we were pressing and pressing and pressing. The free kick was awarded after a good run by Vladimir Smicer, who was cutting in towards the goal. My initial thoughts were, as usual with a free-kick in that sort of area, to get the ball into the danger zone and hope that one of our players get a touch.

Unfortunately for Alaves it was one of their players who got a touch. It went in at the far post and it was all smiles from us.

Jamie Carragher: After what had gone on through the game, I think we were getting a bit tired. We'd played 60-odd games then I think and the last couple of games showed that. I think we made Alaves look a very good team. They were a good team, but they shouldn't have really been competing with us. In the end we ground it out.

Gary McAllister: My initial feeling was just to go and hug all the other players coming towards me and then getting to the fans. I still, to this day, think that there were maybe two or three of our players who didn't realise it was golden goal. I know they won't admit it, but I think there were two or three of our guys who didn't really know that the game was over and that we had won.

Phil Thompson: I don't think anyone could have predicted the outcome of that game. To win it on a golden goal was unbelievable. And the jubilant on-the-field scenes after the game, were so special. The celebrations with the fans, with the players and with the staff, it was wonderful.

Rick Parry: The singing of You'll Never Walk Alone and everybody joining in epitomised Liverpool for me really. That's what this club is all about. It was obviously special and it was obviously something that will live in people's memories forever. Nobody will ever forget being there, ever. And again, to me it was absolutely fantastic because this bond with the supporters is really what separates us from other clubs. You couldn't imagine that happening readily with too many other clubs in quite the same way.

Phil Thompson: Gathering the players together to sing was unbelievable. It just came about so spontaneously.

Gary McAllister: We'd taken Liverpool's name back to the peaks of European football and had matched the occasions that I had grown up watching as an awe-inspired kid.

Steven Gerrard: To contribute at such a young age is what dreams are made of. I grew up watching tapes of all the famous Liverpool teams and players and I had it drilled into me, both on and off the pitch, 'You have to follow the history, you've got to deliver', so there was an element of relief, if you like, when we got those trophies in the bag - that you've added to this clubs great history.

Houllier's heart attack

Liverpool v Leeds United
Anfield
Premier League
13 October 2001

Gerard Houllier: It happened at half-time. If it had happened at the end of the game I would not be here now. At full-time there was unbelievable traffic around Anfield and the ambulance would not have got through. At half-time this was not the case. I was very lucky.

Phil Thompson: There is no doubt that day will remain etched in my mind forever. I knew something wasn't right. I went to the treatment room. On one bed was Emile Heskey who had been injured in the first half. On the other was Gerard looking pale and worried.

Emile Heskey: I actually got brought off at half-time, I think I had a hamstring problem. I was sitting on the doctors bed and Gerard came in. He said to the doctor that he had a pain in his chest.

Gerard Houllier: I thought I had the flu. I wanted to have some vitamins and return to the game. But Dr Waller, the club doctor, stopped me. He was very insistent. He knew. He wanted to take my blood pressure and quickly decided we should go to the hospital. After that, it was a matter of luck. There are only three cardio specialist hospitals in England and one of them is in Broadgreen, just a few miles away. The traffic meant we were there in less than ten minutes.

Phil Thompson: I ran to the dugout and sat down. It suddenly dawned on me that I was now in charge. I was trying to concentrate while worrying about Gerard. I was telling myself that it was possibly just a bit of fatigue. These were tense and hectic times for the club with those expectations still sky high after our trophy haul. Naturally the cameras were focusing on the bench with people wondering where Gerard was. Even the directors did not know what had gone on.

Dietmar Hamann: I was suspended for the game and I sat in the stands next to Michael Owen. Michael and I stayed in our seats during the break and Michael's mobile rang and he answered. As the call went on he began to look concerned. 'That was my mate', he said. 'He's watching Sky and it's just come on the telly that Gerard's ill'. At that stage we didn't know whether it was flu or food poisoning, though sure enough Gerard didn't emerge for the second half and slowly details began to emerge.

Jamie Carragher: I just noticed he wasn't on the bench in the second half. I couldn't understand why but I thought nothing of it. It was only over the next couple of days that we realised the enormity of it.

Gerard Houllier: Again there was more luck. The surgeon who usually operates on such illnesses was meant to be spending the weekend taking his daughter to Leeds. Instead, because he was tired, he stayed in Liverpool. So he was close by – a succession of lucky moments.

Phil Thompson: The specialists told us there was a massive problem with his aorta. It was incredible. Gerard's heart stopped on the operating table – he literally died. But they brought him back to life.

Gerard Houllier: The next day the team was flying out to Kiev for a Champions League match. Imagine if it had happened on the plane. I would have died.

John Arne Riise: When Phil Thompson told us, it was a big shock, but even then we didn't know how serious it was. Obviously, we then learnt more about it and at first you fear the worst but we had to keep playing. He slowly began to get better and we just tried to make his recovery easier by winning as many games as possible.

Jamie Carragher: Phil Thompson was told he would be the caretaker manager until Gerard Houllier came back. Lots of people would have thought, 'I'm the manager now and I'll do things my own way', but he just came in and everything was exactly the same as Gerard Houllier had done.

Phil Thompson: I'd seen what Gerard Houllier had been doing with team selection and in team talks, which was going to be the hardest thing I'd ever done. His team talks were immaculate, very inspiring.

Danny Murphy: He [Houllier] made you feel motivated, passionate and ready for the job in hand. A good talker. But Phil Thompson stood up to the test really well.

Fowler sold to Leeds

November 2001

Robbie Fowler: If I was honest, it was probably on and off for two years. I was hearing so many rumours that I wanted to leave, that I was going to leave and that the club didn't want me. But it was not until other clubs started showing an interest that I realised it was pointless for me to be sitting on the bench all the time. I was picking up wages for doing nothing so I wanted to come away and start afresh somewhere else. I felt I needed it to be honest because if anything I think I was maybe going a little bit stale towards the end at Liverpool.

Rick Parry: Robbie wasn't content to be – as he perceived – number three, he wanted to be playing every week, he felt it certainly wasn't enhancing his England chances. At the end of the day therefore, Robbie made it clear that he wanted to find a new opportunity, he wasn't content with the situation. That being the case it was a case of trying to put a deal together as soon as possible and a deal that benefited both parties.

Jamie Redknapp: There's always a time in a player's career when you feel that you need a change to give you that extra push. Sometimes you can be here too long and I think Robbie felt that.

Rick Parry: The deal was done and it was straightforward and it was amicable. We genuinely wished Robbie all the best and we parted on good terms, which was really how these things should be done.

Robbie Fowler: I was gutted. It had people thinking, 'Oh he's wanted to go', and things like that, but I'd been at Liverpool since I was eleven and obviously when the time comes for you to go, then it's upsetting. Obviously I didn't cry because you tend not to show people your emotions, but I felt like crying because a big part of me had been taken away. I said I wanted to go because I wanted to play first team football, but obviously deep down, I didn't want to go. It was a massive wrench to leave.

Rick Parry: Having taken the decision that it was right for Robbie to move on, and it was right for the club to get a fee, it wasn't an issue frankly that it was Leeds. We didn't mind where it was. The only thing we were worried about was Liverpool and the strength in Liverpool's team. At the end of the day Leeds was the only offer on the table, so it wasn't as if there was a great deal of choice in the matter. Of course, it was Robbie's choice, so it's not like people could say he shouldn't have been sold to a competitor. There's no way Robbie would have wanted to go to a lesser team or a second grade team, and we respect that. It was never a worry for us. I think if you've decided it was right for a player to move and he's not committing himself long term and wants to move, that's ok, you move on and you have confidence in the players that you have.

Robbie Fowler: If I could change anything, I think it would probably be my last game. It was against Sunderland at Anfield and I got brought off at half-time. We were winning 1-0 but we'd had a man sent-off. There's no way I can describe it. For me, that was horrible, the fact I didn't get to say a proper goodbye to the fans. If there was one thing I could change it would have been that.

Owen wins the Ballon d'Or

December 2001

Michael Owen: I didn't have a clue how big it was until a good few years later. I always remember Gerard Houllier saying to me, 'Do you realise what you have won? Do you realise just how big a trophy this is?' I was like, 'Yes boss, I'm so happy'. But I didn't really. I thought it was just another trophy. It's not until you read down the list of players who'd won it, that so few British players had won it and that it's now dominated by the likes of Messi and Ronaldo, that you realise just what a special trophy it is to win. It's something I am very proud of and if anyone comes around to my house the first thing they ask is if they can have a look at the Ballon'Dor. It was a huge achievement but, and I know everyone says this, football is a team game and I was just the beneficiary really of an amazingly successful year with Liverpool. Yes, I scored a fair few goals and helped Liverpool win the trophies but it was down to that team being so successful and then, sprinkled on top, the three goals for England in Munich. It was just one of those years when everything fell into place.

Houllier's return

Liverpool v AS Roma
Anfield
Champions League second group phase
19 March 2002

Gerard Houllier: As soon as I was out of intensive care, which was probably one week after my operation, I kept in touch with Phil and the staff on a regular basis. The surgeon may not have been happy with that but the club staff and my brother quickly understood that there was no point in trying to prevent me from doing so. When you care about things you give it your all, even if it is limited energy. That contact helped me to recover.

Sammy Lee: He was never away. Even during his illness, he was never away, any of the staff will tell you that. He was in constant contact with us and we'd often go to his apartment. Although people probably advised him that wasn't the best way to go about his rehabilitation he did it anyway.

Jamie Carragher: We didn't know the manager was coming back until we went down for our tea on the day of the game. And seeing him there gave everyone a lift.

John Arne Riise: We knew nothing about him coming back beforehand. It was quite a shock when we first saw him because he had changed so much, physically. Apart from that though, he looked good. He spoke to us and it gave us that extra kick to go on and play a good game.

Gerard Houllier: I knew as soon as we drew away in Barcelona that I would be back for the Roma game. I knew it would be a special night. I told the players it would be a special night and that they would be special themselves that evening. I wanted to amongst them and be close to them all of the time for this occasion.

Phil Thompson: He was ready and it was a very emotional night for him, the players and the fans. It was great for him and I was very pleased. It gave everyone a lift because Gerard inspires the players and the fans. If there was any night he was going to come back it was this one.

Gerard Houllier: Why did I come back for the Roma game without letting the press know? Because my concern was that the spotlight would be more about my comeback than the team itself and that it would act as a distraction. I didn't want to risk even one per cent loss of focus for that game. The game against Roma was something special and I always had a feeling that it would be.

Phil Thompson: When he got on the bus to go to the game you could tell the players were lifted. It made for a magical night. I just knew we wouldn't be beaten. You could feel the passion rolling around the stadium.

Jamie Carragher: In the days leading up to the match there was a lot of talk about the famous St Etienne game here in 1977 and the lads were determined to put on a show.

Steven Gerrard: We needed to win by two clear goals to remain in Europe. He would admit now that he came back too soon, but the fact he did showed the strength of the bond he had with the club. His presence helped us that night with Jari Litmanen scoring a penalty and then Emile Heskey sealing our progress.

Emile Heskey: It was very important to get the second goal. We had to get it because before that we didn't have the result we needed. It was a great cross into the box and I managed to get my head on it. It was brilliant to see the ball go in. It was a great team display.

Sammy Lee: For me, Liverpool reached a new level in that game. Both on the pitch and off the pitch. The work rate of the players was phenomenal and [Fabio] Capello said himself that he'd never seen a Liverpool team play to that tempo before. We made such quality opposition as Roma look second best to us on the night.

Jamie Carragher: They'd only lost twice all season so to beat them 2-0 and put ourselves into to the next round was superb.

Gerard Houllier: I have spoken to Fabio Capello since and he told me that when he saw me, he realised Liverpool would win. The reaction from the players was spectacular.

Sammy Lee: It was a wonderful, wonderful occasion – helped in large portions by the crowd. This crowd at Anfield know that once they get behind the team they are like a twelfth man. They really are and I can't stress that enough. We know the importance of the supporters and we believe that ours are the best. We're the real peoples club.

Phil Thompson: This was a special atmosphere only Anfield can produce. This was St Etienne part two and the fans cheered every tackle. It was one of the greatest nights in this football club's history.

Dietmar Hamann: We had the ability to win the competition that year or, at least, reach the final. We lost to Bayer Leverkusen in the quarter final after Houllier took me off. It was viewed as a controversial decision at the time because we were protecting a lead, I was a defensive player and Vladimir Smicer came on – an attacker. For me, I think that was the beginning of the end for the manager.

Falling short in the league

2001/02

Michael Owen: We'd had a great season the year before, winning all the trophies and beating a lot of top teams along the way so I remember us thinking during that summer of 2001, 'Another little push, buy one or two new players and we'll have a chance of the title'.

Gerard Houllier: We finished ahead of Manchester United and with 80 points. In the previous decade Liverpool had not finished ahead of Manchester United, so when that happens you'd expect to win the title. Unfortunately, that year Arsenal went on an incredible run.

Sami Hyypia: Arsenal were unbelievable that season. We finished with a good points tally but only finished second so ultimately it wasn't good enough. It was very disappointing because we played really well that season. Unfortunately for us, they played brilliantly.

Gary McAllister: It would have been enough to win the league in many seasons. Arsenal went and won their last 13 games to finish with 87 points and that kind of run is scary. So Gerard was very close to bringing the title to Liverpool.

Michael Owen: It's amazing, you can have such a good season, come second in the league with a really good points total yet finish the season empty-handed. It was a really big disappointment.

Steven Gerrard: After all the highs we had grown used to, the disappointment was numbing.

Jamie Carragher: Every year under Gerard we had progression and we thought, 'Right, the next step is to win the Premier League'. But we couldn't take it on and it just seemed to fall away. It was probably then that we realised we were on a bit of a decline.

Gerard Houllier: Had it not been for my illness, would Liverpool have won the league? I wish I knew for certain.

Gary McAllister: I just think that we needed to take a few more risks and that team, who had some wonderful footballers, could have taken the Premiership. If we could have found a middle ground between the expansive stuff that was played under Roy Evans and the more measured play under Gerard then we could have done it, I have no doubt about that.

Captain Stevie

In October 2003 Steven Gerrard was appointed Liverpool captain, taking over from Sami Hyypia. It was to prove an inspired decision and Gerrard went on to become the longest-serving skipper in the club's history.

Steven Gerrard: That was one of the best days of my life. At the time, I'll be honest with you, I thought maybe it was a little bit too early. I was still young, still learning and still making mistakes. I obviously dreamed of one day being the captain, but not at that age. I wasn't expecting the captaincy at all. To become the captain of one of the superpowers of Europe, which Liverpool is, at just 23, was a huge responsibility. Obviously, Gerard Houllier thought I was ready for it and a lot of the players thought I was ready for it.

Gerard Houllier: He was a natural-born leader, he had great influence and I appointed him captain at the age of 23. He was the type of player you wanted to follow. You could go to war with him. He could pull you out of difficult situations.

Sami Hyypia: Many people thought I'd be angry about this. Of course, I was disappointed but I knew what it meant to Stevie so it wasn't the end of the world for me. The captaincy is not seen as important in Finland as it is in England and whether I was captain or not didn't affect me as a player. Gerard spoke to me to explain his reasons but he didn't have to. If he [the manager] wanted Stevie to be his captain then that was up to him and I was fine with it. I remember Stevie didn't really want to face me in training that morning. He was a bit strange around me but I just said to him, 'Congratulations, you deserve it and if you ever need my help I'll be there for you'. So it was never a problem.

Steven Gerrard: That was just typical Sami Hyypia, the ultimate professional. At the time I was slightly worried and concerned it might affect my relationship with Sami. I was maybe losing a good mate and a good teammate. But, he was brilliant with me. He shook my hand and said, 'You were always going to get it one day it might as well be now and if you ever need anyone for help or advice I'm always here for you'. Sami was world class for this club since the first day he walked in and certainly like that when he had to pass the armband to me.

Jamie Carragher: And as soon as he got that captain's armband there was no way anyone was ever going to take it off him again. He was made to be Liverpool captain, because of his ability and the way he played the game, being a local lad, and the position he played – in the centre of park. He just ticked every box.

Steven Gerrard: What followed in my Liverpool career was all down to me getting the captaincy early. I'd say that from 23 to, probably, 30 I felt invincible on a football pitch. Without being big-headed I felt like I could play against anyone in the world.

We always win in Wales

Liverpool v Manchester United
Millennium Stadium, Cardiff
Worthington Cup final
2 March 2003

Michael Owen: The Millennium Stadium was a place we felt comfortable playing in. As a striker with pace, there were plenty of wide open spaces to run in to.

Jerzy Dudek: It was my first cup final for Liverpool and as the team coach approached the stadium I could not believe the number of our supporters on the streets. In the build-up to the match I had never experienced such intense hype before. I realised at that moment just how big the club is and how much it means to the fans to win trophies.

Dietmar Hamann: This was an odd one for me. Houllier had decided to play the youngsters in the earlier rounds of the competition and before the final I hadn't played a single game in the League Cup. Having got to the final though the manager was taking no chances and he wanted to put out his strongest side.

Phil Thompson: Everyone was tipping Manchester United to win. Sometimes you look at these things and enjoy the role of underdog. Our fans were anything but downbeat. They had banners throughout the Liverpool sections and we painted the place in our red and white. There were very few flags in comparison in the United areas.

Jerzy Dudek: The atmosphere was exceptional. The roof was closed due to the bad weather and that made the noise levels even louder. I thought the roof might come off when Stevie scored the first goal of the game near the end of the first half.

Steven Gerrard: There aren't many better feelings than scoring against Manchester United, especially in a major final. My goal had a bit of luck to it, taking a deflection off David Beckham and looping into the top corner. But I'll settle for that. Days like this are everything I dreamed of as a kid; winning silverware, scoring a goal and celebrating with my mates.

Danny Murphy: I remember playing on the left and Houllier told me I was playing there to help John Arne Riise out, who was up against David Beckham and Gary Neville. I did very little going forward that day but played very well defensively.

Steven Gerrard: At that time under Gerard Houllier, Liverpool had the Indian sign over United. We used to play a diamond formation in midfield, with a holding player for security and then we would end up outnumbering them in the middle. On a big pitch like Cardiff, or at Old Trafford, having more bodies in the middle helped.

Phil Thompson: They put us under pressure and I thought about an interesting comment the boss had made. Jerzy Dudek had blundered against them at Anfield earlier in the season, but Gerard said, 'He will be our saviour today'. He was to be absolutely right.

Jerzy Dudek: We knew United would come back at us though and that's exactly what happened. I had to make four important saves - one from Veron, one from Scholes and two from van Nistelrooy – before Michael ran clean through and made it 2-0. Game over – and the noise levels were deafening. Finals are all about the end-result not individual performances, but when it was announced that I was man-of-the-match it was very special for me.

Michael Owen: It gave me another happy personal memory from Cardiff and enabled us to feel that we had salvaged something from an average season, bearing in mind that expectations were at an all-time high following our second-place finish the season before.

Phil Thompson: The scenes on the final whistle were brilliant. Someone sent me a copy of the Manchester Evening News after the game in which Alex Ferguson was suggesting this cup wasn't top of their agenda. Maybe not, but when Liverpool and United meet, both clubs desperately want the right result. We got it and it was oh so sweet.

Au revoir Houllier

May 2004

Rick Parry: It certainly wasn't a knee-jerk reaction to let him go. In 2002, we were seven points off the title. In 2003, we were 19 points away and in 2004, although we came fourth and got into the Champions League, we were 30 points behind. There were more than ten defeats in each of those seasons and we had won less than half of the games. Bearing in mind it was our aspiration to be winning, or, at the very least, be contenders, to be in a position where by Christmas we were out of the running for the title was unacceptable. There was nothing to suggest that trend was going to turn.

Jamie Carragher: Towards the end, Houllier wasn't as aggressive, decisive and clinical. He wasn't himself. There were things that he wouldn't have let go a few years before. Maybe he realised he was clinging on to his job and needed people on his side. It happens to a lot of managers. When they go into a club, they know they have a certain amount of time to shape things. They can be combative. But as time passes, you probably need to be more of a politician while maintaining your integrity. Otherwise the politics of the club can drag you down. You become paranoid and lose your focus.

Steven Gerrard: Gerard did so much for Liverpool in a short space of time that maintaining those high standards becomes more difficult. Nobody takes into account that other teams improve as well and that the competition to win trophies becomes fiercer. At times, Gerard found himself under pressure and there were the inevitable whispers that he had lost the dressing room.

Jerzy Dudek: We won nothing in 2003/04 and finished fourth after a 1-1 draw against Newcastle United on the last day of the season. It was enough to qualify for the Champions League, but the writing was on the wall. A few days later, when I was on holiday, I discovered that Gerard Houllier had been sacked. Quite frankly, I wasn't surprised.

Phil Thompson: Your time at a football club is determined by your signings and results and both of these went against us.

Gerard Houllier: You have to get results and we probably got too many good results early on. It raised expectations too early. Due to our success in 2001 and when we then finished second in 2002, everyone automatically assumed we'd simply win the title in 2003. You can have regrets but what do they achieve? Sometimes you think that some of your signings didn't work out or they didn't reach the level that was expected of them or the level that they were capable of achieving but I left with far more positive pictures than regrets. I have no remorse. I regret that sometimes we were a little unfortunate at times but that happens. I know I can look myself in the mirror and honestly say that I tried my best at all times for the good of Liverpool Football Club.

Hola Rafa!

June 2004

Rafael Benitez: As I prepared to take over at Anfield I did not simply spend my time examining the squad and analysing potential signings; I had an entire language and culture to learn. I knew Liverpool Football Club was special. I did not know quite how special until I arrived. The fans were warm and welcoming from my very first day.

Rick Parry: The process was relatively straightforward. We wanted to win the league. So the first credential we looked for was someone who'd won one. There were only two people around with experience of winning the Premier League; Alex Ferguson and Arsene Wenger. Neither of them were going to come to Liverpool. So we then looked further afield, at people who had experiences of winning leagues in Germany, Italy and Spain. That brought us to Rafa Benitez. If you analysed what he'd achieved in Valencia, there were parallels with Liverpool in terms of not having the riches of the clubs they were competing with for trophies.

Jamie Carragher: When Rafa came in, it was like Houllier all over again – he took to me straight away. He'd won two La Liga titles with Valencia, a team I knew all about. I'd played against them twice and watched them loads on TV. When Rafa was appointed, I thought, 'Yes! What a team', and he was the manager of it. I was made up. It was really bold of Liverpool to go and get him.

Rick Parry: Valencia had played against us in the Champions League, as well as in pre-season, and they'd played us off the park. They were very attractive to watch, despite the limited resources. There wasn't much else to it. Rafa ticked all the boxes. He stood out.

Steven Gerrard: Within half an hour of meeting Rafa Benitez for the first time, it became apparent that Liverpool would be doing things differently and that I would have to get used to some changes as well. He requested a meeting with myself, Jamie Carragher and Michael Owen when we were out at Euro 2004 in Portugal. Straight away you could notice the difference. He was hands off and there was going to be a bit of distance between the players and the manager. It didn't matter who you were, a big player or just starting out. Everyone had to pull in the same direction. It is about results. And I was sure we could get them under Rafa.

Owen to Madrid

August 2004

Michael Owen: Myself, Carra, Stevie... we were all big mates, came through the youth set-up together and you think you are going to be at one club forever. I thought exactly the same. Then, one summer, my agent phoned me and said, 'Real Madrid are interested in signing you'. It just sent my head spinning. I was in America at the time, rooming with Carra, and I said, 'You'll never believe this...' and he was like, 'Oh my god what are you going to do? You can't go, you'll never get in the team!' Seriously though, we had a good conversation about it and I kept changing my mind. Yes, no, yes, no. One minute it was a no, then it was yes.

Steven Gerrard: Losing Michael was a huge blow for the club and also for me on a personal level. He was someone I had played alongside since we were kids at the Vernon Sangster Sports Centre just setting out on our careers. I knew his runs, exactly where he wanted the ball and I knew he was a player we would find hard to replace. Michael had one year on his contract and was more impatient than me for change. He wanted to get on in his career and found the lure of Real too hard to turn down.

Michael Owen: You can have no regrets, but I was driving to the airport and thought, 'Oh sugar'. I never wanted to leave Liverpool. That needs to be stressed. If I could have gone over for a week, put the kit on, played with all those stars in that stadium, and then come back to Liverpool I would have been happy. I thought I'd be like Rushie and come back after a year. That's what got me through. I spoke to Rick Parry and although it could never be put into a contract it was almost a sort of gentleman's handshake, if you like, that when I leave Madrid, be it in a year or two years, I'd re-sign for Liverpool. It was like, yes that's going to happen and that probably tipped the balance for me to say, 'Right, yes, I'm going to give it a bash'. I would have regretted it all my life if I'd have said no and always wondered, 'What if?'

Jamie Carragher: I'm sure if Michael could turn back the clock he would have stayed at Liverpool. Deep down, I think most footballers want to feel loved. That's more important than anything to me. If I was advising a young player, I'd tell them to think about their legacy – how you're thought of at the end of your career.

Michael Owen: I nearly did come back. I met Rafael Benitez [in 2005]. We had a secret meeting in Bruno Cheyrou's house. Everything was sorted. I'd taken a wage cut, my agent was in the room with

Rick Parry while me and Rafa were talking about how I was going to play and what we were going to do the next season. And then, Newcastle came in with a £16 million bid and Real Madrid said that unless Liverpool could match that I was going nowhere. I said to Rick Parry if you can go to £12 million, I'll call their bluff because I wanted this move so much. Fair play to Liverpool, they'd sold me for £8 million and were willing to buy me back for £10 million a year later. But that was that. I was left in an impossible situation. I had to sign for Newcastle but was hoping we could reconvene in a year or two. Of course, that never happened and it was a nightmare that I could never play for the club again. It was so close. We all wanted it to happen but circumstances dictated otherwise.

You beauty!

Liverpool v Olympiacos
Anfield
Champions League group phase
8 December 2004

With just four minutes remaining, Liverpool were seemingly on their way out of the Champions League before the knockout rounds even began. Cue an unforgettable moment of divine intervention from the club's talismanic captain.

Steven Gerrard: As the ball bounced towards me I knew that, if I got my body angle right and connected cleanly, I could score. It was still a difficult ball to hit but I caught it like a dream. As soon as it left my foot I knew it was going in because of the contact I'd made. It was as sweet as one of those golf shots where you nail it and you don't even feel it. It was a big, big goal for me and the club.

Jamie Carragher: Stevie was the type of player who was capable of producing moments in a game that take your breath away and one the greatest moments was his goal against Olympiacos – because what comes after that couldn't have happened without it.

Steven Gerrard: The goal was so important. We didn't think it was going to come. The lift and boost it gave us, to go on and achieve what we done, was massive.

Rafael Benitez: It was a massive game for us and that goal, the way it was scored and the celebrations with the fans in front of the Kop, was so special. For me it was one of the key moments in our Champions League run that season. It was the start of the belief.

Steven Gerrard: I was showered with plaudits afterwards, but without the efforts of [Florent Sinama] Pongolle and [Neil] Mellor and the rest of the team, the game would have gone long before I got involved.

Neil Mellor: I was the one who headed the ball towards Stevie. I was right behind it when it flew in. What a goal! The keeper had no chance. Just talking about that moment makes the hairs stand up on my arms.

Garcia's ghost goal

Liverpool v Chelsea
Anfield
Champions League semi-final second leg
3 May 2005

Steven Gerrard: The supporters took the atmosphere to a new level that night. Forty-five minutes before the kick-off the stadium was rocking. Probably the best atmosphere I've experienced at Anfield. The feelings I was getting inside my body were incredible.

Jamie Carragher: There was a big difference between the teams. They finished 37 points ahead of us. Eleven versus eleven they were a better team. But we had Anfield. We had the crowd. There was just something special about it and it made the hairs on the back of your neck stand up. I just remember everyone swinging their scarves. The supporters were so defiant. That's the picture I have of that night.

Luis Garcia: We were so up for it. When we played Chelsea we always wanted to press them like crazy. Really get into them and stop them getting that rhythm going. I must say, it was so much easier to press them that night because of the noise our fans made. I'm sure it affected Chelsea's players as much as it helped us.

Jamie Carragher: That was the most intense game we ever played. It was the fact that every game we played against them in Europe was so keenly fought and tight. Both the 2005 and 2007 games were terrifying. Because of the away goals rule they were so nerve-wracking and on each occasion, had they scored at Anfield we would have lost. As a defender you're thinking, we can't make one mistake here. We just can't. You focus all right but it is so draining.

Luis Garcia: It was such an amazing evening. To score against Chelsea so early was key. They were a great team but very tactical. Mourinho would have drilled them all with a game plan, but we upset that with my goal and suddenly everything was different.

Rafael Benitez: It was a goal, of that I am certain. My secretary, Sheila, told me as much after the game. She had been sitting in the section for club employees, roughly level with the goal line at the Kop end. It crossed the line, she said. I have no reason to doubt her. She was always incredibly reliable.

Luis Garcia: We will never know but for me it was in. I saw the ball cross the line. That's why I started running away to celebrate.

Steven Gerrard: Chelsea were furious – Mourinho most of all. He raged about the, 'ghost goal', returning to it repeatedly over the next ten years, but he could not change the result.

Dietmar Hamann: Even now I still get goosebumps thinking about it. For the final 15 minutes the Liverpool fans basically kept the ball out of the net – that was after they helped it in for Luis Garcia's goal too.

John Arne Riise: I remember the fourth official putting the board up for injury time and it said there were six minutes left on the clock. It was the longest six minutes in the world but the atmosphere during this time was unbelievable.

Dietmar Hamann: Those last minutes ticked by very slowly. Chelsea could still go through with just one goal, and deep into added time Eidur Gudjohnsen had the chance... It was a chance he definitely should have taken.

Jamie Carragher: I was on the line but not quite sure of my angles as it flew past me and the post. Everything stands still for a second as he pulls his foot back. No way back had he scored. So tense. For a second, my heart was in my mouth. I thought we had thrown everything away that we had worked so hard all season to achieve. When his shot whistled past the post, it was a signal that we were going to the final and, for me, it was the sign that we were going to do it.

Dietmar Hamann: Anfield erupted in a way it hadn't erupted for more than 20 years. Liverpool were back where they belonged – in the final of the Champions League. It was a truly momentous victory.

John Arne Riise: If I remember rightly, I stripped down to my underpants after the game. I gave the fans everything. That night will never be forgotten. It was unbelievable. Nobody expected us to beat Chelsea over those two games and get to the final. In the dressing room afterwards it was crazy.

The miracle of Istanbul

Liverpool v AC Milan
Ataturk Stadium, Istanbul
Champions League final
25 May 2005

Steven Gerrard: The best game I've ever played in for club and country by a million miles. The way the game happened and the way we come back. The excitement of it all, to lift the trophy above my head and the homecoming. Everything to do with that game is something that will live with me for the rest of my life. The proudest day I've ever had in a football shirt by a mile.

Jamie Carragher: For me, that's not just the greatest European Cup final of all time, it's one of the great games of all time. You think of Brazil against Italy in the 1970 World Cup final and the famous Real Madrid European Cup final and there's maybe two or three others, but Istanbul is right up there with them. To be involved in a game like that is something special and even now I have to pinch myself when I see clips of it on TV.

Steven Gerrard: AC Milan are one of the giants of European football. They were used to success, used to competing and winning the Champions League. We were underdogs on the night, they were littered with world-class players. At that stage in 2005 they probably had the best player in the world in Kaka, Maldini was still consistent as ever, Pirlo, Seedorf, Shevchenko, just world-class talent basically. We didn't really have many big stars, we just had a fantastic coach in Rafa and a well organised team that was prepared to fight like men for anything. We showed throughout the journey that no matter who we were put up against we always managed to get over the line and we did it in miracle fashion on that night.

Xabi Alonso: It wasn't our best Liverpool team, probably two years later we were better but that's football. In Germany, in Spain, America, Japan, China, Thailand and wherever... everyone remembers that game. It's part of history. It will forever be in the books. I can't really explain how it happened but we got it, we got it – for a fifth time.

Jamie Carragher: The way we'd got there, we'd kept a lot of clean sheets, you go back to the Juventus game and the semi-final with Chelsea, so we thought it might be a 1-0 victory either way. That's how we felt but, of course, that went out of the window after the first minute.

Xabi Alonso: It was a crazy night. We were so enthusiastic before the game but the first half was really hard and it was difficult going in 3-0 down at the interval.

Steven Gerrard: From the first whistle, especially until half-time we were completely dominated. It was men against boys, they were causing us endless problems and at half-time I'm thinking just keep the scoreline down, let's just try and get a bit of pride, get a bit of respect back, and try to get a goal.

Vladimir Smicer: I don't think we played that bad. They scored three good goals. I can't say we were unlucky but things just didn't go our way. Maybe we should have had a penalty when it was only 1-0, Nesta handled the ball from a Garcia shot I think. From that, they broke and scored a second. AC Milan deserved to be leading at the break, without a doubt, but I do think 3-0 was a bit harsh on us.

Sami Hyypia: I think we always had a belief that we could win it, right throughout that season, even from the group stage. After then beating some big teams and getting to the final, the belief was getting stronger. Of course, you have to keep believing even when things are not going right but by half-time at the Ataturk that belief was almost gone.

Jamie Carragher: If someone had said to me then, 'This will finish 3-0', I would have taken it. That sounds mad now that we won, but at the time I just wanted to stop the rot. I really was thinking this could finish six.

John Arne Riise: I was thinking I wanted to go home after the first half. It was horrible. I don't think we played that bad. It was just that they seemed to score with every chance they had. When you're three down at half-time in the Champions League final you think the worst but Liverpool is such a special club, one that never gives up. If we were going to lose three-nil we may as well lose six-nil. The message was to just go out and play so we went back out there really fired up. Football-wise, it turned out to be the best night of my life.

Jamie Carragher: Rafa was brilliant here. We were getting battered, everyone was panicking and two players had had to go off injured. We could have lost our heads completely but Rafa remained cool.

Rafael Benitez: At half-time we needed to do something and decided to make some changes. There is no way we could have went back out and lost by four or five goals in front of our wonderful fans. Once we started thinking and believing we could do it, anything was possible.

Djimi Traore: When we were back in the dressing room the Milan players were outside already celebrating that they were champions, celebrating the victory. That really got to us and gave us the hunger to come back at them.

Rafael Benitez: I was last in the dressing room. I didn't hear Milan celebrate but Alex Miller did. He told the players they were celebrating winning the cup. That was a good thing for us.

Luis Garcia: We were sitting in the dressing room and we could clearly hear thousands of fans singing You'll Never Walk Alone. Can you imagine how that felt? We were 3-0 down in the Champions League final and all we could hear were 45,000 people letting us know they still believed in us. We knew they had endured a long journey and made so many sacrifices to be there. It was at that point we started to believe too.

Pako Ayesteran: We couldn't change things in the first half because of the problems with Harry's injury but he [Benitez] came up with a great solution at half time. Didi started winning the second ball and that became a great help.

Jamie Carragher: The best thing the manager did that the night was bringing on The Kaiser [Didi Hamann]. What a performance from Didi. When he wasn't there in the first half Kaka caused us all the problems. We couldn't control him when he just kept breaking at our defence but Didi did. When we got the goal Milan just seemed to go.

Djimi Traore: Once we scored the first one they were scared, and they fell back. When we brought Didi on it gave us a lot of experience in midfield and it really disrupted them.

Sami Hyypia: We suddenly decided to give them a game. Six minutes in the second half changed the course of history and gave us our belief back.

Rafael Benitez: Stevie's goal, like his one against Olympiacos, was the beginning of the belief.

Steven Gerrard: I have scored better goals and come up with more eye-catching strikes, but, without doubt, this is the most important goal-scoring intervention of my entire career. I checked my initial run because John Arne Riise's first cross was blocked, then I gambled on going into the box again. What is surprising is how much space I had between Jaap Stam and Alessandro Nesta. The header was instinctive. I went for accuracy rather than power because the cross was that good.

Vladimir Smicer: When Stevie scored our first my only thought was, 'Great, at least we've given something back to the fans, something for them to cheer'. So that was good, but it was only when I scored that I thought, 'We can do this'. Of course it was the most important goal in my career. When I saw Didi receive the ball to my left I knew he was going to pass it to me so I was well aware of the situation around me. There was no-one in front of me so I had space to run in... I hit it well. I didn't score too many goals from outside the box during my career but fortunately this was one of them. It put us back in the game and gave us a chance.

Rafael Benitez: Milan were teetering, crumbling. At half-time they had been certain of victory... now they found themselves trying to hold back a red tide.

Jamie Carragher: They shit themselves then. We were right back in it. I still didn't celebrate, I was urging us all on and from that moment each and every one of us wanted the ball, we were all so up for it and you couldn't help but feel that we were going to get that third goal.

Steven Gerrard: I screamed at Milan Baros to nudge the ball into my path as I looked to burst into the area. His touch was perfect and Gennaro Gattuso put a hand on my back, pushed me off balance and sent me crashing to the floor. I wanted to take the spot-kick and for a large part of that season I was our designated penalty taker. But Rafa had a thing where he named different penalty takers for different games. He named Xabi as the penalty taker for the final before the game and while I was personally gutted, I knew Xabi was deadly. Okay, Dida saved his first attempt but when he fired the rebound into the roof of the net our comeback was complete.

Xabi Alonso: The last game in the Premier League, Stevie missed a penalty against Tottenham so Rafa said in the pre-match talk that in the case of a penalty it will be Xabi or Harry Kewell. Harry was not on the pitch so I was the one. It was my first professional penalty. I'd never taken one at Sociedad so it was my first one. There was a lot of responsibility on me. I was more tense than nervous. It was a moment that was probably going to mark the rest of my career. Unluckily I missed it but I got the rebound. It was the quickest five metres I've ever run. After scoring that third goal it seemed as though our name was on the trophy. It's a final that is in the memory of every football supporter. The greatest comeback ever.

Rafael Benitez: On the bench, we could barely believe our eyes. My staff and our substitutes streamed around me, celebrating, dancing, jumping. It had taken six minutes. Watched by the unbelieving eyes of the world, the unthinkable had happened. We had fought back from the dead.

Steven Gerrard: When we went to 3-3 there was a small little thought, creeping in, 'Is it going to be our night the way it turned round?' But even then there were still stages in that second-half where they were getting back on top and they battered us again in extra-time as well.

Jamie Carragher: We were having problems when they made some substitutions. Smicer was playing wing-back, a role he wasn't really suited to, so when Serginho came on, Stevie had to be put there. It was adrenaline that kept us going. Milan had upped their game and we were tiring. Those incredible six minutes had taken it out of us, both physically, and, more importantly, emotionally. We were hanging on with less than ten minutes to go.

Steven Gerrard: When Jerzy made that double save from Shevchenko, just before he hit it, I thought, 'goal', and I knew that would be the end of it but then when it went over the bar, I thought maybe it was going to be our day.

Jamie Carragher: When Jerzy made that save from Shevchenko I thought we would go on to win it because Shevchenko is a top striker and he put in a top performance. There was no way he was going to miss that chance. I was just waiting for the ball to hit the back of the net. When it stayed out, you begin to think these things happen for a reason. I couldn't believe that once again we were still in the game. I just grabbed Jerzy and told him I loved him. I meant it too.

Jerzy Dudek: My brother phoned me the morning after the game and asked me had I seen the match again? I said no and he said, 'You need to see it because your save from Shevchenko was the hand of the God'. I told him I didn't know how I did it.

Djimi Traore: We had so many injuries at the end of normal time and in extra-time. We were well prepared and physically ready for the game, but the tension and the mental fatigue were too much. It was a question of praying for penalties and we were desperately hanging on. We showed grit, determination and bravery. We were strong mentally.

Steven Gerrard: When you talk about last ditch tackles, putting your body on the line, fighting through the pain, digging in and showing desire when everything is against you – no-one epitomised fighting for the badge more than Jamie Carragher on that night.

Jamie Carragher: I was playing the most important game of my life, there was no way I was going to leave that pitch because of cramp.

Jerzy Dudek: Before the penalties, Carra came up to me like he was crazy - as always! He said, 'Jerzy, Jerzy - remember Bruce [Grobbelaar]. He did crazy things to put them off and you have to do the same. Dance, do anything, put them off'.

Djimi Traore: We didn't decide before the game who was going to take the penalties as we never expected it to get that far. Rafa asked all the players if they wanted to take one but I said, 'No thank you'.

Steven Gerrard: The boss asked me if I wanted to take a penalty, I said I did and he put me on fifth. I thought, 'Thanks a lot, pal', my arse was going, I was all over the place!

Jerzy Dudek: We had studied the Milan penalty takers on video and knew which way they kicked the ball but when it came to it, I dived the other way to the way I'd been instructed.

John Arne Riise: I was carrying an injury at the time which meant that I couldn't blast the penalty, which I'd normally do. I had to place it and their keeper [Dida] saved it. That was a nightmare, even though we won the cup, it still left me demoralised.

Jerzy Dudek: When Vladi scored I didn't realise if Shevchenko didn't score we had won. I just had my focus and desire to try and stop every penalty. I saw him walking up and saw the fear in his eyes. I managed to save it and I then saw Jamie and the other players running towards me and I realised it was finished... it was a beautiful moment. Everyone came to me, the kit men, the physios and it was fantastic. There was no one single hero, we were all heroes to come back from 3-0 down and to win on penalties was something special.

Jamie Carragher: When Shevchenko missed that pen, we all took off from the halfway line. There were probably 40,000 Liverpool supporters in the stadium and yet the exact place I ran to was where all my family and friends were celebrating. It was unbelievable because I honestly hadn't a clue where they were in the stadium. I went so mad that I must have had a bit of a blackout. I just crashed to the floor somewhere and I can't remember a single thing that was going on around me for a few moments. What I do remember as I was lying on the floor was that I started to cramp up again!

Steven Gerrard: Lifting the Champions League trophy above my head as the captain of my team... it's something that lives with you forever. I felt like my heart was going to come out of my chest. It was one of those adrenaline moments where you can feel your heart pumping but you can see it as well. Time just stood still really. The guy who was giving me it, he was taking too long, I just wanted to go over and grab it myself. I just wanted to get my hands on it. You get lost in the moment. It's almost like when you score a goal and you're celebrating, you look back on it and think, 'What was I doing then?' You're just lost in your emotions. As captain, it was great for me personally and I felt so lucky to be in that position. But I'm not a selfish person or a selfish player and I realised at that moment what it meant to so many other people so I lifted it for everyone really.

Jerzy Dudek: We celebrated into the night and it was magnificent. We had a few drinks, well maybe a bit more than a few!

Vladimir Smicer: I celebrated with the largest cigar you have ever seen. I went with the fans to dance in the streets. It was incredible to be with the fans. I just wanted to share with them what I felt. It was the greatest night of our lives. I didn't go to bed at all. There is no need for sleep after a night like this. I just wanted to go out on a high. The cup ended up with Stevie G in his room. His girlfriend wasn't here, so he had the cup in his bed instead.

Steven Gerrard: I slept with the cup in my hotel room. I did not want it out of my sight. When I woke up and someone took it away, I felt I had lost a part of me.

Sami Hyypia: I was so happy, the happiest I had ever been at that stage in my life. It is every footballer's dream to win the Champions League at least once and we'd done it.

Rafael Benitez: This was without doubt my biggest night in football. I was as delighted as anyone, though perhaps I was not as elaborate in my celebrations as some of the players. It is a mixture of relief – at having won when all seemed lost – and incredible pride at having achieved something you have worked so hard for, over the course of a season, over the course of a career. When you work so hard and succeed it feels even better.

Jamie Carragher: So we then had the homecoming and I think there were 750,000 to one million people on the streets. It touched everyone. Even people who weren't football fans. It's one of those moments people remember where they were. To give those people that much joy and happiness – I think that's the special thing.

Steven Gerrard: When we got home, on the bus journey around the city... I think that's when the sheer scale of what we had done really hit home. The amount of people in the city centre... I think it was about half a million, they were on top of buildings and everything. We actually couldn't move outside St George's Hall, people were banging on the side of the bus and it was shaking. That's when it hit you. I think in years to come this achievement is going to get even bigger. You'd think it would fade but because it's so big and the way the game went, it seems to be getting bigger all the time. It sends out a message to anyone competing sport-wise to never, ever, ever give up.

Gerrard's u-turn

During the summer of 2005, a dark cloud threatened to dampen the euphoria of Liverpool's remarkable Champions League triumph – inspirational captain Steven Gerrard was seemingly on his way to Chelsea.

Steven Gerrard: I was getting bad vibes and bad feelings. It was uncomfortable. I'd just lifted the Champions League, I'd contributed and helped us get there. It was probably one of the best seasons, form-wise, I'd had. Other people were getting rewarded with contracts and I had less than two years to go on mine. Maybe it was a bit of a mixture of insecurity on my behalf but I didn't feel any love from people above me at the club. That was strange considering what we'd just achieved.

Jamie Carragher: Stevie was seriously thinking about Chelsea and I'd say to him, 'Yeah but Liverpool is one of those clubs you can't walk away from'. He couldn't sign for another English club, although I think he knew that. Especially being a local player. He'd come home from Chelsea with three or four Premier League medals but when he was 40, where was he going to go for a pint or a meal in town? Nobody was going to ask him about them because Liverpool people wouldn't be interested. In fact, we'd be fuming about it.

Steven Gerrard: I wanted to stay. But I heard nothing all through June and the first few days of July. It gave Chelsea, and especially Jose Mourinho, a chance to really get into my head. I'm still not sure, all these years later, why there was no approach from Liverpool to me. There was neglect in my situation. I don't know who was to blame. Should they have offered me a contract after the Champions League final? Yes. I think so. I still feel they should have come to me in the very next week and said, 'Let's sort this out'. It would have killed off all the speculation and saved everyone a lot of heartache. My head was messed up. On July 5, I told Struan [Gerrard's agent] to issue a verbal transfer request.

Rafael Benitez: We met him that night, me, David [Moores] and Rick [Parry]. We tried, all three of us, to persuade him to think about what this meant. Steven was not taking this decision lightly. This was possibly the hardest decision of his life and it was easy to see the toll it had taken on him. I told him to go and speak to his family, to see what they wanted, to consider what leaving Liverpool meant. He said he would go away and sleep on his decision.

Steven Gerrard: I was suffocated by stress. My energy had gone, lost during all those frustrating trips in and out of Benítez' office. My head was banging. I was eating paracetamol like Smarties... It was the lowest point of my career. I broke down. Panic breakdown, complete mess... Could I hand in that Liverpool armband? Could I look the father I adore in the eye again? Could I really put on a Chelsea shirt and face Liverpool in front of the Kop?... No. No. No. I couldn't jump over the edge of the cliff. I could see the great possibilities of Chelsea, but my heart wouldn't let me leave Liverpool. Finally, my mind was made up. I'd walked through the storm. At eleven p.m., I called Struan. 'Tell Rick I want to sign', I told him. 'I want to stay'. Struan contacted Rick. 'Is that offer still available?' 'Yes'. 'Then Stevie will sign it'. Thank God it was over. My heart stopped racing and I relaxed. I put the paracetamol away. I awoke on the morning of Wednesday 6 July with a smile on my face for the first time in weeks.

Rafael Benitez: I do not know what happened with Stevie that evening. I don't know who he talked to, or what was said, or what made him change his mind. All that matters is that he did change his mind.

Jamie Carragher: When the news came through on the TV, I nearly choked on my cornflakes.

The world's end

Liverpool v Sao Paulo
Yokohama, Japan
FIFA World Club Championship final
18 December 2005

Steven Gerrard: To be crowned the best team on the planet was a huge incentive for us, more so because the great Liverpool teams of the past had always failed to get their hands on the trophy. We could have made history had we won. How we came up short I don't know. We battered Brazilian side Sao Paulo in the final but lost 1-0. We had three goals dubiously disallowed and it felt as if the officials were against us. It was a major blow. Rafa was fuming afterwards.

Rafael Benitez: We did everything we could. We hit the bar twice, through Luis Garcia and Harry Kewell. We controlled possession completely. Diego Lugano, their captain, should have been sent off for tripping up Steven as he bore down on goal. We had seventeen corners. Rogerio Ceni, their goalkeeper, saved shot after shot. Even when he couldn't, the linesman rescued them. Luis [Garcia], Sami Hyypia and Sinama [Pongolle] all saw goals ruled out for offside in the second half. I could not fault the effort of any of the players. We were by far the better team, but that would count for nothing when the final whistle blew. We would not be champions of the world.

God's return

January 2006

Robbie Fowler: Rick Parry just put the contract in front of me and I signed it. And to this day I didn't know what I was getting, and I really, really mean that. I wanted to be back at Liverpool more than anything. I went downstairs and I'm not ashamed to admit I let out the biggest shriek in the car. It was like waking up on Christmas morning when you see a present that you want. I was just so overwhelmed. I could not believe that I was playing for Liverpool again. I remember being asked what number I'd be wearing and I said, 'It's not about the name and number on the back, it's about the badge on the front'. It just came to me off the top of my head and it's since become a famous quote. I'm proud of that one. To put that red shirt on again though was just brilliant. It was quite an emotional moment. It had been my own choice to leave and I never thought I was going to get a chance to play for the greatest club again. I did and it was special.

The Gerrard final

Liverpool v West Ham United
Millennium Stadium, Cardiff
FA Cup final
13 May 2006

Jamie Carragher: Another great comeback. That's when Stevie was as good as anyone in world football. He scored two and created another. Without him, there's not a chance we'd have won that cup. It was the Gerrard final.

Steven Gerrard: I think over 90 minutes and then extra-time, it's probably the best I've played for Liverpool. I get a lot of credit for that game because I got a couple of goals and played well, but when I look back it was certainly a team effort.

Jamie Carragher: We were big favourites and fancied our chances of beating West Ham. It didn't exactly go to plan but we got over the line in the end. Of course, I scored the own goal early on, then Pepe spilled the ball and Dean Ashton scored. All kinds of things were going through our heads at this point. We'd built ourselves up to play in this cup final and suddenly, after only 20-30 minutes, we found ourselves two down.

Steven Gerrard: I remember it going pear-shaped at the beginning and the part Jamie Carragher played in that, with his own goal, really got to me because I didn't want the game to finish with him the villain. I knew what it would've done to him if it had ended like that. It wasn't all his fault though. As a team we didn't start the game well at all and I think we almost underestimated West Ham. We were expected to turn up and blow them away, but credit to them, they started the game much better than us and deservedly went ahead.

Rafael Benitez: At first, I was a little bit disappointed because we had an idea going into the game but made some mistakes and had to change things. We had confidence and knew we could do it... but it was important to get the goal before half-time.

Jamie Carragher: The thinking was we had to get one back before half-time. Cisse then scored and we're back in the game. We believed we could win it then and even more so when Stevie scored to make it 2-2.

Steven Gerrard: I think my first one, Peter Crouch has got to take a lot of credit for that. I love playing with target men, especially around that time when I was an attacking midfielder, and I used to like striking the ball from the edge of the box. Crouchy was brilliant to play off, you didn't have to shout or communicate with him. He had fantastic vision and awareness and I managed to get a lovely connection on a half volley which went into the roof of the net, I was really pleased with that one.

Jamie Carragher: Konchesky then scored what I can only describe as a freak goal. I always remember the feeling as it went in. I just thought, 'Oh no'. But Stevie was right next to me and he said, 'We've still got time to equalise'. I just didn't think he'd leave it that late.

Steven Gerrard: My second one, that was a bit of a strange goal really because I wouldn't usually try my luck from that far out at that stage of a game. That's what we were always told by our coaches, if you're chasing a game late doors don't panic and don't shoot from too far out, always go out wide to build the play and start again, be a team player. At that point though, I was so tired and exhausted. It was a warm day and I had cramp in every major muscle in my legs. I just thought sod it, I'm going to hit it as hard as I can and, thankfully, I got an unbelievable connection on the ball. I knew it had a chance of working the keeper as soon as it left my foot, but to see the net bulge from that distance was a special moment for me.

Jamie Carragher: I was actually in the box when he shot. I don't know why, we were all just piling forward. I should really have been on the halfway line but that's what happens when your heart rules your head and you're so desperate you'll do anything to help us get back in the game.

Dietmar Hamann: Obviously Stevie got us into extra time with that fantastic strike from 30-yards but then I remember giving a free-kick away in our right-back position. It was a stupid free-kick to concede. I didn't mean to do it and I just hoped I wouldn't be punished for it. As it happened the ball came in, took a deflection off someone's head and Pepe had to make a fingertip save onto the post which kept us in the game.

Pepe Reina: I was really disappointed with my performance during the first 90 minutes. I was very nervous and didn't play well at all. Thankfully, Stevie, with his goals, had given me an opportunity to redeem myself and in extra-time I remember making a really good save in the last minute. So in the end I was proud, of my performance in those extra 30 minutes and the shoot-out that followed.

Steven Gerrard: It just felt like it was a mountain to climb from start to finish but that was probably one of the best Liverpool teams I've played in, around that 2005-06 era. It was a team that never ever knew when it was beaten, always coming back through difficult moments. Again, we had to go to penalties to win it but we got there in the end.

Dietmar Hamann: On the day West Ham were magnificent, they outplayed us for 120 minutes. For the first time ever I actually felt a bit sorry for the opposition because they did nothing wrong that day. They probably didn't have many players who had played in a cup final before, but they didn't panic and done everything they needed to do. Once it went to penalties though I was pretty confident we could do it because we'd been here before and had momentum in our favour.

Pepe Reina: As a goalkeeper, in situations like this you just have to stay calm and try your best to guess right. It's a lottery and I got lucky. Those saves meant we won the game, but even though I was delighted for myself, for the team and for the fans, I still had this nagging feeling that I had almost cost us the game.

Steven Gerrard: Once it went to penalties, with his [Reina's] record, I was confident.

Rafael Benitez: Once again, we would draw a final 3-3. Once again we would be thankful to our goalkeeper in a penalty shoot-out. Once again, Steven would end the season lifting a trophy... and winning the FA Cup ensured the club finished the season feeling happy, jubilant.

Steven Gerrard: Lifting the European Cup is the ultimate but the FA Cup was special too. I'd played in the final before but to lift the trophy as captain of Liverpool Football Club is a feeling I can't describe.

Looking back now, I can see that I scaled my absolute shimmering peak that afternoon. Beyond even the goals and assist, I produced a performance where everything fell into place for me.

Agony in Athens

Liverpool v AC Milan
Olympic Stadium, Athens
Champions League final
23 May 2007

Jamie Carragher: I felt totally sick after that game. Losing in Athens is the thing that disappoints me the most about my career. To win the European Cup once is a great achievement but there aren't many people who have won it twice and that would have been something totally unbelievable. I'd say we went into it as slight favourites. Milan were obviously out for revenge but I thought we'd edge it.

Steven Gerrard: The feeling was the complete opposite to two years before. It was heartbreaking, one of the lowest points of my career. I thought we started well and were in control, just how we like to be, but when you do that you have got to score. Instead they got the first goal with a bit of luck and it was a big lift for them.

Rafael Benitez: It was only rotten luck that sent us into half-time a goal down. Herbert Fandel, the German referee, harshly penalised Xabi Alonso on the edge of the box for a very soft foul on Kaka. Pirlo stepped up to take the free-kick. He hit it well enough but Reina would have had the shot covered had it not clipped Inzaghi on its way through. The slight touch, far from deliberate, wrong-footed our goalkeeper. Milan, out of nowhere, led, just a minute before the referee blew his whistle for the interval. It was a considerable blow.

Pepe Reina: For all our dominance it was frustrating that we went in 1-0 down at half-time. All the same we still felt at the interval that we could get back into the game and go on and win it. Inzaghi got a second in the 82nd minute and I can still remember the noise in the stadium when he scored it. A dramatic sound effect was played over the tannoy. That sound will live with me forever.

Rafael Benitez: We poured forward, but Milan, to their credit, stood firm. Two years on they were more cautious. They knew what we could do to them if they gave us even the slightest opportunity. We pulled one back, a header from Kuyt. For just a second, everything stopped. This could be a comeback even more remarkable than Istanbul. We had just moments to find another goal. To take it into extra-time. And then, it was over. All that work, all that effort. Over. We were beaten.

Jamie Carragher: We shouldn't have lost but I don't know if we actually did enough to win it. I've never watched that game back so I don't really know what went on in it or whether I could have done something different. It would just be too painful to watch again.

Steven Gerrard: It was a missed opportunity. The team selection wasn't right that night. In my opinion, there wasn't enough pace in the starting line-up to hurt Milan, plus we gave them two soft goals. If we had been sliced apart, then I would have accepted defeat, however reluctantly. But that night still fills me with regrets.

Pepe Reina: There is no doubt about it, losing was devastating. Looking back, they certainly got a bit of luck. Maybe after what happened in Istanbul, fate went in their favour.

Steven Gerrard: I could hardly bear to think about it afterwards. We gave everything but it wasn't to be. The irony is that AC Milan played better in Istanbul than in Athens two years later. That's football and the night belonged to Milan. They had gained their revenge.

El Nino phenomenon

July 2007

Fernando Torres: Rafa called me. I was walking with my dogs and my friend in the park. My mobile phone showed an English number and I thought it was Pepe or Xabi. On the other side of the phone was Rafa to tell me that he wants me to play for Liverpool. It was very important for me that the manager called me and said I could be an important player in one of the best teams in Europe. Liverpool had played two European finals in three years. Benitez was there, Alonso and Reina. It was a club where I felt it would be quite easy for me to adapt. The relationship between the fans and the team was also something I was looking for. It was difficult to leave Atletico. But it was not difficult to choose Liverpool.

Rafael Benitez: He would become, at the time, the most expensive signing in Liverpool's history. But we knew we had found the player we wanted, we needed. He had pace, he was good in the air and, most of all, he had tremendous hunger, to improve himself, to win trophies. He was the right age, and he was within our budget. He fitted the bill perfectly.

Steven Gerrard: It seems strange to admit but I had doubts about whether Fernando Torres would be a success at Liverpool. But what a signing he proved to be. I used to walk onto the pitch every single game convinced I was going to set up a goal for him or score myself. Sometimes I didn't. Mostly it seemed I did. I felt invincible with him in the team alongside me.

So near, yet so far

2007-2009

Fernando Torres: At times I believe we were the best team in Europe. We were not lucky enough to win the Premier League, though we were so close. We also lost in a Champions League semi-final. I think the team was great. You can see that by the players.

Xabi Alonso: They were my happiest times at Liverpool: Pep to Agger, Agger to me, me to Stevie and Stevie to Torres. Sometimes it would take less than ten seconds. The spine in that team was the best I've played in. You also have Carra and Mascherano in the side – top class players. There was skill, steel and speed; it was very competitive, very intense. Very, very determined and committed.

Steven Gerrard: It was a team of men. From front to back. It had probably one of the strongest spines in world football at that time. It's only looking back now that I really appreciate just how good my team-mates were then. Players like Mascherano, Alonso, Carragher, Hyypia, Torres, Reina. They were all big men, big men you want to share a football pitch with because you know you have every chance of beating anyone.

Pepe Reina: We had gone into the 2008/09 season hungry for silverware. After coming so close in Athens, and winning nothing in 2008, we were all desperate to bring a trophy back to Anfield. There was no bigger prize than the Premier League trophy.

Jamie Carragher: When you've won everything domestically, won the Champions League and then played in another final, the next step is to go and win the league. That's what we wanted to do and we were almost there in 2009 but it just seemed to fall away from there.

Pepe Reina: We were in touching distance of the Holy Grail but fell just short. It was the closest Liverpool had come to winning the league since their last championship in 1990, but when it came down to it we just didn't have enough to make the difference.

Xabi Alonso: We were so close and it still hurts in my heart that we were not able to make it. However, my memories of that season are still fantastic. I was playing well and the team was playing well.

Pepe Reina: The highlight for most people will probably always be the 4-1 win against United at Old Trafford, a really special day for everyone associated with the club. That it was their biggest home defeat for 17 years says it all. Teams don't go to Old Trafford and do to them what we did that day. I can remember looking at the massive scoreboard after Andrea Dossena scored our fourth goal after coming on as substitute and it just looked beautiful. I took a picture of it in my mind and it has remained there ever since, a memory of a great day that showed just how good we were at that time.

Steven Gerrard: We produced a spell of football around the March of that season that was as good as anything I can remember in my time. We were swatting teams aside. Good teams as well. We were confident of going to Old Trafford because we had just beaten Real Madrid 4-0 in the Champions League, but no-one expected us to beat Manchester United 4-1 on their own patch. This was when Fernando Torres was at his peak, scaring the life out of defenders such as Nemanja Vidic and Rio Ferdinand.

Rafael Benitez: That fortnight, in which we twice beat Madrid, humiliated our fiercest rivals and then comprehensively overcame Villa, may have been the best two weeks of my time at Liverpool, Istanbul apart. We produced four stunning performances against top-quality opposition. It was a tremendous achievement, and one we hoped would bring us at least one of the two trophies we desired most come the end of the season. It was not to be.

Xabi Alonso: In 2005, we won the Champions League with a not-so-good team. In 2007, we lost the Champions League final with a better team and a more convincing performance. In 2009, we played the best football and lost the least amount of games but still did not win the league. That is the beauty of football, I guess. It is not a straight line.

Pepe Reina: The problem for us was that we drew too many games, especially during a 10-week spell either side of Christmas when we dropped fourteen points from nine games. When you do that the chances are that it is likely to prove costly in the end and it did. It is a pity we could not end as champions, but sometimes you just have to accept that you have given everything and another team has finished ahead of you. It was painful, of course. The feeling was made even worse by the fact that we had been pipped at the post by Manchester United, our biggest rivals.

Rafael Benitez: We reached a club record total of 86 points in a 38-game season. We had scored more goals, too, than we had ever managed in the Premier League era. We had come so close to ending Liverpool's long wait for a championship. We failed by the slenderest of margins.

Xabi Alonso: This side did not win anything together but we felt we could win everything. We had a few stupid draws at home and in the end that's why we did not win the league. We always had that feeling, that belief and confidence. Nobody scared us. We went to the Bernabeu and won. We went to Old Trafford and won. We went to Stamford Bridge and won: big games, big occasions that define seasons. It frustrates me so, so much.

Jamie Carragher: On a few occasions we had one of the best teams in Europe. The problem was so did Manchester United, so did Chelsea and so did Arsenal. In Alex Ferguson, Jose Mourinho and Arsene Wenger, they had some of the greatest managers. That's who we were coming up against. So it wasn't easy. It was tough.

Fernando Torres: We had a team to dream about but one that still needed building. The spine was there. Providing we kept that, I knew we could compete with anyone. Reina, Carragher, Agger, Skrtel, Alonso, Mascherano, Gerrard, and then me. It was strong, very powerful. We were difficult to beat and nobody wanted to play against us. We were not far away from being champions of England and champions of Europe. But we needed to keep the team.

Steven Gerrard: From 2005 to 2009 we should've won more, we come close. If we had stayed together, I'm convinced that team would have won a couple of league titles. And that kills me.

Boardroom turmoil

As the end of noughties approached, Liverpool found itself in the headlines for events off the pitch as much as on it. In 2007 an American consortium led by George Gillett and Tom Hicks took control of the club from long-time owner David Moores, and so began a worrying period of instability.

Rick Parry: The ownership issue was totally debilitating and distracting. Unfortunately, the two owners from America had two very different sets of values and very different mindsets. When you've got two owners with different philosophies, you can't have a single philosophy by definition. That makes life incredibly difficult.

Rafael Benitez: It seemed as though David and Rick had chosen well when they'd agreed to sell the club. In those first few conversations, they [Hicks and Gillett] were desperate for information on how

I wanted the club to progress. We talked about the need to sign new players, my wish to see the Academy revamped so that we might start bringing through more local, home-grown players, the heirs to Gerrard and Carragher, how I thought we might improve the structure of the club and, of course, their ideas for the stadium. There was no sign then, in those first few months, of what was to come.

Rick Parry: George, I think, genuinely did want to do things the right way and was trying to understand the club's values. I don't think it ever mattered to Tom. I don't think it bothered him at all.

Rafael Benitez: I heard a host of rumours and whispers from people in the game. Hicks and Gillett, they told me, had met with Jurgen Klinsmann, the former German national team manager, to see if he would be interested in managing Liverpool. My friends, people I trust, whose information is usually correct, told me my own employers were planning to replace me. Whenever I challenged anyone about it, they denied it, but I knew it was true.

Rick Parry: Clearly Rafa was hurt and understandably so. That became a very difficult period. They weren't trying to do anything malicious in approaching Klinsmann. In football everything gets blown up. They had a very straightforward mindset that Rafa was making a play in the media about the possibility of going to Real Madrid. So they took him literally and explored other options in case he did. It was one of Rafa's initiatives that backfired. He was thinking if he threatened to leave, it might strengthen his position. Instead it was the reverse.

Jamie Carragher: It bothered me deeply that things weren't as they should have been. I thought a lot about the club, the direction it was going in, the way it was run and how it was perceived from the outside. There were things that Liverpool should have been doing in a certain way, the correct way. You associated class and dignity with Liverpool.

Rick Parry: When David was in charge, we scrupulously had a monthly board meeting. That stopped under the new regime. Occasionally, they flew in with an entourage and we'd have an agenda for the day. There were other meetings in New York but they were few and far between. Sometimes there were telephone conversations – occasionally with both but more often with just one. It tended to be more with George.

Rafael Benitez: They were evasive. They would not give me the go-ahead to start talking to players and agents to see if they wanted to join us. I was communicating with the owners mainly be email, and it was hard to get a clear response from them about what we would be able to do.

Rick Parry: When George was supporting Rafa, Tom wasn't. And then vice-versa. It must have been confusing for Rafa. One thing I passionately believe in is, if you are determined to establish a high-performing winning culture, you need a single philosophy from the top down, which we absolutely didn't have. There was a complete split at the top. How on earth we maintained a spell of relative success until 2009, I have no idea.

Rafael Benitez: It all came to a head, of course, in that famous press conference at Melwood, when I repeated the phrase Hicks had sent to me in answer to a succession of questions from confused reporters. It was not something our media team were expecting, but my intention was always the same; to do the best thing for the club.

Jamie Carragher: Of course, it was frustrating. Me and Stevie would speak in the room about what was going on off the pitch. We'd never say anything publicly because you always have to be behind the club, no matter who's in charge. You just play. That's your job and what you're paid to do. Everybody else was fighting. If the players got involved, what's left?

Steven Gerrard: I thought long and hard, most days if not every day, about whether me coming out and saying something publicly would help the situation. Behind the scenes me and Jamie Carragher were constantly asking questions and saying this needs to stop, but we are not the type of players to go and do exclusives in the papers and add fuel to the fire. It was a delicate situation. In an ideal scenario you want total togetherness at a football club but it happened and there was nothing we, as players could do. Once a game actually starts you're not thinking about what's going on behind the scenes with the owners and the managers, you just want to give it your best and try to win for the fans.

Rafael Benitez: Liverpool, though, was no longer a football club. It was a business. The money, which we wanted to use to take Liverpool on to the next level, was all gone. For five years I had been a football manager at Liverpool. By the start of my sixth, it was clear I had become something else entirely. That was supposed to be our year, the season it all came together. Instead it was a long, hard campaign, a battle from start to finish. I was suddenly supposed to be a bank manager. Decisions were being made to appease the banks, not the fans. That is how serious the situation with the owners, Tom Hicks and George Gillett, had become.

Steven Gerrard: I get angry and frustrated when I think about how Liverpool Football Club lurched towards High Court battles off the pitch and slipped down the Premier League on it. We were immersed in a cycle of mediocrity on the field and open warfare between the supporters and the owners off it. No one – certainly not the fans or the players – wanted Hicks and Gillett any more, but they were hanging on to the club for grim death, aware hundreds of millions were riding on whether they could sell it or not.

The Fenway era

2010-2017

A fresh start

Much-needed stability on and off the pitch was Liverpool's number one objective as the club entered the present decade and, on both fronts, so far, it's been achieved.

Rafa's time is up

June 2010

Rafael Benitez: As the season drew to a close, I was informed on three occasions that I would have a meeting with Mr Broughton [the new chairman]. When we did eventually meet, after the final game of our campaign, it was clear that we did not share the same vision for the future of the club. It was at that point that it became evident what was about to happen. It was obvious that they had decided that my time at Anfield was up and wanted to come to an arrangement as quickly as possible. I was not in a hurry to leave Liverpool - quite the opposite, I wanted to stay.

Jamie Carragher: Rafa Benitez had a major influence on my career. I played my best football under him so I'll always be eternally grateful for that. His legacy as Liverpool manager will always be there because we achieved some fantastic things but I think there's a time in everyone's managerial shelf life at a club when it time for a parting of the ways.

Rafael Benitez: It was while I was on holiday in Italy that I next heard from the club. Their lawyers had contacted mine to offer me a settlement. It was confirmation that the directors of the team I had worked so hard to turn into a force at home and abroad no longer wanted my services. I was disappointed, hurt and sad. I would not be given the chance to try to solve the problems that had arisen during the season, to complete the six years of work I had put into the club.

Steven Gerrard: Rafa Benitez is the best coach I played for. He undoubtedly made me a better player and I respect him. But I understand why he was sacked by Liverpool in the summer of 2010. Everything felt a mess at that point and it was the right time for a change. Rafa had become embroiled in fights with different people at the club and lost his focus on what his strengths were. His job was to coach the team, it wasn't to get into political battles and it seemed best for everyone – the club, the players and also Rafa – that there was a break and the slate wiped clean.

Hodgson lasts seven months

June 2010 to January 2011

Martin Broughton: We didn't start off with a first choice. We wanted to have a proper and professional process. We didn't say A was favourite or B was favourite. We talked to quite a lot of people. There were a lot of applicants and we approached some others. There were a number of telephone interviews to get a shortlist. Then there were a number of face-to-face interviews which Christian Purslow and Kenny Dalglish carried out. They put their conclusions to the board and the board agreed it would be a good idea for me and Christian to meet the last two... Roy [Hodgson] was our choice.

Steven Gerrard: I feared for Roy Hodgson almost as soon as he became Liverpool's new manager. I feared for him because he was not Kenny Dalglish [and the club's fans wanted Dalglish]. From the moment the club overlooked Kenny as a replacement for Rafa, it was always going to be difficult for Roy.

Jamie Carragher: I think it's fair to say when Roy Hodgson came into the club it wasn't accepted one hundred per cent by the supporters. There was a few sceptical supporters out there, no doubt, but the results weren't good enough really. Some of the signings he brought in didn't perform and the pressure just grew.

Pepe Reina: If I am honest, Roy was not the manager who I wanted to replace Rafa Benitez... but part of me can still understand it. Hodgson had done a great job with Fulham, he had taken them to the Europa League final in the season before he joined us and he had a lot of experience in England and in Europe. I met him for the first time after coming back from my holidays. We had a short chat, I offered to help him in any way I could and he came across as a really nice man. We were all confident at the time. But our sense of optimism was to be short-lived.

Steven Gerrard: You could smell pretty quickly that it wasn't going to work out. We lost to Northampton in the Carling Cup and Blackpool at home in the Premier League and were soon on a downward trajectory. The atmosphere was deteriorating.

Pepe Reina: There were so many games at Anfield where we just were not good enough and we were allowing our opponents, quite often teams that Liverpool should be expecting to beat and dominating, to set the tempo and dictate the play. That wasn't right. The way we played just wasn't good enough. It cannot all be pinned on the manager. None of us were playing well so it wasn't just Hodgson's fault. The players also have to take responsibility for what went wrong. In his final game as Liverpool manager away to Blackburn on January 5, 2011, none of us could walk off that pitch and say that we had given our best. The mood in the team was not right... it was one of those bad days when it felt like something was going to have to change.

Steven Gerrard: As much as I was disappointed that things didn't work out for Roy Hodgson, at Liverpool Football Club, when results are not good, inevitably changes will happen no matter who is in charge. Things couldn't carry on like they were. We were in the middle of the table and not certain of climbing it, which is ridiculous when you consider the quality of players we still had.

New owners

6 October 2010

Ian Ayre: People sometimes forget how bad it was [under Hicks and Gillett]. I speak to people now and they have really short memories... when you think about that day when we tipped it over the edge and finally pulled it back.

Martin Broughton: The board decided to accept NESV's offer on the basis that it best met the criteria we set out originally for a new owner. [NESV would later become Fenway Sports Group].

Tom Werner: The club was going through bankruptcy. It needed stewards who were going to come in, save it and protect it, and hopefully improve it. I think our legacy, hopefully, will be that we left the club, whenever that is, in better shape than when we found it.

Return of the King

The first big decision made by Liverpool's new American owners was to remove Roy Hodgson as manager and replace him with club icon, Kenny Dalglish.

8 January 2011

Kenny Dalglish: I wouldn't tell a lie, I loved coming back, I was immensely proud to come back into the fold at the club, but there was also a tremendous amount of sympathy that a good man in Roy had lost his job.

Steven Gerrard: Liverpool supporters have a powerful voice and when they speak, you have to listen. It was clear who they wanted to take over, they had been singing Kenny's name as early into the season as October, and I knew Kenny walking through the door in January 2011 would give everyone a lift.

Kenny Dalglish: When I was asked to return it was a no-brainer. I never thought I'd get to manage Liverpool again so when the chance came along, I didn't need asking twice. Just to be back in amongst the people at Anfield meant a huge amount to me and my family.

Jamie Carragher: Kenny came in and galvanised everyone.

Pepe Reina: The beauty of Kenny's appointment was that it brought a calmness to the situation that no other manager could have brought. When you are a club legend and hero to the fans and the players then you are going to be given time to get things right and you are even going to get some understanding when things don't work out. That was really important at the time because obviously under Hodgson we had been playing under a manager who had been under a lot of pressure. The owners were right to bring him back, not just because results got better, but because Kenny is Kenny and he means a lot to everyone at the club. His presence created a calmness that we really needed because it had not been there for some time.

Kenny Dalglish: When I came back in the only thing I had in my mind was to go about it the way I'd gone about it before. We knew that we weren't in the best place. It's not always the manager's fault but the manager is the one who has to carry the can for it. The players also had something to prove, that they were better than they had been. So I got in and just had to try and help them regain a bit of confidence in themselves, give them a wee bit of a boost. We had the game at Old Trafford on the Sunday, then Stevie Clarke joined us the following day. We got in amongst the players and started to make them feel comfortable.

Lucas Leiva: When Kenny came back I would say he helped to turn things around. For myself, he was fantastic. He just gave me all the confidence I needed to go and play and show my skill.

Steven Gerrard: To get the chance to play for Kenny, who was a great friend of mine and someone who had given me great advice throughout my career, was something special. In an instant, the club was united again. Everyone was on the same page, no-one was fighting and the club's new owners made money available for transfers.

Deadline day drama

31 January 2011

Despite weeks of speculation, the transfer window was drawing to a close and all seemed quiet at Anfield until a frantic final day of business saw the completion of three high-profile deals. Fernando Torres left, while Andy Carroll and Luis Suarez arrived.

Kenny Dalglish: It was all left to the last minute but that's normally how it happens nowadays. An important factor was that both players wanted to come here. Liverpool was their first choice. It was a busy 48 hour period but one that was very beneficial to the football club.

Luis Suarez: The first thing I thought about was the prospect of playing with Steven Gerrard and with Fernando Torres. All the years playing in Holland and watching those two score goals on television, all the times I had played as Liverpool on the Playstation, I never really imagined I would be playing alongside those players in real life. I didn't expect the sale of Fernando... and to never even get to train with him was a real shame. When I spoke to Fernando, he told me I was moving to a great club and a great city. He told me he was sure I was going to be happy here, but he had made his mind up to leave.

Fernando Torres: I didn't feel as good as three seasons before, not just physically but mentally. There were too many things to think about, too many promises, too many false hopes. Obviously, I was not playing the same way because I was feeling the apprehension about everything that happened. Sometimes people have to change things in their lives. You wake up in the morning, go into the training ground and say, 'I don't feel the same way as I did, I need a new challenge, a new opportunity'. And one day, one of the best teams in the country call you and want you and it's really easy to think, 'I cannot lose this opportunity, I have to join them'. I'm sure it was the best option for both.

Kenny Dalglish: We were disappointed to see him go but as a football club we had to move on.

Luis Suarez: As soon as Fernando was sold, another big signing came. I first met Andy Carroll in the hotel while I was waiting for my deal to go through and although I didn't say it to him, I was thinking, 'I'm glad you're here'. If Liverpool had sold Torres and only signed me, it would have been, 'Suarez comes to replace Torres'. Andy was like a human shield. He cost more than me so all the talk was of him replacing Fernando. I wasn't really talked about that much.

Andy Carroll: I was a bit surprised when I first heard about the move and didn't really know what was going on but once I knew it was for real I realised it was a great opportunity and that I had to take it. To be wanted by a club like Liverpool and to become their number nine was a great feeling.

Luis Suarez: When I was little, the name Liverpool was one of the biggest in Europe and renowned throughout the world so when I found out the club's interest in me I was never in doubt because it's the dream for every player. It really was a special moment when I finally put pen to paper. They gave me the opportunity to play in the Premier League and just a few days later I got the chance to make my Anfield debut.

Suarez scores on his debut

Liverpool v Stoke City
Anfield
Premier League
2 February 2011

Luis Suarez: Fortunately I was able to play and get on the scoresheet. It was just marvellous. I started off on the subs bench. I'd only had chance for one training session with my team-mates. I remember when I was clean through on the keeper. I was a bit surprised as it was pretty much my first touch of the game. It was a dream debut for me. Just to be on the field for just a few minutes and manage to score in front of the Kop – that's what dreams are made of. These are moments that stick with you, and remain in your memory, and make you love the club even more.

Jamie Carragher: He had a great goals record at Ajax but there have been lots of players like that who've come over from Holland to England. Some have transformed the league, like Van Nistelrooy but then you look at Kezman who went to Chelsea, so you can never be quite sure. There's always a question mark when players come from the Dutch league but with Luis we knew straight away that we had a special player. I know people say it takes time to settle but all the great foreign players Liverpool have had, more often than not, hit the ground running and he was one of them.

Steven Gerrard: He didn't surprise me because I'd watched a lot of footage of Luis before he came and was well aware of him. So, I was expecting him to be a good player. I just didn't expect him to be as good as he was... I didn't realise we were getting one of the best players in the world.

Luis Suarez: Whenever I went out onto the pitch with Liverpool I would give absolutely everything and wanted to do my very best so the club could get back to the level where it deserved to be. The supporters knew I always tried my utmost for the team and gave one hundred per cent.

Steven Gerrard: He's the best by...well, I wouldn't like to disrespect anyone and put a distance on it but let's just say comfortably. He ticks every box. Work-rate, fighter, winner, goalscorer, creator, warrior, you can't say that about many players. I used to love playing with him, he was an absolute dream for a midfielder. His movement was fantastic. There are very few people you go into a football match with and you think we're probably going to win this game because of one person but he was that type of player. He was just a one-off warrior. An absolute monster of a footballer.

Luis Suarez: I think I managed to make a good impression at the club. I am one of the privileged footballers to have had the chance to play at Liverpool and all that I experienced there represents one of the best times of my life. They were incredible and unforgettable times.

Wembley winners once again

Liverpool v Cardiff City
Wembley
Carling Cup final
26 February 2012

Craig Bellamy: Before the match, the manager showed us a short film that illustrated what Wembley meant to Liverpool and what it meant to the club being back there. I sat there watching Shankly talking and Kenny scoring that magnificent winner against Bruges in the 1978 European Cup final. And I thought about all my years of growing up and wanting to be part of this club. When the film ended, there were tears in my eyes.

Jamie Carragher: I can't think of us ever having an easy final. I always thought it was going to be a difficult game. When there's a game of this importance at Wembley, it's always going to be like this.

Craig Bellamy: We knew it was going to be difficult. Finals always are. We thought we'd won it then they fought back and were outstanding all the way through.

Luis Suarez: The truth is that on the day we didn't play well and they played incredibly, they were brilliant. For them to take us to a penalty shoot-out, with the players we had, was impressive.

Martin Skrtel: It was a great game in a beautiful stadium with an unbelievable atmosphere. I think we deserved it. It wasn't easy because they equalised with two minutes to go, but we just tried to keep our heads up and we got it on penalties.

Craig Bellamy: Kuyt scored a fantastic goal and the game needed that. He gave us a big lift. He told us to keep believing and continue with our normal approach. Then he scored a penalty in the shoot-out as well.

Dirk Kuyt: I knew when it came to my penalty that I had to score. I had cleared off the line thirty seconds from the end as well and scored in extra-time, so it was a good afternoon for me and the team.

Jamie Carragher: It was brilliant. It had been a dream of mine to play at Wembley for Liverpool. I'd been there as a kid, but to actually play there and to come on in the League Cup final was great.

Steven Gerrard: I think some people try and knock the League Cup and try to disrespect it but for me, when you're representing Liverpool in a cup final, a major cup final, especially under Kenny Dalglish, I don't think anyone can disrespect that. Again, we done it the tough way, penalty shoot-out. I actually missed a penalty but I lifted the cup so it doesn't matter.

Dirk Kuyt: Even when Steven missed his penalty, I said to him we would still get back into it as there were a number of penalties to be taken. We never stopped believing and that is why we won the trophy.

Kenny Dalglish: I don't think anyone who has ever won a trophy has come away from it saying they didn't enjoy it. To win a trophy at Wembley again clearly meant a lot to the fans. I don't see that as anything but a positive.

Luis Suarez: We were relieved more than anything else. Proud, too, because it had been a long time since the club had won a trophy. And we did feel that we deserved to win the trophy because of how we had got there. The final might not have been impressive, but our journey there had been.

Jamie Carragher: James, my son, got on the pitch at the end. I just got lucky in that when we were running around the pitch he was there. I wasn't sure whether he was high up in the stand or not, but he was on the lower tier, so he could get on. It's something he'll remember for the rest of his life. It's something I'll remember for the rest of my life. I remember taking him up to help us lift the trophy and I think he was trying to lift it before Stevie. Typical Carragher!

Steven Gerrard: I think going up the steps at Wembley adds that little bit more magic than Cardiff. Obviously, Cardiff was like a second home for us, we won an awful lot of trophies there. To walk up those steps was great for me personally and great because it meant we'd won another cup but the most special thing about it was that we'd won it under Kenny Dalglish. It's almost as if you were going up to get the prize to pass on to the king and not many people can they say they've done that so it was a special feeling.

Kenny Dalglish: That was for everyone at Liverpool Football Club. It had been a wee while since something had been chalked up on the board. Winning a cup final against Cardiff at Wembley and walking away with the Carling Cup was a day to remember.

Steven Gerrard: When you become a player for Liverpool there's a responsibility to add to the history that players like him [Kenny] helped create. So when you actually get a cup in your hands it's a relief. It's almost not enjoyable when you're carrying it out because you want it so much that you become scared of failing. That certainly happened at times to some of the Liverpool teams I played in.

Gerrard's derby hat-trick

Liverpool v Everton
Anfield
FA Premier League
13 March 2012

Steven Gerrard: To get a hat-trick against Everton was a big high in my career. I've had many, many highs but that one was certainly right up there. For myself personally, I've had an unbelievable amount of stick off Everton fans; in the city, at traffic lights, in restaurants... wherever I go I face Evertonians and the majority of the time it's good banter. But to score a hat-trick against them was very satisfying from my point of view.

Luis Suarez: Scoring goals in the derby against Everton was sweet but to also play in the derby when Gerrard scored a hat-trick and I provided two or three assists for him was a special moment too, even though I didn't score.

Bursting the blue bubble

Liverpool v Everton
Wembley
FA Cup semi-final
14 April 2012

Jamie Carragher: It was that big a game for me that for a few days before I couldn't sleep. I just couldn't stop thinking about it and I mustn't have been a nice person for my wife and kids to be around at home in those days leading up to it. For me, there was too much riding on it. It was definitely one of the most important games of my life.

Craig Bellamy: Everton were ahead of us in the league by the time the match came around in April and their fans convinced themselves this was the occasion when they were going to get one over on us. There was a lot of talk that there was finally going to be a shift in the balance of power on Merseyside and that Everton were ready to take over the leading role.

Jamie Carragher: It was like a final. The thought of losing that game... it would have been devastating. We weren't doing well and Everton were flying. Everyone fancied Everton.

Craig Bellamy: What drove me on was not just pride in the club but seeing the nerves that were afflicting Jamie Carragher and Steven Gerrard. We got the train down to London and I sat at the same table as them. They were petrified at the thought of losing to Everton.

Kenny Dalglish: I thought the players were fantastic in that game. We started really brightly, passed and moved. Then they [Everton] got a goal. In the second half though we showed a tremendous desire not to lose and got ourselves back into it.

Andy Carroll: Obviously it was disappointing to go a goal down but we came out in the second half and showed them what we're about. At 1-0 we kept calm, kept at it and got an equaliser through Luis with a great finish.

Steven Gerrard: It was a difficult game, we knew it was going to be tough but as the game went on we got stronger. Our response to going a goal down was superb. I won't lie to you, at half-time we were worried. We had to stick together and we did that. We were superb in the second half and could have ran out winners by two or three goals in the end.

Andy Carroll: I had a few chances and should have put one away before I did but I kept working hard and eventually got my goal when Craig [Bellamy] put a great ball in for me. It's always great feeling to score, no matter where it is, but to score the winner at Wembley against Everton was even better. It doesn't get much better.

Jamie Carragher: It was a great, great win that. Probably as big as anything in my career to be honest. We were a goal down at half-time too so to do what we did that day, well, it was such a special day for Liverpudlians and I was just glad that I was part of it.

Craig Bellamy: I had only been on for three minutes. I bent the free-kick in and Andy Carroll glanced it in. There were a few minutes of injury time but Everton didn't threaten us at all. When the final whistle went I looked for Carra straight away. He was on his hands and knees on the floor. I ran over to him and gave him a pat on back. 'Thank fuck for that', he said.

Jamie Carragher: Even though I'd already won two FA Cup finals, winning this felt better. There was no medal or trophy at the end of it but losing this game would have felt worse than anything I'd experienced. To come through and win it was such a relief. I was so glad when it was over. But even though we won, to think that we might have lost still makes me sick to my stomach and I get nervous, even now, thinking about what would have happened.

Denied a Wembley double

Liverpool v Chelsea
Wembley
FA Cup final
5 May 2012

Steven Gerrard: It still nags away at me as to why, as a team, we didn't turn up for the first hour of the final against Chelsea. There is no explanation for it. We knew what was at stake. It was inconceivable that we should be so insipid.

Kenny Dalglish: I don't think the first hour was a true reflection of the quality we had out there. Whether it was a lack of experience in the situation... maybe they were just a wee bit nervous, a lot of them were relatively young and inexperienced at this level. Chelsea had been through the course before. Maybe that was it.

Steven Gerrard: When we eventually woke up, of course, we pushed Chelsea close and the debate about whether Andy Carroll's header crossed the line or not raged afterwards. If we had come back to 2-2 and forced extra-time, I am sure we would have won. Roberto Di Matteo's side were out on their feet at that point.

Luis Suarez: Didier Drogba beat us on his own. We'd had chances to draw level at 2-1, with Andy Carroll having one cleared off the line, but Drogba was astonishing that day. He would jump between our two centre-backs, all alone, and come down with the ball every time. I knew he was a great player, but that day he still surprised me. We just couldn't stop him.

Kenny Dalglish: If you're playing against a team of the quality of Chelsea, you cannot give them a two-goal start and expect to give yourself an opportunity to get something from the game. We were excellent for the last half hour but the game lasts 90 minutes.

Steven Gerrard: The manner of our comeback left me only with regrets. If only we had started like we had finished. If only. Those two small words are the worst for any footballer.

Kenny's leaves for a second time

May 2012

Luis Suarez: I was in Uruguay when I found out that he had been sacked and it really hurt because he had been very close to me. When he lost his job it was hard to take.

Jamie Carragher: In Kenny's second season we got to two cup finals, won one of them. I think to lose his job in these circumstances was harsh.

Steven Gerrard: Reaching two finals and winning one trophy did not mask our league position, but it wasn't the worst season either. Liverpool is about winning silverware. It was important to return to that standard. What the decision to dismiss Kenny shows is that the Americans are not afraid of making big calls, good or bad.

Ian Ayre: If you don't believe the results are right and feel 37 points off the champions and 17 points off Champions League pace is a long distance you have to make a change. The history the club was built on was about success and that means success in the league, which leads to Champions League football, and also winning trophies. No-one is saying we didn't enjoy winning the Carling Cup and getting to the FA Cup final but ultimately the backbone of football now is the Premier League and European football at the highest level.

Within touching distance of the Holy Grail

2013/14

After succeeding Kenny Dalglish as manager at Anfield, Brendan Rodgers came as close as anyone to landing Liverpool's long-awaited first Premier League title.

Brendan Rodgers: We were not expected to even get in the top four but I felt the group we had, gained great momentum as the season went on and it would have been brilliant for Steven Gerrard to have lifted that Premier League trophy. It was a great sadness that we failed to do so.

Steven Gerrard: It's heart-breaking for me and I hate talking about it. It's such a huge low in my career. For me and for everyone at the club. We got so close and the journey we were on was unbelievably enjoyable. I genuinely though it was our turn. I thought this was going to be it, the one I haven't got. But we gave it everything we could. We had an unbelievable team, spearheaded by Luis [Suarez] and Daniel [Sturridge]. But it just didn't happen, we just fell short at the end. It's heart-breaking and it will be for a long, long time.

Luis Suarez: Being so close to winning the Premier League title yet being left with the frustration of missing out, having done everything we could to get our hands on the trophy... it just wasn't to be, but when I look back it was an amazing season and there really were lots of great times.

Brendan Rodgers: We had a number of remarkable performances throughout the season. Just look at some of the scorelines - 3-0 Manchester United, 4-0 Everton, 5-1 Arsenal, 4-0 and 5-0 Tottenham. I look back on that day as the moment the players truly believed in how we work. I just think it was the one which gave the team the belief in how we had been working. We had been improving and developing really well. We had been growing as a team but I felt that was the first away game where, against a rival, we were able to demonstrate our ideas of football. Tottenham are deemed a rival and they were deemed a club ahead of where Liverpool were.

Lucas Leiva: It was a fantastic season, for myself it started really well. We started on a good run and by Christmas time we were top of the league, although we dropped a little bit after defeat to Manchester City and Chelsea. Then we had that crazy run. The team was playing really well and it was fantastic. We were winning games and scoring goals, getting results that nobody expected; like in the derby, the Arsenal game and the Man United game. We really thought that we were going to do it. I remember away to West Ham, I came on at half-time and helped us to a very important win. To be involved in that team that season was a great experience but, of course, in the end it didn't happen. We were close but not close enough. It was really sad.

Brendan Rodgers: I think people looked at the last few games and asked the question, 'Could we handle pressure?' For me, when you win twelve games out of your last 14 in the run in, you can handle the pressure. It's unfair to look at Steven's slip against Chelsea, as a real significant factor in why we didn't go on to win the league. Titles are not won or lost in one particular game; it's over the course of 38. We all shared the pain felt by the supporters that we didn't finish as champions but I feel immense pride that we were able to push right to the very end.

Kolo Toure: Nobody expected us to be where we were. I think we did everything we could but at the end City won it. We fought right until the end. What was the difference? Experience. You need the bad times to have the good times after.

Luis Suarez: Our aim was to qualify for the Champions League but then we got into a position when we thought we could win the league. To lose the title was very sad but it was still one of the best years we had.

Klopp to the Kop

October 2015

Within weeks of parting company with Brendan Rodgers, Liverpool announced the appointment of former Borussia Dortmund boss Jurgen Klopp as the club's new manager.

Jurgen Klopp: I have no other words for this. It was a crazy day with everything that happened in Germany and all that happened here when we landed. It was an absolutely great feeling for me and a big honour to be here. One of the best moments in my life, I have to say.

Ian Ayre: We met as a group – the owners and myself – and talked about the attributes we would want in the next Liverpool manager and all of the ambition and things we want to achieve as a club. His [Klopp's] name rose to the top in terms of the attributes he has, what he could bring and the sort of person he is. Having got all of those boxes ticked, it was then about getting Jurgen and I'm pleased to say we achieved that.

Jurgen Klopp: I always thought about working in England because of the kind of football and the intensity of the football, and Liverpool was first choice. It was not the most difficult decision. I had six very, very cool years at Dortmund and one hard year in the last one, but as a package it was perfect. But I wanted to do something new. I ended my contract with Dortmund and I thought about what I would do in the future – I had to develop myself, think about all the things that had happened in the last 15 years but then I had a holiday for four months and it was enough. It was great, but it was enough. The owners have a dream and I have a dream, and so there was not too much they had to say so I could be here.

Ian Ayre: In terms of did we get the right man for the job? There is absolutely no question. That stands out a mile. I don't think you could pick a better character to fit this club. When you come to a football club from another country and another league, it is very difficult to be accepted. To get so many people behind him so quickly is great testament to the person he is.

Reds pass Yellow Wall

Liverpool v Borussia Dortmund
Anfield
Europa League quarter-final second leg
14 April 2016

Within months of taking charge at Anfield Jurgen Klopp masterminded an exciting run to the Europa League final. On route to Basel, fate decreed that he'd face his former club in an intriguing quarter-final tie, the second leg of which will live long in the memory.

Jurgen Klopp: For us, it was historically important. The whole tie was special. When they made the draw and we got Dortmund everyone said, 'Unlucky, the best team in the competition'. But we knew that over two legs anything was possible. We had watched a lot of their games up to that point but only as a kind of supporter. Once the draw was made we watched their games more serious... The more we watched them, the more we analysed them, we really thought, 'Okay, they are beatable'.

James Milner: It had everything. They are a top team and to come back against them like we did was special. There was an unbelievable atmosphere, even on the way into the ground. To go two down early on was difficult but the desire and drive of the boys to come back... you can't speak highly enough of everyone involved, from the players, staff and fans. The club, as a whole, came together to inspire that comeback.

Divock Origi: When we came in [to the stadium] the atmosphere was special. The supporters received us very warmly. At the beginning of the game, even if it was difficult, it felt very special. The manager was very calm, surprisingly calm. That's the class of a big manager, you could see no panic, no stress, he believed in us and in the end it helped. He gave us belief and we tried to reward that, the belief of the fans, everything.

Jurgen Klopp: We were really good away to Dortmund when we drew there. Then at Anfield, even when we were 2-0 and 3-1 down, we had more chances than all the teams who had played against Dortmund before us that year combined. We knew how to play against them. The only problem was that we had conceded two goals from counter-attacks and another when we should have defended much better.

Dejan Lovren: We didn't expect we would start like this. We will say it was a shit start but we never stopped believing. We never stopped believing in ourselves, we told ourselves at half time we just had to believe.

Divock Origi: The manager just said that we lived to play in evenings like this. We had nothing to lose. We just had to go. We had to play and show our qualities and believe in ourselves that at the end we could win. At half-time he told us we just had to do everything to make it a special evening, one to tell your children and grandchildren about.

Jurgen Klopp: We knew that if we stayed cool we would create chances and that if we created chances we could still win the game. If you can score, you can change the result. We actually felt more confident than you can imagine, even at half-time. I'm not sure about the players but I did and I gave them the message that it was not over.

James Milner: Getting back into the game at the start of the second half only for them to score again... it would have been easy to roll over then but there was a belief to keep going and the crowd drove us on.

Divock Origi: In football, there's no secret. You have to play with your whole heart and give everything. A lot of teams have qualities but when you have a good manager who is tactically strong, and have a good club with good fans, then there's no secret. You can achieve great things.

Jurgen Klopp: I believe in atmosphere and this was the perfect proof of what atmosphere can create. Without noise and without a crowd there was no chance in this game, even though we were good. I've said it a few times but it was the best half-an-hour I ever had in football.

James Milner: At 3-3 and with time running out, you could feel the tension in the ground. Everyone was willing us on, they just wanted us to get forward and get the ball in the box but it was important to have that clarity. Sometimes you just have to be that bit more patient, keep calm and make the right decisions. Studge made a great run from a short free-kick, I got it back and just managed to put a cross over to the far post. It was a great header by Dejan and it sparked great scenes.

Dejan Lovren: You know, when the ball was in the air and I was there, I thought, 'This is the time, it's now or never'. I don't know... it was a relief I would say. A relief in me. Difficult to describe. Emotions. Angry. Relief. Powerful in the moment... all of those things together. That moment you connect, every player needs it. I was so proud and angry, I felt I was saying, 'Yeah, that's me, that's the Dejan you know, who is the fighter until the end, who will never say that it's over'. One of the best days of my life was moving to Liverpool, but that goal is the best moment of my career to be honest.

Jurgen Klopp: When you watch it back, what happened was a really magic night. We will never forget it, for sure. It was outstanding. I loved it.

Liverpool v Sevilla
St Jakob Park Stadion, Basel
Europa League final
18 May 2016

Jurgen Klopp: When I think about the Sevilla final we were good in the first half. We deserved in the first half to win the game. We scored a second goal which was disallowed and we had one or two penalty situations. With a little bit of luck we have a penalty. If we were 2-0 or 3-0 up then Sevilla has no chance because it was an intense season for both teams. But in the second half after one minute... ok, we made a mistake but other teams made bigger mistakes in other games and the opponent didn't score. That changed the game.

Simon Mignolet: We went into half-time with the best result we could have had. We played good football in the first half and created chances. You want to build on that in the second half but it was a big blow to concede so early. Afterwards they played some good football and scored the goals to win the game unfortunately.

Daniel Sturridge: It's hard to put into words what happened out there. As a team, we were unlucky. I felt like in the first half we worked very hard and put everything into it and in the second half we probably got stunned a little bit with the goal. From there, I wouldn't say it was an uphill struggle, but it was probably the experience we kind of lacked in terms of keeping calm. It's one of those games where you take it on the chin.

James Milner: It was devastating losing the game and the most disappointing thing is we didn't show nowhere near what we were about or play anywhere near our capabilities. That's probably the biggest thing for me. Second half we never started at all. We came out and gave a sloppy goal away and never really got back into the game. We said all the right things at half-time about being switched on, but we didn't show that.

Jurgen Klopp: We couldn't strike back and on that night nobody in a Liverpool shirt - no supporter or anyone - could strike back. It was the opposite of the Dortmund game. The crowd stopped believing immediately, we had no petrol in the engine anymore, so it was a really disappointing night.

New look Anfield

Liverpool's new Main Stand was opened amid much acclaim in September 2016. The imposing three-tiered structure had been several years in the making and represented a unique feat of engineering. The team ran out in front of it for the first time against reigning champions Leicester and marked the occasion with a 4-1 win.

Jurgen Klopp: Everyone was excited about the new stand. The atmosphere was unbelievable. The weather was good and the performance was brilliant. It was a wonderful day and we thought immediately, 'It's louder'.

Ian Ayre: This is the spiritual home of Liverpool Football Club. We're all proud of the stadium and we've all got memories of the stadium. Wherever I've gone in the world people have always talked about Anfield and will always talk about Anfield, maybe even a bit more now. It's such a unique place with a unique atmosphere.

Tom Werner: When we first came in there was a lot of uncertainty over whether to remain at Anfield or not. There were a lot of missteps before we came in. There was a lot of scepticism when we talked about our plan we intended to execute.

Ian Ayre: I'd been here [at the club] through two lots of ownerships so there was a lot of work done on prior schemes. We went through a process of studying all the options and when FSG bought the club it was always the desire of the owners to stay at Anfield if we could.

Tom Werner: It's such a special place. The first time I came here... I'd heard so much about it, it's a place where you can feel the history. To us, it was important to try and figure out a solution to keep the club at Anfield. We knew there would be some extraordinary challenges about it. But why would you leave if you could figure out a solution? There were a lot of very specific ideas we had and we were trying to replicate the historic feeling of Anfield.

Ian Ayre: Maintaining the unique Anfield feel and that unique heritage of Liverpool at Anfield was always a key part of the planning process. We had a lot of discussions. I remember talking to John Henry about certain parts and the type of brick we used that needed to match the brick in other parts of the stand. I suppose at the heart of it should be two things; one is that it looked as though it was always part of Anfield and secondly that it's the best in class that Liverpool supporters can feel proud of.

Tom Werner: I am extremely proud of what's been achieved. We have solved a problem which was a real challenge for the club. In the end it's about winning on the pitch and I think this will contribute to that.

Liverpool's youngest goalscorer

Liverpool v Leeds United
Anfield
League Cup fifth round
29 November 2016

At just 17 years and 45 days old Ben Woodburn became the youngest goalscorer in Liverpool's history when he netted in the 81st minute to seal a 2-0 win.

Ben Woodburn: My Anfield goal? I just went home with my family and went to a mate's house to play a bit of FIFA. I was trying to re-enact that goal! If someone had offered me back in August the season

I went on to have, I would definitely have taken it. I tried to work my hardest all year and luckily it paid off with the chances the manager has given me.

Jurgen Klopp: First of all I said to him, 'Well done but it's not too difficult – I would have scored too!' That is maybe the truth! Ben Woodburn is so very young and all of us who care about this player and his situation must protect him and not put extra pressure on him. We know what Ben is capable of and what he is already able to do. My first job is help these boys to be the best, in this case Ben Woodburn. At Kirkby and Melwood there will be no pressure or added spotlight. We want him to learn and develop at his pace, free from pressure.

Ben Woodburn: At the time it was obviously an unbelievable moment for me and everyone around me. Those things happen in football, though, so you can't allow yourself to get caught up in it. That said, I've probably seen it back a few times! It is nice to watch. My phone just blew up with messages, WhatsApps, tags, likes… everything. All of my family and friends got in touch, it just went a bit mad. I managed to reply to everyone who'd messaged me, but it took a while! The next day, I was training and it was straight back to normal. The lads who'd started the game were on a recovery session and I was training normally, so it was just back to my usual routines.

Oh Mane, Mane!

Everton v Liverpool
Goodison Park
Premier League
19 December 2016

Liverpool's big summer signing of 2016 was Senegal striker Sadio Mane and he proved to be an instant hit with the fans, not least for the last-minute winner he scored on his Merseyside derby debut.

Sadio Mane: This day was just amazing. To score that goal… it was for the fans, which is why I ran straight towards them to celebrate. I was a little bit lucky but I wish to always be lucky and score goals for the team. It wasn't an easy game but I think we deserved to win because we created a lot of chances before getting the goal. We were facing a very good team and we had to keep going to the end. But that's what we did and got the win. I'm thankful and very happy to score the winning goal for the team. I feel lucky to be here, in a great team with great players. I am young and think I can only get better.

Jordan Henderson: He had a big influence on us. He works so hard for the team and, with his energy, he always poses a threat. His pace can get him behind defenders and it helps stretch teams when we're on the counter-attack. He got the players and fans player of the year, and was also named in the Premier league team of the year, which shows just how good he was.

Securing Champions League qualification

2016/17

Jurgen Klopp: I'm not sure if that [finishing in the top four] was the target of all the Liverpool supporters, but I think pretty much the second best. We all know we had no European football, but for us, it was not that much an advantage because we had injuries. Without injuries, like Chelsea, - and I don't want to make it too big - we could have had a few points more and it would have looked a little bit different. We had these injuries, but in the first part of the season I knew we were ready. I knew after we beat Arsenal [on the opening day], it should be possible. In a lot of games, we played really outstandingly good football and that showed what we can do. But that doesn't mean anything because there are a lot of games to go after this moment. It was long, it was really long. We all know what happened in January, I'm not sure all of us agree why, but the explanation is injuries and too many games. We cannot change this, it happened, then the problem in February was that we suffered from the games in January, but then in March we were back on track and got to 76 points, so that's it. 76 points, that's an outstanding number. I was really happy with this.

Jordan Henderson: In all aspects of the game I think that we've become more mature as a team. Everyone worked hard throughout the season and we got our just rewards at the end by getting in the top four. Since I've been here we've only been in the Champions League once so it was a good achievement. At the same time we've still got a lot to improve on. We want more. We've got to keep winning, we want silverware and we want to be the best team. So yeah, it's a step in the right direction for us, one that will help us develop as a squad, but we're not finished yet.

Gerrard returns to his roots

After two years with LA Galaxy, Steven Gerrard returned to Liverpool in 2017 to begin a new career at the Academy, coaching those who hope to follow in his illustrious footsteps.

Steven Gerrard: It is a fantastic feeling to be back working for the club. To get the role of under-18 manager is a big gig, one I'm really excited about. I still don't know whether I will be a top coach, no-one knows just yet. I'm still learning. It's the beginning of the journey.

Alex Inglethorpe: If I was to pick one individual who embodies the characteristics and values we are looking to instil into our organisation at Kirkby, it would be Steven Gerrard. For him to have been so enthusiastic about being part of what we are looking to do is simply great news for everyone connected to the club. I don't think it would surprise anyone to know that Steven had a host of great options, in terms of what to do next in his career, including playing, management and coaching. But it's been evident from the first meeting with him that his heart and head belongs here.

Steven Gerrard: I don't think I need to explain to people what this football club means to me, but when I knew coming back was a serious option I wanted to make sure it was a substantive role and a role in which I could really help the organisation.

Alex Inglethorpe: He has shown great humility in making it clear from the outset he wants a role where he can contribute to Liverpool; it's typical of him that his priority has been defining the role so it helps the club, ahead of himself. He has expressed a desire to learn from us and manage a young team. The benefits to us will be immense. This is a substantial role and one which makes the academy and the club in general stronger and better.

Steven Gerrard: It feels like completing the circle; returning to the place where professionally it all began. However, this isn't a decision based on emotion - it's about what I can offer and contribute to Liverpool.

LFC 125: the past, the present and the future

Phil Thompson: Liverpool is such a special football club and it has been for 125 years. It's a great to be a Liverpool fan. You see the Kop, you see our flags and you see our history. In a sporting sense, Liverpool Football Club has given me an absolute wonderful life. It's a club that has provided us with some fantastic highs and a few lows. As both a former player and a fan, to know I've played a part in this makes me feel very privileged and proud, Liverpool FC means everything to me and long may it continue.

Roy Evans: We're going in the right direction. We've never won this Premier League, which drives me up the wall. I'd have liked to have won it personally but didn't and that still haunts me so I'd love to see that happen in the next few years, especially with the manager we've got here now. Everything Jurgen says I like, but when you manage a club like Liverpool you have to win trophies because that's the standard that has been set for many, many years.

Tom Werner: We want to honour the past but we believe there's an extremely bright future. This club now has a remarkable manager who is world class, we have a number of world class players on the team… and we continue to strive every day to make the club stronger and better. 'We are obviously in a very competitive league and a competitive world, and we want to be the best.'

Peter Moore: The key is to celebrate our past but also use it as a platform to look forward and continue to shape our story. Today there are people all over the world who support Liverpool FC passionately – as I did living in San Francisco for many years – and there are those who were fortunate enough to grow up a stone's throw from Anfield for whom the stadium is a second home. We are a global football club but one with a local heart.

Trent Alexander-Arnold: There haven't been too many local lads who have come through the first team since the likes of Steven Gerrard and Jamie Carragher, and I think that whenever we get Scousers in the team it's always a good thing. But there is a lot of quality coming from elsewhere as well. Everyone knows you have to fight for your place at Liverpool. It's a competitive game and you have to learn your position. It doesn't matter if you're a Scouser or not, if you're worthy of the shirt then you'll wear it. If you aren't, you won't.

Jordan Henderson: Playing for a club with our history definitely has an impact on you as a player. Being the current captain probably hammers that home even more, but it's always around you. When we play in the Champions League we wear a badge on the shirt with the number '5' on it. Every day at Melwood we walk in past the European Cup, a bust of Bill Shankly and a wall marking all the trophies the club has won. It's the same at Anfield – and, by the way, rightly so. Who wouldn't be proud of this history? Hopefully we can add more success and create new history, stories and memories for the supporters – that's what we'll work hard every day to do.

Trent Alexander-Arnold: It's hard to put into words what the club means to me. My whole life just revolves around it. Everywhere you go in the city you see Liverpool fans, then, when you come into training you're with the team. It makes you realise the size of the club that you're playing for. There's not a day that goes by when I don't see a Liverpool shirt somewhere and that brings a smile to my face knowing that I'm playing for the club I love. It's a special, special club and to be as successful as we have been in the last 125 years is a result of a lot of hard work by many, many people. We're looking to bring more success in the years to come and hopefully I can be part of that.

The Red Journey

who's who

Alan A'Court: Liverpool player, 1953-64.

John Aldridge: Liverpool player, 1987-89.

Trent Alexander-Arnold: Liverpool player, 2016-present.

Xabi Alonso: Liverpool player, 2004-09.

Alf Arrowsmith: Liverpool player, 1961-68.

Charlie Ashcroft: Liverpool player 1946-55.

Pako Ayesteran: Liverpool assistant manager, 2004-07.

Ian Ayre: Liverpool commercial director, 2007-11; Liverpool managing director, 2011-14; Liverpool chief executive, 2014-17.

Phil Babb: Liverpool player, 1994-99.

Jack Balmer: Liverpool player, 1935-52.

William Barclay: Liverpool secretary/ manager, 1892-95.

John Barnes: Liverpool player, 1987-97.

Peter Beardsley: Liverpool player, 1987-91.

Jim Beglin: Liverpool player, 1984-87.

Craig Bellamy: Liverpool player, 2006-07 & 2011-12.

Rafael Benitez: Liverpool manager, 2004-10.

Patrik Berger: Liverpool player, 1996-2003.

Louis Bimpson: Liverpool player, 1953-59.

Tom [Tiny] Bradshaw: Liverpool player, 1930-37.

Martin Broughton: Liverpool chairman, 2010.

Matt Busby: Liverpool player, 1936-45.

Gerry Byrne: Liverpool player, 1957-69.

Ian Callaghan: Liverpool player, 1960-78.

Kenneth Campbell: Liverpool player, 1912-20.

Jamie Carragher: Liverpool player, 1997-2013.

Andy Carroll: Liverpool player, 2011-12.

Jimmy Case: Liverpool player, 1975-81.

Ray Clemence: Liverpool player, 1968-81.

Nigel Clough: Liverpool player, 1993-95.

Stan Collymore: Liverpool player, 1995-97.

Peter Cormack: Liverpool player, 1972-75.

Kenny Dalglish: Liverpool player, 1977-90; Liverpool manager 1985-91 & 2011-12.

Julian Dicks: Liverpool player, 1993-94.

Jerzy Dudek: Liverpool player, 2001-07.

Cyril Done: Liverpool player, 1939-52.

Roy Evans: Liverpool player, 1970-73; Liverpool reserve team coach, 1974-83; Liverpool first team coach, 1983-92; Liverpool assistant manager, 1993-94; Liverpool manager, 1994-98.

Joe Fagan: Liverpool reserve team coach, 1958-71; Liverpool first team coach 1971-79; Liverpool assistant manager, 1979-83; Liverpool manager, 1983-85.

David Fairclough: Liverpool player 1975-83.

Robbie Fowler: Liverpool player, 1993-2001 & 2006-07.

Jim Furnell: Liverpool player, 1962-63.

Luis Garcia: Liverpool player, 2004-07.

Howard Gayle: Liverpool player, 1980-81.

Steven Gerrard: Liverpool player, 1998-2015; Liverpool academy coach 2017-present.

Gary Gillespie: Liverpool player, 1984-91.

Bobby Graham: Liverpool player, 1964-72.

Arthur Goddard: Liverpool player, 1902-14.

Bruce Grobbelaar: Liverpool player, 1981-94.

Brian Hall: Liverpool player, 1969-76.

Dietmar Hamann: Liverpool player, 1999-2006.

Alan Hansen: Liverpool player, 1977-90.

Sam Hardy: Liverpool player, 1905-12.

Steve Heighway: Liverpool player, 1970-81; Liverpool Youth Development Officer, 1989-98; Liverpool academy director, 1998-2007.

Jordan Henderson: Liverpool player, 2011-present.

Emile Heskey: Liverpool player, 2000-04.

Joe Hewitt: Liverpool player, 1904-09.

Dave Hickson: Liverpool player, 1959-61.

Ray Houghton: Liverpool player 1987-92.

John Houlding: Liverpool president, 1892-1902; Liverpool chairman, 1892-96.

Gerard Houllier: Liverpool manager, 1998-2004.

Emlyn Hughes: Liverpool player, 1967-79.

Laurie Hughes: Liverpool player, 1946-57.

Roger Hunt: Liverpool player, 1959-69.

Sami Hyypia: Liverpool player, 1999-2009.

Paul Ince: Liverpool player, 1997-99.

Alex Inglethorpe: Liverpool academy coach, 2012-14; Liverpool academy director 2014-present.

David James: Liverpool player, 1992-99.

David Johnson: Liverpool player, 1976-82.

Craig Johnston: Liverpool player, 1981-88.

Bill Jones: Liverpool player, 1946-54.

Joey Jones: Liverpool player, 1975-78.

Rob Jones: Liverpool player, 1991-98.

George Kay: Liverpool manager, 1936-51.

Kevin Keegan: Liverpool player, 1971-77.

Ray Kennedy: Liverpool player, 1974-82.

Alan Kennedy: Liverpool player, 1978-85.

Jurgen Klopp: Liverpool manager, 2015-present.

Dirk Kuyt: Liverpool player, 2006-12.

Ray Lambert: Liverpool player, 1946-55.

Chris Lawler: Liverpool player, 1963-75.

Tommy Lawrence: Liverpool player, 1962-71.

Mark Lawrenson: Liverpool player, 1981-88.

Sammy Lee: Liverpool player, 1978-86; Liverpool reserve team coach, 1992-98; Liverpool first team coach, 1998-2004 & 2008-11.

Lucas Leiva: Liverpool player, 2007-17.

Kevin Lewis: Liverpool player, 1960-63.

Billy Liddell: Liverpool player, 1946-60.

Alec Lindsay: Liverpool player, 1969-77.

Larry Lloyd: Liverpool player, 1969-74.

Ephraim Longworth: Liverpool player, 1910-28.

Dejan Lovren: Liverpool player, 2014-present.

Donald Mackinlay: Liverpool player, 1910-28.

Gary McAllister: Liverpool player, 2000-02.

Jason McAteer: Liverpool player, 1995-99.

Terry McDermott: Liverpool player, 1974-82.

Jimmy McDougall: Liverpool player, 1928-38.

Steve McMahon: Liverpool player, 1985-91.

Steve McManaman: Liverpool player, 1990-99.

Sadio Mane: Liverpool player, 2016-present.

Mike Marsh: Liverpool player, 1989-93; Liverpool academy coach, 2009-12; Liverpool first team coach, 2012-15.

Erik Meijer: Liverpool player, 1999-2000.

Jimmy Melia: Liverpool player, 1955-64.

Simon Mignolet: Liverpool player, 2013-present.

Gordon Milne: Liverpool player, 1960-67.

James Milner: Liverpool player, 2015-present.

Jan Molby: Liverpool player, 1984-95.

Peter Moore: Liverpool chief executive, 2017-present.

Ronnie Moran: Liverpool player, 1952-65; Liverpool reserve team coach, 1971-74; Liverpool first team coach, 1974-98 [including two spells as caretaker manager].

Danny Murphy: Liverpool player, 1997-2004.

Phil Neal: Liverpool player, 1974-85.

Steve Nicol: Liverpool player, 1982-94.

Berry Nieuwenhuys: Liverpool player, 1933-47.

Michael Owen: Liverpool player, 1997-2004.

Divock Origi: Liverpool player, 2015-present.

Bob Paisley: Liverpool player, 1946-54; Liverpool reserve team coach, 1954-57; Liverpool first team coach, 1957-74; Liverpool manager, 1974-83.

Stan Palk: Liverpool player, 1947-48.

Rick Parry: Liverpool chief executive, 1998-2009.

George Patterson: Liverpool assistant secretary, 1908-15; Liverpool secretary/manager, 1915-19; Liverpool secretary, 1920-28; Liverpool manager, 1928-36.

Jimmy Payne: Liverpool player, 1948-56.

Alex Raisbeck: Liverpool player, 1898-1909.

Jamie Redknapp: Liverpool player, 1991-2001.

Karl-Heinz Reidle: Liverpool player, 1997-99.

Pepe Reina: Liverpool player, 2005-13.

John Arne Riise: Liverpool player, 2001-2008.

Peter Robinson: Liverpool secretary/chief executive, 1965-99.

Brendan Rodgers: Liverpool manager, 2012-15.

Ronnie Rosenthal: Liverpool player, 1990-93.

Neil Ruddock: Liverpool player, 1993-97.

Ian Rush: Liverpool player, 1980-87 & 1988-96.

Ian St John: Liverpool player, 1961-71.

Dean Saunders: Liverpool player, 1991-92.

Roy Saunders: Liverpool player, 1953-58.

Tom Saunders: Liverpool youth development officer/scout, 1968-86; Liverpool director, 1993-2001.

John Scales: Liverpool player, 1994-96.

Elisha Scott: Liverpool player, 1912-34.

Bill Shankly: Liverpool manager, 1959-74.

Martin Skrtel: Liverpool player, 2008-16.

Vladimir Smicer: Liverpool player, 1999-2005.

John Smith: Liverpool chairman, 1973-90.

Tommy Smith: Liverpool player, 1963-78.

Graeme Souness: Liverpool player, 1978-84; Liverpool manager, 1991-94.

David Speedie: Liverpool player, 1991.

Eddie Spicer: Liverpool player, 1946-53.

Steve Staunton: Liverpool player, 1988-91 & 1998-2000.

Willie Stevenson: Liverpool player, 1962-67.

Geoff Strong: Liverpool player, 1964-70.

Albert Stubbins: Liverpool player, 1946-53.

Daniel Sturridge: Liverpool player, 2013-present.

Luis Suarez: Liverpool player, 2011-14.

Nick Tanner: Liverpool player, 1989-92.

Phil Taylor: Liverpool player, 1936-54; Liverpool first team coach, 1954-56; Liverpool manager, 1956-59.

Michael Thomas: Liverpool player, 1991-98.

David Thompson: Liverpool player, 1996-2000.

Peter Thompson: Liverpool player, 1963-72.

Phil Thompson: Liverpool player, 1972-83; Liverpool reserve team coach, 1986-93; Liverpool assistant manager, 1998-2004 [including spell as caretaker manager].

Fernando Torres: Liverpool player, 2007-2011.

John Toshack: Liverpool player, 1970-77.

Kolo Toure: Liverpool player, 2013-16.

Djimi Traore: Liverpool player, 1999-2006.

Geoff Twentyman: Liverpool player, 1953-59; Liverpool chief scout 1967-86.

Gordon Wallace: Liverpool player, 1962-65.

Mark Walters: Liverpool player, 1991-95.

Tom Watson: Liverpool secretary/manager, 1896-1915.

Don Welsh: Liverpool manager, 1951-56.

Tom Werner: Liverpool chairman, 2010-present.

Ronnie Whelan: Liverpool player, 1981-94.

Ben Woodburn: Liverpool player, 2016-present.

Mark Wright: Liverpool player, 1991-97.

Ron Yeats: Liverpool player, 1961-71; Liverpool chief scout, 1986-2006.

Note: Playing careers are measured from a player's first team debut to their final game for Liverpool.

Bibliography

The following have all been
a valuable source of reference when
compiling The Red Journey...

Books

A'Court, Alan & Hargraves, Ian – **Alan A'Court My Life In Football** [Bluecoat Press, 2003]

Anderson, Jeff with Done, Stephen – **The Official Liverpool FC Illustrated History** [Carlton Books, 2014]

Ashton, Ken – **The Liverpool FC Book** [Stanley Paul, 1967]

Balague, Guillem – **A Season On The Brink: Rafael Benitez, Liverpool and the Path to European Glory** [Weidenfeld Nicolson, 2005]

Baldursson, Arnie & Magnusson, Gudmundur – **Liverpool The Complete Record** [deCoubertin Books, 2011]

Baldursson, Arnie & Magnusson, Gudmundur – **Liverpool Encyclopedia** [deCoubertin Books, 2013]

Barnes, John – **John Barnes: The Autobiography** [Headline, 1999]

Bowler, David – **Shanks: The Authorised Biography** [Orion, 1996]

Busby, Matt – **Matt Busby: My Story** [Souvenir Press, 1957]

Beardsley, Peter – **Peter Beardsley: My Life Story** [CollinsWillow, 1995]

Bellamy, Craig – **Craig Bellamy – Goodfella, My Autobiography** [Trinity Mirror Sport Media 2013]

Benitez, Rafael – **Champions League Dreams** [Headline, 2012]

Callaghan, Ian & Keith, John – **Cally: A Football Phenomenon** [Quartet, 1974]

Carragher, Jamie – **Carra: My Autobiography** [Bantam, 2008]

Case, Jimmy & Smart, Andrew – **Hard Case: The Autobiography Of Jimmy Case** [John Blake Publishing 2014]

Corbett, James & Hickson, Dave – **The Cannonball Kid** [deCoubertin Books, 2014]

Dalglish, Kenny – **Dalglish: My Autobiography** [Hodder & Stoughton, 1996]

Dalglish, Kenny – **Kenny Dalglish, My Life** [Trinity Mirror Sport Media, 2013]

Dalglish, Kenny – **Kenny Dalglish: My Liverpool Home** [Hodder & Stoughton, 2010]

Dudek, Jerzy – **Jerzy Dudek, A Big Pole In Our Goal: My Autobiography** [Trinity Mirror Sport Media, 2016]

Fagan, Andrew & Platt, Mark – **Joe Fagan Reluctant Champion: The Authorised Biography** [Aurum Press, 2011]

Fairclough, David – **Supersub: The Story Of Football's Most Famous Number 12** [deCoubertin Books, 2015]

Gerrard, Steven – **Steven Gerrard: My Liverpool Story** [Headline, 2012]

Gerrard, Steven – **Steven Gerrard: My Story** [Penguin, 2015]

Fowler, Robbie – **Fowler: My Autobiography** [Macmillan, 2005]

Hale, Steve & Thompson, Phil – **The Shankly Years: A Revolution In Football** [Ebury Press, 1998]

Hamann, Dietmar – **The Didi Man: My Love Affair With Liverpool** [Headline, 2012]

Hansen, Alan – **A Matter of Opinion** [Partridge, 1999]

Hansen, Alan & Gallacher, Ken – **Tall, Dark and Hansen: Ten Years At Anfield** [Mainstream, 1988]

Hanssen, Kjell – **Dicky Sams: Liverpool... in Blue and White** [Sportsblikk, 2009]

Herbert, Ian – **Quiet Genius: Bob Paisley, British Football's Greatest Manager** [Bloomsbury Sport, 2017]

Hughes, Chris – **Toshack: FourFourTwo Great Footballers** [Virgin Books, 2002]

Hughes, Emlyn – **Crazy Horse** [Arthur Baker Limited, 1980]

Hughes, Simon – **Men In White Suits, Liverpool FC in the 1990s: The Players' Stories** [Bantam, 2015]

Hughes, Simon – **Red Machine, Liverpool FC in the 1980s: The Players' Stories** [Mainstream, 2013]

Hughes, Simon – **Ring Of Fire, Liverpool FC into the 21st Century: The Players' Stories** [Bantam, 2016]

Johnston, Craig & Jameson, Neil – **Walk Alone: The Craig Johnston Story** [Fleetfoot Books, 1990]

Keegan, Kevin – **Kevin Keegan My Autobiography** [Ted Smart, 1997]

Keith, John – **Billy Liddell: The Legend Who Carried The Kop** [Robson Books, 2003]

Keith, John – **Bob Paisley Manager Of The Millennium** [Robson Books, 1999]

Keith, John – **The Essential Shankly** [Robson Books, 2001]

Kelly, Stephen F – **Bill Shankly It's Much More Important Than That** [Virgin Books, 1997]

Kelly, Stephen F – **The Boot Room Boys** [Collins Willow, 1999]

Lawson, Hedley – **Elisha Scott's Diaries & Press Cuttings: His Life Story** [Hedley Lawson, 2012]

Liddell, Billy – **Billy Liddell: My Soccer Story** [Stanley Paul, 1960]

Liverpool Football Club – **Liverpool FC: The Historic Treble** [Carlton, 2001]

Lloyd, Larry & Wright, Rita – **Larry Lloyd: Hard Man Hard Game** [John Blake Publishing, 2009]

McDermott, Terry – **Terry Mac: Living For The Moment, My Autobiography** [Trinity Mirror Sport Media, 2017]

Moynihan, Leo – **Liverpool Cult Heroes** [Pitch Publishing, 2014]

Moynihan, Leo – **Match Of My Life Liverpool** [Know The Score Books, 2005]

Neal, Phil – **Life At The Kop** [Macdonald Queen Anne Press, 1986]

Nicol, Steve – **Stevie Nicol: My Autobiography, 5 League titles and a packet of crisps** [Trinity Mirror Sport Media, 2016]

Owen, Michael – Michael Owen: Off The Record, My Autobiography [CollinsWillow, 2004]

Paisley, Bob – *50 Golden Reds* [Front Page Books, 1990]

Paisley, Bob – **Bob Paisley: A Lifetime In Football** [Arthur Baker Limited, 1983]

Paisley, Bob – **Bob Paisley's Liverpool Scrapbook** [Souvenir Press, 1979]

Paisley, Bob – My 50 Golden Reds [Front Page Books, 1990]

Pead, Brian – **Liverpool: A Complete Record** [Breedon Books, 1988]

Platt, Mark – **Cup Kings 1965** [Bluecoat Press, 2000]

Platt, Mark – **Cup Kings 1977** [Bluecoat Press, 2003]

Platt, Mark & Shaw, Gary – **At The End Of The Storm** [Gary Shaw, 2009]

Ponting, Ivan – **Liverpool Player By Player** [Crowood Press, 1990]

Ponting, Ivan & Hale, Steve – **Liverpool In Europe** [Guinness Publishing, 1992]

Ponting, Ivan & Hale, Steve – **Sir Roger: The Life And Times Of Roger Hunt** [Bluecoat Press]

Ponting, Ivan & Hale, Steve – **The Boot Room: An Anfield Legend** [Bluecoat Press, 1994]

Reina, Pepe – **Pepe: My Autobiography** [Trinity Mirror Sport Media, 2011]

Rush, Ian – **Rush: The Autobiography** [Ebury Press, 2008]

Shankly, Bill & Roberts, John – **Shankly** [Arthur Baker Limited, 1976]

Smith, Tommy – **Tommy Smith: Anfield Iron The Autobiography** [Bantam Press, 2008]

Smith, Tommy & Rogers, Ken – **Over The Top: My Anfield Secrets** [Breedon Books, 1998]

Souness, Graeme – **No Half Measures** [Collins Willow, 1985]

Souness, Graeme – **Souness: The Management Years** [Andre Deutsch, 1999]

St John, Ian – **Boom At The Kop** [The Sportsmans Book Club, 1967]

St John, Ian – **The Saint: My Autobiography** [Hodder & Stoughton, 2005]

Thompson, Phil – **Shankly** [Bluecoat Press, 1993]

Thompson, Phil – **Thommo: Stand Up Pinocchio** [Trinity Mirror Sport Media, 2005]

Trinity Mirror Sport Media – **Liverpool Secrets Behind The Shankly Gates** [Trinity Mirror Sport Media, 2005]

Ward, Andrew & Taylor, Rogan with Williams, John – **Three Sides Of The Mersey: An Oral History Of Everton, Liverpool & Tranmere Rovers** [Robson Books, 1993]

Whelan, Ronnie & Conlon, Tommy – **Walk On, My Life In Red** [Simon & Schuster 2011]

Williams, John – **Red Men: Liverpool Football Club The Biography** [Maintstream, 2010]

Newspapers/Magazines

Liverpool Echo
Liverpool Mercury
Evening Express
Daily Post
Daily Express
Daily Mail
The Guardian
The Times
The Independent
Dundee Courier
Weekly News
Cricket & Football Field
Field Sports
Kop Newspaper
XTRA Time
Liverpool FC Matchday Programmes
Liverpool FC Official Magazine
Charles Buchan's Football Monthly

Websites

liverpoolfc.com
lfchistory.net
playupliverpool.com

Television

LFC TV
Liverpool Official History DVD
BBC
ITV
Sky Sports

Roll of honour

We are Liverpool

Arthur Platt	Paul Crowley	Frank Crowley	Keira Dutton
Jack Platt	Geir Olav Kittelsrud	Mogens Nielsen	John Platt
Ella Platt	Harald Pettersen	Steve Parry	Ian Platt
Tom Platt	John - Paul Tooley	Torfinn Simonsen	Adam Platt
Andrew Cahill	Jørgen Ringestad	Rita Irene Stenersen	Tommy Platt
Matthew Cahill	Kieran Mulvaney	Yumiko Tumaru	Keith Platt
Macy-Jo Priestley	Ola Helgedagsrud	Brian Martin	David Platt
JJ Priestley	Timothy J. F. Wilding	John Connors	Peter Dalton
Lewis Priestley	Anthony Barnes and	Steve Ault	Tom Dalton
Lilly Kinsella	Katie Ditch	Stuart Brennan	Norman Woods
Lois Priestley	Mike Donnelly	Graham Duncan	June Woods
Daniel Priestley	Robert Gallagher	Forbes Duff	Stephen Woods
Stephen Priestley	Hans Magne Opsahl	Mike Lepic	Joe Woods
Leslie Priestley	Nick Hadkiss	David Locke	Sam Woods
James & Joseph Price	John Koutoupis	William Corbett	Ian Woods
Andrew Priestley	Alisha Weiss	Arnie Baldursson	Adam Woods
Tom Priestley	Fred Mc Donogh	Gudmundur Magnusson	Thomas Woods
Alex Bibby	Les Wright	Ragnhild Lund Ansnes	Oliver Woods
23 Foundation	Neil Lussey	Jostein Ansnes	Janet Hudson
Clive R Cockram	Paul Tremarco	Andrew Coulton	Terry Lindsay
George T Renshaw	Tore Hansen	Joseph Wright	Peter Lindsay
John Corrigan	Adam Lowendahl	Jayden O'Sullivan-Bowe	Graham Lindsay
Al & Sal Mather	Rune Myrvang	Terry Kinsella	Ted Lindsay
Chetan Murarji	Brian McLaughlin	Mike Kinsella	Alex Lindsay
Mark Thomas	Christophe Cogghe	Garry Kinsella	John Caveen
D L Z Wong	Gayner Lepic	Ryan Kinsella	David Caveen
Tim Richards	Ken Solomon	Lawrence Price	Jacob Caveen
Mark Townsend	Stephen Astall	James Price	Kitty McGowan
William McGinnigle	Paul Schofield	Joseph Price	Glenn Armstrong
Ian Howarth	Tony Bowden	Gary Martin	Alex McGowan
Marcus Francis Howarth	Donna Carpenter	Callum Neilson	Vicky Perrin
Benjamin and	James Carroll	Paul Neilson	Ian McGowan
Zephyr Locksley Lai	Avtar Colar	John Lyons	Lyn McGowan
Philip Brough	Roger Danielsberg	Owen Dutton	Jack McGowan
Gina Heywood	Dean Evans	Aimee Dutton	Joe McGowan
Craig Stenhouse	Frode Furuli	Max Dutton	Harry McGowan
Malcolm Berry	Kenneth Giske	Ben Dutton	Michael McGowan
Michael Holloway	Danielle McNally	Zack Dutton	Frankie McGowan

Lee Brown	Joe Bradshaw	Paul Anderson	Gary Knott
Annie Brown	Tony Davis	Phil Welsh	Anthony Knott
Lydia Brown	Jimmy Golding	Michael Welsh	Samuel Gillespie
Peter Catling	Maisy Hughes	Stephen Woolley	Joseph Gillespie
Lin Catling	Chris Hughes	Stan Green	Arthur Milton
Liam Catling	Christopher Hughes	Rob Green	Kevin Keegan Milton
Rob Dolphin	Joey Hughes	Andrew Green	Keith Coker
Sophie Dolphin	Blain Hughes	Bobby Green	Dom Dransfield
Emily Dolphin	Teigan Hughes	Charlie Green	Mandie Dransfield
Paul Kennerley	Lewis Hughes	Rob Hinds	Jake Hargreaves
Sean Kennerley	Lee Connor	Daniel Mohammed	Phil Caffrey
Sam Kennerley	Ben Connor	Ian McHale	Janine Burnett
Harry Kennerley	Adam Causer	Neil McHale	Darren Williams
Ava Kennerley	Danny Boult	Liam McNeely	John Williams
Craig Thomas	Lee Anfield	Alison Heaton	Mary Caffrey
Connar Thomas	Charlie Anfield	Alf Ratcliffe	Colin Wareing
Lee Thomas	Isabella Anfield	Michael Goulding	Kyle Wareing
Alan Campbell	Ben Clancy	Faye Mates-Goulding	Colin Morton Snr
Charlie Campbell	Max Clancy	Gary Roberts	Ann McHale
Connie Campbell	Lucy Clancy	Ben Roberts	Colin Morton Jnr
Simon Morton	Dave Motherwell	Brian (Yozza) Hughes	Owen Morton
Thomas Morton	Ste Motherwell	Jamie Cass	Jeannie Durrans Morton
John Holligan	Alex Motherwell	Joe Cass	Abbie Morton
Steven Holligan	Brian McGreevy	Stefan Seaton	Janet Morton
Michael Holligan	Archie Skerritt	Clifford Ferguson	Lesley Morton
Jason Turton	Graham Nugent	Patricia (Ann) Jones	Ken Hardman
Luke Riley Turton	Tony Cocker	Vinny Jones Snr	Mark Hardman
Albert Davin	Azri 'Ace' Abdullah	Vinny Jones	Les McMaster
Tony Grimes	John Foley Snr	Julie Grant	Frank McKinney
Harry Grimes	John Foley Jnr	Lauren Grant	Leon Hymas
Elliot Grimes	Ian Foley	Daniel Grant	Svein Indrevaer
Jeffrey Moran	Oliver Foley	George McKenna	Ste Evans
Gary Shaw	Joshua Foley	Michael Deane	Dylan Evans
Les Shaw	Joseph Foley	Hat Scarf or a Badge	Ellie Thomas
Stephen Hughes	James Stewart	Harry Deane	Lilly Thomas
Frank Beardwood	Paul McShane	Michael Browne	Sean Surridge
Oliver Lea	Peter Molyneux	Michael James Browne	Oliver Wells
Tony Kennils	Kieran Molyneux	Owen Williams	Paul Tremarco Snr
Jan Kennils	Ryan Molyneux	Rob Glover	Gerard Tremarco
Bex Kennils	James Molyneux	Samuel McClelland	Jimmy Tremarco
Luci Kennils	Thomas Molyneux	Eddie Morland	Paul Tremarco Jnr
Phillip Gordon	Dave Molyneux	John Morland	Michael Tremarco
David Brown	Harry Molyneux	Kevin Morland	Matty Cass
Andrew Brown	Robert Miller	Liam Wells	Jamie Cass
Ben Brown	Rose Elizabeth Miller	Syd Ogwin	Oscar Cass
Tony Randles	Joseph Paul Rees Miller	Michaela Knott	Les Fletcher

David Lim	Gary Swift	Tony Mottram	Steve Hunter
Tony Teo	Mark Kidd	Michelle Mottram	Barry Hibbert
Kelvin Chin	Steve Dineley	James Burke	Norman Hibbert
Kenneth Teo	James Dineley	Darren Lea	Stephen Hibbert
Mark Seah	Tommy Lee	Billy Lea	James Hibbert
Amos Tan	Dave Wood Snr	Herbert Garner	Ian Hibbert
David Rylands	David Wood Jnr	Geoffrey Balmer	Laurence Connolly
Peter Rylands	Andy Walker	Henry 'Harry' Lyness	Bobby Wilcox
James Rylands	Mattie Walker	Eric Hooton	Lenny Woods
Philip Irving	Ken Walker	Peter Hooton	Jon McGrail
Phil Irving	Michael Hall	Ed Fitzsimons	Conor McGrail
Cieran Irving	Brian Hall Snr	Terry Garner	Mike Hinden
Ian Irving	Brian Hall Jnr	John Garner	Hudson Barnes
Lewis Irving	Joseph Hall	Janet Garner	Raina Barnes
Patrick Irving	George Johnson	Kerry Garner	Peter Barnes
David Caton	Alan Johnson	Kirsty Garner	Ben Barnes
Niall Caton	Lewis Johnson	Evon Garner	Martin Walker
Dave Rawsthorne	William Shaw	Frankie Fayer Jnr	Fraya Walker
Mick Rawsthorne	Harry Badrock Snr	Nathan Jones	Peter McDowall
Jason Sealeaf	Harry Badrock Jnr	Oliver Jones	Frankie McDowall
Alan Sealeaf	Brian Johnson	Reece Jones	Jim Gardiner
Charlie Broley	Derek Johnson	John Monaghan	George Jones
Sandra Broley	Michael Hanley	Stephen Monaghan	Mary Jones
Alan Broley	Mark Volante	Joe Monaghan	Alan Jones
Peter Hughes	Sue Volante	John Nicolson	Phil Jones
Phil Hughes	Sophia Volante	Keith Culvin	Tony Davin
Neil (Yozza) Hughes	Charlie Volante	Geoff Brittles	John Byrne
David Holmes	Gerry Blayney	Tony Robb	Paul Byrne
Julie Holmes	Phil Reade	Joe Pickup	George Scott
Isobel Holmes	Brian Reade	Ste Pickup	Gavin Scott
Grace Holmes	Nassos Siotropos	Hayley Hammond	Calum Scott
Harry Smith	Luqman Guee	Ian Saddington	Charlie Scott
David Fairclough	Henry Eileen Han	Jake Saddington	Gary Rourke
Henry Fairclough	Sheldon Xavier	Layla Saddington	Linda Rourke
Eddie Lawson	Joey Howard	Albert Vinten	Lee Rourke
Les Lawson	James Best	Tony O'Brien	Claire Rourke
Jamie Lawson	Alan Best	Michael O'Brien	Jonathan Bamber
Deborah Norton	William Dixon	Dave Henry	Billy Healey
Josh Norton	Adam Dixon	Tony Caveney	William 'Bill' Howell
John Ball	Gramme Dixon	Jacob Hoy	Billy Howell
Brian Beamond	Harry Newbold	Alex Hoy	Jimmy Areabi
George Rowlands	Joey Howard	Stan Cotton	Ian Killey
Gary Rawlinson	James Best	Eddie Cotton	Iain Mccormack
Eddie Serjeant	Alan Best	John Cotton	David Muirhead
Roy Serjeant	Glyn John McHale	Terry Cotton	Oke Akpogheneta
Steve Minshull	Maureen Jean McHale	Graham Agg	Wayne Tucker

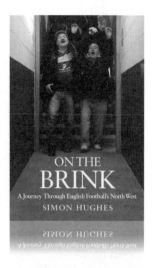

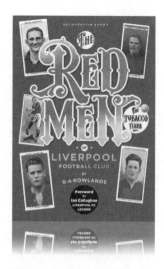

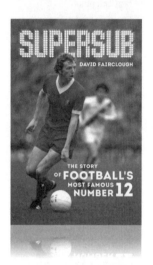

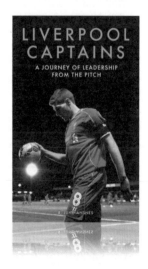

*Further reading
available from*

DECOUBERTIN.CO.UK